Play Therapy

Play Therapy
for Preschool Children

Edited by

Charles E. Schaefer

American Psychological Association

Washington, DC

Published by
American Psychological Association
750 First Street, NE
Washington, DC 20002
www.apa.org

To order
APA Order Department
P.O. Box 92984
Washington, DC 20090-2984
Tel: (800) 374-2721; Direct: (202) 336-5510
Fax: (202) 336-5502; TDD/TTY: (202) 336-6123
Online: www.apa.org/books/
E-mail: order@apa.org

In the U.K., Europe, Africa, and the Middle East, copies may be ordered from
American Psychological Association
3 Henrietta Street
Covent Garden, London
WC2E 8LU England

Typeset in Goudy by Circle Graphics, Inc., Columbia, MD

Printer: Maple-Vail Book Manufacturing, York, PA
Cover Designer: Minker Design, Sarasota, FL
Technical/Production Editor: Harriet Kaplan

The opinions and statements published are the responsibility of the authors, and such opinions and statements do not necessarily represent the policies of the American Psychological Association.

Library of Congress Cataloging-in-Publication Data

Play therapy for preschool children / edited by Charles E. Schaefer. — 1st ed.
    p. cm.
  Includes bibliographical references and index.
  ISBN-13: 978-1-4338-0566-0
  ISBN-10: 1-4338-0566-9
 1. Play therapy. 2. Child psychotherapy. I. Schaefer, Charles E.
  RJ505.P6P534 2009
  618.92'891653—dc22
                                    2009018742

British Library Cataloguing-in-Publication Data
A CIP record is available from the British Library.

Printed in the United States of America
First Edition

CONTENTS

CONTRIBUTORS

Claudia Avina, Harbor-UCLA Medical Center, Torrance, CA

Helen E. Benedict, Baylor University, Waco, TX

Corissa L. Callahan, University of Florida, Gainesville

Meena Dasari, New York University School of Medicine, New York

Manuela A. Diaz, Child Trauma Research Program, University of California, San Francisco

Sheila Eyberg, University of Florida, Gainesville

Jill C. Fodstad, Louisiana State University, Baton Rouge

Hilda R. Glazer, Capella University, Minneapolis, MN

Kristi Gibbs, University of Tennessee at Chattanooga

Katherine A. Gioia, Illinois State University, Normal

Paris Goodyear-Brown, Paris & Me: Counseling for Kids, Brentwood, TN

Eric J. Green, The Chicago School of Professional Psychology, Chicago, IL

Susan M. Knell, Spectrum Psychological Associates, Mayfield Village, OH

Alicia F. Lieberman, Child Trauma Research Program, University of California, San Francisco, and San Francisco General Hospital, San Francisco, CA

Johnny L. Matson, Louisiana State University, Baton Rouge

Julie Blundon Nash, Institute of Living, Hartford, CT

David Neufeld, University of California, Berkeley, and San Francisco State University, San Francisco, CA

M. Jamila Reid, Parenting Clinic of the University of Washington, Seattle

Charles E. Schaefer, Fairleigh Dickinson University, Teaneck, NJ

Diana Schofield, Virginia Treatment Center for Children, Richmond

Janine Shelby, University of California, Los Angeles

Monica L. Stevens, University of Florida, Gainesville

Renée M. Tobin, Illinois State University, Normal

Heather Warnick, Harbor-UCLA Medical Center, Torrance, CA

Carolyn Webster-Stratton, Parenting Clinic of the University of Washington, Seattle

Pamela Wolfberg, San Francisco State University, San Francisco, CA

Play Therapy

INTRODUCTION

CHARLES E. SCHAEFER

In recent years, a number of efficacious play therapy approaches with preschool children ages 3 to 5 have been identified. The purpose of this book is to present current play interventions for preventing and resolving the most common psychological disorders of preschool children. The goal is to provide students and practitioners with a state-of-the-art handbook of developmentally appropriate play interventions for this important but often neglected age group.

PLAY AND THE PRESCHOOL CHILD

Play is the predominant activity of preschool children—their favorite way to spend time. Play helps them learn, form relationships, and manage stress. Moreover, it facilitates self-expression, enables children to derive meaning from experiences, and helps them solidify a sense of self. Also, numerous studies have identified play as the leading activity in accelerating young children's cognitive, emotional, and social development.

Although all children benefit from playful activity, a substantial number exhibit behavior problems requiring therapeutic services. Traditionally,

3

the most widely used psychotherapeutic approach with preschoolers has been play therapy. Among the main reasons why play therapy is the treatment of choice with these young children are these:

- Play is the natural language of childhood. Young children have not yet acquired the words to adequately express their thoughts and feelings, but they can readily play them out.
- The emergence of fantasy play in 3- to 5-year-old children is a key developmental acquisition. Fantasy play provides a unique window into the child's inner world of thoughts, feelings, and conflicts.
- Young children tend to resist interacting with an adult therapist, but rapport and a therapeutic alliance can usually be formed through enjoyable play interactions.

The field of early intervention has been expanding rapidly because of the demand by parents, professionals, and legislators for services that are effective in preventing or resolving preschool children's problematic behaviors. The preschool period (ages 3 to 5) lays a critical foundation for the child's later growth, development, and psychological well-being. When psychological disturbances are identified and treated in early childhood before they become entrenched and magnified, the negative impact on the child's future self-development and adjustment is mitigated or negated. Without early intervention, many of the emerging adjustment problems of young children become persistent and intractable.

A number of therapeutic approaches for children represent downward extensions of strategies developed for adults. However, children are not little adults and respond best when interventions are specifically created for or adapted to their developmental level. The play therapies contained in this book are all designed to meet the development needs, tasks, and abilities of preschool children.

ABOUT PLAY THERAPY

For more than a hundred years now, child therapists and other professionals have recognized and used the therapeutic powers of play with young children. Play therapy is the earliest and most popular form of child psychotherapy. It encompasses a number of theoretical models that have been used to treat a broad range of psychiatric disorders. Play therapy is currently being applied across the life cycle, from infants and toddlers (Schaefer, Kelly-Zion, McCormack, & Ohnogi, 2008) to elderly people (Schaefer, 2003b). However, it continues to be most extensively used with preschool children. A brief review of the core concepts of play therapy follows.

Definition and History of Play Therapy

The Association for Play Therapy has defined *play therapy* as "the systematic use of a theoretical model to establish an interpersonal process wherein trained play therapists use the therapeutic powers of play to help clients prevent or resolve psychosocial difficulties and achieve optimal growth and development" (Association for Play Therapy, Board of Directors, 1997, p. 14). Play therapy has its earliest roots in psychoanalysis. In observing children, Sigmund Freud noticed that they would repeatedly relive traumatic experiences in their play. By so doing, they could purge themselves of negative feelings associated with the event and achieve mastery over it. He termed this healing process *abreaction*. Hermine Hug-Hellmuth, Melanie Klein, and Anna Freud pioneered the development of the psychoanalytic play technique in England in the early 1900s. Hug-Hellmuth (1921) was the first to propose that play was central in child analysis and to use play materials to facilitate children's self-expression. Klein (1932) believed that play allows direct access to the child's unconscious and that play for a child is like free association for adults. Anna Freud (1946) found that play was invaluable in establishing an alliance with a child.

In the 1950s, Carl Rogers (1951) brought person-centered psychotherapy into the mainstream in the United States. Rogers advocated three core conditions as being needed by therapists in conducting therapy, namely unconditional positive regard, congruence (authenticity and genuineness), and empathic understanding. He believed that when these conditions were present in the therapeutic relationship, the client's inherent growth and healing forces were released.

Virginia Axline (1969) later adapted this nondirective relationship approach for child clients. This child-centered play therapy offers the child an opportunity to express feelings by using play as language and toys as words (Landreth, 2002). According to Axline, the eight principles that guide the therapist in conducting child-centered, nondirective play therapy are as follows:

1. The therapist must develop a warm, friendly relationship with the child in which good rapport is established as soon as possible.
2. The therapist accepts the child exactly as he or she is.
3. The therapist establishes a feeling of permissiveness in the relationship so that the child feels free to express her or his feelings completely.
4. The therapist is alert to recognize the feelings the child is expressing and reflects those feelings back to the child in such a manner that the child gains insight into his or her behavior.
5. The therapist maintains a deep respect for the child's ability to solve her or his own problems if given an opportunity to do so.

The responsibility to make choices and to institute change is the child's.

6. The therapist does not attempt to direct the child's actions or conversation in any manner. The child leads the way; the therapist follows.
7. The therapist does not attempt to hurry the therapy along. It is a gradual process and is recognized as such by the therapist.
8. The therapist establishes only those limitations that are necessary to anchor the therapy to the world of reality and to make the child aware of his or her responsibility in the relationship.

In recent years, modifications to the child-centered play therapy model have allowed it to be used by parents and other caregivers. In *filial* therapy (Guerney, 1964; Guerney & Guerney, 1989), play therapists train and supervise parents to conduct individual, nondirective play sessions with their child at home. The parent thereby becomes the therapeutic agent, and the therapeutic process can generalize to life outside the playroom. The filial model is cost-effective in terms of therapist time and the long-term reduction of symptoms that is achieved by the enhancement of the parent–child relationship (VanFleet, 2005). Inspired by the success of filial therapy, play therapists have recently developed programs such as kinder therapy to train classroom teachers to administer child-centered play therapy to select students at school (White, Flynt, & Draper, 1997).

In the 1990s, Susan Knell (1993, 1998) wrote about an innovative play therapy approach that integrated cognitive–behavioral strategies with play techniques. This cognitive–behavioral play therapy model represents an adaptation of cognitive and behavioral theories originally proposed by Aaron Beck, Albert Bandura, and others. In practice, a cognitive–behavioral play therapy intervention often contains a modeling component through which coping skills are demonstrated in doll play by the therapist. Through the use of play and stories, the therapist can also indirectly communicate adaptive changes for the child's cognitions. The application of this structured approach by child therapists of different orientations has increased notably over the past decade (Drewes, 2009).

Most recently, because no single play therapy theory has proven sufficient to treat the broad array of childhood disorders, an eclectic model has evolved in which therapists draw on all the major schools of play therapy to select an intervention tailored to the child's individual needs. The basic premise is that one size does not fit all, so play therapists need to be proficient in both directive and nondirective play strategies to successfully match the intervention to the presenting problem. The intervention chapters in this book illustrate the differential application of play theories to resolve specific behavior problems of preschool children.

Schaefer (2002) has termed the eclectic approach *prescriptive play therapy*. The central premise of this prescriptive approach is *prescriptive matching*, that is, an individualized, differential, and focused matching of the therapeutic powers of play to the specific, causative forces underlying the client's presenting problem (Kaduson, Cangelosi, & Schaefer, 1997). A detailed description of the aforementioned psychoanalytic, child-centered, filial, cognitive–behavioral, and prescriptive schools of play therapy, along with other well-known play therapy models—for example, family, group, and attachment-oriented play therapies—can be found in the handbook *Foundations of Play Therapy* (Schaefer, 2003a).

Therapeutic Powers of Play

Each of the diverse theories of play therapy emphasizes one or more of the therapeutic or curative powers of play. *Therapeutic powers* refers to those forces inherent in play that produce therapeutic change and thus the reduction of presenting problems. Yalom (1985) wrote about the "therapeutic factors," or change mechanisms, that he believed to be activated in group psychotherapy. *Universality*—the realization that you are not the only one suffering from a particular problem—is one of his group factors. It is only in the past 10 years that child clinicians and researchers have become interested in the specific mechanisms in play that make it a healing agent. In a literature review I conducted a decade ago (Schaefer, 1999), I described the therapeutic powers of play and identified more than 20 therapeutic powers. A taxonomy of these therapeutic powers is presented in Table 1.

A greater understanding of the therapeutic powers of play will enable practitioners to apply them more effectively in tailoring treatment to the client's needs. There is a pressing need for process-oriented research studies that are designed to identify the specific mediators in play therapy, that is, the therapeutic factors that produce the desired change in the client's behavior.

PLAY THERAPY IN THE 21ST CENTURY

The dynamic field of play therapy has experienced a number of significant changes in recent years. Among these emerging trends are the following:

- the training of paraprofessionals—that is, parents, teachers, and peers—who then directly conduct the play sessions under the supervision of the play therapists, which is cost-effective and improves generalization of treatment effects to the natural environment;

TABLE 1
Therapeutic Powers of Play

Therapeutic power	Description
Self-expression	Play activities facilitate the expression of conscious thoughts and feelings better than words alone.
Access to the unconscious	In play, children reveal unconscious conflicts via the defense mechanism of projection, displacement, and symbolization.
Direct and indirect teaching	Therapists use doll modeling and role play to teach coping skills. They also teach indirectly through storytelling.
Abreaction	Children use play to remember, relive, and work through past traumatic events.
Stress inoculation	The anticipatory anxiety of forthcoming stressful events, like hospitalization, can be lessened by playing out the event in advance.
Counterconditioning	The fun of playing hide and seek in the dark can counteract and overcome fear of the dark.
Catharsis	Emotional release of negative affect can be obtained by pounding clay or bursting balloons.
Positive affect	The fun of playing helps lift one's spirits and contributes to a sense of well-being.
Sublimation	Unacceptable impulses such as aggression can be channeled into acceptable game play, for example, football or tennis.
Attachment–relationship enhancement	Playful interactions have been found to promote attachment and a positive emotional bond between parent and child.
Moral judgment	Piaget (1932) observed that children's spontaneous rule making and rule enforcement during game play helped in the development of mature moral judgment.
Empathy	During role play, children can exercise their capacity for empathy, that is, the ability to see things from another's perspective.
Power–control	Free play provides children the unique experience of feeling powerful and in complete control.
Competence	Play offers children unlimited opportunities to create, such as through stories and worlds constructed in a sand tray, whereby they can gain a sense of competence and self-efficacy.
Sense of self	In nondirective play therapy, children experience unconditional acceptance and complete freedom to be themselves, without fear of evaluation or pressure to change.
Accelerated development	In play, children tend to function at an advanced level of development.

TABLE 1
Therapeutic Powers of Play *(Continued)*

Therapeutic power	Description
Creative problem solving	Play has been found to stimulate creative thinking in children.
Fantasy compensation	Through play, children can gain immediate gratification of their wishes; for example, a weak child can be super strong and a poor child can be rich.
Reality testing	In social pretend play, children often switch back and forth between the roles they are playing and their real selves, thereby strengthening their reality-testing ability.
Behavioral rehearsal	Through the use of puppet and role play, children can practice adaptive behaviors.
Rapport building	When adults play with children, they become more likable and attractive to the children, thus facilitating rapport and alliance formation.

- an increased awareness by play therapists of the need for evidence-based practice, which has led to a substantial increase in the number of well-designed outcome studies of play therapy's effectiveness; and
- increased international interest in the clinical practice of play therapy.

In 1982, Kevin O'Connor and I founded the Association for Play Therapy. This U.S. association grew rapidly and now has more than 5,000 members. Recently, similar national play therapy associations have proliferated in other countries, including England, Ireland, South Korea, Australia, Canada, and Mexico. Clearly, there is growing recognition among the nations of the world of the healing powers of child's play.

ABOUT THE BOOK

This book's focus is the clinical practice of play therapy with preschool children. Chapter 1 informs the reader of the clinical and developmental issues that are likely to arise in conducting psychotherapy with children this age. The remaining chapters are organized into four main sections for ease of reference. Part I discusses play-based strategies designed to prevent emerging problems from escalating. Part II contains play interventions for internalizing disorders, including fears and anxieties, posttraumatic stress, and childhood grief. Part III presents effective play approaches for disruptive disorders, such as oppositional–defiant behaviors. Part IV covers play interventions for preschoolers with significant developmental delays, including children on the autistic spectrum.

The book is intended as a practical resource for beginning and experienced child therapists. In particular, professionals in the fields of psychology, psychiatry, counseling, social work, and occupational therapy will benefit from reading this book. It will also be of interest to teachers, parents, and others who are interested in improving young children's mental health.

REFERENCES

Axline, V. M. (1969). *Play therapy*. New York: Ballantine.

Association for Play Therapy, Board of Directors. (1997). Minutes. *Association for Play Therapy Newsletter, 16*, p. 14.

Drewes, A. (Ed.). (2009). *Blending play therapy with cognitive behavioral therapy*. Hoboken, NJ: Wiley.

Freud, A. (1946). *The psychological treatment of children*. London: Imago.

Guerney, B. (1964). Filial therapy: Description and rationale. *Journal of Consulting Psychology, 28*, 304–310.

Guerney, L., & Guerney, B. (1989). Child relationship enhancement. *Person-Centered Review, 4*, 344–357.

Hug-Hellmuth, H. (1921). On the technique of child analysis. *International Journal of Psychoanalysis, 2*, 287.

Kaduson, H., Cangelosi, D., & Schaefer, C. (1997). *The playing cure: Individualized play therapy for specific childhood problems*. Northvale, NJ: Jason Aronson.

Klein, M. (1932). *The psychoanalysis of children*. London: Hogarth.

Knell, S. M. (1993). *Cognitive–behavioral play therapy*. Northvale, NJ: Jason Aronson.

Knell, S. M. (1998). Cognitive–behavioral play therapy. *Journal of Clinical Child Psychology, 27*, 28–33.

Landreth, G. (2002). *Play therapy: The art of the relationship* (2nd ed.). New York: Brunner-Routledge.

Piaget, J. (1932). *The moral judgment of the child*. New York: Harcourt.

Rogers, C. (1951). *Client-centered therapy: Its current practice, implications, and theory*. Boston: Houghton Mifflin.

Schaefer, C. E. (1999). *The therapeutic powers of play*. Northvale, NJ: Aronson.

Schaefer, C. E. (2002). Prescriptive play therapy. *International Journal of Play Therapy, 10*(2), 57–73.

Schaefer, C. E. (Ed.). (2003a). *Foundations of play therapy*. Hoboken, NJ: Wiley.

Schaefer, C. E. (Ed.). (2003b). *Play therapy with adults*. Hoboken, NJ: Wiley.

Schaefer, C. E., Kelly-Zion, S., McCormack, J., & Ohnogi, A. (2008). *Play therapy for very young children*. New York: Aronson.

White, J., Flynt, M., & Draper, K. (1997). Kinder therapy: Teachers as therapeutic agents. *International Journal of Play Therapy, 6,* 33–49.

VanFleet, R. (2005). *Filial therapy: Strengthening parent–child relationships through play*. (2nd ed.). Sarasota, FL: Professional Resource Press.

Yalom, I. D. (1985). *The theory and practice of group psychotherapy*. New York: Basic Books.

I

PLAY-BASED PREVENTION PROGRAMS

1

CLINICAL AND DEVELOPMENTAL ISSUES IN PSYCHOTHERAPY WITH PRESCHOOL CHILDREN: LAYING THE GROUNDWORK FOR PLAY THERAPY

JULIE BLUNDON NASH AND CHARLES E. SCHAEFER

Many questions are often raised in regard to psychotherapy with preschool children. Do children simply grow out of problem behaviors, or are some behaviors pathological? Can preschool-age children be reliably diagnosed with disorders listed in the *Diagnostic and Statistical Manual of Mental Disorders* (4th ed., text revision [*DSM–IV–TR*]; American Psychiatric Association, 2000)? How does one accurately assess symptoms in a child who may have limited language and reporting skills? How does the family's involvement affect the child's treatment? Are there any evidence-based treatments available for children of this age group In this chapter, we review these and other clinical and developmental issues relevant to therapeutic interventions for the preschool-age child that all child therapists need to keep in mind when offering services to young children and their families.

CLINICAL ISSUES

The clinical issues covered here include the prevalence of psychopathology in young children, barriers to treatment, diagnostic and assessment issues, and parent involvement in treatment.

Prevalence of Psychopathology

Prevalence rates of pathologies are difficult to determine for this age group, and multiple studies have found a variety of rates. The variation ranges from 5% to 26% and is primarily the result of methodological differences in the studies (Brauner & Stephens, 2006). Overall, the most representative studies have suggested the probable occurrence of any DSM–IV–TR disorder in preschool children to be 21.4%, a figure that includes both single and comorbid disorders (Lavigne et al., 1996). This rate is consistent with prevalence rates for older children, suggesting that preschool-age children's emotional and behavioral problems occur at comparable levels.

More specifically, common clinical presentations include attention deficit/ hyperactivity, disruptive behavior, mood, and anxiety disorders (Wilens et al., 2002). Wilens et al. (2002), in a sample of 200 clinically referred youngsters, found that 86% met criteria for a diagnosis of attention-deficit/hyperactivity disorder (ADHD). They also found that 43% met criteria for a mood disorder, and 28% met criteria for an anxiety disorder. These rates are significantly lower when nonclinically referred children are observed. Lavigne et al. (1996) evaluated 510 of 3,860 preschool-age children who were screened through their pediatricians. Of this population, 2% met criteria for ADHD, and almost all of these children had other comorbid conditions. In terms of emotional disorders, 0.3% of children met the criteria for depression not otherwise specified, and 0.5% to 0.7% met the criteria for an anxiety disorder. Oppositional defiant disorder was the most prevalent symptom pattern in this sample, with 16.8% of these children meeting the criteria.

Will these behavioral, social, and emotional problems diminish with the passage of time? Research has indicated that this is not always the natural progression. Numerous studies have shown that serious externalizing and internalizing problems in preschoolers often persist (Campbell, Pierce, Moore, Marakovitz, & Newby, 1996; Lavigne et al., 1998; Pierce, Ewing, & Campbell, 1999). Although prevalence rates vary across studies, as many as 50% of children who show such problems in the preschool years still show some problems by elementary school, and these problems continue into later years as well (Campbell, 1995; Gimpel & Holland, 2003; Lavigne et al., 1998). If left untreated, some symptoms can persist throughout the life span. More specifically, symptoms of ADHD, obsessive–compulsive disorder, depression, psychotic disorders, and bipolar disorder are likely to be maintained over the life span, as are disorders on the autism spectrum (Hechtman, 1996). It is important to recognize that even if we now know that behaviors can be stable over the life span, research into the causal mechanisms is still needed (Campbell, 2002).

The early emergence of behavioral and developmental problems in children poses the challenge of determining which of these children will outgrow the problems over time and which children are at risk of their continuation and escalation. Researchers have sought to address this challenge. For example, Campbell, Shaw, and Gilliom (2000) investigated early externalizing behavior problems of toddlers and preschoolers. They found that boys with especially high levels of early hyperactivity and aggression, coupled with high levels of negative, inconsistent parenting practices and high degrees of family stress and adversity, are most likely to evidence continuing problems at school entry. Findings from a number of other studies, both epidemiological and high risk, have supported this observation (e.g., Achenbach, Edelbrock, & Howell, 1987; Campbell et al., 1996; Lavigne et al., 1998).

Barriers to Treatment

Whether parents will seek help for children's problems remains a question. Although availability of services is often a concern, the two most common barriers to seeking help are parents thinking the child will grow out of the problem behaviors and believing that they should be able to handle the problems as parents (Pavuluri, Luk, & McGee, 1996). Parents may also be unsure of the differences between their children's behaviors and those of normally developing children, or they may be concerned about the stigma of psychological treatment (Brauner & Stephens, 2006). Low socioeconomic status, low social support, poor maternal mental health, and parental separation are additional barriers to seeking treatment for children (Feehan, Stanton, McGee, & Silva, 1990; Pavuluri et al., 1996).

When children show anxious or depressive symptoms, especially those lasting for more than a year, or have experienced negative life events, parents are more likely to seek treatment (Douma, Dekker, De Ruiter, Verhulst, & Koot, 2006). Research has indicated that although 19% of parents of preschool children with disordered behavior seek help (Pavuluri et al., 1996), this rises to 55% of parents who observe problem behaviors in their 10- to 18-year-old children (Douma et al., 2006). Parents of younger children are more likely to seek help if their children are male, but this difference disappears as children become older (Feehan et al., 1990).

Once in treatment, parents' adherence to the therapist's recommendations becomes a concern. If parents perceive numerous barriers to the recommendations—such as competing time demands, trouble accessing the service, disagreement with the recommendation, or financial concerns—they are less likely to pursue the treatment (MacNaughton & Rodrigue, 2001).

Diagnostic Issues

In regard to the clinical diagnosis of preschool children, a number of significant questions have been raised. The primary issues are whether

DSM–IV–TR criteria can be reliably applied to preschoolers or whether these criteria need to be modified for young children. There is also the issue of whether children's problem behaviors are pathological and stable or developmental and transient and thus not in need of treatment. To determine whether a child demonstrates problem behaviors at a pathological level, the frequency, chronicity, context, and constellation of symptoms should all be considered. Studies have also indicated that the types of problems children exhibit change depending on the child's age (Campbell, 2002).

Because the manifestation of symptoms varies across developmental trajectories, conformation to the DSM–IV–TR classification system is difficult (Keenan & Wakschlag, 2002). Some of the concerns about using the DSM–IV–TR to diagnose children include the rapid changes that occur in the preschool age period, individual differences in rate of development, and the differentiation of problem behaviors as being characteristic of the child as opposed to relational difficulties. For example, research has found developmental differences in the manifestation of symptoms among 3- to 5-year-olds, especially when anxiety and fears are considered (Spence, Rapee, McDonald, & Ingram, 2001). Other issues with using DSM–IV–TR criteria for diagnosis are the need for clinically significant distress, which preschool children are not likely to report, and the necessary duration of symptoms. Also, when diagnosing preschoolers, clinicians should not consider the full array of DSM–IV–TR disorders because some disorders, such as schizophrenia, are not seen in this age group.

Difficulties in accurately and reliably diagnosing preschool children with DSM–IV–TR diagnostic criteria are common. Prevalence rates of any disorder, including anxiety, mood, and behavior disorders, range from 14% to 26.4% when clinical interviews and subsequent clinical judgment are used diagnostically (Egger & Angold, 2006). When the DSM–IV–TR criteria were used in clinical interviews, up to 76% of preschool-age children with clinically significant symptoms of major depressive disorder were not diagnosed (Luby et al., 2002).

These results highlight the need for developmentally appropriate diagnostic criteria, for which there continues to be no general consensus. Current examples include the Classification of Child and Adolescent Mental Diagnoses in Primary Care (American Academy of Pediatrics, 1996), the Diagnostic and Classification of Mental Health and Developmental Disorders of Infancy and Early Childhood (DC:0–3; National Center for Clinical and Infant Programs, 1994), and Research Diagnostic Criteria—Preschool Age (Task Force on Research Diagnostic Criteria, 2003). The Classification of Child and Adolescent Mental Diagnoses in Primary Care was developed to provide a stronger developmental distinction for diagnostic categories for young children, including family and social contexts (American Academy of Pediatrics, 1996). The Research Diag-

nostic Criteria—Preschool Age includes clearly specified diagnostic criteria for this age group that were developed for research use (Task Force on Research Diagnostic Criteria, 2003), whereas the DC:0–3 includes constellations of disorders that are not included in the *DSM–IV–TR*, as well as some that parallel criteria in the *DSM–IV–TR*. The DC:0–3 proposes a five-axis diagnosis that highlights the child's development, as well as contextual issues including family relationships (National Center for Clinical Infant Programs, 1994). Initial steps have been taken to measure the DC:0–3's validity; these steps suggest that many of the diagnoses are valid (Evangelista & McLellan, 2004).

Assessment Issues

The typical concerns about using standardized assessment measures relate to developmentally appropriate limitations with preschool-age children, which include their attention spans, which are shorter than those of older children; their temperament differences; and their difficulty in comprehending time when determining dates of symptom onset and duration. The ability to judge when to inhibit a response and when to be more open is different in younger children, as is language fluency. Although children are often seen as inaccurate reporters of their own symptoms, some research has suggested that preschool-age children can provide useful information about core depressive symptoms (Luby, Belden, Sullivan, & Spitznagel, 2007). However, it is important to have multiple informants during an assessment because children function differently across settings, and using a variety of raters can show these differences (Campbell, 2002).

Over the years, developmentally appropriate assessment measures have been created. The first of such measures were parent and teacher reports of children's behaviors (Achenbach et al., 1987; Angold & Egger, 2007; Behar, 1977; Richman et al., 1974). Since then, researchers have developed diagnostic interviews that are appropriate for this age group, as well as observational assessments. Self-report measures for children and direct interviews have been found useful, as have methods of coding responses to puppet-based interviews and story stems (Angold & Egger, 2007).

A few measures have been developed that are specifically intended for preschool-age children. The Preschool Age Psychiatric Assessment (PAPA; Egger & Angold, 2004) is a structured parent interview intended for parents of children between the ages of 2 and 5. This assessment consists of diagnostic modules that allow an interviewer to determine *DSM–IV–TR* diagnoses and levels of impairment. The PAPA also allows interviewers to consider developmental levels and problem areas that may not be identified in the *DSM–IV–TR*. Research has indicated that this is a reliable assessment tool for preschoolers.

Interviews using puppets and dolls have also proven useful. The Berkeley puppet interview has been used to show that preschool children's reports of depressive symptoms can predict their functioning 6 months later (Luby et al., 2007). This particular technique requires specific puppets and training, but children and practitioners can use ordinary puppets or materials to promote interactions. By speaking through puppets or dolls, children often feel more comfortable and psychologically safe in responding to sensitive topics.

Free play can also be used during assessment to observe numerous themes and behaviors. For example, how children enter the playroom, content of play, preferences, interactions, and energy level can all give information not only about the child's abilities and developmental level but also about what life is like for a particular child or difficulties he or she may be experiencing. Dollhouses, art supplies, a sandbox, miniature toys, puppets, play telephones, costumes, and the like are useful for engaging children in free play. As Sattler (1998) pointed out, play can be used to assess a child's ability to adapt and solve problems, as well as a child's quality of creativity, interpersonal interactions, and thought processes.

Parent Involvement in Treatment

Parents have proven to be a major resource for influencing preschool-age children's behavior (Nixon, 2002), and interventions that use parents as active partners in producing change in their preschool-age children have dominated the literature. The combination of ineffective parenting behaviors, family dysfunction, and child characteristics or vulnerabilities typically leads to problem behaviors that are persistent rather than transient. This biopsychosocial model suggests that how children's behaviors change and develop over time depends not only on the child's predispositions, but also on the caretaker's responsiveness to and accommodation of the child's needs. With appropriately engaged and responsive caretakers, as well as a stimulating environment, young children can show significant resilience in the face of early stressors (Campbell, 2002).

Research based in attachment theory has suggested that children's relationships with their caregivers form the basis of many long-term social behaviors and relationships (Bowlby, 1969; Thompson, 1998; Waters, Weinfield, & Hamilton, 2000; Weinfield, Sroufe, & Egeland, 2000). A secure attachment in the 1st year of life provides a model for later relationships and a feeling of safety and comfort for the helpless infant.

The parent–child relationship changes when children enter the preschool years. Infants are dependent on their parents for all aspects of caretaking, whereas preschool-age children are becoming more autonomous and focused on exploring their worlds. During these years, parents must learn to set limits and give children guidelines for appropriate behavior (Campbell, 2002). This allows children to safely and comfortably interact with new situations and people and thus to learn about social and behavioral norms. Parents' ability to provide such limits while maintaining a positive relationship helps children to develop self-control and other necessary skills for positive development (Kochanska, 1997; Patterson, DeBaryshe, & Ramsey, 1989).

Children who experience conflictual rather than positive relationships with their caretakers have been shown to have persistent behavioral and emotional problems (Campbell, 1995, 1997; Campbell et al., 1996; DeKlyen, Speltz, & Greenberg, 1998). Research has also found that children raised without effective limit setting and appropriate discipline are prone to exhibit self-centered and oppositional behaviors (Aunola & Nurmi, 2005).

These findings indicate that a parenting style that includes love and warmth, as well as consistent limits, can have a positive impact on children's clinical presentation. Accordingly, therapeutic interventions that support the development and maintenance of parent–child interactions featuring both warmth and structure—that is, an authoritative parenting style—are quite effective with preschool children. Observation of parent–child interactions during play is a useful way of determining a parent's style of child rearing (Blundon & Schaefer, 2006).

If children are developing along typical trajectories, parenting classes can be useful to help parents continue to promote positive development (Powell, Dunlap, & Fox, 2004). Parent management training has proven effective in reducing both oppositional and conduct problems in preschoolers (Eyberg, 1992). Interventions that use parent training usually combine behavior modification strategies with relationship enhancement practices. This combination allows parents to improve in both discipline and positive interactions with their children. Parent training is reciprocal because mental health professionals share their knowledge of effective parenting and parents share their experience of what works and does not work in influencing their children (Briesmeister & Schaefer, 1998). Subsequent chapters focus on a variety of play-based parent training interventions that can be used to target specific problems of preschool-age children.

Empirically Supported Interventions

The empirically supported intervention movement originated in the medical field, wherein scientists and practitioners began looking for treatments that had research supporting their effectiveness. Policymakers hoped that evidence-based practice would combat rising health care costs, improve quality of care and training, and boost consumer satisfaction (Fertuck, 2007). One significant concern of practitioners, however, is that third-party payers will only use lists of specified, empirically supported interventions to guide payment for services while neglecting clinical expertise and client preferences.

In 2005, the American Psychological Association (APA) developed a task force to consider how to integrate research with evidence in psychological interventions, as well as to consider the roles of clinical expertise and patient values in decision making. APA (2005) suggested that combination of empirically supported interventions and patient needs should guide treatment decision. Although some treatments have been empirically validated and supported, more efforts are needed to examine the impact of clinical judgment and skill on clinical outcomes (Fertuck, 2007).

Numerous empirical studies support the efficacy of play therapy. These studies include interventions for individual children, groups of children, and parent–child dyads. Meta-analyses of play therapy have found that effect sizes range from moderate to large, indicating that play therapy has resulted in significant positive changes in children's behavior (LeBlanc & Ritchie, 2001). LeBlanc and Ritchie (2001) found that the inclusion of parents in treatment led to higher, more positive outcomes in play therapy. Bratton, Ray, Rhine, and Jones (2005) also noted that training parents to be cotherapists, as in filial play therapy, leads to higher effect sizes.

DEVELOPMENTAL ISSUES

Developmental issues related to psychotherapy for young children include the development of play and emotional regulation in preschoolers, the use of metaphors, and creating a therapeutic alliance.

Play Development During the Preschool Years

There are substantial changes in the nature of children's play during these early years. In normal development, children progress from parallel play around age 3 to more cooperative and social play around age 4. Play themes begin to include movement between reality and fantasy. At this time, children are beginning to take other people's perspectives in their play and are able to engage in more shared imagination play than when they were younger. By age 5, children are exhibiting more make-believe play and continuing to develop more cooperative play (Schaefer & DiGeronimo, 2000). Frequent engagement in pretend play has important implications for preschoolers' cognitive, emotional, and social growth (Gordon, 1993). Pretend play is particularly useful for developing the perspective-taking ability needed for successful positive peer interactions (Bergen, 2002). By age 5, children begin to enjoy playing simple games, such as Candyland, which further develops social skills such as turn taking and good sportsmanship.

It is also important to recognize the developmental need for substantial free play in early childhood. Play allows children to learn about their worlds and master challenges, improve physical development, think creatively, and interact with others in a positive way. With children's worlds becoming more academically driven and hurried, child-directed play is typically one of the first items that parents and teachers take off of children's schedules. This can contribute to stress, anxiety, and depression, all of which negatively affect functioning not only in the childhood years but also throughout development (Ginsburg, 2007).

Development of Emotional Regulation in Preschoolers

During the preschool years, a major developmental task is to understand, identify, and regulate one's emotions. When children are able to control their emotions, their peers rate them as more friendly and likable (Denham & Weissberg, 2004). A major way in which young children learn to modulate the frequency and intensity of their emotional reactions is pretend play. Research has shown that those children who exhibit emotional regulation during pretend play are more likely to show similar skills in daily life (Galyer & Evans, 2001). Further research has suggested that this is particularly true for girls, although engaging in more pretend play, particularly with caregivers, is linked to higher understanding of emotions by children of both genders (Lindsey & Colwell, 2003).

Pretend play with peers is also important, especially with peers who are slightly more advanced. By routinely playing with someone who has more experience, children are able to develop more frequent, appropriate, and adaptive emotional displays. This play also leads to improvements in children's level of empathy and ability to identify their own emotional states and needs in nonplay interactions (Galyer & Evans, 2001). Sociodramatic play, wherein preschoolers enact different roles in a skit, has proven particularly effective in boosting emotional regulation in impulsive children (Elias & Berk, 2002). Further details on the role of sociodramatic play in fostering self-regulation in young children can be found in chapter 9 of this volume by Katherine A. Gioia and Renee Tobin.

Developmental Perspective on the Use of Metaphors With Preschoolers

Research has suggested that preschool-age children are able to understand metaphors and literal sentences at comparable levels (Pearson, 1990). This suggests that metaphors in therapy with children are possible, and in fact, children prefer to use metaphors to complete tasks such as relaxation

(Heffner, Greco, & Eifert, 2003). One example of an appropriate therapeutic metaphor for relaxation is for the child to pretend he or she is a turtle going into its shell, rather than the literal wording to squeeze the shoulders upward (Heffner, et al., 2003). The use of a specific metaphor must be tailored to the child's individual interests, experiences, and characteristics.

There are some differences in the characteristics of children who respond well to metaphors. For example, children with higher cognitive functioning show greater responsiveness on these tasks (Heffner et al., 2003). Such children are likely somewhat older, and research has suggested that older preschool children, specifically boys, show greater comprehension of metaphors than do younger children (Lutzer, 1991). This suggests that as children's language and abstract reasoning skills develop, the use of metaphor becomes a more salient and effective treatment option.

Forming a Therapeutic Alliance With Preschoolers: A Developmental Perspective

Developing a therapeutic alliance with a child is the first and probably most important task of a child therapist. Young children lack awareness of their psychological problems and typically do not self-refer themselves or come voluntarily to therapy. Moreover, they frequently are quite anxious about meeting with a strange adult and thus strongly resist entering treatment.

Bordin (1994) proposed that a critical aspect of forming a working therapeutic alliance with a client is the development of a bond of mutual liking. Developmentally, the best way to forge such a bond with a child is by engaging in the child's favorite and most enjoyable activity—play. Through play, a pleasure bond is formed between therapist and child, which leads to the child's liking of the therapist and willingness to engage in the therapy process.

Apart from play, what else can the therapist do to promote an alliance with a young child? In a study of play therapists, Nalavany, Ryan, Gomory, and Lacasse (2005) found that they considered Rogerian theory—which emphasizes therapist warmth, genuineness, empathy, and respect—a vital nonspecific factor in developing a therapeutic alliance with children. Also, when the therapist takes a nondirective stance in the play, the child is able to form a positive alliance at his or her own pace.

SUMMARY AND CONCLUSIONS

In conclusion, a number of clinical issues need to be considered in therapeutic interventions with preschool-age children. Preschool-age children show emotional and behavioral concerns of a clinically significant nature that, when left untreated, can persist throughout the life span. Diagnostic criteria are being developed that can more accurately and appropriately identify these difficulties. However, there are barriers to initiating treatment that have yet to be overcome. Providing information to parents about the differences and stability of problem behaviors versus normative development can be useful, as can providing access to treatment and positively affecting the parent–child relationship.

A number of developmental perspectives can enhance treatment effectiveness. These include changes in the nature of children's play during the preschool years, the effective use of metaphors, and the use of play to form a therapeutic alliance with the child. The following chapters discuss a variety of effective treatments that can be used with this population, including filial therapy, cognitive–behavioral play therapy, sand tray therapy, parent–child interaction therapy, and child-centered play therapy.

REFERENCES

Achenbach, T. M., Edelbrock, C., & Howell, C. T. (1987). Empirically based assessment of the behavioral/emotional problems of 2- and 3-year old children. *Journal of Abnormal Child Psychology, 15,* 629–650.

American Academy of Pediatrics. (1996). *The classification of child and adolescent mental diagnoses in primary care (DSM-PC).* Elk Grove, IL: Author.

American Psychiatric Association. (2000). *Diagnostic and statistical manual of mental disorders* (4th ed., text revision). Washington, DC: Author.

American Psychological Association. (2005). *Report of the 2005 Presidential Task Force on Evidence-Based Practice.* Washington, DC: Author.

Angold, A., & Egger, H. L. (2007). Preschool psychopathology: Lessons for the life-span. *Journal of Child Psychology and Psychiatry, 48,* 961–966.

Aunola, K., & Nurmi, J. (2005). The role of parenting styles in children's problem behavior. *Child Development, 76,* 1144–1159.

Behar, L. (1977). The Preschool Behavior Questionnaire. *Journal of Abnormal Child Psychology, 5,* 265–275.

Bergen, D. (2002). The role of pretend play in children's cognitive development. *Early Childhood Research and Practice, 4,* Article 2. Retrieved May 20, 2008, from http://ecrp.uiuc.edu/v4n1/bergen.html

Blundon, J. A., & Schaefer, C. E. (2006). The role of parent–child play in children's development. *Psychology and Education, 43,* 1–10.

Bordin, E. S. (1994). *The working alliance.* New York: Wiley.

Bowlby, J. S. (1969). *Attachment and loss: Vol. I. Attachment.* New York: Basic Books.

Bratton, S. C., Ray, D., Rhine, T., & Jones, L. (2005). The efficacy of play therapy with children: A meta-analytic review of treatment outcomes. *Professional Psychology: Research and Practice, 36,* 376–390.

Brauner, C. B., & Stephens, C. B. (2006). Estimating the prevalence of early childhood serious emotional/behavioral disorders: Challenges and recommendations [Special report]. *Public Health Reports, 121,* 303–310.

Briesmeister, J. M., & Schaefer, C. E. (1998). *Handbook of parent training* (2nd ed.). New York: Wiley.

Campbell, S. B. (1995). Behavior problems in preschool children: A review of recent research. *Journal of Child Psychology and Psychiatry, 36,* 113–149.

Campbell, S. B. (1997). Behavior problems in preschool children: Developmental and family issues. In T. Ollendick & R. Prinz (Eds.), *Advances in clinical child psychology* (Vol. 19, pp. 1–26). New York: Plenum Press.

Campbell, S. B. (2002). *Behavior problems in preschool children.* New York: Guilford Press.

Campbell, S. B., Pierce, E. W., Moore, G., Marakovitz, S., & Newby, K. (1996). Boys' externalizing problems at elementary school: Pathways from early behavior problems, maternal control, and family stress. *Development and Psychopathology, 8,* 701–720.

Campbell, S. B., Shaw, D. S., & Gilliom, M. (2000). Early externalizing behavior problems: Toddlers and preschoolers at risk for later maladjustment. *Development and Psychopathology, 12,* 467–488.

DeKlyen, M., Speltz, M. L., & Greenberg, M. T. (1998). Fathering and early onset conduct problems: Positive and negative parenting, father–son attachment, and marital conflict. *Clinical Child and Family Psychology Review, 1,* 3–22.

Denham, S. A., & Weissberg, R. P. (2004). Social-emotional learning in early childhood: What we know and where to go from here. In E. Chesebrough, P. King, T. P. Gullotta, & M. Bloom (Eds.), *A blueprint for the promotion of prosocial behavior in early childhood* (pp. 13–50). New York: Kluwer Academic/Plenum Publishers.

Douma, J. C., Dekker, M. C., De Ruiter, K. P., Verhulst, F. C., & Koot, H. M. (2006). Help-seeking process of parents for psychopathology in youth with moderate to borderline intellectual disabilities. *Journal of the American Academy of Child & Adolescent Psychiatry, 45,* 1232–1242.

Egger, H. L., & Angold, A. (2004). The Preschool Age Psychiatric Assessment (PAPA): A structured parent interview for diagnosing psychiatric disorders in preschool children. In R. DelCarmen-Wiggens & A. Carter (Eds.), *Handbook of infant, toddler, and preschool mental health assessment* (pp. 223–243). New York: Oxford University Press.

Egger, H. L., & Angold, A. (2006). Common emotional and behavioral disorders in preschool children: Presentation, nosology, and epidemiology. *Journal of Child Psychology and Psychiatry, 47,* 313–337.

Elias, C., & Berk, L. E. (2002). Self-regulation in young children: Is there a role for sociodramatic play? *Early Childhood Research Quarterly, 17,* 216–238.

Evangelista, N., & McLellan, M. J. (2004). The zero to three diagnostic system: A framework for considering emotional and behavioral problems in young children. *School Psychology Review, 33,* 159–173.

Eyberg, S. M. (1992). Parent and teacher behavior inventories for the assessment of conduct problem behaviors in children. In L. VandeCreek, S. Knapp, & T. L. Jackson (Eds.), *Innovations in clinical practice: A source book* (Vol. 11, pp. 261–270). Sarasota, FL: Professional Resource Press.

Feehan, M., Stanton, W., McGee, R., & Silva, P. A. (1990). Parental help-seeking for behavioural and emotional problems in childhood and adolescence. *Community Health Studies, 14*, 303–309.

Fertuck, E. A. (2007). [Review of the book *Evidence-based psychotherapy: Where theory and practice meet*]. *Psychotherapy: Theory, Research, Practice, Training, 44*, 115–120.

Galyer, K. T., & Evans, I. M. (2001). Pretend play and the development of emotion regulation in preschool children. *Early Child Development and Care, 166*, 93–108.

Gimpel, G. A., & Holland, M. L. (2003). *Emotional and behavioral problems of young children: Effective interventions in the preschool and kindergarten years.* New York: Guilford Press.

Ginsburg, K. R. (2007). The importance of play in promoting healthy child development and maintaining strong parent–child bonds. *Pediatrics, 119*, 182–191.

Gordon, D. E. (1993). The inhibition of pretend play and its implications for development. *Human Development, 36*, 215–234.

Hechtman, L. (1996). *Do they grow out of it? Long-term outcomes of childhood disorders.* Washington, DC: American Psychiatric Publishing.

Heffner, M., Greco, L. A., & Eifert, G. H. (2003). Pretend you are a turtle: Children's responses to metaphorical versus literal relaxation instructions. *Child & Family Behavior Therapy, 25*, 19–33.

Keenan, K., & Wakschlag, L. S. (2002). Can a valid diagnosis of disruptive behavior disorder be made in preschool children? *American Journal of Psychiatry, 159*, 351–358.

Kochanska, G. (1997). Mutually responsive orientation between mothers and their young children: Implications for early socialization. *Child Development, 68*, 94–112.

Lavigne, J. V., Arend, R., Rosenbaum, D., Binns, H., Christoffel, K. K., & Gibbons, R. D. (1998). Psychiatric disorders with onset in the preschool years: I. Stability of diagnoses. *Journal of the American Academy of Child & Adolescent Psychiatry, 37*, 1246–1254.

Lavigne, J. V., Gibbons, R. D., Christoffel, K. K., Arend, R., Rosenbaum, D., Binns, H., et al. (1996). Prevalence rates and correlates of psychiatric disorders among preschool children. *Journal of the American Academy of Child & Adolescent Psychiatry, 35*, 204–214.

LeBlanc, M., & Ritchie, M. (2001). A meta-analysis of play therapy outcomes. *Counselling Psychology Quarterly, 14*, 149–163.

Lindsey, E. W., & Colwell, M. J. (2003). Preschoolers' emotional competence: Links to pretend and physical play. *Child Study Journal, 33*, 39–52.

Luby, J. L., Belden, A., Sullivan, J., & Spitznagel, E. (2007). Preschoolers' contribution to their diagnosis of depression and anxiety: Uses and limits of young child self-reports of symptoms. *Child Psychiatry and Human Development, 38*, 321–338.

Luby, J. L., Heffelfinger, A. K., Mrakotsky, C., Hessler, M. J., Brown, K. M., & Hildebrand, T. (2002). Preschool major depressive disorder: Preliminary validation for developmentally modified *DSM–V* criteria. *Journal of the American Academy of Child & Adolescent Psychiatry, 41*, 928–937.

Lutzer, V. D. (1991). Gender differences in preschoolers' ability to interpret common metaphors. *Journal of Creative Behavior, 25*, 69–74.

MacNaughton, K. L., & Rodrigue, J. R. (2001). Predicting adherence to recommendations by parents of clinic-referred children. *Journal of Consulting and Clinical Psychology, 69*, 262–270.

Nalavany, B. A., Ryan, S. D., Gomory, T., & Lacasse, J. R. (2005). Mapping the characteristics of a "good" play therapist. *International Journal of Play Therapy, 14*, 27–50.

National Center for Clinical Infant Programs. (1994). *0-3: Diagnostic classification of mental health and developmental disorders of infancy and early childhood*. Arlington, VA: Author.

Nixon, R. (2002). Treatment of behavior problems in preschoolers: A review of parent training programs. *Clinical Psychology Review, 22*, 525–546.

Patterson, G. R., DeBaryshe, B., & Ramsey, E. (1989). A developmental perspective on antisocial behavior. *American Psychologist, 44*, 329–335.

Pavuluri, M. N., Luk, S., & McGee, R. (1996). Help-seeking for behavior problems by parents of preschool children: A community study. *Journal of the American Academy of Child & Adolescent Psychiatry, 35*, 215–222.

Pearson, B. Z. (1990). The comprehension of metaphor by preschool children. *Journal of Child Language, 17*, 185–203.

Pierce, E. W., Ewing, L. J., & Campbell, S. B. (1999). Diagnostic status and symptomatic behavior of hard-to-manage preschool children in middle childhood and early adolescence. *Journal of Clinical Child Psychology, 28*, 44–57.

Powell, D., Dunlap, G., & Fox, L. (2006). Prevention and intervention for the challenging behaviors of toddlers and preschoolers. *Infants & Young Children, 19*, 25–35.

Richman, N., Stevenson, J. E., Graham, P. J., Ridgely, M. S., Goldman, H. H., & Talbott, J. A. C. (1974). Prevalence of behaviour problems in 3-year-old children: An epidemiological study in a London borough. *Journal of Child Psychology and Psychiatry, 16*, 277–287.

Sattler, J. M. (1998). *Clinical and forensic interviewing of children and families*. San Diego: Author.

Schaefer, C. E., & DiGeronimo, T. F. (2000). *Ages & stages*. New York: Wiley.

Spence, S. H., Rapee, R., McDonald, C., & Ingram, M. (2001). The structure of anxiety symptoms among preschoolers. *Behaviour Research and Therapy, 39*, 1293–1316.

Task Force on Research Diagnostic Criteria: Infancy and Preschool. (2003). Research diagnostic criteria for infants and preschool children: The process and empirical support. *Journal of the American Academy of Child & Adolescent Psychiatry, 42*, 1504–1512.

Thompson, R. A. (1998). Early socio-personality development. In W. Damon (Series Ed.) & N. Eisenberg (Vol. Ed.), *Handbook of child psychology: Vol. 3. Social, emotional, and personality development* (5th ed., pp. 25–104). New York: Wiley.

Waters, E., Weinfield, N. A., & Hamilton, C. E. (2000). The stability of attachment security from infancy to adolescence and early adulthood: General discussion. *Child Development, 71*, 703–706.

Weinfield, N. S., Sroufe, L. A., & Egeland, B. (2000). Attachment from infancy to early adulthood in a high risk sample: Continuity, discontinuity, and their correlates. *Child Development, 71*, 695–702.

Wilens, T. E., Biederman, J., Brown, S., Monuteaux, M., Prince, J., & Spencer, T. J. (2002). Patterns of psychopathology and dysfunction in clinically referred preschoolers. *Journal of Developmental & Behavioral Pediatrics, 23*(Suppl. 1), S31–S36.

2

EVIDENCE SUPPORTING THE BENEFIT OF PLAY FOR MILD TO MODERATE BEHAVIOR PROBLEMS OF PRESCHOOL CHILDREN

CHARLES E. SCHAEFER

Play interventions have proven effective in reducing or resolving a number of common problems of preschoolers, such as anxious and aggressive behaviors. If the healing powers of play are applied to these problems when they are of mild to moderate intensity, they are less likely to escalate into serious disorders. In this chapter, I describe a range of evidence-based play interventions for these subclinical difficulties. Often, parents and teachers can be trained by professionals to implement these play interventions in the natural environment. The first part of the chapter focuses on preschool children's common fears and anxieties, and the second part addresses aggressive behavior problems.

ANXIETY AND FEARFULNESS

Anxiety problems are the most common psychological disorders of childhood. Play researchers have devoted more attention to studying these difficulties than to any other childhood disorder. Consequently, a wide variety of evidence-based play interventions are now available for resolving young children's anxieties and fears. The following research findings should aid practitioners in both preventing and treating these troublesome behaviors.

Anticipatory Anxiety

Play activities have proven very beneficial in preparing young children for common stressful events and thus inoculating preschoolers to the anxiety these stressors trigger. Levy (1959) found that few parents prepare their children for life's common stressful experiences such as a doctor or dentist visit, starting school, or hospitalization. According to Levy, most parents view these events as part of living and do not believe their children need special preparation or training to cope.

However, stress theorists and researchers have asserted that the most effective means of preparing children for life's numerous stressful events is an active preparatory process in which parents and caregivers give information ahead of time. The goal is to inform children about what they will be experiencing and to give them coping skills.

Play is a particularly effective means of preparing young children for forthcoming stressful experiences. For a child about to start school for the first time, a toy schoolhouse, school bus, and miniature dolls can be used by parent and child to play out the sequence of events involved in attending school (e.g., getting on the bus, greeting the teacher) and to model with the dolls effective ways to handle these situations. The major therapeutic benefits of this preparatory pretend play are to (a) make the strange familiar, (b) practice coping skills, (c) listen to the child's concerns, and (d) correct any misperceptions the child might have about the situation.

Most of the research on stress inoculation play has focused on its application with children about to undergo medical procedures. Burstein and Meichenbaum (1979) gave children facing minor surgery the option of playing with either a medically related or nonmedically related toy. They found that children who were least anxious before the surgery had spent significantly more time playing with the medically related toys 1 week before surgery. These children also reported significantly less postoperative anxiety a week after surgery. Burstein and Meichenbaum concluded that the low-anxiety children engaged in the "work of worrying," namely, cognitive anticipation of what the procedure would be like and rehearsal of coping skills.

According to the "work-of-worrying" concept first proposed by Janis (1958), a person will be better able to tolerate pain and suffering if he or she worries about it beforehand rather than maintaining an expectation of personal invulnerability. Simply put, forewarned is forearmed. In studying the reactions of adult preoperative surgery patients, Janis found that a moderate amount of anticipatory fear about the impending operation permitted patients to develop effective inner defenses. In contrast, situations in which patients did not worry beforehand made them less able to cope with the pain and discomfort following surgery.

Cassell (1965) presented additional research support for stress inoculation play. She found that children (ages 3–11) hospitalized for cardiac catheterization showed less stress responses to the procedure if a nurse played out the procedure the day before. Using miniature hospital play toys and puppets, the nurse demonstrated the sequence of the upcoming medical procedure. Then the child played the role of the doctor performing the procedure, and the nurse played the role of the child. This role reversal allowed the child to experience a sense of power and control that was not possible during the actual procedure.

Cassell (1965) noted that the children who participated in this preoperative play preparation exhibited fewer stress responses during the procedure than a no-treatment control group. They also expressed more willingness to return to the hospital for further treatment.

The beneficial effects of encouraging children to play out impending medical procedures (e.g., needle injections, surgery, anesthesia) on lowering their anxiety during and after the procedure have been replicated by a growing number of investigators (e.g., Hatava, Olsson, & Lagerkransr, 2000; Johnson & Stockdale, 1975; Li, Lopez, & Lee, 2007; Pressdee, May, Eastman, & Grier, 1997; Schwartz, 1983; Young & Fu, 1988; Zahr, 1998).

When compared with traditional ways (verbal, written, film) of preparing children for medical procedures, fantasy play with medical toys, equipment, and procedures has proven to be the most effective. Thus, play preparation has become the evidence-based intervention of choice for these children. Research findings have indicated that play preparation for very young children (ages 3–5) should take place the day before the medical procedure and for children ages 6 to 12, 5 to 7 days before.

Also noteworthy is the finding by Patel et al. (2006) that the use of handheld video games significantly reduced the anxiety level of preschoolers undergoing outpatient surgery. Video game play is now being widely applied in health care settings to distract children by providing an enjoyable and familiar activity.

Apart from medical play, parents can use preparatory fantasy play to reduce the stress of many other life events. Kramer (1996), for instance, found that 3- to 5-year-old firstborn children who, the month before the birth of a sibling, used fantasy play to enact their concerns tended to interact more positively with their sibling at 6 months and 14 months after the birth. The fantasy play seemed to serve a preparatory function by helping the children more realistically anticipate the changes that would occur with the new child's arrival.

Play can be invaluable not only to prepare the child for the birth of a sibling but to assist the mother and child in maintaining a close relationship after the arrival of the new baby. Baydar, Greek, and Brooks-Gunn (1997) studied the effect of the birth of a sibling on the interaction between the mother and the older child over the first 6 years of life. They found in a national sample of more than 400 children that positive interactions between the mother and the older child diminished after the birth, especially if the birth interval was short and the mother increasingly adopted a controlling parenting style. One way to prevent such a deterioration in the parent–older child relationship would be for the mother to schedule regular, special play times with the older child during which the mother adopts a warm, nondirective, child-centered approach during the play interactions.

Chronically Ill Children

Chronic illness or disability in children can produce considerable stress and trigger burdensome fears and anxieties. Play can be an antidote to this distress. Chronically ill children in the hospital, for example, have reported that health care personnel help them adapt by being in a positive mood, displaying a sense of humor, and distracting them by playing games with them (Boyd & Hunsberger, 1998). Clearly, hospitalized children's need to play and feel joy is particularly strong.

Playful fantasy can also be a coping resource for chronically ill preschool children. Johnson, Whitt, and Martin (1987) found that when parents trained their ill children to be more imaginative, the children's anxiety level was reduced to a more normal level. The brief, parent-administered intervention consisted of having the children engage in playful fantasies for 15 minutes a day over a 2-week period. The fantasy exercises were selected from Richard DeMille's (1967) book *Put Your Mother on the Ceiling*. Chronically ill children in an attention control group maintained their previously elevated anxiety level. The parents and the children stated that they found the fantasy play to be both practical and enjoyable as a home-based intervention.

Separation Anxiety

Separation protest (i.e., brief, mild upset on separation from the mother) is a normal behavior of young children (ages 9 months to 3 years). *Separation anxiety* refers to a more pronounced and prolonged distress of the child after separation.

One of the earliest studies of the effect of play on separation anxiety was conducted by Barnett (1984). She found that if preschoolers who were exhibiting separation anxiety in the classroom were allowed to engage in fantasy play, their anxiety level was significantly reduced. A control group of children with separation anxiety who were read stories by their teachers after separation did not show a similar reduction in anxiety.

Milos and Reiss (1982) also found that preschool children with high separation anxiety who were assisted in playing out separation themes in their classroom fantasy play reduced their level of anxiety. A control group of children with high separation anxiety who played with toys irrelevant to separation themes (blocks, puzzles, crayons) did not show a comparable reduction in anxiety. The authors noted that the more the play of the children with separation anxiety focused on separation themes and attempts to resolve the anxiety, the lower their scores were on the posttest anxiety measures.

Providing preschoolers with transitional objects has proven to be another effective way to reduce their separation anxiety. The ability to derive comfort from an object that reminds the child of the mother (e.g., soft stuffed animals or dolls) begins as early as 5 to 9 months and continues to be a significant aid through the preschool years. Triebenbacher and Tegano (1993) found that young children who used transitional objects, such as teddy bears, showed less anxiety when separated from their mothers at child care centers compared with a group of children who were not attached to such objects.

In other studies (Passman & Weisberg, 1975; Ybarra, Passman, & Eisenberg, 2000), 3-year-old children attached to transitional objects were able to handle the stress of being alone in novel settings, for example, pediatric outpatient exam rooms, as well as if their mothers were present in the rooms. Moreover, a study by Boniface and Graham (1979) revealed that 3-year-olds who insisted on having a specific soft object present at bedtime or at times of stress had fewer sleep disturbances and were more independent than 3-year-olds who did not insist on such objects.

Notwithstanding the research supporting the benefit that preschoolers derive from their attachment to dolls and other soft objects, survey research has found that only about 40% of U.S. parents have a positive attitude toward transitional object use by their young children. Public education about the proven benefits of transitional object use by young children would be helpful in this regard.

Another strategy to prepare very young children for parental separations is for parents to play simple games with the child, such as peekaboo, jack-in-the-box, and hide-and-seek. Such game play demonstrates to children that although familiar objects leave or disappear, they can be counted on to soon return. Beginning in infancy, separation and reunion games can be played with children on a regular basis to help them deal with the stress of separations from caretakers.

Anxiety Dreams

An *anxiety dream* or *nightmare* is a scary dream that awakens the sleeper. Most preschool children will report occasional nightmares, and about 5% experience them weekly. The peak age for the occurrence of nightmares in children is 3 to 6 years. The typical nightmare of preschool children is that they are being chased by a frightening object, such as a monster, and cannot escape.

Halliday (1987) identified four anxiety-producing features common to the nightmare experience, namely, the nightmare's uncontrollability, its perceived sense of reality, the dreadful and anxiety-producing storyline, and the great significance or meaning that it seems to have. Halliday suggested that any intervention that can give relief from one or more of these factors should provide a reduction in nightmare distress.

The *Senoi dream technique* is often used by therapists and parents to help children with nightmares. The Senoi Indians, a native tribe of Malaysia, originated this approach, which basically involves rescripting the nightmare's storyline. A child who is experiencing recurring nightmares is advised by the parents to think of a way to change the dream's ending to make it less scary, for example, make friends with the monster, have the monster fall into a trap or fly away, or call on a dream helper or superhero for help in overcoming the scary object. To make the scary object more concrete, external, and manageable, toys, dolls, or puppets can be used to rehearse the rescripting. During the day, the child plays out a more satisfying ending for the dream using the play objects. This enactment of a positive dream ending should be repeated for 3 consecutive days to solidify the child's perceived sense of control of the nightmare. If the nightmare returns, the play rehearsal is repeated for another 3 consecutive days. Halliday (1995) reported the successful application of this technique with young children. Krakow, Sandoval, Schrader, and Keuhne (2001) found this imagery rehearsal strategy to be effective in reducing the chronic nightmares of teenage girls and sexually abused women. It seems that teaching children, adolescents, and adults to imagine a positive ending to their nightmares is a clinically feasible and cost-effective approach.

Fears and Phobias

Nighttime fears are among the most common types of fear preschoolers experience; they encompass fears of intruders, the dark, imaginary creatures, and environmental threats such as house fires. These fears can cause significant interference with the child's functioning as well as much distress for the child and the family.

In a study by Muris, Merckelbach, Ollendick, King, and Bogie (2001), children reported that they found the following strategies helpful in coping with night frights:

- think to oneself that there is really nothing to be afraid of;
- call Mom or Dad into the room and ask them to sit close by;

- hug a pillow or soft doll;
- pray;
- try to stay up later;
- use distraction (e.g., read a book);
- check the bedroom to see whether someone is there; and
- try to go right to sleep.

An alternate strategy for combating fear that has proven more effective is *systematic desensitization*. In the systematic desensitization procedure, behaviors incompatible with fear (e.g., relaxation, pleasure, play) are used to counteract the fear. Santacruz, Mendez, and Sanchez-Meca (2006) found that a game-play desensitization intervention was superior to bibliotherapy in overcoming darkness phobia in a group of 4- to 8-year-olds. In the game-play procedure, parents were trained to play games with their fearful child for 20 minutes each week for 3 weeks.

In the handkerchief game, a blindfolded child tried to find a toy in his or her bedroom; in the toy-in-the-dark-room game, the child went into his or her dark bedroom to find a hidden toy; in the animal friend game, the child in a dark room guessed the animal sounds the parent made from another room; in the Olympiad of brave game, the child pretended to be a brave character and tried to stay alone in a dark room for longer and longer times, starting with 5 seconds. Santacruz et al. (2006) reported that the improvement the children showed in darkness phobia because of this intervention was maintained at a 1-year follow-up.

Emotive imagery, a variant of systematic desensitization, has also been used to reduce nighttime fears in children. Jackson and King (1981) used emotive imagery to treat a 5-year-old child with trauma-induced fears of darkness, noises, and shadows. Because the child's favorite superhero was Batman, the therapist created a fear hierarchy and then asked the child to imagine that he and Batman had joined forces and that he was appointed a special agent. Next, the child was asked to close his eyes and to imagine the fear-producing images in a graduated fashion (least to most scary) while accompanied by Batman. After only four sessions of emotive imagery, the child showed considerable improvement, and his gains were maintained at an 18-month follow-up.

Fear of animals is another very common childhood fear. Kuroda (1969) treated the fear of frogs in preschoolers by in vivo play desensitization. In a gamelike format, the children were helped to sing songs and tell stories about frogs and to dramatize the movements of frogs via dance. This playful desensitization procedure was found to be highly effective compared with a wait-list control group. In a second study, Kuroda reduced children's fear of cats by means of the same procedure.

Similarly, Croghan and Musante (1975) treated a 7-year-old boy with a phobia of high buildings by means of play desensitization. Games played in front of a feared building included throwing snowballs at the building, kicking the building and noticing that it did not kick back, and jumping over the cracks in the sidewalk in front of the building. After six play sessions, the therapist reported that the boy's fear of tall buildings subsided, and no difficulty was evident a year later.

For children exhibiting fearfulness after experiencing a single-incident stressor, a therapeutic power of play in which they will often engage on their own is abreaction. *Abreactive* play involves repeatedly reenacting a stressful real-life event in one's fantasy play. Barnett and Storm (1981), for example, observed that children ages 3 to 5 who were anxious after watching a scary movie tended to reenact the movie's distressing theme over and over in their play, with toys representing the movie's characters. This repetitive abreactive play decreased their physiological anxiety, whereas the anxiety level of a no-treatment control group remained stable. Barnett and Storm noted that if given a variety of toys, preschool children who have experienced a stressful event are likely to choose toys that allow them to face their anxiety by playfully reenacting the stressful situation. In so doing, they are able to gradually assimilate and master the mild to moderate stresses of life.

Galante and Foa (1986) also applied an abreactive play approach to help young children after an earthquake devastated their Italian village. During seven monthly play sessions, the children were given the opportunity to reenact the earthquake experience using miniature toys. To recreate the quake, they shook tables to topple toy houses. The children then pretended to be firemen or rescue workers who helped the survivors and rebuilt the village. Through this reenactment play, they could safely release their feelings about the disaster and gain a sense of mastery over it. Compared with untreated children from another damaged village, children who received this group play therapy showed a significant reduction in their anxiety symptoms. Gains were maintained at an 18-month follow-up.

Hurricane victims have also benefited from abreactive play. Saylor, Swenson, and Powell (1992) found that preschoolers who had experienced Hurricane Hugo in 1989 tended to spontaneously play out themes related to the hurricane. For instance, 8 weeks after the storm, a mother reported that her 4-year-old son repeatedly replayed the Hugo event with every medium available, including broccoli spears at dinner. The spears represented the trees being ravaged again and again by winds that reached 175 miles per hour.

Maqwaza, Killian, Petersen, and Pellay (1993) studied a group of preschoolers who were living amid chronic violence in South Africa. They found that the more the children were able to express their experiences through play and drawings, the less they suffered from trauma symptoms.

AGGRESSIVE BEHAVIORS

Preschool children who initiate physical and verbal aggressiveness in conflict situations with their peers tend to be deficient in interpersonal awareness, perspective-taking abilities, and cooperative behaviors. These social competence defects place them at risk for subsequent social and academic difficulties. Empirically supported play interventions have been identified for use with aggressive preschoolers both in groups and individually.

Udwin (1983) evaluated the effectiveness of imaginative play training for 34 aggressive preschoolers who had a history of physical child abuse or neglect. In the 10 imaginative play sessions, the trainers prompted the children to engage in fantasy play with puppets and to participate in sociodramatic play with their peers. The sociodramatic play involved taking roles and acting out scenarios and story lines such as "A Trip to the Moon" and "Goldilocks and the Three Bears." Compared with an attention control group, the fantasy-trained children significantly increased their cooperative peer interactions and decreased their aggressiveness.

Sociodramatic play training has been found by other investigators (Connolly & Doyle, 1984; Saltz, Dixon, & Johnson, 1977) to strengthen the preschool child's emerging social skills of empathy, role taking, self-control, sharing, and cooperation. In a pioneering study, Smilansky (1968) found that in disadvantaged preschoolers, sociodramatic play training increased positive affect, verbal fluency, and empathy and decreased aggressiveness toward peers.

Cooperative game play has also been found to be an effective intervention for reducing preschool children's aggressive behavior. Davitz (1952) trained 20 preschool children to play cooperatively (e.g., jointly draw a mural on a wall, jointly build a tower with blocks). The children, in groups of four, received seven cooperative play sessions each lasting 30 minutes. Compared with a no-treatment control group, the experimental group showed less aggression toward their peers after the training.

Bay-Hinitz, Peterson, and Quilitch (1994) conducted another study to determine whether aggressive preschool children who learned to play cooperative games would subsequently show less aggression toward others. Seventy children ages 4 to 5 were taught to play cooperative games in which a successful outcome depended on all the players assisting one another to achieve a common goal. The cooperative play resulted in decreased aggressive behaviors in the children's free play. Wolfe (1983) also noted a decrease in aggressive behaviors when teachers reinforced cooperative play among preschool children.

Because aggressive fantasies tend to lead to aggressive behaviors, another effective strategy is to restrict the occurrence of such fantasies. A study by Sherburne (1988) discovered that when preschool teachers required a child to play alone on a small rug in the classroom if the child displayed any violent or aggressive theme play (bombing, shooting, killing), the frequency of the violent theme play decreased, as did the child's number of overt aggressive acts. Other studies have reported that the more preschoolers watch violent television shows or play violent video games, the more violent fantasies they show in their pretend play and the more aggressive and destructive behaviors they exhibit in real life (Schaefer & Harrison, 2004).

Frances Gardner (1987; Gardner et al., 2003) observed the mother–child interactions of 60 3-year-old children in their homes in a study done in England. She found that the amount of spontaneous joint play between mother and child at age 3 predicted individual improvement in conduct problems at age 4. Noteworthy was the finding that this association was independent of the initial level of the child's conduct problems, hyperactivity, social class, maternal depression, and frequency of negative mother–child interactions. The amount of time the child spent unoccupied and not interacting with the mother independently predicted a worsening of the aggressive problems over time. Time spent by the child in other activities, including joint conversation and solitary play, did not predict a change in conduct behavior over time.

Gardner and colleagues (Gardner, 1987; Gardner et al., 2003) also studied *joint play*, in which the mother not only provided the child time and materials to play but became actively involved in the play. The play was reciprocal and cooperative—sometimes the mother initiated and directed the play and sometimes the child did. They both responded to each other's requests and suggestions. The researchers concluded that such cooperative play seemed to provide for the child a training ground for harmonious rather than conflicted, aggressive relationships that then generalized to peer interactions. A number of other researchers (Chandani, Prince, & Scott, 1999; Kochanska, Forman, Aksan, & Dunbar, 2005; Russell & Russell, 1996) have similarly found that a high frequency of joint play between mothers and their preschoolers is associated with a low rate of behavior problems in the children. Quality joint play was defined by Kochanska et al. (2005) as being characterized by two specific interactions by the play partners: (a) mutual responsiveness to each other's requests and directives and (b) shared positive affect.

The convergence of evidence by different investigators highlights the importance of joint play between mothers and their preschool children for promoting prosocial (cooperation) rather than antisocial (fighting) tendencies in the children.

OVERWEIGHT CHILDREN

The past 2 decades have shown a rapidly rising prevalence of children who are overweight or obese. Childhood obesity is associated with cardiovascular morbidity, diabetes, and a range of other medical conditions. Overweight and obesity in preschool children precedes a marked fall in self-esteem by the late primary grades. This is not surprising because these children are subject to elevated teasing and bullying by peers (Hesketh, Wake, & Waters, 2004). Also noteworthy is the finding that a 5-year-old who is obese has 8 times the risk of a 5-year-old who is not obese of suffering from obesity in adulthood.

The preschool years are increasingly being recognized as an important period for intervention efforts. Increased physical activity play is one way to combat children's weight problems by increasing their energy expenditure to match their energy intake.

Because physical activity is so enjoyable to children, they will be internally motivated to maintain an increase in this behavior. Burdette and Whitaker (2005) recommended using the word *play* rather than *exercise* or *sports* when encouraging young children to engage in active, unstructured outdoor movement. The word *play* helps them view the activity more positively.

In regard to children's use of leisure time, there are sedentary and passive pursuits—such as watching television, using the computer, and playing videogames—that compete with active outdoor play. For example, compared with preschool children who watch fewer than 2 hours of television a day, those who watch 2 hours or more spend an average of 30 minutes less time each day playing outdoors (Rideout, Vandewater, & Wartella, 2003).

Clearly, free play—particularly unstructured, outdoor physical play—needs to be restored to the lives of preschool children. Parents and teachers can assume a key role in both encouraging and modeling such active play for young children.

SUMMARY

Play interventions are often the most developmentally appropriate ways to treat preschool children. Child clinicians now have a wide array of play interventions to apply to the emerging behavior problems of young children. This chapter has summarized the empirical support for the effectiveness of play interventions for anxious, aggressive, and overweight preschoolers.

REFERENCES

Barnett, L. (1984). Young children's resolution of distress through play. *Journal of Child Psychology and Psychiatry, 25,* 477–483.

Barnett, L., & Storm, B. (1981). Play, pleasure and pain: The reduction of anxiety through play. *Leisure Science, 4,* 161–175.

Baydar, N., Greek, A., & Brooks-Gunn, J. (1997). A longitudinal study of the effects of the birth of a sibling during the first 6 years of life. *Journal of Marriage and the Family, 59*, 931–956.

Bay-Hinitz, A., Peterson, R., & Quilitch, H. (1994). Cooperative games: A way to modify aggressive and cooperative behavior in young children. *Journal of Applied Behavior Analysis, 27*, 435–444.

Boniface, D., & Graham, P. (1979). The three-year-old and his attachment to a special soft object. *Journal of Child Psychology and Psychiatry, 20*, 217–224.

Boyd, J. R., & Hunsberger, M. (1988). Chronically ill children coping with repeated hospitalizations: Their perceptions and suggested interventions. *Journal of Pediatric Nursing, 13*, 330–342.

Burdette, H., & Whitaker, R. (2005). Resurrecting free play in young children. *Archives of Pediatric & Adolescent Medicine, 159*, 46–50.

Burstein, S., & Meichenbaum, D. (1979). The work of worrying in children undergoing surgery. *Journal of Abnormal Child Psychology, 7*, 121–132.

Cassell, S. (1965). Effect of brief puppet therapy upon the emotional responses of children undergoing cardiac catheterization. *Journal of Consulting and Clinical Psychology, 29*, 1–8.

Chandani, K., Prince, M., & Scott, S. (1999). Development and initial validation of the Parent–Child Joint Activity Scale: A measure of joint engagement in activities between parent and child. *International Journal of Methods in Psychiatric Research, 8*, 219–228.

Connolly, J., & Doyle, A. (1984). Relation of fantasy play to social competence. *Developmental Psychology, 20*, 797–806.

Croghan, L., & Musante, G. (1975). The elimination of a boy's high-building phobia by in vivo desensitization and game playing. *Journal of Behavior Therapy and Experimental Psychology, 6*, 87–88.

Davitz, J. L. (1952). The effects of previous training on post-frustration behavior. *Journal of Abnormal and Social Psychology, 47*, 309–315.

DeMille, R. (1967). *Put your mother on the ceiling: Children's imagination games.* New York: Viking Press.

Galante, R., & Foa, E. (1986). An epidemiological study of psychic trauma and treatment effectiveness after a natural disaster. *Journal of the American Academy of Child & Adolescent Psychiatry, 25*, 357–363.

Gardner, F. (1987). Positive interaction between mothers and conduct problem children: Is there training for harmony as well as fighting? *Journal of Abnormal Child Psychology, 15*, 283–293.

Gardner, F., Ward, S., Burton, J., & Wilson, L. (2003). The role of mother–child joint play in the early development of children's conduct problems: A longitudinal study. *Social Development, 12*, 361–378.

Halliday, G. (1987). Direct psychological therapies for nightmares: A review. *Clinical Psychology Review, 7*, 501–523.

Halliday, G. (1995). Treating nightmares in children. In C.E. Schaefer (Ed.), *Clinical handbook of sleep disorders in children* (pp. 149–175). Northvale, NJ: Jason Aronson.

Hatava, P., Olsson, G., & Lagerkransr, M. (2000). Preoperative psychological preparation for children undergoing ENT operations: A comparison of two methods. *Paediatric Anaesthesia, 10*, 477–486.

Hesketh, K., Wake, M., & Waters, E. (2004). Body mass index and parent-reported self-esteem in elementary school children: Evidence for a causal relationship. *International Journal of Obesity, 28*, 1223–1227.

Jackson, H., & King, N. (1981). The emotive imagery treatment of a child's trauma-induced phobia. *Journal of Behavior Therapy and Experimental Psychology, 12*, 325–328.

Janis, I. (1958). *Psychological stress*. New York: Wiley.

Johnson, M., Whitt, J., & Martin, B. (1987). The effect of fantasy facilitation on anxiety in chronically ill and healthy children. *Journal of Pediatric Psychology, 12*, 273–283.

Johnson, P., & Stockdale, D. (1975). Effects of puppet therapy on palmer sweating of hospitalized children. *Johns Hopkins Medical Journal, 137*, 1–5.

Kochanska, G., Forman, D., Aksan, S., & Dunbar, S. (2005). Pathways to conscience: Early mother–child mutually responsive orientation and children's moral emotion, conduct, and cognition. *Journal of Child Psychology and Psychiatry, 46*, 19–34.

Krakow, B., Sandoval, D., Schrader, R., & Keuhne, B. (2001). Treatment of chronic nightmares in adjudicated adolescent girls in a residential facility. *Journal of Adolescent Health, 29*, 94–100.

Kramer, L. (1996). What's real in children's fantasy? Fantasy play across the transition to becoming a sibling. *Journal of Child Psychology and Psychiatry, 37*, 329–337.

Kuroda, J. (1969). Elimination of children's fear of animals by the method of experimental desensitization: An application of learning theory to child psychology. *Psychologia, 12*, 161–165.

Levy, E. (1959). Children's behavior under stress and its relation to training by parents to respond to stress situations. *Child Development, 30*, 307–324.

Li, H., Lopez, V., & Lee, T. (2007). Effects of preoperative, therapeutic play on outcomes of children undergoing day surgery. *Research in Nursing & Health, 30*, 320–332.

Maqwaza, A., Killian, B., Petersen, I., & Pellay, Y. (1993). The effects of chronic violence on preschool children living in South African townships. *Child Abuse & Neglect, 17*, 795–803.

Milos, M., & Reiss, S. (1982). Effects of three play conditions on separation anxiety in young children. *Journal of Consulting and Clinical Psychology, 50,* 389–395.

Muris, P., Merckelbach, H., Ollendick, T., King, N., & Bogie, N. (2001). Children's nighttime fears. *Behavior Research and Therapy, 39,* 13–28.

Passman, R., & Weisberg, P. (1975). Mothers and blankets as agents for promoting play and exploration in young children in a novel environment. *Journal of Consulting and Clinical Psychology, 53,* 603–611.

Patel, A., Schieble, T., Davidson, M., Tran, N., Schoenberg, C., Delphin, E., & Bennett, A. (2006). Distraction with a hand-held video game reduces pediatric preoperative anxiety. *Pediatric Anesthesia, 16,* 1019–1027.

Pressdee, D., May, L., Eastman, E., & Grier, D. (1997). The use of play therapy in the preparation of children undergoing MR imaging. *Clinical Radiology, 52,* 945–947.

Rideout, V., Vandewater, V., & Wartella, E. (2003). *Zero to six: Electronic media in the lives of infants, toddlers, and preschoolers.* Menlo Park, CA: Henry J. Kaiser Family Foundation.

Russell, A., & Russell, G. (1996). Positive parenting and boys' and girls' misbehavior during home observation. *International Journal of Behavior Development, 19,* 291–307.

Saltz, E., Dixon, D., & Johnson, J. (1977). Training disadvantaged preschoolers on various fantasy activities: Effects on cognitive functioning and impulse control. *Child Development, 48,* 367–380.

Santacruz, I., Mendez, F., & Sanchez-Meca, J. (2006). Play therapy applied by parents for children with darkness phobia: Comparison of two programmes. *Child & Family Behavior Therapy, 28,* 19–35.

Saylor, C., Swenson, C., & Powell, P. (1992). Hurricane Hugo blows down the broccoli: Preschoolers post-disaster play and adjustment. *Child Psychiatry & Human Development, 22,* 139–149.

Schaefer, C.E., & Harrison, W. (2004). The effects of violent fantasy on children's aggressive behavior. *Psychology & Education, 41,* 35–41.

Schwartz, B. (1983). Effects of psychological preparation on children hospitalized for dental operations. *Journal of Pediatrics, 103,* 634–638.

Sherburne, S. (1988). Decreasing violent or aggressive play theme play among preschool children with behavior problems. *Child Maltreatment, 7,* 187–197.

Smilansky, S. (1968). *The effects of sociodramatic play on disadvantaged preschool children.* New York: Wiley.

Triebenbacher, S., & Tegano, D. (1993). Children's use of transitional objects during daily separation from significant caretakers. *Perceptual and Motor Skills, 76,* 89–90.

Udwin, O. (1983). Imaginative play training as an intervention method with institutionalized preschool children. *British Journal of Educational Psychology, 53,* 32–39.

Wolfe, V. (1983). Teaching cooperative play to behavior problem preschool children. *Education & Treatment of Children, 6*, 1–9.

Ybarra, G., Passman, R., & Eisenberg, C. (2000). The presence of security blankets or mothers (or both) affects distress during pediatric examinations. *Journal of Consulting and Clinical Psychology, 68*, 322–336.

Young, M., & Fu, V. (1988). Influence of play and temperament on the young child's response to pain. *Children's Health Care, 16*, 209–215.

Zahr, L. (1998). Therapeutic play for hospitalized preschoolers in Lebanon. *Pediatric Nursing, 24*, 449–454.

3

PLAY THERAPY FOR INSECURELY ATTACHED PRESCHOOL CHILDREN

HELEN E. BENEDICT AND DIANA SCHOFIELD

Development of an attachment relationship is one of the primary developmental tasks of the first 3 years of life (Bowlby, 1988). Many preschool children emerge from toddlerhood with an insecure attachment to their primary attachment figure. This relationship can develop as secure or insecure in a variety of ways, depending on the relational environment in interaction with the basic endowment of the child (Ainsworth, Blehar, Waters, & Wall, 1978; Cicchetti, Toth, & Lynch, 1995). A secure infant attachment relationship serves developmentally as a basic foundation for much of preschool and later development; a child with an insecure attachment is at risk for subsequent problems in emotional, behavioral, cognitive, and social development (Kobak, Cassidy, Lyons-Ruth, & Ziv, 2006). Therefore, an insecurely attached preschool child is vulnerable to developmental problems both in the preschool period itself and throughout later development (T. G. O'Connor, 2006).

Play therapy, specifically a relationship-based approach, is ideally suited for treating attachment problems in preschool children (Benedict, 2006; Benedict & Hastings, 2002). Alternatively labeled *attachment-based play therapy* or *object-relations play therapy*, this approach initially focuses on building a secure-base relationship with the child. Once a secure-base relationship is formed, the focus is on helping the child with affective and behavioral regulation and challenging negative internal working models. The relationship-based model presented here also focuses on adapting each phase of treatment to the specific subtypes of attachment problems seen, whether secure-base distortions or disorders of nonattachment.

Before discussing this play therapy further, we present a detailed description of attachment problems in the preschool-age period. Following this description, we provide an overview of the play therapy approach. After a discussion of the developmental issues specific to this preschool population, we present the model's specific clinical procedures. We examine empirical support for using play therapy with preschool children with attachment problems and close with a case example of this approach.

Both clinicians and researchers have identified certain behavioral and developmental patterns common to preschool children with attachment problems. First, these children have difficulties with self-regulation of both affect and behavior (Schore, 1994; Sroufe, 1996). Affect regulation problems can present as difficulty with transitions, tendency to tantrums or meltdowns when stressed by such things as challenging tasks or thwarted desires, and exaggerated reactivity in emotional expression. Behaviorally, such dysregulation tends to be expressed either by inhibited, constricted behavior or by poorly controlled behaviors, including aggressiveness, hyperactivity, and poor attention or focus. Second, these children are slow to trust adults (Zeanah & Boris, 2000). Third, by preschool age, these children have already begun to develop stable negative internal working models, or prototypes used in interactions, of the self and others. Whereas children with secure attachments form positive internal working models of the self (e.g., "I am lovable") and others ("Grownups are safe and make me feel good"), attachment-troubled children see themselves as bad or unlovable and others as frightening and dangerous (Bowlby, 1988).

Attachment-based play therapy was developed specifically to treat children with attachment problems. According to this model, *attachment* is defined as the special intimacy and closeness between the child and the caregiver that develops during the 1st year of life (Bowlby, 1988). This initial attachment relationship, which develops through interaction with a sensitive caregiver, serves to both protect (as a safe haven) and empower (as a secure base) the infant. As the infant experiences more of the world, the initial attachment behaviors develop into internal working models of the self and others that serve to guide relationships throughout life. A vast body of research has established both the importance of attachment to social and emotional development and the pathways by which attachment develops (for a summary, see Kobak et al., 2006).

Developmental research has clearly identified four distinct, relatively stable attachment patterns that can be identified as early as 1 year of age: secure, avoidant, resistant, and disorganized (Ainsworth et al., 1978; Main &

Solomon, 1990). The latter three all represent some form of insecure attachment. Clinicians have further refined these distinctions to highlight subtle distinctions in the ways in which insecurely attached children present clinically during the preschool years (Bretherton, Ridgeway, & Cassidy, 1990; Crittenden, 1992; Teti, 1999). Zeanah and Boris (2000) proposed three categories of attachment problems for clinical use: disorders of nonattachment, secure-base distortions, and disrupted attachment disorders. They made further distinctions within each of these three categories to elaborate clinically rich portraits of the kinds of problems seen in insecurely attached preschool children.

Disorders of nonattachment, the first broad category, are relatively rarely seen in most clinical settings. Within disorders of nonattachment, there are two subcategories, inhibited and disinhibited. In both of these, the child appears to have failed to develop a specific attachment to a preferred attachment figure and shows disturbances in seeking comfort, showing affect, cooperation, exploration, and self-regulation.

In the Zeanah and Boris (2000) system, there are four subtypes of secure-base distortions, all of which are characterized by an attachment relationship that includes some distortion in the caregiver's ability to serve as a secure base for the child's exploration of the world and as a safe haven when the child becomes distressed (Cooper, Hoffman, Powell, & Marvin, 2005). The first of these subtypes is *self-endangerment*. Children in this subcategory tend to explore freely but do not maintain a safe haven; thus, they are often reckless, engaging in provocative and dangerous behavior and frequently showing either self-directed or adult-directed aggression. The second subtype of secure-base distortion is *clinging–inhibited*. These children, who present very similarly to children with the resistant attachment pattern described originally by Ainsworth et al. (1978), are clingy, uncomfortable separating from the caregiver, and inhibited and generally avoid exploration of the environment in favor of remaining close to the caregiver. The third subtype, *hypercompliance*, is most similar to the disorganized attachment category first described by Main and Solomon (1990). These children are not clingy, but they also do not explore freely. Instead, they are emotionally constricted and hypervigilant, sometimes showing "frozen watchfulness." The final subtype is *role reversal* and is characterized by parentified behavior, in which the child seems preoccupied with the primary caregiver's well-being and exhibits an inverted relationship with him or her by being either overly controlling or overly solicitous (Teti, 1999).

The third broad category proposed by Zeanah and Boris (2000) is *disrupted attachment*. This category is reserved for children who have had their initial attachment relationship severed through such experiences as death of the caregiver, abandonment, or removal by child protective services with subsequent foster care or adoption. The best approach to understanding the clinical needs of children experiencing disrupted attachment is to examine both previous attachment relationships and the current caregiver–child relationship. Any of the nonattached or secure-base distortion attachment patterns might apply to the disruption situation. Thus, preschool children with attachment problems can present clinically with a variety of symptoms and behaviors requiring treatment.

The attachment-based play therapy model is informed by attachment theory, as described earlier (Bowlby, 1988; Siegel, 1999), and by the importance of regulatory capacities (Cicchetti et al., 1995; Schore, 1994), the treatment of trauma (Hughes, 2006a, 2007), and object relations theory (Mahler & Furer,1968; Mahler, Pine, & Berman, 1975; Winnicott, 1971). The major assumption of Bowlby's (1988) attachment theory is that the child's first few years with a primary caregiver shape the child's *internal working models* (IWMs; self-constructs and expectations and templates for interaction with the environment). Trevarthen, Aitken, Vanderkerkhove, Delafield-Butt, and Nagy (2006) and Cicchetti et al. (2005) also contributed to the attachment literature by maintaining that the presence or lack of intersubjectivity between a child and the primary caregiver shapes the child's view of him- or herself and how the child comes to know him- or herself as an "I." To the extent that the caregiver is attuned and positive in expression toward the infant, the child will most likely grow up with a positive, coherent sense of self. A child whose caregivers neglect him or her tends to have a fragmented, disjointed sense of self. Literature about regulatory capacities in traumatized children indicates that a primary caregiver's ability to regulate the child directly relates to the development of coregulation in the dyad, and ultimately to the development of a child's ability to regulate him- or herself. Nonoptimal caregivers who do not regulate their children do not foster coregulation, and those children do not learn to regulate themselves very well, if at all.

Attachment problems, in this view, represent some degree of developmental failure in that the child's IWMs are distorted or negative. As such, the IWMs do not effectively guide the child in exploring safely, developing new relationships, seeking needed comfort, or handling stress. Treatment of attachment problems, therefore, must address and ultimately alter the distorted or negative IWMs. Because IWMs develop and evolve within relationships, treatment should initially establish a solid relationship between the therapist and the child and then, using a variety of techniques, work therapeutically to challenge and ultimately repair problematic IWMs.

DEVELOPMENTAL ISSUES

Developmentally, preschoolers share several characteristics that influence both the types of emotional and behavioral problems seen and the features of effective therapeutic interventions for this age group (Benedict, 1993;

Campbell, 1995). In general, preschool children's difficulties are relatively undifferentiated in the sense that problems are likely to be expressed by both internalizing (e.g., anxiety, depression, withdrawal) and externalizing (e.g. acting out, aggression, impulsivity) symptoms (Achenbach, 1982). This contrasts sharply with school-age children, who are likely to have symptoms that are, for the most part, either internalizing or externalizing (Achenbach & Rescorla, 2000). In terms of therapeutic needs, preschool children need interventions that can address both types of symptoms. Play therapy, in which the therapist is highly accepting of the child and provides a relatively unstructured setting, is an ideal therapeutic approach to address this wide range of symptoms (K. J. O'Connor, 2000; Schaefer, 1993).

Second, preschool children are typically rather unmodulated in the expression of distress; when problems arise, feelings are likely to be highly intense and behaviors relatively out of control when compared with those of older children (Benedict, 1993; Hewitt, 1999). This appears to be the result of preschoolers' limited coping strategies, their newly emerging self-regulatory skills that can easily be overwhelmed by feelings and experiences, and their limited ability to inhibit impulses (Rothbaum & Weisz, 1989; Schore, 1994). Play therapy, again, appears ideally suited to the preschooler's limited ability to modulate feelings and behaviors. Play therapy provides a therapeutic setting in which children can use a naturally occurring and familiar means of communication, play, to express problems (Elkind, 2007; Schaefer, 1993). Within play, it is safe to express feelings and behaviors that might not be acceptable in a less protected environment.

The third characteristic of preschool children that especially influences the choice of therapeutic intervention is the preschool child's relative openness and lack of defensiveness about both feelings and problems (Trad, 1989). It is usually not until the school years that children become defensive and aware of the social implications of having problems. Although this lack of defensiveness makes preschool children typically open to therapy, it also leaves them vulnerable to being overwhelmed when therapy focuses on distressing ideas and events. Play therapy uses play, specifically the metaphors expressed within play, to address these concerns, thus providing the emotional distance needed by the child to work through the distressing feelings, memories, and behaviors (T. G. O'Connor, 2006).

The fourth developmental issue that informs both the problems seen in and the therapeutic needs of preschool children concerns the child's deep embeddedness in the home and, to a lesser degree, school environment. The preschool child is still largely dependent on the caregiver for basic needs and for most emotional needs (Hewitt, 1999). When the child has attachment problems, these problems will trace back to the child–caregiver relationship whether they are expressed within the home or displaced onto a child–teacher relationship at school. Attachment-based play therapy addresses this aspect of preschool development through the caregiver component of the approach, which can take the form of working in play with both the caregiver and the child or working with the child in play while working with the caregiver in other ways.

A final developmental consideration that clearly reinforces the notion that play is the best medium for working with preschool children is the cognitive and linguistic limitations that characterize preschool children. One such limitation concerns language. Language ability, especially expressive language, develops rapidly and steadily over the preschool period. Only as children reach ages 5 and 6 does the expression of ideas, feelings, and activities become both fluid and automatic. On a similar note, preschoolers tend to display an intense reliance on a concrete understanding of their world. Abstract concepts such as causality and time present major challenges for preschool children because their notions of causality are quite primitive. They tend to rely on simple associations in time or space to explain events, and their egocentric viewpoint leads them to see themselves as responsible for or causing any negative events or traumas they experience. Thus, the therapist is likely to encounter children who believe that such stressful events as their caregiver's divorce, their father's death, or their caregiver's fighting is because of either the child's refusal to do something or the child's misbehavior. All of these constraints limit the usefulness of therapeutic approaches that rely primarily on verbal and cognitive techniques. Preschool children can most easily change their thinking and behavior through play, in which they can use metaphor and overt actions as they process difficult events, feelings, or behaviors.

PLAY INTERVENTION PROCEDURES

Play intervention procedures for insecurely attached preschool children can be divided into two groups: procedures that are informed by the developmental issues outlined earlier and that are needed by all preschool children, and play procedures specifically needed for insecurely attached children. The general procedures, including the therapist's responsive approach, appropriate limits to provide safety, cognitive adaptations made by the therapists, and the importance of reliance on child-generated metaphors, are described first. Then several additional procedures specific to the needs of insecurely attached preschool children are elaborated.

Play therapy for all preschoolers should be child responsive. That is, any actions, verbalizations, or interventions by the therapist should be in direct response to the child's play. Only the child can lead the play toward the issues and concerns around which the child needs to play. Although this approach is largely nondirective in nature, it does involve the therapist's actively intervening in the play in a child-responsive fashion so as to support the goals of play therapy. Such interventions typically take the form of invitations (Gil, 1991). Within play therapy, an invitation can be a reflection, a description of the feelings or motives of a character in the play, or a suggestion for a new direction for the play. Such interventions are invitational in that they are gently offered so the child can respond or not as the child chooses. There are no negative consequences for the child, such as feeling that the therapist will be disappointed or angry if the child ignores the invitation. The therapist remains warm, accepting, and deeply invested in the child and the child's play regardless of the child's response to an invitation.

Second, the tendency for preschool children to be unmodulated in emotional and behavioral expression requires the play therapist to have procedures for setting appropriate limits and maintaining safety in the playroom. In the approach discussed in this chapter, limit setting is always in response to threats to the child's or the therapist's safety (Benedict & Narcavage, 1997). Basically, all emotional and behavioral expression is accepted from the child except when it might hurt either the child or the therapist. In this sense, play therapy should be nondirective in nature, and limits should be used only when absolutely necessary. Then the therapist provides only the amount of direction and control needed to restore safety and tries to do so without interrupting the child's play. For example, if the child begins to climb on an unsafe structure in the room, such as narrow shelves, the therapist might go over to the child and stand ready to support the child if needed, saying, "I'm going to stand here to be sure you are safe." The special concerns about maintaining a safe environment for insecurely attached preschool children are discussed in more detail later in this chapter.

Another procedure needed by all preschoolers concerns the cognitive limitations that preschool children routinely experience. These limitations require therapists to adjust their language to the child's level. Using overly complex sentences and vocabulary above the child's developmental level should be avoided. Similarly, cognitive limits would imply that the therapist refrain from asking questions, especially about why things are happening, and avoid cognitive approaches that rely on reasoning.

Finally, the preschool child's comfort with play, coupled with the child's lack of defensiveness, determines the type of play most helpful within play therapy for preschoolers. Pretend play and social role play allow the child to reproduce remembered events and relationships through metaphor. Preschool children can understand and manipulate play metaphors long before they can verbalize and discuss the same memories, events, and feelings (Hewitt, 1999). Experiencing through play metaphors the issues and concerns that have led the child to be distressed enables new understandings, solutions to problems, and healing of affects to take place. The child-responsive play therapist facilitates this process by following the child's metaphors rather than introducing the therapist's metaphors. By respecting the child's play themes, the therapist helps the child create distance from distressing ideas or feelings, thus providing a safe place for the child.

Play therapy for insecurely attached preschool children requires specific procedures beyond those needed by all preschoolers. Children with attachment problems need therapy to focus initially on the development of a *secure-base relationship*, in which the child is provided a space where he or she can safely explore relationships and work through traumatic experiences with another person (Becker-Weidman, 2005). In addition, these children also need the therapist to appropriately challenge, and ultimately alter, the distorted IWMs that are characteristic of attachment problems. Establishing a secure-base relationship with this population presents special challenges to the therapist. As discussed earlier, insecurely attached preschool children are poorly regulated in affect and behavior; slow to form new relationships, especially with adults; and burdened with emerging IWMs that portray both the child and adults in negative ways. All of these characteristics potentially interfere with developing a strong therapist–child relationship. Several play procedures are used to overcome this challenge.

The first procedure is the therapist's attitude or stance. The therapist must be genuinely warm and accepting of the child. At a minimum, the therapist must show full acceptance of all of the child's thoughts, feelings, and behaviors, even uncomfortable behaviors such as regression, aggression, withdrawal, and failure to maintain appropriate boundaries. Such acceptance should not be confused with permissiveness, which allows all behaviors without providing for the child's psychological and physical safety. The therapist should hold constant a warm, positive regard for the child but use the additional procedures described in the following paragraphs to provide to the child the needed security.

Another play procedure essential for establishing a secure-base relationship between the child and the therapist is constancy. For the insecurely attached child to trust the therapist, the therapist must be constant for the child. This requires that the therapist maintain consistency of both self and the play therapy setting. The therapist must show the same warm and accepting attitude and the same play procedures session after session. Furthermore, the therapist needs to demonstrate to the child that their relationship contains shared memories of things that have occurred previously in play therapy. This can be done by making such comments as "I remember the first time you came here, you weren't so sure you wanted to play with that baby." The setting also needs to be constant in key ways. The rules of the playroom, the way the materials are made available, and the play materials themselves need to be consistent. Even if one is using a portable playroom, one can establish constancy through which toys are made available and how the toys are set up in the room. Similarly, having a predictable time and place for therapy helps the child experience the therapist's constancy. For these children, even something as small as introducing a new toy into the playroom can be unsettling and requires that the therapist overtly prepare the child for any such changes.

A third relationship-enhancing play procedure needed by insecurely attached children is therapist attunement. *Attunement* is the creation of a state of intersubjectivity between therapist and child in which they each sense the other's intimate emotions through shared experiences (Trevarthen et al., 2006). This is captured in part by the child-responsive nature of interventions. It is also seen in the therapist's occasional reflections that show that the therapist's full attention is engaged with the child. Finally, attunement requires that the therapist match the vitality, or emotional intensity, of the child's affect (Hughes, 2006a). By matching the vitality or intensity of the child's affect, the child feels understood or "felt" by the therapist, thus enabling the child to feel safe in exploring his or her emotions as they occur.

A fourth play procedure essential for insecurely attached children, especially ones who have experienced interpersonal trauma in the original attachment relationship, is to ensure the child's sense of safety in the play therapy setting. All of the previous procedures, warmth and acceptance, constancy, and attunement contribute to this sense of safety. However, for these children, these interventions are not enough. Active provision of both physical and psychological safety is required for the therapist–child relationship to serve as a secure base for the child. Of these latter, physical safety is the easiest for the therapist to provide. This can be done by setting limits (as described earlier) or by physically being close and able to directly maintain the child's safety. It should be noted, however, that many insecurely attached children are at greater physical risk in play therapy than are preschool children with other kinds of problems, both because of their poor behavioral self-regulation and their tendency to be reckless (Zeanah & Boris, 2000).

Providing psychological safety is more challenging for the therapist. Because insecurely attached preschool children consistently show poor self-regulation of both behavior and affect, they need the therapist to provide some of the regulation that is missing to feel safe. The difficulty the therapist faces is finding ways to regulate the child without being overly controlling or directive. The basic mechanism for regulating the child's affect is to first use attunement to match the child's vitality affect and, through empathic communication, establish a state of intersubjectivity with the child. At that point, the therapist can begin to shift the child's dysregulated vitality affect to a more regulated state through their interaction. In other words, the therapist "captures" the child by matching the child's excitement or intense affect and creating for the child a sense that the therapist fully empathizes with the child's feelings. Then the therapist gently leads the child by lowering his or her own affect vitality. The child can now "borrow" the therapist's affective regulation until the child is again in control and can again self-regulate.

Once the secure-base relationship is established, the therapist begins to implement play procedures designed to challenge the child's maladaptive IWMs. The first way this is accomplished is through the developing relationship between the therapist and child. The play procedures outlined in the process of developing the secure-base relationship make the therapist's very presence and ongoing interaction a challenge to the IWMs. The child initially enters the therapeutic relationship with IWMs, or expectations, about adults and the ways in which they typically respond to the child. When the therapist does not conform to the expectation of a harsh, rejecting, angry adult predicted by the child's negative IWM, this challenges the model's veracity. This challenging process is often difficult for the therapist to sustain because the child needs to continually test the therapist to see whether it is genuine. The child will engage in behaviors that have in the past incurred adult disapproval, rejection, or withdrawal. The resulting oppositional, angry, destructive, or withdrawing behaviors on the part of the child require the therapist to continually self-monitor so that the therapeutic stance is always genuinely empathic and maintained without interference from any anxieties, anger, confidence lapses, or withdrawal feelings coming from the therapist's personal life (Hughes, 2006b).

During the working phase of therapy, there are additional play procedures available to the therapist. One such procedure is the use of invitations to expose the child to a different way of viewing things and events in his or her world. This approach uses an age-appropriate cognitive invitation to help alter the child's IWMs. For example, if the child pretends to be the mommy who is mean to and inconsistent with the child, as played by the therapist, one minute and nice and caring the next, the therapist–child might say in a pretend child's voice, "I am all mixed up; sometimes you're a nice mommy and sometimes you're a mean mommy," thus providing an opportunity for the child to accept that mommy behavior is sometimes very confusing or to understand that sometimes mommy can be nice, countering the all-or-nothing thinking of the preschool child. Another, more action-based procedure is when the therapist provides an invitation for things to work out differently in a frequently played scenario. This is usually only initiated by the therapist after the child has played the scene many times, always with the same maladaptive outcome.

When working with insecurely attached preschool children, the therapist needs to be fully aware of the challenges termination poses for the child. Termination basically has two components. First, the child–caregiver relationship needs to be strengthened so that the changes in the child's IWMs that first occurred within the therapist–child relationship can now extend to the caregiver–child relationship. Second, the child needs to experience the ending of the relationship with the therapist in a healthy way.

Although detailing all of the ways in which one can work to help caregivers be more attuned and effective in their relationship with the child so that the child can transfer the altered IWMs from the therapist–child relationship to that with the primary caregiver is beyond the scope of this chapter, we briefly discuss this aspect of termination here. Fostering the relationship between the child and the primary caregiver is a crucial goal for the child's therapy. Hopefully, throughout the course of the play therapy, the therapist has found ways to work with the caregiver. As the play therapy proceeds, the child becomes more able to engage in a healthy relationship. The primary caregiver, at this same time, needs to be able to sustain his or her part of a secure-base relationship with the child. Early in therapy, the secure-base therapist–child relationship is often extremely intense and important to the child, who originally entered therapy because there was not an adequate secure-base relationship in place with the primary caregiver. Terminating that relationship without having healed the caregiver–child relationship to some degree can be traumatic for the child. Thus, to prepare for termination, the therapist needs to use play procedures that help the child apply his or her newly altered and healthier IWMs to the primary caregiver. In this play therapy approach, if the caregiver has not been part of the play therapy sessions up to this point, he or she typically joins the sessions, giving the therapist an opportunity to help the dyad develop a secure attachment relationship.

The termination process, which takes place only after the caregiver–child work described earlier has been accomplished, involves helping the child move out of the therapist–child relationship. Several specific play procedures are used to make the process a healthy one. First, the therapist needs to set aside several sessions, ranging from four to eight depending on the particular child's needs, for termination to take place and discuss the termination process with both the child and the primary caregiver. It is particularly crucial to help the caregiver understand the importance of termination because most parents do not easily understand why saying goodbye to this relationship should take so much time. Second, the therapist, often working directly with the child, needs to plan a marking event, such as a good-bye party or a "therapy graduation party," for the final session. Preschool children need a concrete event to help them process the termination, and they are quite familiar with parties to mark other important events such as birthdays. Third, the therapist needs to prepare a transitional object for the child to take home. At its simplest, this can simply be a photo of the child and therapist together. For longer term cases, it might be beneficial to write a therapy book for the child. A *therapy book* is a simple book that tells the narrative of the child's therapy, beginning with meeting the therapist, describing in developmentally appropriate ways the therapeutic work and celebrating the child's progress, preferably in the child's words (e.g., "I don't get scared anymore"). It can easily be illustrated with line drawings, clip art, or actual photos. Finally, the therapist needs to be ready to respond to several issues typically presented in the play of insecurely attached preschool children in termination. These include sadness over the impending loss, which the therapist needs to affirm for both the child and the therapist, anger at the therapist for stopping, and joy at feeling more competent and regulated. It is also common for children to "recapitulate" their experience by playing themes from early in therapy with the newer healthier resolution. The therapist can use this play to help the child understand how memories become part of who we are and that these memories will not go away even when the child is no longer seeing the therapist.

EMPIRICAL SUPPORT

At present, no efficacy or effectiveness studies specifically examining attachment-based play therapy with insecurely attached preschool children are available in the literature. This is the result of two interfacing issues: the relative newness of efficacy research on play therapy and the lack of consensus about diagnostic issues around attachment problems. On the latter issue, there is considerable agreement that insecure attachment in infancy and early childhood puts the child at risk for later developmental problems and that some sort of intervention is indicated, particularly in the case of disorganized attachment or complex trauma. Many different types of interventions have now been developed and presented in the literature, with varying degrees of outcome research completed. This small body of literature is one of three general sources of support for attachment-based play therapy and is discussed here, along with the other two types of research, efficacy and effectiveness research with play therapy in general and research supporting the theoretical underpinnings of attachment-based play therapy.

The past 20 years have seen a significant increase in available empirical support for play therapy (Ray, 2006). A meta-analysis of this body of research conducted recently showed a moderate effect size for play therapy as measured by a decrease in symptoms and/or an increase in self-esteem (Bratton & Ray, 2005). Ray (2006) concluded that play therapy is effective, especially with young children, the age group targeted by attachment-based play therapy. Her review of research suggested that play therapy effectiveness is enhanced when there is a significant parent component to the therapy, which is again consistent with the approach presented in this chapter.

The second source of empirical support for the attachment-based play therapy model presented here derives from research demonstrating effectiveness with non–play-based attachment interventions with young children. One example of this is the strong evidence base for *circle-of-security* intervention (Cooper et al., 2005). This approach uses videotapes of the parent and child playing together and negotiating a separation to modify parents' behavior toward greater attunement with their child. This research has demonstrated significant changes in parent–child attachment as a result of the intervention. Similar findings have been reported by Timmer, Urquiza, Zebell, and McGrath (2005) using parent–child interaction therapy, a well-established empirically supported therapy for young children with behavior problems. Their most recent studies have suggested that much of the change reported in children's behavior appears to be strongly influenced by what they call "Level 3 interpretations," comments designed to help parents be more sensitive to their children and given to mothers during the interactive play phase of therapy (A. Urquiza, personal communication, October 12, 2007). Thus, this work seems to support the importance of a focus on parental attunement to the child, a key tenet of attachment-based play therapy. Still another approach used with children with attachment problems has implications for the approach presented in this chapter. Specifically, dyadic developmental psychotherapy, developed by Daniel Hughes (2006a, 2007), has been tested in some recent studies. This approach, which is playful but not play therapy per se, is most frequently used with school-age children and adolescents. The studies have shown that children with attachment problems receiving dyadic developmental psychotherapy showed greater improvement than children receiving treatment using a variety of approaches, but not dyadic developmental psychotherapy, within the community both at the end of treatment and at multiyear follow-up (Becker-Weidman & Hughes, 2008). Attachment-based play therapy shares the same theoretical base as dyadic developmental psychotherapy, and the same basic precepts inform the therapist's behavior.

The final source of empirical support for attachment-based play therapy presented here derives from the literature on the development of secure and insecure attachments. There is a wealth of research supporting the notion of distorted IWMs in insecurely attached children and adults (Kobak et al., 2006). Other research has clearly shown the importance of a secure-base relationship in shifting IWMs and in helping the individual develop a capacity for attachment in relationships (Dozier, Higley, Albus, & Nutter, 2002).

CASE ILLUSTRATION

Brycen, a 4-year-old boy, has lived with his father, Pete, and the father's significant other, Julie, since he was 2 and a half. Before this he lived with his biological mother, Tiffany, while Pete was deployed in Afghanistan. When

Pete returned, he met his son for the first time. He learned from both sets of grandparents that Brycen had been both physically abused and neglected in Tiffany's care, and he took Brycen to live with him at that time. By the time of referral, Brycen had formed some attachment to both new parents but presented with symptoms of traumatic attachment disorder.

Brycen had severe behavioral problems at school, including aggressive outbursts and screaming. At home, he had explosive tantrums and was unable to communicate easily with his father. Other symptoms included episodes of smearing feces and defecating in the bathtub; some sexualized behaviors with Julie, which she was able to stop; fights with neighborhood children; eating everything, including bugs, dirt, and grass; and continual defiance and testing of Julie. Julie has been staying home to be with Brycen; he is clearly attached to her and considers her his mother. He calls his biological mother "Tiffany" on the rare occasions when he refers to her. Julie describes Brycen as lovable and as a "ball of energy" from the time he wakes up at "top speed." Brycen's parents report showed concerns with hyperactivity and distractibility, aggression, depression, and adaptability. They reported that Brycen did not adjust smoothly to changes in the physical and social environments and tended to respond with perseveration, overreactions, or avoidance. Brycen appeared to have difficulty calming when upset and problems with anger, emotional self-control, executive functioning, and low resiliency. He also had problems with nightmares, bedwetting, and defiance. According to the Zeanah and Boris (2000) system, Brycen has a disrupted attachment that appears to have been a disorder of nonattachment (disinhibited type) when he lived with his biological mother that has evolved to a secure-base distortion with both self-endangering and hypervigilant features with Julie.

It appears that Brycen's substantial trauma history shaped his brain development and, thus, his emotional, cognitive, and behavioral functioning. Brycen's IWMs, his sense of self and other, and his subsequent style of interacting with his environment were shaped in the first few years with his biological mother. Given the reported abuse and neglect Brycen withstood from birth to age 3, it appears that Brycen views the world as random, chaotic, and not attuned to his needs. He appears to view himself as having little efficacy in the world and a sense of badness and aloneness, which is very frightening for children. Brycen's presentation suggests that he was not kept safe and did not have his basic needs met. He appears to respond to the world around him with a heightened state of arousal, hypervigilance, and a need to control his environment. It is likely that he did not have appropriate limits set for him or a sense of physical or psychological safety. Cognitively, his IWMs have manifested themselves in a lack of cause-and-effect thinking, decreased logic, and increased distortions of thought. Brycen may tend to live a fragmented life by separating parts of himself into a "good boy" or a "bad kid." Emotionally, he appears to have little ability to manage his own emotions, fears, or anxieties. Behaviorally, Brycen's state of dysregulation appears to discharge emotion before thought. Brycen's adaptations to his previous environment are no longer functional in his current environment, where his caregivers are attuned to his needs and physical and emotional states. This profound lack of regulation (brought on by a lack of coregulation and intersubjectivity in the first few years of life) has resulted in behavior problems in school and at home with Brycen's new primary caregiver, Julie. Despite no longer having a need for his defensive strategies, Brycen tends to use them automatically, and these strategies are maladaptive in his current environment.

The plan for therapy for Brycen included individual play therapy coupled with parenting guidance with Julie. In the play therapy, the goal was to create a securely attached therapeutic relationship and then, using the metaphor of play, to provide titrated exposure to trauma themes and meaning making. Brycen was expected to be able to use the therapist as a new object, who would be able to reflect his own goodness; help him develop a positive and efficacious sense of self; and regulate him in session, ultimately teaching him to regulate himself. An important goal of therapy was to also treat Brycen's untreated trauma, allowing him to gradually play out the most accessible to the least accessible scenarios and themes as his sense of safety in session would allow, so that his life narrative could become better articulated and real rather than pent up in implicit memories. It was also important to gradually reshape Brycen's IWMs through the therapeutic relationship (i.e., creating safety, maintaining constancy) and regulate him so that he could learn to regulate himself and use strategies for coping when he was feeling dysregulated. Another goal of therapy was to give a "voice" to Brycen's behavior and help him to be able to identify and verbalize his own feelings so that he may be able to more effectively communicate his needs to others.

The parenting guidance provided Julie was largely informed by the circle-of-security intervention (Cooper et al., 2005) and Zeanah, Larrieu, Heller, and Valliere's (2000) notion of the parent representation of the child. The intervention works to support the parent as the secure base or safe haven from which a child explores and to which he or she returns for comfort. Julie was provided psychoeducation to help her support, facilitate, and enjoy the exploration with Brycen. When the cue from Brycen indicated a need for comfort, Julie was encouraged to protect, delight in him, and help organize his feelings. An additional assumption of the circle-of-security intervention is that sometimes children "miscue" and act as if they need to explore or be distant when in fact they are in need of comfort, or vice versa. Incorrect interpretation of the child's cues often leads to inappropriate responses on the part of the caregiver. The intervention included reframing some of Julie's interpretations of Brycen's behaviors and designing tailored interventions for her to implement at home.

Good rapport and a therapeutic relationship were quickly established, and Brycen evidenced initial themes of independence and dominance as he attempted to establish a sense of safety in therapy; he made great efforts to control every detail of his environment. His initial sessions were characterized by scattered, unresolved play with hints of death and nurturance themes, reflecting his fears and internal conflicts. Brycen evidenced a great deal of ambivalence in his play, and this continued throughout the 26 sessions of therapy. Initially, he appeared to play out the most accessible themes first, those related to danger and mastery, which he more easily tolerated in his consciousness. He made consistent efforts to test constancy and safety, which again reflected his ambivalence about his ability to be safe on the basis of what he knew about the world from his first few years of life.

In the 13th session, Brycen moved to working on a deeper level as he began to verbalize some details about his trauma and life with Tiffany, his biological mother, and immediately became dysregulated in session. At this point, the therapist began to make observations of Brycen's dysregulation more explicit in session, naming it ("I can tell you're getting a little too excited, and I'm going to help you calm down") and teaching him tools to use to help himself calm. He accepted the therapist's attempts to regulate and comfort him and provide some structure to his emotional disturbance. In subsequent sessions, Brycen played out themes involving kidnapping, danger, and protection of "good" characters against "bad" characters.

During his 17th session, Brycen stated that his biological mother fed him beer and acknowledged that beer was for adults, not for children. He went on to state that his biological mother was "mean" and that she was an "alcoholic." When asked what the word *alcoholic* meant, Brycen stated that it meant "someone who drank too much alcohol." This session was preceded by increased dysregulation at home (e.g., nightmares, more tantrums, and some beginning verbalization of remembered incidents with Tiffany), a pattern subsequently seen before all of his trauma work in the play therapy. Throughout the last 23 sessions, Brycen increasingly allowed the therapist to help him regulate his emotions, to nurture him, and to set appropriate limits for him in the context of the growing therapeutic bond. As the attachment bond deepened, Brycen made fewer efforts to test the therapist's ability to keep him safe, and he subsequently exhibited a higher level of trust.

It became clear through therapy that whenever Brycen thought or spoke about his biological mother, Tiffany, the emotional experience had a dysregulating effect on him, which could be seen in his bad dreams at home and increased agitation in his play therapy sessions. This dysregulation appears to have had cognitive, emotional, and physiological consequences for Brycen because he was not able to function adaptively or age appropriately when he was in such a state.

At the time of this writing, Brycen continues in therapy, so the final outcome cannot be reported. However, even after only 26 sessions, Brycen has greatly improved in some of the areas his parents identified as problematic. For example, he does not frequently engage in impulsive and dangerous behavior, although he still has problems with impulsivity. Brycen does not try to light matches or cut his own hair, as he tried to do previously. Additionally, Brycen no longer eats inedible items or aggresses toward Julie. His communication skills have greatly improved, and this gain, in combination with Julie's more accurate interpretation of Brycen's cues, has created more understanding and stability in the mother–son dyad. Brycen has become more accepting of limits, and Julie has become more flexible in her redirection of Brycen when he gets stuck. Although his tantrums have continued, Julie has developed attachment-focused interventions to help Brycen calm more easily and reconnect with her so that his emotional upset can be quieted and he can return to a more adaptive level of functioning.

CONCLUSION AND FUTURE DIRECTIONS

The explosion of recent research on the development of attachment and on attachment problems as they present clinically has drawn our attention to this important problem. Research has increasingly informed therapists' attempts to intervene with attachment problems effectively, and this chapter has presented an approach, based on this research. This play therapy approach that is based both on attachment and developmental research and theory has shown promise in the clinical setting for helping young children who have problems in their attachment relationships. The results of outcome studies with conceptually similar approaches with older children and their families are encouraging. However, better definitions of the clinical presentations of attachment problems, especially as they relate to various types of interpersonal trauma such as abuse, neglect, or exposure to violence, are greatly needed. Despite the methodological challenges of careful outcome research, studies of this and other approaches, especially those using the natural language of young children, play, must be conducted if we hope to help these children effectively.

REFERENCES

Achenbach, T. M. (1982). *Developmental psychopathology* (2nd ed.). New York: Wiley.

Achenbach, T. M., & Rescorla, L. (2000). *Manual for the ASEBA preschool forms and profiles*. Burlington: University of Vermont, Research Center for Children, Youth, and Families.

Ainsworth, M. D. S., Blehar, M. C., Waters, E., & Wall, S. (1978). *Patterns of attachment: A psychological study of the strange situation*. Hillsdale, NJ: Erlbaum.

Becker-Weidman, A. (2005). Dyadic developmental psychotherapy: The theory. In A. Becker-Weidman & D. Shell (Eds.), *Creating capacity for attachment: Dyadic developmental psychotherapy in the treatment of trauma-attachment disorders* (pp. 7–32). Oklahoma City, OK: Wood 'N' Barnes.

Becker-Weidman, A., & Hughes, D. (2008). Dyadic developmental psychotherapy: An evidence-based treatment for children with complex trauma and disorders of attachment. *Child & Family Social Work, 13,* 329–337.

Benedict, H. E. (1993, October). *Play therapy with preschool children: A developmental–dynamic approach*. Paper presented at the Annual Meeting of the Association for Play Therapy, Atlanta, GA.

Benedict, H. E. (2006). Object relations play therapy: Applications to attachment problems and relational trauma. In C. E. Schaefer & H. G. Kaduson (Eds.), *Contemporary play therapy: Theory, research, and practice* (pp. 3–27). New York. Guilford Press.

Benedict, H. E., & Hastings, L. (2002). Object-relations play therapy. In J. Magnavita (Ed.), *Comprehensive handbook of psychotherapy: Vol. 1. Psychodynamic/object relations* (pp. 47–80). New York: Wiley.

Benedict, H. E., & Narcavage, C. (1997). *Healing children through play therapy: Therapeutic responses available to the clinician*. Unpublished manuscript, Baylor University, Waco, TX.

Bowlby, J. (1988). *A secure base: Parent–child attachment and healthy human development*. New York: Basic Books.

Bratton, S., & Ray, D. (2005). The efficacy of play therapy with children: A meta-analytic review of treatment outcomes. *Professional Psychology: Research and Practice, 36,* 376–390.

Bretherton, I., Ridgeway, D., & Cassidy, J. (1990). Assessing internal working models of the attachment relationship: An attachment story completion task for 3-year-olds. In M. T. Greenberg, D. Cicchetti, & E. M. Cummings (Eds.), *Attachment in the preschool years: Theory, research, and intervention* (pp. 273–308). Chicago: University of Chicago Press.

Campbell, S. B. (1995). Behavior problems in preschool children: A review of recent research. *Journal of Child Psychology and Psychiatry, 36* 113–129.

Cicchetti, D., Toth, S. L., & Lynch, M. (1995). Bowlby's dream comes full circle: The application of attachment theory to risk and psychopathology. In T. H. Ollendick & R. J. Prinz (Eds.), *Advances in clinical child psychology* (Vol. 17, pp. 1–75) New York: Plenum Press.

Cooper, G., Hoffman, K., Powell, B., & Marvin, R. (2005). The circle of security intervention: Differential diagnosis and differential treatment. In L. J. Berlin, Y. Ziv, L. Amaya-Jackson, & M. Greenberg (Eds.), *Enhancing early attachments: Theory, research, intervention, and policy* (pp. 127–151). New York: Guilford Press.

Crittenden, P. M. (1992). Quality of attachment in the preschool years. *Development and Psychopathology, 4,* 209–241.

Dozier, M., Higley, E., Albus, K., & Nutter, AQ. (2002). Intervening with foster infants' caregivers: Targeting three critical needs. *Infant Mental Health Journal, 23*, 541–554.

Elkind, D. (2007). *The power of play: How spontaneous, imaginative activities lead to happier, healthier children.* Cambridge, MA: Da Capo Press.

Gil, E. (1991). *The healing power of play: Working with abused children.* New York: Guilford Press.

Hewitt, S. K. (1999). *Assessing allegations of sexual abuse in preschool children: Understanding small voices.* Thousand Oaks, CA: Sage.

Hughes, D. (2006a). *Building the bonds of attachment: Awakening love in deeply troubled children* (2nd ed.). Lanham, MD: Rowan-Littlefield.

Hughes, D. (July, 2006b). *Clinical training in the psychological treatment of children with trauma-attachment problems: Beginning level.* Waterville, ME: Colby College.

Hughes, D. (2007). *Attachment-focused family therapy.* New York: Norton.

Kobak, R., Cassidy, J., Lyons-Ruth, K., & Ziv, Y. (2006). Attachment, stress, and psychopathology: A developmental pathways model. In D. Cicchetti & D. J. Cohen (Eds.), *Developmental psychopathology: Vol. 1. Theory and method* (2nd ed., pp. 333–369). New York: Wiley.

Mahler, M. S., & Furer, M. (1968). *On human symbiosis and the vicissitudes of individuation.* New York: International Universities Press.

Mahler, M. S., Pine, F., & Bergman, A. (1975). *The psychological birth of the human infant: Symbiosis and individuation.* New York: Basic Books.

Main, M., & Solomon, J. (1990). Procedures for identifying infants as disorganized/disoriented during the Ainsworth Strange Situation. In M. T. Greenberg, D. Cicchetti, & E. M. Cummings (Eds.), *Attachment in the preschool years: Theory, research, and intervention* (pp. 121–160). Chicago: University of Chicago Press.

O'Connor, K. J. (2000). *The play therapy primer* (2nd ed.). New York: Wiley.

O'Connor, T. G. (2006). The persisting effects of early experiences on psychological development. In D. Cicchetti & D. J. Cohen (Eds.), *Developmental psychopathology: Vol. 3. Risk, disorder, and adaptation* (2nd ed., pp. 202–234). New York: Wiley.

Ray, D. C. (2006). Evidence-based play therapy. In C. E. Schaefer & H. G. Kaduson (Eds.), *Contemporary play therapy: Theory, research, and practice* (pp. 136–157). New York: Guilford Press.

Rothbaum, F., & Weisz, J. R. (1989). *Child psychopathology and the quest for control.* Newbury Park, CA: Sage.

Schaefer, C. E. (Ed.). (1993). *The therapeutic powers of play.* Northvale, NJ: Jason Aronson.

Schore, A. N. (1994). *Affect regulations and the origin of the self: The neurobiology of emotional development.* Hillsdale, NJ: Erlbaum.

Siegel, D. J. (1999). *The developing mind: Toward a neurobiology of interpersonal experience.* New York: Guilford Press.

Sroufe, L. A. (1996). *Emotional development: The organization of emotional life in the early years*. New York: Cambridge University Press.

Teti, D. (1999). Conceptualizations of disorganization in the preschool years. In J. Solomon & C. George (Eds.), *Attachment disorganization* (pp. 214–242). New York: Guilford Press.

Timmer, S. G., Urquiza, A. J., Zebell, N. M., & McGrath, J. M. (2005). Parent–child interaction therapy: Application to maltreating parent–child dyads. *Child Abuse and Neglect, 29*, 825–942.

Trad, P. V. (1989). *The preschool child: Assessment, diagnosis, and treatment*. New York: Wiley.

Trevarthen, C., Aitken, K. J., Vanderkerkhove, M., Delafield-Butt, J., & Nagy, E. (2006). Collaborative regulations of vitality in early childhood: Stress in intimate relationships and postnatal psychopathology. In D. Cicchetti & D. J. Cohen (Eds.), *Developmental psychopathology: Vol. 2. Developmental neuroscience* (2nd ed., pp. 65–126). New York: Wiley.

Winnicott, D. W. (1971). *Playing and reality*. London: Tavistock.

Zeanah, C. H., & Boris, N. W. (2000). Disturbances and disorders of attachment in early childhood. In C. H. Zeanah (Ed.), *Handbook of infant mental health* (2nd ed., pp. 353–368). New York: Guilford Press.

Zeanah, C. H., Larrieu, J. A., Heller, S. S., & Valliere, J. (2000). Infant–parent relationship assessment. In C. H. Zeanah (Ed.), *Handbook of infant mental health* (2nd ed., pp. 222–235). New York: Guilford Press.

II

PLAY INTERVENTIONS FOR INTERNALIZING DISORDERS

4

POSTTRAUMATIC PARENTING: A PARENT–CHILD DYADIC TREATMENT FOR YOUNG CHILDREN'S POSTTRAUMATIC ADJUSTMENT

JANINE SHELBY, CLAUDIA AVINA, AND HEATHER WARNICK

The relationship between parenting and children's posttraumatic adjustment has long been recognized by both clinicians and researchers. However, parent–child dyadic treatments that expressly address the needs of traumatized children have only recently begun to emerge. In this chapter, we propose the Posttraumatic Parenting (PP) program, a parent–child dyadic treatment specifically designed for young trauma survivors. The PP program blends elements of existing parent–child dyadic treatments with trauma-focused interventions to create an evidence-informed posttraumatic treatment for 3- to 8-year-old children and their nonoffending caregivers. The PP program was designed to be a practical, engaging, and developmentally appropriate approach to the posttraumatic treatment of young children. In the PP treatment, parents receive in vivo coaching as they interact with their children in activities selected to correspond to specific domains important in posttraumatic parent–child relationships (see Emde, 1989; Larrieu & Bellow, 2004; Zeanah et al., 1997).

In this chapter, we briefly review several research-based parent–child treatments, accentuating the parenting domains emphasized in each of these programs. We then describe the theoretical underpinnings of the PP program and how it blends theory, existing research-based treatments, and posttraumatic interventions. Although we have not yet published research

69

data on the PP program, we believe that it holds value as an evidence-informed therapy option for young survivors and their caregivers.

TRAUMA AND PARENTING

The caregiver–child relationship has long been identified in research as an important factor in childhood psychological adjustment and mental health (Crockenberg & Leerkes, 2000; Zeanah, Larrieu, Heller, & Valliere, 2000). In a number of studies, children's trauma symptoms have been shown to be related to such factors as family functioning, parental reactions, and social support (Cohen & Mannarino, 1993, 1998; Deblinger, Stauffer, & Steer, 2001; Silverman & La Greca, 2002; Vernberg, 2002). Similarly, parental involvement in the treatment has been linked to positive child outcomes for both trauma-related (Cohen & Mannarino, 1993; Deblinger, McLeer, & Henry, 1990) and other types of childhood treatment (LeBlanc & Ritchie, 1999; Urquiza & McNeil, 1996).

Our clinical work in the Child Trauma Clinic at Harbor-UCLA Medical Center has led us to increase our focus on interventions that occur at the parent–child level. When caregivers of traumatized youngsters use specific posttraumatic parenting strategies, we have found that the children's anxiety can often be greatly reduced. As advocates for the use of a variety of research-based treatments to serve diverse populations of young survivors, we suggest that the PP program can be used to supplement other treatment methods (e.g., individual, family, or parent collateral therapies) or, if it is the most clinically relevant treatment, as the primary treatment approach. We believe that the PP program is unique among burgeoning parent–child dyadic treatments because of its emphasis on and scope of interventions specifically targeting parent–child posttraumatic interactions.

PARENT–CHILD DYADIC TREATMENTS

Numerous treatments exist that focus on the interactions between caregivers and children (e.g., family therapies, parent education programs, parent–child dyadic treatments). In the pages that follow, we review some of these treatments, identifying the domains of parenting emphasized in each. This review is not intended to serve as an exhaustive discussion of all parenting intervention programs. Rather, we selected these treatments on the basis of their empirical foundation, their relevance to posttraumatic parenting, and our familiarity with them. Elements of these existing, established treatments were integrated into the PP treatment. See Table 4.1 for an overview.

TABLE 4.1
Comparison of Selected Parent–Child Dyadic Treatments

Treatment elements	Parent–child interaction therapy	Filial therapy	Child–parent psychotherapy	Child–parent relationship therapy	Posttraumatic parenting
Type of treatment	Dyadic	Initial therapist–child session, several individual collateral sessions, and later dyadic parent–child sessions	Dyadic, with collateral parent sessions as needed	Dyadic, with collateral parent training and optional video demonstrations	Dyadic, with collateral parent sessions as needed
Length	Not time limited	Varies	50 sessions	10 sessions	Not time limited
Goals	Enhance the child–parent relationships and improve parenting techniques.	Enhance the parent–child relationship through child-directed play.	Instill trust and safety.	Enhance the parent–child relationship through child-directed play.	Reduce posttraumatic symptoms, enhance caregiver skill, and promote safety.
Domains of treatment	1. Increase positive interactions between child and caregiver. 2. Reduce dysfunctional relationship patterns. 3. Improve parental behavioral management techniques. 4. Enhance parental support of appropriate child play.	Vary slightly across treatments, but generally involve teaching parents the abilities to structure, engage in, and enhance understanding of child-led play experiences. Specific parenting skills taught include reflective listening, recognizing and responding to chil-	1. Play. 2. Address sensorimotor disorganization and disruption of biological rhythms. 3. Reduce fearfulness. 4. Reduce reckless, self-endangering, and accident-prone behavior. 5. Reduce aggression.	Same as other filial therapy approaches	Enhance parental ability to provide protection, comfort, instrumental care, nurturance and empathy, emotional availability, discipline, play, and teaching.

(continues)

TABLE 4.1
Comparison of Selected Parent–Child Dyadic Treatments *(Continued)*

Treatment elements	Parent–child interaction therapy	Filial therapy	Child–parent psychotherapy	Child–parent relationship therapy	Posttraumatic parenting
		dren's feelings, therapeutic limit setting, and building children's self-esteem.	6. Remove punitive and critical parenting practices. 7. Address the relationship with the perpetrator of the violence, absent father, or both.		
Randomized controlled trials	Multiple	Yes	Yes	Yes; per authors, child–parent relationship therapy protocol was used and published as a filial therapy study.	Currently underway
Ages	2–7 (studies exist supporting the use of parent–child interaction therapy with older children as well)	3–10, but can vary across specific treatment models	Infancy and early childhood	2–10	3–8

Parent–Child Interaction Therapy and Parent–Child Attunement Therapy

Parent–child interaction therapy (PCIT; Herschell, Calzada, Eyberg, & McNeil, 2002; Urquiza & McNeil, 1996) and the version modified for younger children (i.e., ages 1 to 3), parent–child attunement therapy (PCAT; Dombrowski, Timmer, Blacker, & Urquiza, 2005), are parent–child dyadic therapies that are designed to enhance the child–parent relationship and improve parenting techniques. Treatment goals are obtained by increasing positive interactions between children and their caregivers, reducing dysfunctional relationship patterns, improving behavioral management techniques, and enhancing parental support of appropriate child play. In the treatment, the parent is provided in vivo coaching by the therapist to follow the child's lead in play, make nondirective types of communications (e.g., describing the child's behaviors, imitating the child's play, using reflective statements), praise positive child behaviors, ignore undesirable child behaviors, and engage in effective parenting skills (e.g., issuing effective directives). The therapist observes parent–child interactions through a one-way mirror and provides feedback to the parent using bug-in-the-ear technology. The coaching progresses from initial explicit instructions regarding what the parent should say or do to a later stage in which the parent generates most of the responses to the child as the therapist primarily reinforces previously learned successful parenting practices. PCAT is similar to PCIT but was specifically designed to meet the developmental needs of children ages 1 to 3, particularly those with trauma-related attachment problems.

PCIT has received a great deal of empirical support for the reduction of disruptive behaviors (Eisenstadt, Eyberg, McNeil, Newcomb, & Funderburk, 1993), disruptive behaviors among children with mental retardation (Bagner & Eyberg, 2007), child abuse (Urquiza & McNeil, 1996), and several other clinical issues (for a review, see Herschell et al., 2002). In recent studies, PCIT has also been found to reduce separation anxiety symptoms (Pincus, Santucci, Ehrenreich, & Eyberg, 2008) and PTSD symptoms among youngsters (Urquiza, 2007). Preliminary support for PCAT has been established in a published case study (Dombrowski et al., 2005).

Filial Therapy

Filial therapy is a parent–child dyadic treatment in which parents are taught to engage in child-directed play with their children. Therapists train and supervise parents to conduct child-led play sessions as a means of both treating the presenting problem and strengthening the parent–child relationship. This training takes place through a number of modalities, including didactic or coaching sessions with parents, parental observation of the therapist interacting with the child (i.e., modeling-based teaching), observation of the parent's own interactions with the child via video recording, and role play rehearsals between therapist and parent. In filial therapy, parents participate in preliminary training in which they must demonstrate mastery of specific skills before participating in play sessions with their children. Play sessions are first held in the therapeutic setting and are later conducted by the parent in the home with the child (for a detailed review of filial therapy, see VanFleet, 2005).

Several offshoots or variations of filial therapy have emerged, including filial play therapy, filial family therapy, child relationship enhancement family therapy, and child–parent relationship therapy (CPRT). The goal of these treatments is consistent with the humanistic philosophy to teach a parent to "be" with the child rather than attempt to control or change specific behaviors or problems (Bratton, Landreth, Kellam, & Blackard, 2006). One example of this class of treatments is CPRT (Bratton et al., 2006), a 10-session manualized treatment program in which parents are taught specific play-based skills and instructed to engage in play with their children at home. The specific skills emphasized in CPRT include (a) structuring, in which parents inform children about and enforce boundaries of the play sessions; (b) empathic listening and reflection that conveys understanding of the children's emotions; and (c) engaging in child-led play. Parents are trained to notice both explicit and subtle cues provided by the child during play that provide information regarding how the child may be perceiving the play and other, more broad life experiences.

Following the initial sessions in which parents are oriented to the basic humanistic principles of the treatment model, parents are taught to structure home play sessions, including what toys to make available to the child. Parents are then coached to structure the play sessions, participate in and understand the child's communications, and unconditionally accept the child's feelings and experiences. Emphasis is placed on facilitating the child's autonomy and decision-making abilities, reflecting the child's feelings and wishes, building self-esteem through encouragement, and enhancing parental limit setting (Bratton et al., 2006). Feedback to the parent is provided via observation of videotaped parent–child play sessions. Educational videotapes that exemplify core concepts of the treatment model are available as optional teaching supplements. Although disciplinary skills are not the primary focus of these treatments, parental limit setting is integrated into the treatment by enhancing parents' ability to explicitly communicate parameters of the play sessions and set appropriate limits (e.g., the child is not allowed to harm him- or herself) during play sessions.

Empirical examination of filial therapy dates back to the 1960s (Andronico & Guerney, 1969; Stover & Guerney, 1967), but these early case studies and small-scale research studies have more recently been supplemented by additional research. Published studies supporting this 60-year-old method and its affiliates include outcomes such as increased parental empathic interactions with the child (Andronico & Guerney, 1969; Bratton & Landreth, 1995; Lee & Landreth, 2003; Smith & Landreth, 2004; Stover & Guerney, 1967), parental satisfaction with the parent–child relationship (Glazer-Waldman, Zimmerman, Landreth, & Norton, 1992), and reduced childhood behavior problems (Bratton & Landreth, 2005; Harris & Landreth, 1997; Smith & Landreth, 2004; Tew, Landreth, Joiner, & Solt, 2002).

Child–Parent Psychotherapy

Child–parent psychotherapy (CPP; Lieberman & Van Horn, 2005) is a parent–child dyadic therapy that focuses on improving young children's mental health by improving parental attunement to children's emotional experiences. Parent–child dyads participate in weekly play sessions facilitated by the therapist, who may also provide collateral parent sessions when needed. The therapist's role is to observe, explain, and interpret the experience of both the child and the parent as they interact in play sessions. Emphasis is placed on helping the parent link present parenting behaviors with the parent's own childhood experiences. In the therapy, the parent learns to respond appropriately and competently to the child's emotional expressions. The core treatment objectives are to modify maladaptive behaviors in the child, the parent, or their relationship; increase developmentally appropriate activities; and construct a joint family narrative that facilitates a hopeful, trusting relationship between parent and child.

This intervention is grounded in Fraiberg's (1980; Fraiberg, Adelson, & Shapiro, 1975; Lieberman, 1992, 2004; Lieberman & Van Horn, 2008) theory that parents behave according to representational models of their own attachment relationships from childhood. From this perspective, it is hypothesized that benevolent child-rearing practices (e.g., those in which the child feels loved, accepted, worthy, and secure) create an imprinted experience that provides a young child with a sense of well-being that protects against traumatic experiences (Lieberman, Padron, Van Horn, & Harris, 2005). A parent's use of benevolent and nonbenevolent practices is seen as a series of unconscious enactments of experiences endured during the parent's early history. The treatment emphasizes parents' ability to bring these unconscious experiences into consciousness and connect their parenting practices to their own childhood experiences to best meet the child's needs.

There is emerging empirical support for CPP's effectiveness, specifically with young children exposed to trauma. Lieberman, Van Horn, and Ghosh Ippen (2005) found that among 75 domestic violence–exposed preschooler–

parent dyads, child behavior problems, symptoms of traumatic stress, maternal psychiatric symptoms, and avoidance decreased after participating in CPP treatment for 1 year compared with a control condition of case management and individual treatment. Additional reductions in child behavior problems as well as the maintenance of improvements in maternal symptoms were found at a 6-month follow-up for the CPP treatment group (Lieberman, Ghosh Ippen, & Van Horn, 2006). Alternate versions of CPP, including infant–parent psychotherapy and toddler–parent psychotherapy, have been empirically evaluated and demonstrate positive effects on the secure attachment of young children across various populations (Cicchetti, Rogosch, & Toth 1997).

Trauma-Focused Cognitive–Behavioral Therapy

Although not exclusively a parent–child dyadic treatment and therefore not the focus of this chapter, trauma-focused cognitive–behavioral therapy (CBT; Cohen & Mannarino, 1996; Cohen, Mannarino, & Deblinger, 2006) has an extensive evidentiary base and includes a corresponding parent-focused component. Trauma-focused CBT has been widely demonstrated to reduce posttraumatic stress disorder symptoms among sexually abused children. In this treatment, traumatized youngsters receive individual CBT sessions, but collateral and conjoint work with the nonoffending caregiver is also emphasized. The components of the collateral parent sessions include the following:

- psychoeducation;
- enhancement of parenting skills (e.g., use of praise, ignoring, the time-out technique);
- parental relaxation training;
- enhancement of parental affective expression and modulation (e.g., thought interruption and positive distractions);
- parental education regarding the cognitive triangle (i.e., the interrelationship between thoughts, feelings, and behavior); and
- enhancement of parental ability to provide a safe environment, listen noncritically to the child's trauma narrative, and discuss the child's trauma narrative in helpful ways.

In conjoint sessions, the nonoffending caregiver and victimized child focus on their attributions regarding the abuse, the child's sense of safety, sexuality, and how to enhance future safety and development.

Dyadic Treatment Components

Although the parent–child dyadic treatments we have described (i.e., PCIT, filial therapy and CPRT, and CPP) differ in several respects, they share the following two common elements: (a) Parent–child interactive play is used as a therapeutic medium and (b) the parent–child relationship is the principal target of the intervention. A pronounced difference between these treatments and trauma-focused CBT is that the dyadic treatments include a focus on parent–child play-based interactions. Variations among the parent–child dyadic treatments also exist, including which specific areas are emphasized (e.g., enhancing the parent–child relationship, improving parents' disciplinary effectiveness, the caregiver's own developmental experiences), the number of parenting domains emphasized (i.e., ranging from a more narrow focus on parent–child play-based interactions to a more broad focus on multiple parenting domains), the manner in which feedback is delivered to the parent (e.g., in vivo coaching, therapist modeling, collateral session with the parent), and the degree to which specific symptoms or parent behaviors are targeted for intervention.

Posttraumatic Parenting Program

The PP program was designed to blend theory, existing research-based treatments, and parenting-specific posttraumatic interventions. The program is a structured, evidence-informed, parent–child dyadic treatment for young traumatized children and their nonoffending caregivers. In this approach, 3- to 8-year-old children and their guardians participate in specifically selected play and other activities while receiving in vivo coaching from the therapist. The fundamental belief underlying this model is that many young survivors show both symptom reduction and improved adjustment when their parents effectively engage in behaviors that promote safety, comfort, and well-being. The PP program also accentuates the caregiver's ability to engage in play, teaching, nonviolent discipline, and other parental behaviors that are particularly important to symptom reduction and adjustment among recently traumatized children. Although many of these parental behaviors may seem intuitive, we have found that many caregivers from our clinical population do not routinely engage in these activities and that coaching them to do so often results in powerful benefit to the young survivors. Similar to the play-based dyadic treatments described earlier, in the PP program the parent–child play interactions are included in the treatment, which encompasses seven additional areas of focus. In the PP program, a total of eight specific parenting domains are targeted, and all therapeutic interventions are delivered on the basis of each caregiver–child dyad's individual needs. These domains, suggested by Larrieu and Bellow (2004), are as follows: emotional availability; nurturance–empathic responsiveness; protection; comfort; teaching; play; discipline; and instrumental care, structure, and routines (see Table 4.2). We positioned the domains such that those

TABLE 4.2
Parenting Domains and Associated Positive Child Outcomes

Phase	Domain	Outcome
1	Protection	Vigilance, self-protection, and safety
	Comfort	Comfort seeking
2	Instrumental care, structure, and routines	Self-regulation and predictability
	Nurturance–empathic responsiveness	Security, trust, and self-esteem
	Emotional availability	Emotion regulation
3	Play	Play and imagination
	Discipline	Limit setting, self-control, and cooperation
4	Teaching	Learning, curiosity, and mastery

with the most urgency (i.e., protection) would be addressed first. Next, we outline each domain in more detail.

Protection (Parent) and Vigilance, Self-Protection, and Safety (Child)

This domain involves parental ability to protect children from dangerous situations or harm. It is critical in the assessment of caregiver–child relationships in which there has been abuse or trauma, particularly when the parent's inability to protect the child from harm was a contributing factor to the abuse. The child's developmental tasks within this domain are to develop an awareness of his or her environment and surroundings and to accurately recognize threats to safety (i.e., vigilance). Another aspect of this domain includes the ability to keep oneself free from danger or harm (i.e., self-protection), which is closely related to the parent's capacity to ensure a safe environment for the child.

Comforting (Parent) and Comfort Seeking (Child)

The ability to provide comfort to the child is the key aspect of this domain. Specific to trauma, this includes the provision of solace and comfort to the child to reduce the child's distress when dealing with upsetting or difficult material or circumstances (Larrieu & Bellow, 2004). Furthermore, this domain involves parental tolerance of the parent's own internal discomfort regarding the child's pain or distress and the ability to respond in an effective manner despite this discomfort. Following a traumatic event, the comforting skills included in this domain may be particularly difficult for avoidant parents who may themselves have difficulty acknowledging and coping with the traumatic event. This domain also involves the child's ability to signal the caretaker when he or she needs to be comforted or soothed, such that the parent is able to adequately recognize this need and offer comfort.

Instrumental Care, Structure, and Routines (Parent)
and Self-Regulation–Predictability (Child)

Instrumental care is the domain related to the parent's ability to meet the child's basic needs, including the provision of food, shelter, clothing, and other essential resources. This domain also includes creating a sense of structure and routine and establishing a predictable schedule for the child. This consistency helps to facilitate the child's self-regulation skills and promotes the child's subjective experience of reassurance, safety, and trust. Following a traumatic event, families may experience disruption in their usual routines and structure, and they sometimes experience a loss of valuable resources, such as home, work, quality child care, or transportation.

Emotional Availability (Parent) and Emotion Regulation (Child)

This domain is defined by the parent's ability to accurately label his or her own emotional experiences and to share an appropriate range of emotions with the child. This domain also includes the parent's ability to correctly interpret and label the child's emotions. The parent's task is to assist the child in learning how to accurately identify, adequately manage, and express his or her own emotions. The parental ability to be emotionally available to the child is regarded as closely related to the child's ability to effectively regulate his or her own emotions (Larrieu & Bellow, 2004).

Nurturance–Empathic Responsiveness (Parent) and Security, Trust,
and Self-Esteem (Child)

Empathic responsiveness represents the parent's ability to respond sensitively to the child's perceived emotional experience. This domain involves the parental ability to provide support and encouragement, which promotes the child's development of a sense of security, trust, and the belief that others will behave as expected (Larrieu & Bellow, 2004). Self-esteem, as related to this domain, involves the child's beliefs and emotions regarding his or her own self-worth.

Play (Parent) and Play–Imagination (Child)

In addition to its value as a pleasurable activity that helps to promote happiness, cognitive skills, and problem solving, play is an important way for children to explore and learn about their surroundings. Parents' tasks in this domain are to help their children have fun, experiment with different social roles, solve problems in play scenarios, and learn more about themselves and the world around them (Larrieu & Bellow, 2004). Caregiver–child play also offers the dyad the opportunity to spend positive, noncritical time together. The parent's specific role includes (a) allowing the child to make his or her own choices in the play, (b) following the child's lead, and (c) remaining within the child's metaphor (Larrieu & Bellow, 2004). The success of the parent–child dyad in this domain is determined by both children's willingness to demonstrate certain themes (e.g., negative feelings, material related to the traumatic event) and parents' responses to those themes. Following a traumatic event, this domain is important to allow children the opportunity to share their trauma-related experiences and potential resolutions with their parents via play.

Discipline–Limit Setting (Parent) and Self-Control–Cooperation (Child)

This domain involves the parent's skill in helping the child understand the limits of his or her abilities, the consequences of his or her actions, and the boundaries of self and others. Through the use of discipline and limit setting, the child develops self-control and the ability to set self-imposed limits to internally regulate his or her own behavior. This domain is critical in posttraumatic parenting because excessive, overly harsh, or physical discipline may be a trauma trigger for the child. In contrast, the child whose caregivers offer lax or inconsistent discipline may create a different sort of hardship—an overwhelmed child who needs assistance to inhibit inappropriate, unproductive, or dangerous behaviors.

Teaching (Parent) and Learning–Curiosity–Mastery (Child)

Teaching children about the world around them and how to successfully negotiate problems are also elements of helpful posttraumatic parenting. Successful teaching requires having an awareness of the child's ability level and a willingness to provide support, encouragement, and problem-solving strategies to complete tasks that may be slightly more difficult than those to which the child is accustomed. This domain is relevant to posttraumatic parenting particularly with regard to how and what parents teach their children regarding adaptive coping skills. By being exposed to age-appropriate challenging situations and accomplishable tasks, the child gains experiences that foster future success and mastery (Larrieu & Bellow, 2004).

Posttraumatic Parenting Treatment Structure

The eight parenting domains we have just described provide the theoretical basis for the specific interventions offered to caregiver–child dyads. These interventions are provided experientially—rather than didactically—to the extent possible. Interventions are also behavioral and specific and often implemented with visual aids and activities designed to benefit parents with a range of learning styles.

After completing a preliminary psychodiagnostic assessment of the child, including a thorough developmental history, the rationale for the treatment is provided to the parent and the child. Predyadic collateral therapy is provided to the caregiver alone to assess and address safety-related issues and the parent's ability to ensure the child's basic well-being. During the dyadic portion of the treatment, the therapist asks the caregiver and child to engage in intrasession assignments, individually depicted on colorful index cards to make them more engaging. These cards specify particular activities that correspond to each of the eight parenting domains described by Larrieu and Bellow (2004) and summarized in Table 4.2. During the first administration of the cards, the caregiver–child dyad completes at least two tasks related to each domain. During the initial PP skills session (or across a couple of sessions, if necessary) a baseline of parenting skills in each domain is established, and the treatment is targeted toward underdeveloped domain-specific parenting skills. As the treatment progresses, additional parenting task cards are provided for the targeted domains to enhance, refine, and reinforce parenting skills that assist in the child's posttraumatic adjustment. As parents strengthen their skills in each domain, the therapist monitors domain skills for several sessions to ensure that the treatment gains are robust while the dyad progresses to a focus on additional domains.

In the PP program, the eight domains are typically addressed with the parent–child dyad in four phases. Also, the domains involving those parenting skills likely to emerge relatively quickly (e.g., establishing routines, engaging in comforting behaviors) were hierarchically placed earlier in the treatment than those that require longer term work to address (e.g., empathy, emotional availability). However, there is flexibility in the model for the therapist to alter the suggested hierarchy to focus on the domains most relevant to the caregiver–child dyad.

To assess the effectiveness of the parent–child dyad on each task, we use a rating scale similar to that used in the Structured Clinical Interview for *DSM–IV* Axis I Disorders (First, Spitzer, Gibbon & Williams, 1997), in which the clinician rates the respondent regarding criteria that are present, subthreshold, or absent (First et al., 1997). A "present" rating indicates, for example, that the parent is able to successfully make comforting statements to or engage in comforting behaviors with the child, who evidences signs of being comforted. Because we consider both the parent's and the child's competency to demonstrate or perform specific tasks in the various domains, we suggest that the parent and child be scored separately for competency within each given area. Some children respond surprisingly well (e.g., as if they feel comforted) to parental behaviors that would not be expected to comfort a child and do not demonstrate competency in the domain (e.g., a parent who responds to a child's comfort seeking with a painfully hard pat on the back). Separating the parent–child assessment ratings allows a clinical focus on the individual areas of intervention necessary for each member of the dyad.

When parents do not demonstrate competencies in each domain, the domain is targeted by having the parent engage in additional, increasingly specific activities within the same domain until competency is achieved. For example, if a parent does not demonstrate a strong ability to comfort the child in response to a task card soliciting demonstration of comforting behaviors, the parent then receives a follow-up card asking the parent to engage in more specific activities with the child (e.g., "Offer your child a hug," "Reassure your child that you will do everything you can to keep him or her safe"). Throughout the treatment, the activities related to each domain begin with general tasks (e.g., "Do something to show that you love your child") that are followed by more specific, skill-building tasks if the parent does not demonstrate competency. That is, the parent receives live coaching and is offered increasingly specific versions of the same task (e.g., "Move closer to your child," "Look into her eyes," "Use a warm and caring tone," "Say 'I love you'") until competency in the domain is obtained. As indicated in the examples provided earlier, live coaching includes feedback on verbal and nonverbal communication. Additional examples of intrasession parenting tasks related to each domain are described in Table 4.3.

CONCLUSION

Although there is only anecdotal and theoretical support for the PP model at this time, we nevertheless believe that PP provides a unique and useful treatment option as part of a field that has yet to widely research posttraumatic treatments for young children. We designed the PP program to be a practical, engaging, clinician-friendly treatment option for caregiver–child dyads in need of targeted parenting interventions. On the basis of our preliminary work in a university hospital outpatient clinic, we have anecdotally observed dramatic reductions in childhood posttraumatic stress as well as positive outcomes in factors such as the traumatized child's sense of safety, comfort, nurturance, and delight. We believe that as a play-based intervention, this treatment goes one step beyond mere symptom reduction by providing a structure for future positive experiences in caregiver–child interactions and developmentally appropriate communication.

This treatment was not designed to replace other research-based approaches. We offer the PP program as an evidence-informed, additional treatment option that the therapist may use to complement, addend, or preface other more established posttraumatic treatments. Although we have had success using this approach to isolate and enhance parenting skills specifically

TABLE 4.3
Sample Parent–Child Treatment Activities for Each Domain

Phase	Parenting domain	Selected collateral session activities	Selected dyadic intrasession tasks
1	Protection	Discussion of child's level of safety; parent rating of danger level in sample vignettes and video-taped samples; family genogram of abuse	Tell your child what you will do to keep him or her safe. Tell your child how important his or her safety is to you.
	Comforting	Video demonstrations, role-plays	Do something that is comforting to or with your child; tell your child that the two of you will get through this and that you will both be okay.
2	Instrumental care	Discuss family routine, healthy meals, exposure to media violence, emotionally and physically safe child care, and other instrumental care issues.	Make a plan with your child for a bedtime routine.
	Emotional availability	Affect psychoeducation; reflection skills training; discussion of child's posttraumatic feeling	Play with your child for 10 minutes; reflect your child's feelings during the play.
	Nurturance and empathy	Collateral session activities	Tell your child three things that you like about her or him; make empathic statements for play characters.
3	Play	Parent training regarding core child-led play skills	Play with your child for 5 minutes; ask your child to put away the toys by him or herself
	Discipline	Parent training regarding core parenting skills related to discipline	Ask your child to put away the toys by him- or herself.
4	Teaching	Parental coping; skill building	Teach your child what he or she can do to feel better when he or she feels upset.

related to posttraumatic parenting, we recognize that the eight domains posited by Larrieu and Bellow (2004) may not be the only areas of relevance in the parent–child relationship and that a clinical observation—especially a brief one—may not accurately represent the complexity of a caregiver's full relationship with the child. Nonetheless, our extremely positive clinical experiences prompt us to offer our initial impressions to contribute to the discussion about how to best help young trauma survivors and their caregivers.

Although we do not yet have published empirical findings to support the efficacy of this parent–child dyadic treatment, we believe that there is indirect support for this type of treatment given the positive findings for other similar treatments (e.g., PCIT, CPRT, and filial therapy). We introduce this treatment on the basis of our belief that these findings combined with our own clinical experiences lend at least preliminary support for PP as we develop its evidentiary base.

REFERENCES

Andronico, M. P., & Guerney, B. G., Jr. (1969). A psychotherapeutic aide in a Head Start Program: I. Theory and practice. *Children, 16*, 14–17.

Bagner, D. M., & Eyberg, S. M. (2007). Parent–child interaction therapy for disruptive behavior in children with mental retardation: A randomized controlled trial. *Journal of Clinical Child and Adolescent Psychology, 36*, 418–429.

Bratton, S., & Landreth, G. (1995). Filial therapy with single parents: Effects on parental acceptance, empathy, and stress. *International Journal of Play Therapy, 4*, 61–80.

Bratton, S., Landreth, G., Kellam, T., & Blackard, S.R. (2006). *Child parent relationship therapy (CPRT) treatment manual: A 10-session filial therapy model for training parents*. New York: Routledge.

Cicchetti, D., Rogosch, F. A., & Toh, S. L. (1997). Ontogenesis, depressotypic organization, and the depressive spectrum. In S. S. Luthar, J. Burack, D. Cicchetti, & J. Weisz (Eds.), *Developmental psychopathology: Perspectives on adjustment, risk, and disorder* (pp. 273–313). New York: Cambridge University Press.

Cohen, J. A., & Mannarino, A. P. (1993). A treatment model for sexually abused preschoolers. *Journal of Interpersonal Violence, 8*, 115–131.

Cohen, J. A., & Mannarino, A. P. (1996). Factors that mediate treatment outcome of sexually abused preschool children. *Journal of the American Academy of Child & Adolescent Psychiatry, 35*, 1402–1410.

Cohen, J. A., & Mannarino, A. P. (1998). Interventions for sexually abused children: Initial treatment outcome findings. *Child Maltreatment, 3*, 17–26.

Cohen, J. A., Mannarino, A. P., & Deblinger, E. (2006). *Treating trauma and traumatic grief in children and adolescents*. New York: Guilford Press.

Crockenberg, S., & Leerkes, E. (2000). Infant social and emotional development in family context. In C. H. Zeanah (Ed.), *Handbook of infant mental health* (2nd ed., pp. 60–90). New York: Guilford Press.

Deblinger, E., McLeer, S.V., & Henry, D. (1990). Cognitive–behavioral treatment for sexually abused children suffering posttraumatic stress: Preliminary findings. *Journal of the American Academy of Child & Adolescent Psychiatry, 29*, 747–752.

Deblinger, E., Stauffer, L. B., & Steer, R. A. (2001). Comparative efficacies of supportive and cognitive–behavioral group therapies for young children who have been sexually abused and their nonoffending mothers. *Child Maltreatment, 6*, 332–343.

Dombrowski, S. C., Timmer, S. G., Blacker, D. M., & Urquiza, A. J. (2005). A positive behavioural intervention for toddlers: Parent–child attunement therapy. *Child Abuse Review, 14*, 132–151.

Eisenstadt, T. H., Eyberg, S., McNeil, C. B., Newcomb, K., & Funderburk, B. (1993). Parent–child interaction therapy with behavior problem children: Relative effectiveness of two stages and overall treatment outcome. *Journal of Clinical Child Psychology, 22*, 42–51

Emde, R. N. (1989). The infant's relationship experience: Developmental and affective aspects. In A. J. Sameroff & R. N. Emde (Eds.), *Relationship disturbances in early childhood: A developmental approach* (pp. 33–51). New York: Basic Books.

First, M. B., Spitzer, R. L., Gibbon, M., &Williams, J. B. W. (1997). *Structured Clinical Interview for DSM–IV Axis I Disorders (SCID-I), Clinician Version, user's guide*. Washington, DC: American Psychiatric Publishing.

Fraiberg, S. (1980). *Clinical studies in infant mental health*. New York: Basic Books.

Fraiberg, S., Adelson, E., & Shapiro, V. (1975). Ghosts in the nursery: A psychoanalytic approach to impaired infant–mother relationships. *Journal of the American Academy of Child & Adolescent Psychiatry, 14*, 387–421.

Glazer-Waldman, H., Zimmerman, J., Landreth, G., & Norton, D. (1992). Filial therapy: An intervention for parents of children with chronic illnesses. *International Journal of Play Therapy, 1*, 31–42.

Harris, Z. I., & Landreth, G. (1997). Filial therapy with incarcerated mothers: A five week model. *International Journal of Play Therapy, 6*, 53–73.

Herschell, A. D., Calzada, E. J., Eyberg, S. M., & McNeil, C. B. (2002). Parent–child interaction therapy: New directions in research. *Cognitive and Behavioral Practice, 9*, 9–16.

Larrieu, J. A., & Bellow, S. M. (2004). Relationship assessment for young traumatized children. In J. D. Osofsky (Ed.), *Young children and trauma: Intervention and trauma* (pp.155–172). New York: Guilford Press.

LeBlanc, M., & Ritchie, M. (1999). Predictors of play therapy outcomes. *International Journal of Play Therapy, 8*, 19–34.

Lee, M., & Landreth, G. (2003). Filial therapy with immigrant Korean parents in the United States. *International Journal of Play Therapy, 12*, 67–85.

Lieberman, A. F. (1992). Infant–parent psychotherapy with toddlers. *Development and Psychopathology, 4*, 559–574.

Lieberman, A. F. (2004). Child–parent psychotherapy: A relationship-based approach to the treatment of mental health disorders in infancy and early childhood. In A. J. Sameroff, S. C. McDonough, & K. L. Rosenblaum (Eds.), Treating *parent–infant relationship problems* (pp. 97–122). New York: Guilford Press.

Lieberman, A. F., Ghosh Ippen, C., & Van Horn, P. (2006). Child–parent psychotherapy: 6-month follow-up of a randomized controlled trial. *Journal of the Academy of Child & Adolescent Psychiatry, 45*, 913–918.

Lieberman, A. F., Padron, E., Van Horn, P., & Harris, W. W. (2005). Angels in the nursery: The intergenerational transmission of benevolent parental influences. *Infant Mental Health Journal, 26*, 504–520.

Lieberman, A. F., & Van Horn, P. (2005). *Don't hit my mommy*. Washington, DC: Zero to Three Press.

Lieberman, A. F., & Van Horn, P. (2008). *Psychotherapy with infants and young children: Repairing the effects of stress and trauma on early attachment*. New York: Guilford Press.

Lieberman, A. F., Van Horn, P. J., & Ghosh Ippen, C. (2005). Toward evidence-based treatment: Child–parent psychotherapy with preschoolers exposed to marital violence. *Journal of the American Academy of Child & Adolescent Psychiatry, 44*, 1241–1248.

Pincus, D. B., Santucci, L. C., Ehrenreich, J., & Eyberg, S. M. (2008). The implementation of modified parent–child interaction therapy for youth with separation anxiety disorder. *Cognitive and Behavioral Practice, 15*, 118–125.

Silverman, W. K., & La Greca, A. M. (2002). Children experiencing disaster: Definitions, reactions, and predictors of outcomes. In A. M. La Greca, W. K. Silverman, E. M. Bernberg, & M. C. Roberts (Eds.), *Helping children cope with disasters and terrorism* (pp. 11–33). Washington, DC: American Psychological Association.

Smith, D. M., & Landreth, G. I. (2004). Filial therapy with teachers of deaf and hard of hearing preschool children. *International Journal of Play Therapy, 13*, 13–33.

Stover, L., & Guerney, B. G., Jr. (1967). The efficacy of training procedures for mothers in filial therapy. *Psychotherapy, 4*, 110–115.

Tew, K., Landreth, G., Joiner, K. D., & Solt, M. D. (2002). Filial therapy with parents of chronically ill children. *International Journal of Play Therapy, 13*, 13–33.

Urquiza, A. J. (2007, October). Parent–child interaction therapy. In J. S. Shelby (Chair), *Evidence-based treatments and play therapy: Innovations and adaptations*. Symposium conducted at the meeting of the Association for Play Therapy, Los Angeles, CA.

Urquiza, A. J., & McNeil, C. B. (1996). Parent–child interaction therapy: An intensive dyadic intervention for physically abusive families. *Child Maltreatment, 1*, 134–144.

VanFleet, R. (2005). *Filial therapy: Strengthening parent–child relationships through play* (2nd ed.). Sarasota, FL: Professional Resource Press.

Vernberg, E. M. (2002). Intervention approaches following disasters. In A. M. La Greca, W. K. Silverman, E. M. Vernberg, & M. C. Roberts (Eds.), *Helping children cope with disaster and terrorism* (pp. 55–72). Washington, DC: American Psychological Association.

Zeanah, C. H., Boris, N. W., Heller, S. S., Hinshaw-Fuselier, S., Larrieu, J. A., Lewis, M., et al. (1997). Relationship assessment in infant mental health. *Infant Mental Health Journal, 18,* 182–197.

Zeanah, C. H., Larrieu, J. A., Heller, S. S., & Valliere, J. (2000). Infant–parent relationship assessment. In C. H. Zeanah (Ed.), *Handbook of infant mental health* (2nd ed., pp. 222–235). New York: Guilford Press.

5

FILIAL PLAY THERAPY FOR GRIEVING PRESCHOOL CHILDREN

HILDA R. GLAZER

Researchers have come to understand that childhood mourning is a normal process and does not necessarily result in psychopathology and developmental dysfunction (Oltjenbruns, 2001). The experience of loss and exposure to trauma can affect the child's development in either a positive or a negative way. Children are resilient and may not have any adverse reactions or negative behavior changes, or the loss may result in psychological distress and behavioral change.

Understanding the impact of loss in a child's life and developing effective interventions is the focus of this chapter. In this chapter, I present filial therapy as an empirically validated intervention for the grieving preschool child. Taking an ecological perspective, I focus on the individual within the environment. Interpersonal relationships, community resources and conditions, and the various systems within which the person functions all affect the way in which he or she copes and problem solves (Collins & Collins, 2005). The child's functioning is then related to the others' reactions and the support available to the child and the family. I begin the chapter with a discussion of developmental issues and play, followed by a discussion of children's grief. Play interventions and filial therapy are presented with supporting research and illustrated by a case study. The chapter ends with suggestions for future directions.

CONCEPTUALIZING INTERVENTIONS
FOR THE PRESCHOOL CHILD

Play is an important part of the child's life. All children use play thera-peutically as a way of dealing with stress (Elkind, 2007) and processing events in their lives. In a therapeutic playroom, the therapist provides a safe place for the child to play and process life events. The relationship that develops between the child and the therapist is a critical piece of that process. The therapist provides the context in which expression occurs. The communica-tion in the playroom is bidirectional, with both the child and the therapist responding to the interaction.

The child has to depend on the adult to see the need for therapy and to make the arrangements. However, when one is working with grieving or traumatized families, it is difficult to separate the adults' experience and response from those of the child. Some adults, in my experience, see the child's response as the same as their own and are unable to differentiate between the two. Helping the adult to differentiate becomes one of the goals of therapy.

When conceptualizing the interventions for a particular child, there are a number of questions that should be raised. These include the following:

- What is the presenting issue?
- How does the family system affect the presenting problem?
- What are this child's needs?
- Who is going to have the greatest impact on the child?
- Which intervention will have the greatest potential to facilitate change?

Changes in behavior are often the presenting reason. All of a sudden, a child cries easily, is clingy, shows regressive behaviors, or acts out in ways that are new to this child and are disturbing at home and preschool. For the preschool child, the answers to the second and third questions are deter-mined through interaction with the family and child and understanding what brought them to therapy. The answer to the fourth question is often the parent rather than the therapist, and one intervention that should be considered in treatment planning with the preschool child is filial therapy. Filial therapy provides the opportunity for the parent to become the child's primary therapist under the guidance of the play therapist. Although still child centered, the intervention uses the attachment bond between parent and child to facilitate change and provide the context for processing. The playroom becomes a place where the parent and child will have some-thing special.

THEORETICAL FOUNDATIONS OF FILIAL THERAPY

Filial therapy, or child–parent relationship training, is a theoretically integrative approach combining elements of psychodynamic, humanistic, behavioral, cognitive, social learning, attachment, and family systems theories. However, the primary theoretical basis is client-centered play therapy. Moustakas (1959), in describing relationship therapy, saw therapy as a unique growth experience created by one person who needs help and another person who accepts the responsibility of offering it. The parallel in filial therapy is that it is based on the parent–child bond and the assumption that the parent has more emotional significance to the child than does the therapist. The parent and child are developmentally linked, and the playroom becomes a place where they learn and grow together. In his experience, Moustakas (1959) found that "parents recognize the significance of their own participation and are eager to explore their relationship with the child, to express their interests and concerns, and to discover new ways of approaching him" (p. 169). My theoretical base—developed while studying under Garry Landreth at the University of North Texas and then in working with Louise Guerney—is client centered with a psychoeducational group therapy model.

Relational–cultural therapy is related theoretically to filial therapy in that many of the guiding or core principles are similar. Relational–cultural therapy is based on a set of core principles that include the following:

- people grow through and toward relationships throughout the life span
- movement toward mutuality rather than movement toward separation characterizes mature functioning
- relational differentiation and elaboration characterize growth
- in growth-fostering relationships, all people contribute, grow or benefit; development is not a one-way street
- therapy relationships are characterized by a special kind of mutuality. (Jordan, 2000, p. 1007)

According to Jordan, the work of relational–cultural therapy is understanding the individual patterns of connections and disconnections. In filial therapy, the relationship between the parent and the child becomes the focus, and often the restoration of that relationship is the goal of therapy. For the child experiencing trauma or loss, the parent and child use the playroom to explore the meaning of the experience for the child, and both the parent and the child learn and grow in the experience. Filial therapy encourages and reinforces that empathy and mutuality. The construct of mutual empathy suggests that both individuals in a relationship are affected by the other (Jordan, 2000). This supports the parent's role in filial therapy because the parent–child bond already exists and is strengthened in the process of the therapeutic encounter in the playroom.

The model for filial therapy is "a competence-oriented psychoeducational framework" (VanFleet, 1994, p. 2) in which therapists teach parents to conduct special playtimes, work with them on development of skills, and eventually help them to integrate the playtimes and parenting skills at home. Training for filial therapy is provided through a number of training institutes and associations, and courses in filial therapy are provided at universities, often within counseling or counseling psychology departments that offer courses in play therapy. As with all therapeutic interventions, filial therapy should not be conducted without proper training.

FILIAL THERAPY MODEL

Filial therapy was developed in the 1960s by Bernard and Louise Guerney at Rutgers University and Pennsylvania State University. In her 2000 article, Louise Guerney reviewed the rationales originally developed by Bernard Guerney in 1964:

- Child problems are often related to a lack of parenting knowledge and skill.
- Playing with their child in a therapeutic role should help parents and children to relate in a more positive and appropriate way.
- There is precedent in the use of play sessions in the work of earlier client-centered therapists.
- Much of the resistance to therapy on the part of parents is eliminated.
- The parent–child relationship is one of the most significant in the child's life; thus, the potential for change is greater with the parent than with a therapist.

Originally applied to children with typical behavior and/or emotional problems in lower middle to middle-class White urban and suburban intact families, variations have focused more on the interaction between parent and child. Foley, Higdon, and White (2006) described filial therapy as "relationship-based therapy model built on the assumption that under certain conditions, a safe and secure context will be created to foster intimacy and understanding between parent and child" (p. 39).

The method has now been applied successfully with many ethnic and racial groups (e.g., Lee & Landreth, 2003); lower income families; divorced, blended, foster, and adoptive families (e.g., Bratton & Landreth, 1995; Glazer & Kottman, 1994); children with chronic illness (e.g., Glazer-Waldman, Zimmerman, Landreth, & Norton, 1992); grieving children (e.g., Glazer, 2006); and parent surrogates in the United States and abroad. The effectiveness of filial therapy has been demonstrated; parents learn to be more accepting of their children, allow them more self-direction, and are more empathic. Louise Guerney (2000) summed it up in this way:

> Based on the variations in application of [filial therapy] that have proven workable across a range of populations, we think that [filial therapy] is a remarkably robust approach that can be shorter or longer, used with groups or individual families (with only a single parent as well), applied in inadequate[ly] sized offices or lovely treatment rooms, and still be depended upon for bringing about desired change. (p. 13)

Filial therapy is conducted in a consistent, manualized approach using the original long approach of the Guerneys, the Landreth 10-week model, the VanFleet model, or modifications of these models (Carmichael, 2006).

DEVELOPMENTAL ISSUES

Each age brings with it new opportunities for growth and new challenges. Children use play to nourish their cognitive, emotional, and social development at all ages (Elkind, 2007). The additional challenge for the preschool child is the development of a sense of competition. These children also develop gender roles and become more independent. Cognitively, they are developing more realistic concepts of the world, learning to follow verbal instructions and pay attention. They are both learning and creating symbols (Elkind, 2007). As they enter preschool, they begin to play with others and learn social rules. Elkind (2007) postulated that three elements are necessary to a happy and productive life: love, play, and work. Of these, "Play is the dominant and directing mode of learning during this age period, and children learn best through self-created learning experiences" (Elkind, 2007, p. 7).

It is important to note that although traumatic experiences such as the death of a loved one will have an impact on preschoolers' lives, not all young children will develop emotional or behavioral problems or psychiatric disorders (Van Horn & Lieberman, 2004). Summarizing the research on resilience, Van Horn and Lieberman (2004) listed three factors that protect development in children who have experienced trauma: (a) a relationship with a caring competent adult, which is the most important; (b) a community safe haven; and (c) the child's internal resources, including easy temperament and average or above-average intelligence. The parent's ability to cope with and respond to the child is critical to the child's ability to cope with the loss. In coping with their own grief, adults are not always able to see the child's grief and may not be able to respond his or her needs.

Grief-Related Developmental Issues

The grief of preschool children must be placed in the context of development. That is, preschool children think about death in a qualitatively different way than do older children. Preschool children do not understand universality of death; they do not see that death is permanent and that death means that all bodily functions cease (Oltjenbruns, 2001). Because the preschool child believes that death is reversible, he or she may ask questions about when the person who died is returning home (Oltjenbruns, 2001) or think that he or she can go visit the person in heaven. This can be distressing to grieving adults.

Death for a child is a nonnormative life event. It confronts the child with crisis. The impact on child development may be positive or negative, and there is the potential for psychological harm as well as the opportunity for growth. Often, preschool children do not have the language capacity to describe their feelings or ask for what they need. They are often unable to draw comfort from the words of others (Oltjenbruns, 2001). Grief is expressed through play and through behavior. The behaviors will vary and will represent the way the child copes with the situation; they are the clues to how the child is coping and his or her emotional state (Oltjenbruns, 2001). But it is also important to note that the preschool child may constrain his or her emotional reactions in response to the caretaker's responses (Oltjenbruns, 2001). How the adults are grieving and coping and how they interact with the child will also affect the child's response. Changes in behavior may occur shortly after the death, and others may appear after some time. Their duration may be either short or long term. Some of the behaviors that may appear include the following:

- Children may exhibit a fear of being separated from the parent: crying, whimpering, screaming, immobility or aimless motion, trembling, frightened facial expressions, and excessive clinging.
- Parents may also notice children returning to behaviors exhibited at earlier ages (regressive behaviors), such as thumb sucking, bedwetting, and fear of darkness.
- Children in this age bracket tend to be strongly affected by parents' reactions to the traumatic event.
- Children may use defense mechanisms of denial and projection.
- Children's explosive emotions may be an outward expression of grief work directed toward anyone available.
- Children tend to be fairly protective of themselves and their emotions when they are with other children.
- In normal mourning, anger expressed toward one target or another is the rule (Bowlby, 1980).

- Children may experience a wave of overwhelming thoughts.
- Children may dream of the person who died.
- Children may show not-uncommon disruption in eating and sleeping patterns.
- Children may feel a sense of insecurity and abandonment and a wish to be protected from future loss.
- Children may feel guilt over being a survivor.
- Children may feel guilt over expressing any kind of joy or happiness in life.

One phenomenon that typically occurs with preschool children is that they appear to vacillate between experiencing their loss and engaging in normal activities (Oltjenbruns, 2001). This is often disconcerting to adults taking care of the child who do not understand that this is typical behavior.

Many children find it important to continue a bond with the deceased person as they deal with and accommodate to the loss (Oltjenbruns, 2001). For example, preschool children may place the deceased person in their drawings, often as an angel-type figure but sometimes as part of the family scene. In reviewing the literature on childhood grief, Oltjenbruns (2001) developed a list of preschool children's psychological reactions that includes emotional distress, separation anxiety, fear that others will also die, death fantasies, learning difficulties (concentration difficulties), and guilt.

In understanding the impact of the loss on the child, it is important to view it in the context of primary and secondary losses. The primary loss is the person who died—the loss of a personally meaningful relationship and perhaps the loss of a primary attachment figure. The secondary losses include those related to changes in life and routine after the death. If the family moves, there is the loss of the house; the child's room; and often the neighborhood, school, and friends. There may be other changes in routine that may be upsetting to the child. One child showed this in her play by taking all of the furniture out of the dollhouse and putting it under the large stuffed animal in the room and then sitting on it. She never said a word to me or her mother about how she felt about moving. She did this a few more times before coming in one day and setting up the dollhouse and putting the family in the car and driving them to the house.

PLAY INTERVENTION PROCEDURES

Parents and caregivers may bring the child in shortly after the death, or they may wait until the child becomes symptomatic. There is no evidence of an impact of delay on outcomes in young children (Van Horn & Lieberman, 2004). The therapeutic value of enactment through symbolic play is that it allows for reworking and mastery of the traumatic events. For the grieving or traumatized child, the therapeutic environment must create a climate for posttraumatic play (Gil, 1991). The child reenacts the events in an effort to master them (Gil, 1991). Often, the child will set up the same play sequence in multiple sessions with nearly identical actions and an identical outcome. The potential benefit of this play is that although the child is remembering events that are frightening or anxiety producing, he or she is going from a passive to an active stance in controlling the reenactment (Gil, 1991). Gil also suggested that in the controlled, safe environment of the playroom, the child is gaining a sense of mastery and empowerment.

When selecting interventions, be careful that the intervention does not cause inadvertent harm. Children may not have the coping strategies to withstand these interventions (Shelby, 2007). Using a nondirective approach allows the child rather than the therapist to choose when to address or process the death.

Another consideration is the change in the family and family system that results as a natural consequence of filial therapy. The changes that occur in the relationship in the playroom transfer or generalize to life outside the playroom and to the family for both the parent and the child engaged in this special playtime.

Toys

The toys in the playroom for filial or play therapy include the following groupings:

- real-life toys,
- acting-out or aggressive toys,
- toys for creative expression,
- family or nurturing toys,
- scary toys, and
- pretend and fantasy toys.

In the playroom, I have found that younger children use toys within reach and often pick a toy that they have at home. So I make sure that some in each category are at eye level and below. The chalkboard and paper and markers are also favorite activities, as are clay and Play-Doh.

Nurturing play is often a theme, with toddlers using the kitchen and clay and paper to make meals. Nurturing play also occurs when the toddlers include me and the parent in their play, such as preparing or giving us dinner. Most of the toddler's play is solitary, however. Some children start the early play sessions by asking me to tell them what each thing they pick up is or what it is for. My response is that in the playroom, they can decide. Often this only continues for two sessions.

Filial Therapy Model

I have modified the 10-week model developed by Garry Landreth (1991) to be flexible and meet the needs of the family and child. The rationale for the change is based on time rather than the elimination of any skill or activity. When therapy is done one on one, less time is needed than with a group. There is a consistent sequence of learning and practice, following the outline developed for our original research on filial therapy (Glazer-Waldman et al., 1992).

In my practice I use play therapy or filial therapy or a combination, and I use two processes: (a) one in which play therapy is conducted for the first three to five sessions and (b) one in which filial therapy begins right away. One of the goals of the first session with the parent is to determine the best intervention for the child on the basis of the presenting problem and the child–family history. One of the factors that determines which process is used is whether the parent or guardian is willing to be part of the process. Another is family dynamics: I look at the relationship between parent and child and note the parent's ability to parent in a loss or trauma situation. Some parents are grieving and unable to participate in filial therapy at the time that I am seeing the family. Others have both the ability and the desire to participate in therapy for their children.

Part of the discussion includes the importance of play to the child developmentally. I explain the process and appropriateness of filial therapy. If the parent agrees to participate in filial therapy, I set a schedule for meetings with the parent and give parents either a workbook with information, articles, and exercises that I developed or the handbook for parents developed by Rise VanFleet (2000).

Session 1

The goal of the first session is to introduce the parent to the goals of filial therapy and to set goals for the parent and child. Behavioral goals with observable outcomes are set so that the parent can see changes. Typical goals may include

- increasing the parent's understanding of his or her child,
- helping parents recognize the importance of play in the child's and the parent's life (VanFleet, 1994),
- establishing an optimal relationship between parent and child,
- improving emotional and behavioral adjustment,
- increasing the parent's warmth toward and trust in the child (VanFleet, 1994), and
- providing a nonthreatening place where the parent can deal with his or her own issues as they relate to the child and parenting (VanFleet, 1994).

Homework for the first week is for the parent to find something new about the child and to list three of the child's strengths. There is also a discussion of the role of play and playing.

Session 2

The objective of the second session is to introduce emotional development and practice basic skills. The homework is reviewed. There is a short review of emotional development and the ways in which people communicate their feelings. On the basis of the parent's interest level, I may suggest readings.

The first two basic skills are reflective listening and tracking. *Reflective listening* is when the therapist or parent repeats what the child has said in a slightly different way. There can also be reflection of feeling in which the therapist or parent says the feeling that appears to be underlying what the child said. The child might say, "I am getting the frogs out; I can't find the Daddy frog." The parent or therapist might say, "You are looking for the frogs, but you have not found the Daddy frog yet." However, if reflecting the feeling, the response might instead be "You are sad that you cannot find the Daddy frog." This skill is typically introduced to the parent by going over a tape of a play therapy session so that the parent can see the skills, critique the actions, and ask questions about the process. Part of the time is spent in the playroom, demonstrating and trying out the skills, with the therapist and the parent taking turns playing the child. *Tracking* is when the therapist responds to what he or she sees in observing the child's play. In line with the previous example, the child may be lining up the frogs with the two larger frogs in front and the others behind. The response might be "You lined the frogs up with the two big ones in front and the smaller ones behind them." Both of these skills demonstrate to the child that the parent is there and that he or she is hearing them and is interested in their world.

The parent's homework for the week is to practice reflective listening and tracking for 5 minutes each (e.g., the parent is challenged to have a 5-minute conversation with another adult without asking any questions). Part of this session and each of the following sessions is for the parents and therapist to talk about family system issues and the parent's concerns.

Session 3

The objective of the third session is to prepare the parent for the special playtimes with his or her child. The first task is to review the homework and then to practice the skills in the playroom with the therapist playing the child's role. The parent's level of skill in tracking and listening determines the day's objective. Parents are asked to role-play these skills as part of the session. Parents judge their own level of comfort with the skills, and the therapist provides feedback about things that were done correctly and things that might be improved. Handouts with the skills broken down into parts are used to provide guides for skills. If the parent's skill level is inadequate, then the third session is spend in review. If the parent's skill level is adequate, then the next step is to review the basic tenets of client-centered play therapy following the principles set out by Axline (1947). The list of toys for filial therapy is shared, and the site for the play session is discussed. Presenting the sessions to the child is one of the major things to review. Presenting the special play-time as truly being a time for parent and child with no interruptions and as a special time for them to be together sends the message that this is an important and unique time for both the parent and the child. One father told me that the time in the car alone together to and from the playroom became important to him and his child and part of the special time that they had together. There is also a discussion of emotional development and naming emotions, leading to a discussion of why we reflect emotions and practice in reflecting emotions. Homework for Week 3 is to buy the toys or collect them in a box, to tell the child about the play sessions, and to practice reflection and tracking.

Session 4

This session is the first with the child in the playroom. In my playroom, I can sit in the hall and see all of the room. An agency playroom may have one-way mirrors with the capability to videotape or communicate with the parent while the session is in progress. The parent and child play for 30 minutes with me watching and videotaping if possible. If necessary, I can interject comments and make suggestions to ease the way for the parent.

Session 5

The objective of the fifth session is to review the first play session and to review and practice skills as needed. The first question to the parent is, "Did anything seem different this week after the play session?" This usually becomes the basis of an important discussion about the parent–child relationship. At this session, limit setting is introduced because it usually comes up in the first-session review. I have a conversation about communication, using some of the rules for communication between parent and child developed by Haim Ginott (1959). The focus is on the following:

1. If you cannot say it in 10 words or fewer, do not say it.
2. Never ask a question to which you already know the answer.
3. Be an emotional thermostat, not a thermometer (i.e., a thermostat can be changed, but a thermometer just takes the measure).

4. It is not what you said, but what you say after what you said (e.g., when you yell because you had a bad day, you can come back and tell the child that you did not mean to yell—it was your bad day speaking).

The following sessions are play sessions in the playroom with review of tapes shortly thereafter. The parent often quickly notices how some of the skills transfer to the rest of the week and the resulting changes in the family system. The transfer from the play session to the rest of the week often seems to the parents to be an important change. Reviewing the original goals for filial therapy often reveals that other positive changes have occurred in the relationship. Often, parents see their child as a separate individual rather than seeing the child's issues and concerns as a reflection of their own.

After there is a comfort level and adequate skill level, the play sessions are moved to the home with the parent videotaping and reviewing the tapes with me. The termination phase of filial therapy begins when the parent and child are conducting the sessions at home, and they begin to see it as part of the weekly routine. During the final session with the parent, I review the goals set at the first session. The value of continuing the play sessions is discussed.

There are follow-up phone calls with the option for additional sessions at 3 and 6 weeks after termination. Parents are usually still doing play sessions and report that they have continued to see filial therapy as reinforcing and strengthening their relationship with their children. Some may have expanded it to their other children and ask how they can use it with older children and teens. The transfer to daily life usually occurs naturally once the parent is comfortable with the skills, and the new way of interacting with the child remains even when the special play sessions end.

EMPIRICAL SUPPORT

In reviewing the research on childhood bereavement, Oltjenbruns (2001) noted shortcomings and issues that included sample selection, data-gathering techniques, not taking into account mediating variables, and weaknesses in the interpretation of data. Another review article by Johnson, Kent, and Leather (2005) concluded that interventions used to strengthen the bond between parent and child are effective and have been used effectively to reduce distress and behavioral difficulties. Guo (2005) reviewed studies on filial therapy, focusing on those using the 10-week model across a variety of cultures, and concluded that filial therapy held promise for therapists in China and throughout the world.

Van Horn and Lieberman (2004) reported that there is research supporting successful treatment of children who have experienced trauma with group and individual interventions. One model that worked was the mother–child group; however, the authors noted that the mother had to be able to recognize the effects of the trauma on the child. In reporting on their earlier research, Van Horn and Lieberman (2004) described the process as one that was specifically developed for children who had witnessed domestic violence. Specific goals of this therapy included normalizing the experience, placing the experience in perspective, and restoring the reciprocity in the relationship between parent and child.

Although a relatively new therapy, filial therapy has been heavily researched since its inception and has been adapted and applied in a variety of settings and with a variety of populations, resulting in a rich quantitative, evidence-based, and qualitative research base supporting its effectiveness. Guerney (2000) noted that between 1971 and 2000, a large number of studies with a variety of populations of children and parents supported filial therapy. The studies by Guerney and others in the 1970s using the original protocol for filial therapy also used the same measures originally developed by Guerney, thus giving the advantage of comparison with those studies and adding support for the effectiveness of the protocol for decreasing negative behaviors such as aggression (Guerney, 2000). Rennie and Landreth (2000) reviewed a number of studies of filial therapy and concluded that filial therapy did promote and enhance the parent–child relationship. Parents could learn the client-centered play therapy skills necessary to become effective therapeutic agents with their children. They found that research supported filial therapy as an effective intervention for increasing parental acceptance, self-esteem, and empathy; making positive changes in the family system; increasing child self-esteem; and decreasing parental stress and child behavior problems. Additionally, Landreth's (1991) 10-week variation has been extensively studied at the University of North Texas and found to be an effective intervention with different populations. In their meta-analysis of play and filial therapy research, Bratton, Ray, Rhine, and Jones (2005) concluded that their research strongly supported the adoption of filial therapy as an effective therapeutic modality in working with children.

A recent qualitative study by Foley et al. (2006) found that the parents who participated in filial therapy attributed positive and progressive meaning to their experience. These parents also reported that they increased their self-awareness, problem-solving resources, and confidence and improved their relationships with their children.

The model's robustness is seen in the research on its application to various settings and populations. For example, research has been published on ethnic and racial groups (e.g., Guo, 2005; Lee & Landreth,

2003); lower income, divorced, blended, foster, and adoptive families (e.g., Bratton & Landreth, 1995; Glazer & Kottman, 1994); children with chronic illness (e.g., Glazer-Waldman et al., 1992); and grieving children (e.g., Glazer, 2006).

The age of children in most of the filial studies reported was 4 to 10 years. Bratton et al. (2005) found a mean of 7 in their meta-analysis. I did not find any research on filial therapy with infants and toddlers. Although there is strong empirical support for filial therapy, more research is needed to solidify it as an evidence-based therapy. Longitudinal research is also needed to determine how long the parents should continue the play sessions and filial therapy's long-term effects on the family.

CASE ILLUSTRATION

A 4-year-old was referred to me because of her 3-year-old sister's death after a short illness. This was traumatic for this family because the illness came on quickly but diagnosis was difficult, and they watched the child decline while it seemed that nothing could be done. Complicating this for the other children in the family is that they lived in a community where another child had died in a similar fashion 2 years before, and the client had played with this child. The client was having nightmares, got angry at others easily, and cried easily. She was clingy with her parents and refused to spend the night at her aunts' or grandparents', which was something that she used to enjoy. The family had a lot of social support, and the mother and father were also seeing a counselor. The mother stated that she wanted to be sure that her children processed this successfully. I brought up filial therapy as a type of intervention to consider, and the mother said she would think about it.

To begin to assess where the child was at the present time, I asked the child to draw trees for me—the three-tree exercise. First, the child is told to draw a tree. This child's tree was straight with a long trunk and branches and leaves at the top. The tree was completely colored in, and grass was drawn at the bottom. On a second sheet of paper, the child is told to draw another tree—a tree in a storm. This child drew the same tree with gray clouds and rain and lightning. Rain was on the tree. To me, it looked like the tree was crying. When I asked her to tell me about the tree, she said that the tree was sad because it was raining hard and there was thunder. Next, on a third sheet of paper, the child is asked to draw a third three— the tree after the storm. This tree was laid out horizontally with no leaves or green. When I asked her to tell me about the tree, she said it was dead, and that was all.

My impression was that this was a sad child. She did not clearly see past the trauma at this time. The goal then became to process the grief with the child and help her begin to see past the death to a life that was okay.[1]

At first, her play was exploratory, and she did not talk to me or make eye contact in the first three sessions. In the fourth session, she drew a picture of her sister and told me that this was her sister in the hospital and that she was now in heaven. She took the picture home with her. Mom called later in the week and told me that she had begun to talk about her sister for the first time since the funeral.

After the second session, the mother talked to me about filial therapy, and I gave her a few articles to read. She called and asked to begin filial therapy. Starting at Week 3, I began filial therapy training with the mother. We met separately during the week for the filial therapy training. At the sixth session with the child, the mother sat behind me while I conducted the play session. At the seventh session, the mother sat in the front and conducted her first play session with my coaching.

The next week, the girl did a sand tray in which she placed animal families with parents and children and said that her family had one person in heaven. It appeared that she was working on the changes in her family. She also drew a picture of her family with an angel-like figure that she told me was her sister in heaven. Her mother reported that she was asking where her sister was and if she could go visit her. The mother told her that no, she could not visit her sister in heaven and that her sister could not visit her.

The sixth session marked a significant change. With her mother in the room, the child used the dollhouse and baby dolls to create a scene that was like a typical family dinner before her sister died. Then one of the dolls got sick, and we heard a running dialogue of the process the child was going through. She was sure the doll was going to die. The mother processed this with the child. At one point, the child sat on her mother's lap and said, "Why did she have to go?" Holding her daughter, the mother said that she did not know the answer. In our session later in the week, the mother related how this concern about illness and death came up again because the girl's father had a cold so she was able to reinforce what she had said in session.

The mother held five more sessions at home, and we talked after each one. Together, mother and daughter began to process their grief and were able to support each other in it.

---

[1]Since the time of this case, I worked with a child who was a year older who drew the three trees and told me that the trees were his dad before, during, and after an illness.

CONCLUSION AND FUTURE DIRECTIONS

Processing grief together through filial therapy strengthens the parent–child bond and enhances the relationship. Following a death in the family, the parent may not be able to be part of this process, in which case play therapy is a viable intervention. Research has supported the value of including the parent in the process.

Filial therapy's potential with a variety of family and child issues is unlimited. Particularly in situations of trauma, loss, and grief, in which the impact is on the family system, filial therapy can be effective in facilitating the family's healing as they process the events together. In supporting the healing process, filial therapy becomes a set of skills that often continue to have a positive impact on the parent–child relationship. The relationship has been changed through play.

The child-centered approach provides the context for using filial therapy with preschool children. The therapist meets the child where he or she is and works with the parent to develop the skills necessary to provide the context in which change can occur and in which the relationship between parent and child can be healed or enhanced. Processing grief can become a positive experience for the parent and child, allowing each to see where the other is at this time. It can also help the parent to differentiate between his or her grief and that of the child.

REFERENCES

Axline, V. (1947). *Play therapy*. Cambridge, MA: Riverside.

Bowlby, J. (1969). *Attachment and loss: Vol. 1. Attachment*. New York: Basic Books.

Bratton, S., & Landreth, G. (1995). Filial therapy with single parents: Effects on parental acceptance, empathy and stress. *International Journal of Play Therapy, 4,* 61–80.

Bratton, S. C., Ray, D., Rhine, T., & Jones, L. (2005). The efficacy of play therapy with children: A meta-analytic review of treatment outcomes. *Professional Psychology: Research and Practice, 36,* 376–390.

Carmichael, K. D. (2006). *Play therapy: An Introduction*. Upper Saddle River, NJ: Pearson.

Collins, B. C., & Collins, T. M. (2005). *Crisis and trauma: Developmental–ecological intervention*. Boston: Houghton Mifflin.

Elkind, D. (2007). *The power of play: How spontaneous, imaginative activities lead to happier, healthier children*. Cambridge, MA: Da Capo Lifelong Books.

Foley, Y. C., Higdon, L., & White, J. F. (2006). A qualitative study of filial therapy: Parent's voices. *International Journal of Play Therapy, 15,* 37–64.

Gil, E. (1991). *The healing power of play: Working with abused children*. New York: Guilford Press.

Ginott, H. G. (1959). *Psychotherapy with children: The living relationship*. Greeley, CO: Carron.

Glazer, H. R. (1999). Children and play in the Holocaust. *Journal of Humanistic Counseling, Education and Development, 37*, 194–199.

Glazer, H. R., & Kottman, T. (1994). Filial therapy: Rebuilding the relationship between parents and children of divorce. *Journal of Humanistic Education and Development, 33*, 4–12.

Glazer-Waldman, H. R., Zimmerman, J. E., Landreth, G. L., & Norton, D. (1992). Filial therapy: An intervention for parents of children with chronic illness. *International Journal of Play Therapy, 1*, 31–42.

Guerney, L. (2000) Filial therapy into the 21st century. *International Journal of Play Therapy, 9*, 1–18.

Guo, Y. (2005). Filial therapy for children's behavioral and emotional problems in mainland China. *Journal of Child and Adolescent Psychiatric Nursing, 18*, 171–180.

Johnson, G., Kent, G., & Leather, J. (2005, January). Strengthening the parent–child relationship: A review of family interventions and their use in medical settings. *Child: Care, Health and Development, 31*, 25–32.

Jordan, J. (2000). The role of mutual empathy in relational/cultural therapy. *Journal of Clinical Psychology, 56*, 1005–1016.

Landreth, G. L. (1991). *Play therapy: The art of the relationship*. Muncie, IN: Accelerated Development.

Lee, M., & Landreth, G. L. (2003). Filial therapy with immigrant Korean parents in the United States. *International Journal of Play Therapy, 12*, 49–66.

Moustakas, C. E. (1959). *Psychotherapy with children: The living relationship*. Greeley, CO: Carron.

Oltjenbruns, K. A. (2001). Developmental content of childhood: Grief and regrief phenomena. In M. S. Stroebe, R. O. Hansson, W. Stroebe, & H. Schut (Eds.), *Handbook of bereavement research: Consequences, coping, and care* (pp. 169–197). Washington, DC: American Psychological Association.

Rennie, R., & Landreth, G. L. (2000). Effects of filial therapy on parent and child behaviors. *International Journal of Play Therapy, 9*, 19–38.

Shelby, J. (2007). Play therapy and evidenced-based practice for traumatized children. *Play Therapy, 2*(3), 29–31.

VanFleet, R. (1994). *Filial therapy: Strengthening parent–child relationships through play*. Sarasota, FL: Practitioner's Resource Press.

VanFleet, R. (2000). *A parent's handbook of filial play therapy*. Boiling Springs, PA: Play Therapy Press.

Van Horn, P., & Lieberman, A. F. (2004). Early intervention with infants, toddlers, and preschoolers. In B. T. Litz (Ed.), *Early intervention for trauma and traumatic loss* (pp. 112–130). New York: Guilford Press.

6

STRATEGIC PLAY THERAPY TECHNIQUES FOR ANXIOUS PRESCHOOLERS

PARIS GOODYEAR-BROWN

"There's a tornado in my tummy." This is the description of anxiety given by a 4-year-old freckle-faced boy named Jake who was brought to treatment by his bewildered and exhausted mother. At the time the family was referred for treatment, Jake had been attending a 2-day-a-week Mother's Day Out program for 3 months. He would wake up on school mornings fighting to stay in bed and resisting getting dressed. On these mornings, his mother would eventually wrangle him into the car, where he would continue to cry all the way to school, making statements like "I feel sick" and "I need to stay with you!" At the time he entered treatment, Jake had vomited in the car or in the parking lot every day before entering his classroom. Jake is a preschooler who struggles with anxiety, and his story is a common one.

Anxiety is an invisible tormentor that can have devastating effects on the physiology, the thought life, and the relational life of our youngest clients. Approximately 6% to 20% of children have an anxiety disorder (Costello, Egger, & Angold, 2004). The epidemiology of anxiety is less clear in the preschool population. This may be accounted for by the common hope held by many parents that their children's anxiety symptoms are just a phase. These parents may wait to seek treatment, hoping that the problem will resolve itself. When a child reaches school age, however, underlying anxiety issues may become more pronounced. Several factors are implicated in anxiety problems in preschoolers, including mother–child attachment patterns (Bowlby, 1988; Brumariu & Kerns, 2008); differences in neurophysiological responsivity (Wehrenberg & Prinz, 2007); genetic predisposition within the family; and parental factors, including parental anxiety, maternal depression, parental reinforcement of avoidant coping strategies, and high parental control (Rapee, 1997; Shortt, Barrett, Dadds, & Fox, 2001; Southam-Gerow, Kendall, & Weersing, 2001). Children with untreated anxiety disorders are at greater risk of developing social and academic impairments. The onset of comorbid diagnoses, particularly other anxiety disorders and depression, may be seen over the life span in addition to an elevated risk of substance abuse (American Academy of Child and Adolescent Psychiatry Official Action, 2007).

In this chapter, I discuss four distinct yet complementary areas of treatment, all of which are corroborated by the growing body of evidence that supports the importance of parents being copartners in the treatment of their children's anxiety problems (Barrett & Farrell, 2007; Barrett & Shortt, 2003; Carr, 2009). The first avenue for the treatment of anxious preschoolers focuses on educating the family about the mechanisms through which anxiety works, in essence, developing a shared language about the problem. The second avenue aims to enhance the supportive dimensions of the parent–child relationship (Bell & Eyberg, 2002; Bratton, Landreth, Kellam, & Blackard, 2006; Brestan & Eyberg, 1998; Jernberg & Booth, 2001; Martin, Snow, & Sullivan, 2008). The third avenue involves teaching the child and parent how to engage in strategies aimed at decreasing the physiological arousal associated with anxiety (Barrett & Shortt, 2003, Kabat-Zinn, 1990). The fourth avenue consists of empowering the preschool child to externalize and then fight fear through cognitive and behavioral play therapy strategies while empowering the parent to be the child's cheerleader (Dacey & Fiore, 2000; Kendall, Aschenbrand, & Hudson, 2003; March & Mulle, 1998; Spencer, DuPont, & DuPont, 2003). Anxiety comes in many shapes and sizes. Clear case conceptualization is critical in designing a treatment plan that uses these four avenues in the most effective combination.

DEVELOPING A SHARED LANGUAGE WITH THE FAMILY

The first critical step in helping families who have an anxious preschooler is to educate the whole family system about the nature of anxiety. Families often need clarification about how fear differs from anxiety. Fear is the normal reaction to a clear and present danger. For example, if someone's fist is coming toward a child's face, the child will experience fear, which will in turn activate the fight-or-flight mechanism that will help him or her avoid the fist. If fear is a child's reaction to the danger that is, anxiety is the child's reaction to the danger that might be (Spencer et al., 2003). The difficulty with anxiety is that the list of what might be is endless, which can leave a child feeling constantly overwhelmed and vigilant.

There are many typical childhood fears, most of which are developmentally appropriate, like fear of the dark, of monsters, or of separating from a parent. Each of these is within the range of typicality during various developmental periods and is usually resolved quickly and to the parent's and child's satisfaction. The essential concept that parents must grasp is that the child's attempt to cope with the anxiety by avoiding it will only exacerbate the problem. When a child avoids an anxiety-producing stimulus, there is an immediate, if fleeting, decrease in anxiety. The child has a momentary experience of feeling better, and this feeling reinforces his or her maladaptive coping strategy (i.e., avoidance).

Many metaphors can be used to communicate to children how anxiety works. For example, the anxiety can be personified as a dragon: The therapist can use a large dragon puppet and talk about how the dragon feeds off the child's anxiety. The dragon's favorite food is the child's avoidance responses. The dragon gets bigger every time its roar (i.e., the anxiety) keeps the child from doing something like going to school. In my office, I keep a giant red-and-gold dragon puppet. It is so large that it can wrap around my preschool-age clients. I also have the very small version of this same puppet. I show both puppets to the child while describing our goal, which is to make the worry dragon smaller and smaller until the child is significantly bigger than the dragon. The way in which a plant grows can serve as another helpful metaphor for the way anxiety grows. Huebner (2006) compared anxiety to a tomato plant. The more the child tends the tomato plant, the larger it grows, until eventually there is an overabundance of tomatoes. In this same way, tending to the anxiety (e.g., through rehearsing worries, avoiding anxiety-producing situations) encourages the growth of the worries.

Another helpful prop is the "worry sphere"—a hollow ball made of plastic connections that can collapse into a very small ball or expand into a very large orb. I often use the worry sphere in the assessment phase of treatment. I expand the sphere to its largest size and then invite the child to choose symbols in the room to represent his or her worries. In one case, a 5-year-old girl's anxiety was centered on her parents' divorce. She chose toys to represent Mom, Dad, herself, and the two homes between which she split her time. We put those symbols inside the worry sphere and then compressed it, giving the little girl an experience of the worries getting smaller and smaller over time.

By the time a child enters treatment for anxiety problems, the anxiety is holding the child captive. The imagery of being bound by anxiety can be made concrete through the use of props in the playroom. The child chooses a self-object that is then wrapped up in twine, ribbon, or metal links. The therapist explains that the child's worries are keeping the child in bondage, but that the strands of worry can be cut off. The child and therapist together articulate the child's worries and begin planning strategies to combat them as they cut through chains and set the self-object free.

Whatever metaphor is used to explain the way in which anxiety works, it can be helpful to give an example to the family, like the one that follows:

> A child is paralyzed with fear at the thought of going to school because he wants to stay with Mom. Mom puts the child in the car seat and drives across town to the school. The child becomes more and more anxious, pleads with Mom to stay home, and starts to cry, screaming, "I can't go to school." Mom accurately perceives the child's distress and does what she believes is best: She turns around and drives home. The child immediately experiences a strong sense of relief, both physiologically and cognitively, as a result of the avoidance. The instant reduction in arousal is perceived by the child as feeling better and actually reinforces avoidance as the best strategy for dealing with anxiety.

One of the most insidious side effects of avoidance is generalization from the initial anxiety-provoking stimuli to a multitude of things or situations that must be avoided. For example, a child who starts out worried about coming into contact with germs may first cope with the anxiety by being careful to avoid touching the toilet seat when going to the bathroom. The immediate sense of safety the child experiences reinforces avoidance as the most effective coping strategy. At some point, it is not enough for the child to avoid touching the toilet seat; now he or she must avoid touching anything in the bathroom. Eventually, this may generalize into the idea that the child cannot use any bathroom other than the one in his or her home, so the child becomes a prisoner in his or her own house, captive to his or her own anxiety.

EFFECTIVE COREGULATION: HELPING PARENTS SOOTHE THEIR CHILDREN

One primary focus of treatment with anxious preschoolers is to hone the parents' ability to contingently respond to the child and more effectively coregulate the child's emotional and physiological responses to situations. In infancy, a baby cries and is held and rocked. The baby learns that he or she will be taken care of. Babies do not know what to call the dysregulation that they experience when they are hungry or cold or need stimulation. Anxiety is one way to describe the sensations that the baby is experiencing. If the discomfort is not quickly alleviated, cortisol stress hormones are released into the baby's body, and the infant experiences heightened physiological arousal.

The parent picks up the upset baby, soothes and rocks and murmurs and pats, and the baby feels better. His or her neurophysiology has been soothed. It is through positive, consistent interactions with their caregiver that children learn self-regulation.

John Bowlby (1973, 1988), Mary Main (1995), and Mary Ainsworth (Ainsworth, Blehar, Waters, & Wall, 1978) were pioneers on the frontier of attachment theory. Out of this research has come a series of classifications that categorizes the ways in which children learn to respond to parental behavior and get their needs met. A *secure attachment pattern* is one in which the parent has been consistently available, both physically and emotionally, and contingently responsive to the infant's needs. If the child is hungry, he or she cries and the mother feeds him. If the child is bored, his or her mother provides stimulation. The child learns that the mother can be trusted and will meet his or her needs. The child sees the parent as a secure base and will freely engage in age-appropriate exploration and return to his or her mother for comfort at times of stress or fear.

Insecure attachment patterns come in several forms. Both avoidant and ambivalent attachment styles can be conceptualized as organized attempts on the child's part to remain close in physical proximity to an attachment figure. In both cases, fear and anxiety activate the attachment system, but the child must use a roundabout method of trying to get his or her needs for survival met. Avoidant infants stay away and look as though they do not need the parent. Ambivalent infants, who are uncertain of the caregiver's response, vacillate between angry, rejecting behavior and clingy behavior. The disorganized attachment pattern is one in which a child has been repeatedly overwhelmed with intense anxiety because of abuse or neglect. As children with insecure attachments grow into toddlers and preschoolers, many anxiety-related symptoms may emerge.

Several play therapy treatment models assist families in becoming more attuned to each other while enhancing their relationship. *Theraplay* (Jernberg & Booth, 2001; Martin et al., 2008) increases attunement between parent and child while strengthening the relationship along four dimensions (structure, nurture, engagement, and challenge). Martin et al. (2008) found that the parent's adeptness at providing these four dimensions correlated with the child's drive for exploration and regulatory capacities. *Parent–child interaction therapy*, a behavioral play therapy model, also works on building a positive relationship between parent and child while shaping the child's prosocial behaviors (Hembree-Kigin & McNeil, 1995). Although there is a wealth of empirical support for the application of parent–child interaction therapy to both oppositional and traumatized children, it is also being studied as a useful intervention for reducing separation anxiety with young children (Pincus & Choate, in press). Another helpful model that focuses on enhancing the relationship between parents and children is *child–parent relationship therapy* (Bratton et al., 2006), a 10-week manualized filial therapy protocol. Each of these treatment protocols helps to build attunement between the parent and the child, thereby enhancing the parent's proficiency in coregulating the child's affect. Ultimately, the contingent responsiveness parents practice in each of these models increases the parent's ability to function as a soothing agent for the child.

Several colleagues and I have designed a set of strategies that help parents respond to their anxious preschoolers in ways that are often counterintuitive.[1] The acronym SOOTHE—soft tone of voice, organize, offer, touch, hear, end and let go—helps parents to remember this skill set.

Soft Tone of Voice

Preschoolers often handle their anxiety by throwing tantrums. Parents may respond to a child's tantrum by becoming louder or more intense in their own vocalizations. However, the elevation of the parent's voice will only feed the escalation of the child's tantrum. When teaching this to parents, I often add "soft tone of face" to the description. What we know about mirror cells in the brain can inform our approach to anxious children. If the parent becomes dysregulated, the child is likely to match the parent's level of dysregulation. If, instead, the parent deliberately speaks in a soft, nurturing (or at least neutral) tone of voice, the child can latch onto this and begin to deescalate. Another way of explaining this to parents is to help them see themselves as anchors. If the child tries to take control by saying no as a way of handling his or her anxiety, the parent may be tempted to respond with his or her own escalation, such as "Yes, you will, young man!" This response can be equated with throwing a ship's anchor up in the air and having it catch in the mainsail. If parents choose instead to lower their voices, use a soothing tone, and remain calm, they will anchor the child's experience beneath the current level of escalation. In a sense, parents can pull their children up to higher levels of reactivity or invite them to deescalate through a strategy as simple as using a soft tone of voice.

Organize

The anxious child often loses the ability to sequence information. Anxious children respond poorly to a lack of structure. Not knowing what is expected can heighten anxiety. Therefore, it is very important that the parents of anxious preschoolers develop schedules and consistent routines. Play thera-

---

[1]The SOOTHE strategies were designed by Linda Ashford, Paris Goodyear-Brown, and Patti van Eys as part of a pilot project funded through the Vanderbilt Kennedy Center for Research on Human Development. These strategies are now part of the treatment protocol NEAR (nurturing engagement for attachment repair).

pists can be very useful in this regard. One activity that can help with the creation or reinforcement of a schedule is the domino rally. Dominos are a wonderful tool for helping families build sequential narratives of everything from trauma histories to schedules and routines. When administering the intervention, I give the family some people-shaped dominoes and ask the child to stand them up one by one as the parent recites the order of events that occur in an average day. Diagnostically, this activity can help the clinician discern whether the family is under- or overscheduled and to modify the schedule as needed.

Another fun way to help families establish a routine is to give them a blank copy of a winding board game. The parents fill in the spaces one by one with the steps of the child's routine, starting at waking up and ending at bedtime. Families can take the finished game home and "play" it again and again. There may be parts of the routine that the child has not learned yet, and repeating the succession of events through game play can provide sequential soothing for the child. *Organize* also refers to the need to provide anxious children with help at transition times. Anxious children do not respond well to change. It can help tremendously to let them know in advance if something in their normal routine will be different on a given day. When a child's play is going to be interrupted to go to the grocery store, it can be very helpful to give the child a warning. The parent can say, "You have 5 more minutes to play, and then we are going to the store." A 2-minute warning may also be helpful.

When anxious children are beginning a new activity like playing soccer for the first time, it can help to prepare them for it. Help parents brainstorm potential trouble spots for their anxious children. An exercise called "Brainstorm the Blow-Ups" is a fun way to help parents to be proactive in scanning the environment for anything that may spike their child's anxiety. As part of teaching the organize concept to parents, I introduce a miniature volcano and talk with the parents about times when the child may have erupted in defiance or had a meltdown because of a specific anxiety-provoking situation. I write down some situations that I believe might be provoke an anxiety response in the child and put them in the volcano. One might read, "Callie will be playing on a soccer team for the first time." Each parent takes a turn pulling one out of the volcano and brainstorming specific parenting strategies that could help to relieve anxiety. Example strategies might include the following: Introduce the child to the coach before the first practice. Allow the child to go see the soccer field where he or she will practice. Kick the ball around with mom or dad on the soccer field. Watch a movie or read a book about soccer.

Offer

Some preschool-age children who struggle with anxiety can be easily overwhelmed by too many choices. Taking an anxious child to the toy store and cheerfully inviting him or her to pick one may result in a total meltdown before the family has left the store. This child is soothed by offering a narrower range of choices. Conversely, some anxious preschoolers compensate for their anxiety by trying to be in control of every decision. These children may have a total meltdown when told exactly what they have to do. This kind of child benefits from having the parent offer choices with parameters. The child who needs to drink some juice can be offered apple juice or orange juice and gets to have some control in the decision while still staying within the boundaries set by the parent. Parents can also offer help, additional structure, or a way out if a child seems to be floundering.

The following is an illustration of a mother offering a way out to her anxious child. Ryan and his mother were halfway through a dyadic assessment. His mother picked up the card reading "Adult and child put lotion on each other." She got out two bottles of lotion and gave one to Ryan. She then said, "I'm going put lotion on you, and you're going to put some on me." Ryan immediately said "No" in a petulant tone of voice and gave her a sulky look. His mother asked, "Where would you like the lotion, on your arms or hands?" Ryan pointed to his hair. She said, "Well, we can't really put lotion on your hair, so how about your arms?" Ryan said "No!" louder (more petulantly) and crossed his arms over his chest. His mother accurately interpreted his response as being driven by anxiety, as opposed to sheer oppositionality, and said, "You know, I forgot that you don't like lotion. Look, I'm rubbing it all into my arms so that there's no more on my hands. How about I just rub your back instead?" She then put out her hand to touch Ryan's back. She offered him a way out of the anxiety-provoking situation while still accomplishing the task of engaging in a nurturing activity together.

Touch

The *T* in SOOTHE is meant to reaffirm the mitigating effect that a simple touch or increased physical proximity can have on anxious children. At the end of the day, for example, when a child is overwrought and exhausted, some cuddle time can have a more soothing effect than words.

Hear

Hear refers to the parent's ongoing job of trying to discern what the child needs when he or she engages in anxiety-driven defiance. For example, a child who is told to put on his or her shoes may refuse. Most parents interpret the refusal as will-based defiance when, in fact, a anxious child may be just learning how to tie his or her shoes and is worried about doing it right and therefore wants to avoid the trial. If the parent hears the child's underlying need correctly, the original command can be modified. The parent could say, "Please go get your shoes, and I will help you put them on."

End and Let Go

Two points are associated with "end and let go." The first point refers to helping the child completely deescalate before returning to the normal activities of life. The importance of the return to baseline became clear to me in my early work at a therapeutic preschool. The program was made up of 3- to 5-year-olds with severe emotional disturbances. They often became dysregulated and lost control of their bodies in ways that required physical restraint. There were a number of occasions on which a child was held until his or her body was relatively calm, and although he or she may still have been grumbling, reintegrated into his or her classroom setting. What we found over and over again was that children who were not completely deescalated would have another violent episode within the hour. Continuing to soothe and de-stimulate the child until he or she had returned to baseline was much more effective. After being fully deescalated, clients were much more likely to tap their inner resources when the next challenging moment occurred.

The second aspect of end and let go has to do with the parents' reaction to a child's meltdown. Once we acknowledge that children with anxiety suffer from neurophysiological dysregulation, it becomes possible to understand how a child's meltdown may actually serve a regulatory function. Some children describe anxiety as a sense of pressure building inside their bodies and actually articulate feeling better after the tantrum. Parents, however, may continue to feel shell shocked and exhausted for hours after a tantrum has occurred. The parent may understandably need some recovery time and may have difficulty being immediately responsive to the child who has just had a meltdown. Unfortunately for the parent, it is directly after the meltdown when a child may feel most vulnerable and even ashamed of his or her irrational behavior. In the aftermath of the storm, reconnecting with the parent both provides immediate soothing to the child and brings a degree of repair to the parent–child relationship. Dan Siegel (Siegel & Hartzell, 2003) has talked about the toxic ruptures that can occur between parents and children when upset occurs in both parties but is never processed. Therefore, although acknowledging the parents' right to their own anger and exhaustion, we ask them to let go of it and remain contingently responsive to the child after meltdowns. These SOOTHE strategies are a useful addition to the skill sets of all parents who have anxious preschoolers and have become a standard part of my practice with these families.

CALMING THE PHYSIOLOGY

I sometimes joke with parents about calming the wild beast, but it is not too far from the goal. The "wild beast" encompasses all the physiological arousal systems that signal us that anxiety is present. Many anxious preschoolers initially present with intense psychosomatic complaints. When I ask a preschooler to talk about what's bothering him or her, it is very common to hear "My tummy hurts all the time," "I have a headache," or "I have a lump in my throat." Any persistent somatic complaint should be checked out by the child's pediatrician, but once the child has been given a clean bill of health, the family can begin to help the child deal with the physiological arousal. Preschool-age children are most acutely aware of the anxiety that they experience on a physical level, but they often need help in making a connection between their physiological arousal and the situation or thoughts that are making them anxious.

For example, a precocious 5-year-old girl is brought to treatment because she cannot go to sleep at night. When questioned about what is bothering her, she says, "I can't breathe at night." She states the physiological symptom because it is the most salient to her. I draw a picture of a brain and ask her what she is thinking about when she has trouble breathing. She responds, "I might stop breathing." When we investigate further, it becomes clear that her grandfather had died the previous summer from natural causes. As the parents tried to explain what had happened, they told her, "He just stopped breathing in the night." The child latched onto this explanation and transformed it into an idiosyncratic fear that became tied to a physiological symptom.

Several play-based strategies that help this little girl combat the anxiety while practicing physiological self-calming are listed in the following paragraphs. Focused breathing is a useful tool for countering physiological arousal (Kabat-Zinn, 1990). An intervention called *using bubbles* is a tried-and-true play therapy strategy that assists the client in learning and practicing deep breathing. The therapist takes a tube of bubbles and says the following:

> Watch what happens to the bubbles when I change my breathing. If I take a quick breath in and out [*therapist demonstrates*], nothing much happens; not many bubbles are made. If I take a deep breath in and breathe out really hard, I can make a lot of little bubbles, which can be a lot of fun. But if I take a deep breath in and I blow out really slowly—so slowly that I almost can't hear my own breath [*therapist demonstrates*]—I can make a great big bubble!

The child usually grabs the bubbles eagerly and says, "Let me try."

This simple play intervention has several therapeutic payoffs. First, bubbles are inherently engaging and fun. The fun of blowing bubbles counters the toxicity of the anxiety and increases the likelihood that the therapeutic homework will be completed. Second, the intervention gives the young child an external focal point for deep breathing, a point in space to focus on while taking diaphragmatic breaths. The idea that the child should blow out really slowly is meant to help the client achieve control over his or her breathing.

The bubbles are given to the child and parent along with the prescription that the child should blow three big bubbles each day. The timing of this practice can vary depending on what time of day the anxiety is most strongly felt. The client who is throwing up on the way to school each day might blow big bubbles in the car on the way to school to counter the escalating physiological response that accompanies anxiety about going to school. The client who has nighttime anxiety might blow bubbles just before bed.

Another prop that can function as an effective external focal point for deep breathing practice is the pinwheel. Children are given their own pinwheels, asked to hold them close to their mouths, and blow. Most children can do this easily . They are then asked to hold the pinwheel an arm's length away and still rotate it with their breath, which requires children to take deeper breaths. These exercises are helpful in retraining children to take deep diaphragmatic breaths that are controlled in both their inhalation and their expulsion of air. Clients can create their own pinwheels with kits purchased from novelty stores. When the child makes his or her own pinwheel, the benefits are multiplied. The creation of his or her own prop increases the child's sense of ownership of the strategy. Moreover, the make-your-own pinwheel allows the child and therapist to personalize it with pictures that trigger relaxation and safety for the client. For example, the therapist might draw a picture of the child's favorite stuffed animal, another of the child's favorite book, and another of the child's favorite food. When the child blows on the pinwheel, she or he will first see these reminders of soothing objects and then see them all blend together as the pinwheel rotates. For sexual abuse survivors who have been traumatized in the night, anxiety is often intensified at bedtime. I give these children special glow-in-the-dark pinwheels. These serve the dual purpose of countering the physiological escalation at bedtime with an antithetical replacement behavior while reminding the child of the safety of the play therapist through the transitional object of the pinwheel.

Biofeedback is another intervention that is helpful for children who are working on calming their physiology. In the course of a biofeedback session, a client measures his or her heart rate, galvanic skin response, blood pressure, or breathing on a continuous basis. The act of increasing his or her awareness of a physiological process allows the client's body to relax. In the play therapy room, a simple stethoscope can routinely be used to help a client focus on noticing the heartbeat and reducing the number of beats per minute. Preschool-age children do this activity best if the therapist and child take turns with the stethoscope. If the child has trouble making out the heartbeats, the therapist can further structure the activity by counting the heartbeats out loud.

Progressive muscle tension and relaxation is another physiological intervention that helps children combat anxiety (Eisen & Kearney, 1995; Wolpe, 1984), and it can be accomplished in a playful way. In my office, we turn on warm lighting and put on some soothing music, and the child is invited to lie down on the floor and relax. I blow bubbles high up into the air, and the child's only job at first is to watch the bubbles float down toward him or her. Then I invite the child to tense and release various muscle groups, starting with the face and moving all the way down to the toes. This activity can become a normal component of sessions. After several repetitions of this progressive body relaxation paired with the visual images of the falling bubbles, a conditioned association is made between the two. When the preschooler begins to hunch his or her shoulders, clench his or her teeth, or give some other signal that the anxiety is taking over, she or he can be reminded to picture the bubbles falling. As the child conjures up a picture of the falling bubbles, his or her body automatically begins to relax. The conditioned somatic response is linked to the image in the child's mind of the bubbles falling. Activating the imagery activates the relaxation response.

Positive imagery is another relaxation tool for anxious children (Cohen, Mannarino, & Deblinger, 2006). The creation of a safe-place or happy-place image can also be very useful as a tool for anxiety management for preschool-age children. These children may have difficulty visualizing an image internally unless it has first been created concretely. The sand tray is an excellent tool that allows the child to create a three-dimensional safe place. I begin by inviting the child to choose a place where he or she felt "really safe and really calm and really good." A severely maltreated or neglected child may have no recollection of a safe place. In this case, the client can create an imaginary safe place. I have the child describe the place in some detail as he or she creates the place in the sand. It is important to ask questions that allow the child to integrate the sensory details of the imagined environment. Questions should target tastes, smells, sounds, and tactile experiences. A safe-place image can also be fleshed out through art or clay work. One preschool child made a whole forest of trees out of green and brown Play-Doh. A picture was taken of it, and the child used this picture as a bridge to solidifying her internal image of a peaceful forest.

Another fun and useful stress inoculation activity for preschoolers, a "menu of soothing strategies," was designed by Janine Shelby (Goodyear-Brown, Riviere, & Shelby, 2004). The therapist begins by introducing the child to a bin full of play food and pretending that the therapist and the child are visiting a restaurant. The child gets to choose what he or she would like for an appetizer, drink, main dish, side dish, and dessert. After this, the therapist creates a menu out of construction paper. I usually name the restaurant after the child, something like "Café Joshua," which seems to delight the child and increase a sense of ownership of the activity. The therapist then makes a list of all the senses and helps the child fill in the menu. Asking the child, "What is a taste that makes you feel really good?" may generate anything from grapes to pizza. The icons for these foods would need to be drawn or cut from magazines so that the child has a pictorial reminder system. Other stimuli are chosen for each sense. Preschool children have chosen the smell of their mother's hair as an olfactory sense memory, the softness of a beloved teddy bear as a tactile sense memory, the sound of their mother singing a lullaby as an auditory sense memory, and so forth. If the child chooses the fabric from his or her special blanket as a texture that makes him or her feel calm, perhaps a square of the fabric can be sent to school in the child's pocket. When the child is feeling anxious, he or she can reach into the pocket, rub the piece of fabric, and experience immediate physiological relief. All these activities are done in various combinations over the course of treatment to help the client recognize that he or she can influence his or her own physiological responses to the environment. This burgeoning sense of control helps the client to fight the anxiety on the sensory front.

EXTERNALIZATION AND COGNITIVE–BEHAVIORAL PLAY THERAPY

The battle against anxiety must also be fought on the cognitive and behavioral fronts. It is important to understand preschoolers' developmental needs when designing a treatment plan for overcoming anxiety. Many cognitive–behavioral procedures such as thought stopping and cognitive restructuring have proven to be effective in decreasing adolescents' anxiety (Chu & Harrison, 2007; Freestone, Ladoucer, Provencher, & Blais, 1995; Kendall et al., 2003; Kendall, Hudson, Gosch, Flannery-Schroeder, & Suveg, 2008; March & Mulle, 1998). For these populations, the majority of work can happen intrapsychically. For example, adolescents can be taught to identify their anxious thoughts as they occur internally and give themselves a nonverbal instruction to stop that thought and practice thought replacement. This adeptness with internal cognitive processes is not possible for preschool children. Preschoolers' developmental needs necessitate a different path to the same end. For this reason, one of the first tasks of treatment with anxious preschoolers is to externalize the anxiety.

Play therapy is the perfect milieu for this work, offering a seemingly endless array of mechanisms for this externalization. A specific figurine might be chosen as the externalized anxiety, or a worry monster can be created with clay or art supplies. The child might choose a puppet to be the externalized anxiety, such as the "worry witch" and "princess perfect." Many times, if the anxiety is trauma induced, clients will choose a perpetrator symbol and contain or manipulate this symbol in ways that give them experiential mastery of the fear. For example, a 3-year-old boy who had been sexually abused by his father continues to suffer from nighttime anxiety. In the playroom, he chooses a two-headed dragon to represent the dad, puts miniature handcuffs on him, and locks him in the jail. This containment, accomplished through the play scenario, gives the child a sense of power in relationship to the perpetrator that could not be managed outside of the playroom.

A 5-year-old boy with generalized anxiety disorder created a three-headed-monster on construction paper to represent his fears. He cut the monster out, glued it to a popsicle stick, and named it Mr. Meanie. Mr. Meanie became the focal point for all the work the client did to combat his fear. In this case, the client was too young to fight the thoughts inside his head, so we gave the enemy a face and a name, and then we used play interventions to build up the arsenal of skills that this little boy could use to fight back.

SOCIAL LEARNING THEORY AND PUPPETS AS PARTNERS

Social learning theory conceptualizes the power of modeling as a vehicle for learning, change, and growth (Bandura, 1976). Children learn a tremendous amount just by watching others act and react to situations. Play therapists can harness the power of modeling to reduce anxiety in children. Puppets can verbalize carefully crafted restructured cognitions that combat the irrational, anxious thoughts with which the child wrestles. The modeling provided by the puppet can give the child practical, alternative ways to handle the fear. One powerful dynamic of having a puppet be the one in distress is that the child is not confronted directly with his or her cognitive distortions; rather, the child is able to observe and is less psychologically defended. The child gets to watch as the therapist educates the "someone like me" who is wrestling with the same problem. The therapist might even enlist the child's help in convincing the puppet of the new information.

The next case example illustrates the power of puppets as partners in fighting anxiety. Sally, a 5-year-old girl, was referred for an intense fear of choking. At the time her distraught mother called, the child had not eaten anything but crackers in 10 days. Sally was losing a significant amount of weight, and everyone was concerned that she might have to be hospitalized if she did not begin to eat soon. After gathering a careful history, it became clear that the child had experienced an episode 2 years earlier in which she choked on a piece of chicken. From that point on, the child would panic at the sight of chicken, and the parents let her avoid this particular food. However, the reinforcement gained from the avoidance of this one particular food eventually generalized to a fear of all chewy foods, then generalized to an aversion to all foods with a certain texture, and so on.

Treatment for this child began with the hint of a tea party and a puppet play. A paint-your-own porcelain tea set was purchased for the session, and the client delighted in getting to paint all the plates and cups herself. Painting the tea cups and saucers served as a very manageable, nonthreatening exposure to the possibility of ingesting some food and drink. The therapist invited a puppet character named Jerry the Giraffe to the tea party, and while the child was painting, Jerry told the therapist that he would not be able to eat at the tea party because he was afraid to swallow leaves. When the therapist asked him what had happened, he described a scenario in which he had pulled too many leaves off a tree branch at one time, tried to swallow them all, and got a leaf stuck somewhere in his long, long throat. The therapist asked questions about how it felt to have the leaf stuck there. The giraffe provided some somatosensory details of his choking event, providing the child with both exposure to the sensory material related to her own choking event and normalization of these sensations. The therapist then asked the giraffe what happened, and Jerry said that he eventually coughed the leaf up. The therapist celebrated the powerful way in which Jerry's "cougher" got rid of the leaf and then educated Jerry about how his body works, specifically describing how our bodies are made to expel objects that get stuck in our throats. All the while, Sally painted and listened closely. Jerry remained unsure of whether he should believe what the therapist was telling him, so he checked with Sally. (In this way, the therapist can invite the child into the play and allow the client to test and possibly integrate the new information.) The little girl nodded shyly at the puppet and later drew a picture of Jerry learning how his throat worked.

For the second session, the therapist brought a variety of foods for a real tea party. Another way to describe this play scenario would be to call it a successive approximation of the behavior that was being targeted, that is, eating an expanded range of foods. Sally went right over to the windowsill to see if the paint-your-own teacups had dried. She began to set up the tea party. She put a cracker on each plate, including Jerry's. Jerry then asked for powdered donuts, and she smiled and put a powdered donut on each plate. Jerry made a mess of his donut and got powdered sugar all over his nose. This made Sally laugh. The intrinsically fun nature of the play serves as a counterbalancing force for the toxicity of the anxiety related to food. In the course of the session, Sally began to nibble on the donut.

A therapist must negotiate many balancing acts when treating anxious children. One of these is the ratio of overt praise given to the child for overcoming the anxiety-provoking situation that she has just mastered versus the casual acceptance of a behavior that is, after all, in the normal range for most children. In this case, Sally was already predisposed to shyness. If the therapist made a victorious expression or otherwise strong reaction when the child began to eat her donut, the therapist would have highlighted the child's departure from her typical pathological response. Sally may have become more anxious with the additional attention, and the encouragement could have had an iatrogenic effect on the child's trial behavior.

WORRIED THOUGHTS AND EXPERIENTIAL MASTERY PLAY

Cognitive restructuring can be a challenging goal to accomplish with preschool-age children. The keys are parental encouragement, modeling, and practice, practice, practice. Anxious children have a great deal of difficulty recognizing their own progress (Dacey & Fiore, 2000). Therefore, they need the people closest to them to be their cheerleaders. Externalizing the anxiety early in treatment helps with this transformation by putting the parent and child on the same team fighting the anxiety monster together.

The child identifies the negative thoughts through a series of play activities. "Where are the Worry Worms?" is a game that playfully invites clients to articulate their worries. I begin by introducing the child to a box of rubber worms. Next, I invite the child to close his or her eyes as I hide the worms around the room. As the client finds each worm, he or she shares one more worried thought that he or she has. Even preschool children can usually identify a simple worried thought that repeats over and over in their heads. One prompt could be "A worried thought is something that you think over and over again that makes you feel bad." A further elaboration would be "You might want to stop thinking about it, but you just can't stop yourself." The child might say, "Mommy might not come back," "I'm scared of the dark," or "A monster will get me!" I write these thoughts down on little pieces of paper that look like a brain. Later, the child can feed the worried thoughts into a battery-operated brain that that I keep in the office. It has teeth and can chomp up worried thoughts. Many of my preschool clients enjoy feeding the worried thoughts to the chomping brain as one symbolic way of getting rid of them. Individual pictures or toy symbols can be made or chosen to represent each worried thought.

A Worry Box can also be designed during the assessment phase of treatment. The therapist introduces a blank box to the child and invites him or her to decorate it with soothing images. These can be drawn or cut out from magazines and glued onto the box. The child's worried thoughts are then written down, and the child places them in the box. The box serves as a containment device. The therapist may say,

> We're going to keep your worried thoughts in this box, and we'll take them out to look at them and learn how to boss them back as we play together. When you go home, you can remember that the worried thoughts are here in the box.

Preschool-age children will sometimes want to put tape around the edges of the box, or wrap it up with lots of string and put a pretend lock on it. The additional manipulation of the box helps the child feel more control over the worried thoughts, offering a sense of containment.

Another play-based assessment tool that can be used to exhaust the list of worries that a child may have is Liana Lowenstein's (1999) intervention, "Butterflies in Your Stomach." The child's body is outlined on a large sheet of butcher paper. The therapist makes the connection between people's worried thoughts and the sensation of butterflies in their stomach. Butterfly templates (or plastic butterflies) are introduced, and the child identifies various worries or anxious thoughts through the butterflies.

Once the anxious thoughts have been identified, I help the child to experience a sense of mastery over the thoughts through experiential mastery play. In other words, I empower the child by giving him or her the experience, in play, of being able to stop the fears. I give the child a whistle or a bicycle horn and tell him that Mr. Scary (or whatever symbol the child created as the concrete externalization of the anxiety) loves to tell him worried thoughts, but he has a secret weakness: He cannot stand loud noises. I will then be the voice of Mr. Scary and repeat the irrational thoughts the child (or the parent, or both) has identified. The child can blow the whistle at any point, and Mr. Scary not only stops speaking, but runs to hide! Children feel an enormous and immediate sense of power by being able to put Mr. Scary on the run. Giggles often punctuate this activity, and the play therapist's role is to keep it silly, light, and empowering for the child. After the child has had the experience of stopping Mr. Scary in his tracks with a sound, the whistle is traded in for a stop sign. I have a big blow-up stop sign that children use in my office, but personalized stop signs can also be made out of construction paper and tongue depressors. When the child holds up the stop sign and says "Stop!" the Worry Monster has to be quiet. These activities are often the genesis of the client's understanding that he or she can do something to manipulate the worried thoughts.

The important part of the intervention is the child's kinesthetic involvement in stopping Mr. Scary from speaking the worried thoughts over and over again. Stop signs can also be used in the sand tray to stop worried trucks. The child can make his or her own stop sign and practice holding it up to stop the Worry Monster from speaking. The stop sign can serve as both a transitional object from the safety and empowerment of the playroom to the child's home or school environment and as a reminder of the therapeutic intervention being practiced. Once the child has developed an awareness of the troublesome thoughts and kinesthetically practiced silencing those thoughts, new replacement thoughts or restructured cognitions can be crafted and rehearsed.

Blank baseball caps are a great way to help preschool-age children practice switching between their worried thoughts and new, helpful thoughts. The therapist presents two unadorned, canvas baseball caps of different colors. The therapist writes the previously identified negative thoughts on various sections of the hat and encourages the child to decorate the hat's brim with pictures or symbols that show how the troublesome thoughts make the child feel. The second hat is adorned with the statements that detail the client's restructured cognitions. The child chooses a puppet to wear the hat with the worried thoughts, and the therapist role-plays the actions the puppet takes while thinking the worried thoughts. The child gets to change the puppet's hat and then watches as the puppet reacts differently to the same scenarios because the puppet is wearing the hat with the helpful thoughts. The child can then wear the hats and role-play the scenarios him- or herself.

Another play therapy intervention that I created to allow children the tactile experience of manipulating and controlling the irrational thoughts is called "Punching Holes in That Theory" (Goodyear-Brown, 2005). The therapist asks the child to describe his or her worst fear or most upsetting anxious thought. The child chooses a brightly colored piece of paper, and the therapist draws a picture of the child's worst fear on it or writes out the words of the anxious thought. The therapist introduces a hole-punching set with many different shape cutters. The therapist can fold the paper in half to ensure that one punch by the child creates two holes in the paper. The child then practices his or her "power words" and replacement cognitions while punching shaped holes in the original statement. The child gets the verbal practice while having the kinesthetic experience of destroying the irrational thought.

Preschool-age children learn primarily through kinesthetic engagement. Therefore, all of their therapeutic learning should be anchored in the manipulation of props. I have created a combination of interventions that requires only a few props but offers the preschool-age child an empowering experience of eradicating the fear. The first intervention is called "Fanning the Flame." The therapist begins by drawing some flames on a whiteboard in the playroom. Most preschoolers have at least a rudimentary understanding of fire and fire safety. The therapist compares the flames to the fears that bother the child. The therapist explains that just like air or wind can make fires grow bigger, paying a lot of attention to our fears makes them grow bigger. The therapist then introduces a traditional fan (make-your-own fan kits can be purchased through various novelty toy companies) and invites the client to list the ways in which people can draw extra attention to their fears. The therapist writes these down or draws pictures of them on the fan. The child gets to hold the fan and move it vigorously in front of the whiteboard while the therapist draws more and more flames on the board. The therapist then exclaims, "Oh, no!

We've made the fear fire worse by paying attention to it. We need to find a way to put the fire out!"

The therapist pulls out a toy fire extinguisher and fireman dress-up clothes and offers them to the child. One prop that holds particular appeal for the preschoolers who visit my playroom is a backpack fire extinguisher with a hose that squirts a significant amount of water with each pump. The child straps on the backpack and gets to squirt water onto the whiteboard while the therapist talks about coping strategies that help fight the fears. By degrees, the flames wash away down the whiteboard, and the child feels a sense of empowerment (Goodyear-Brown, 2005). The next iteration of the activity involves drawing a picture of something that the child actually fears on the whiteboard. The child can then extinguish this fear experientially with the water while being coached in verbalizations that help the child "boss back the fear." The therapist might coach the child to say, "You're not in charge of me; I'm in charge of you!" to the picture while spraying water at it.

PLAY-BASED GRADUATED EXPOSURE AND RESPONSE PREVENTION

Once a child (a) understands the way in which anxiety works, (b) has learned how to calm the physiology, and (c) can fight the fear through various coping strategies described previously, a very precise set of graduated exposures can be structured (Franklin, Rynn, March, & Foa, 2002; March & Mulle, 1998; Morris & March, 2004). The play therapist must get a detailed history of the anxiety-producing stimuli and design a playful, positive series of graduated exposures that lead to a sense of empowerment for the child. Parents who are helping anxious children overcome their fears must balance purposeful, powerful exposures to the anxiety-producing stimuli with lots of positive encouragement and soothing. Couched in playful behaviors, graduated exposures can be designed for a given preschooler's specific set of anxious behaviors. Using the medium of play to approach anxiety-provoking stimuli encourages desensitization and builds on a child's natural competencies. The rewards of play are powerful motivators for children. Moreover, the positive emotions felt while playing counter the anxiety's toxic effects.

For example, the child who is afraid of snakes would normally steer clear of any environment that might risk exposure to snakes. However, the playroom promises many pleasurable experiences, and the enjoyment of the overall space mitigates the fear experienced in being near the toy snakes. As the child remains in the presence of the fear-inducing symbol, the child's physiology has a chance to quiet down, and the child habituates to the snakes' presence. Gradual exposure in this sense may mean that the play therapist consciously has the snakes contained and far removed from where the child is playing for the first few sessions. Over time, the snake toys are presented in closer and closer proximity to the child. As the child learns to tolerate the anxiety provoked by being near the snakes, his or her confidence and self-esteem increase. This learning can then be intentionally generalized to other environments through another conscious series of gradual exposures.

It is best if the parent, child, and therapist all agree together on the series of exposures. Several playful strategies can be used to help parents and children design a set of exposures that will result in mastery of the targeted fear. One such strategy invites the parent–child dyad to build a staircase out of modeling clay. The staircase can be uniform in color or may use a different color for each step. I then ask the family to identify one situation that is "a little bit" scary for the child but could be overcome fairly easily. It is important to make sure that the first few exposures are easy enough for the child that he or she experiences a sense of competence in his or her ability to push through the anxiety. We create toothpick flags for each situation and put them in ascending order along the staircase from the least difficult task to the most difficult task. Another fun way to concretize the set of exposures is to make a ladder out of construction paper, filling in each rung of the ladder with another exposure task. Any number of things can be used to show the child's progress as he or she "climbs" the ladder. A particular favorite of some preschool-age children is a monkey from the old-fashioned Barrel of Monkeys toy. The monkey hooks over each rung of the ladder as the child accomplishes each task. Whenever the monkey moves up a rung on the ladder, the child receives a small, predetermined reward. A ladder can also be made with Magnetix or Kid K'nex and rungs removed and exchanged for rewards as the child chooses to push through each exposure.

CONCLUSION

This chapter serves as an outline for the treatment goals and play therapy interventions that can be used in working with anxious preschoolers. Helping the family system to understand the nature of the illness is the first step. The second step is strengthening the parent–child dyad so that the parent functions in the most soothing and supportive role possible. Once the support systems have been strengthened, the treatment goals are as follows: (a) calming the physiology, (b) externalizing the anxiety, and (c) gaining experiential mastery over the anxiety through play-based articulation of the worried thoughts, followed by thought-stopping and thought-replacement procedures. Some children may need a clearly delineated set of exposures to experience full resolution of their anxiety symptoms. As the termination phase begins, parents and children should review what they have learned with a eye toward maintaining their treatment gains. Last, the therapist should help facilitate celebration of the family's achievements and make a meaningful goodbye.

REFERENCES

Ainsworth, M. D. S., Blehar, M. C., Waters, E., & Wall, S. (1978). *Patterns of attachment: A psychological study of the strange situation.* Hillsdale, NJ: Erlbaum.

American Academy of Child and Adolescent Psychology Official Action. (2007). Practice parameter for the assessment and treatment of children and adolescents with anxiety disorders. *Journal of the American Academy of Child & Adolescent Psychiatry, 46,* 267–283.

Bandura, A. (1976). *Social learning theory.* Upper Saddle River, NJ: Prentice Hall.

Barrett, P., & Farrell, L. (2007). Behavioral family intervention for childhood anxiety. In J. M. Briesmeister & C. E. Schaefer (Eds.), *Handbook of parent training: Helping parents prevent and solve problem behaviors* (pp. 133–164). Hoboken, NJ: Wiley.

Barrett, P., & Shortt, A. L. (2003). Parental involvement in the treatment of anxious children. In A. E. Kazdin & J. R. Weisz (Eds.), *Evidence-based psychotherapies for children and adolescents* (pp. 101–119). New York: Guilford Press.

Bell, S., & Eyberg, S. M. (2002). Parent–child interaction therapy. In L. VandeCreek, S. Knapp, & T. L. Jackson (Eds.), *Innovations in clinical practice: A source book* (Vol. 20, pp. 57–74). Sarasota, FL: Professional Resource Press.

Bowlby, J. (1973). *Attachment and loss: Vol. 1. Attachment.* New York: Basic Books.

Bowlby, J. (1988). *A secure base.* New York: Basic Books.

Bratton, S., Landreth, G., Kellam, T., & Blackard, S. (2006). *Child parent relationship therapy (CPRT): A 10-session filial therapy model for training parents.* New York: Routledge.

Brestan, E., & Eyberg, S. (1998). Effective psychosocial treatments of conduct disordered children and adolescents: 29 years, 82 studies, and 5272 kids. *Journal of Clinical Child Psychology, 27,* 180–189.

Brumariu, L. E., & Kerns, K. A. (2008). Mother–child attachment and social anxiety symptoms in middle childhood. *Journal of Applied Developmental Psychology, 29,* 393–402.

Carr, A. (2009). The effectiveness of family therapy and systematic interventions for child-focused problems. *Journal of Family Therapy, 31,* 3–45.

Chu, B. C., & Harrison, T. L. (2007). Disorder-specific effects of CBT for anxious and depressed youth: A meta-analysis of candidate mediators for change. *Clinical Child and Family Psychology Review, 10,* 352–372.

Cohen, J., Mannarino, A., & Deblinger E. (2006). *Treating trauma and traumatic grief in children and adolescents.* New York: Guilford Press.

Costello, E. J., Egger, H. L., & Angold, A. (2004). Developmental epidemiology of anxiety disorders. In T. H. Ollendick & J. S. March (Eds.), *Phobic and anxiety disorders in children and adolescents* (pp. 631–648). New York: Oxford University Press.

Dacey, J. S., & Fiore, L. B. (2000). *Your anxious child: How parents and teachers can relieve anxiety in children*. San Francisco: Jossey-Bass.

Eisen, A. R., & Kearney, C. A. (1995). *Practitioner's guide to treating fear and anxiety in children and adolescents: A cognitive–behavioral approach*. Northvale, NJ: Jason Aronson.

Franklin, M. E., Rynn, M., March, J. S., & Foa, E. B. (2002). Obsessive–compulsive disorder. In M. Hersen (Ed.). Clinical behavior therapy: Adults and children. (pp. 276–303). Hoboken, NJ: Wiley.

Freestone, M. H, Ladoucer, R., Provencher, M., & Blais, F. (1995). Strategies used with intrusive thoughts: Context, appraisal, mood and efficacy. *Journal of Anxiety Disorders, 9*, 201–215.

Goodyear-Brown, P. (2005). *Digging for buried treasure 2: 52 more prop based play therapy interventions for treating the problems of childhood*. Nashville, TN: Sundog.

Goodyear-Brown, P., Riviere, S., & Shelby, J. (2004). *10 peas in a pod: Prescriptive eclectic play therapy approaches and strategies for treating troubled children* [DVD]. Available from http://www.parisandme.com

Hembree-Kigin, T., & McNeil, C. B. (1995). *Parent child interaction therapy*. New York: Plenum Press.

Huebner, D. (2006). *What to do when you worry too much: A kid's guide to overcoming anxiety*. Washington, DC: Magination Press.

Jernberg, A., & Booth, P. (2001). *Theraplay*. San Francisco: Jossey-Bass.

Kabat-Zinn, J. (1990). *Full catastrophe living: Using the wisdom of your body and mind to face pain, stress and illness*. New York: Delta.

Kendall, P., Aschenbrand, S. G., & Hudson, J. L. (2003). Child-focused treatment of anxiety. In A. E. Kazdin & J. R. Weisz (Eds.), *Evidence-based psychotherapies for children and adolescents* (pp. 81–119). New York: Guilford Press.

Kendall, P. C., Hudson, J. L., Gosch, E., Flannery-Schroeder, E., & Suveg, C. (2008). Cognitive–behavioral therapy for anxiety disordered youth: A randomized clinical trial evaluating child and family modalities. *Journal of Consulting and Clinical Psychology, 76*, 282–297.

Lowenstein, L. (1999). *Creative interventions for troubled children and youth*. Toronto: Champion Press.

Main, M. (1995). Attachment: Overview, with implications for clinical social work. In S. Goldberg, R. Muir, & J. Kerr (Eds.), *Attachment theory: Social, developmental and clinical perspectives* (pp. 407–474). Hillsdale, NJ: Analytic Press.

March, J., & Mulle, K. (1998). *OCD in children and adolescents: A cognitive–behavioral treatment manual*. New York: Guilford Press.

Martin, E., Snow, M., & Sullivan, K. (2008). Patterns of relating between mothers and preschool-age children using the Marschak interaction method rating system. *Early Childhood Development and Care, 178,* 305–314.

Morris, T. L., & March, J. (2004). *Anxiety disorders in children and adolescents* (2nd ed.). New York: Guilford Press.

Pincus, D. B., & Choate, M. L. (in press). Parent child interaction approaches to the treatment of separation anxiety in young preschoolers. *Cognitive and Behavioral Practice.*

Rapee, R. M. (1997). Potential role of childrearing practices in the development of anxiety and depression. *Clinical Psychology Review, 17,* 47–68.

Shortt, A. L., Barrett, P. M., Dadds, M. R., & Fox, T. (2001). The influence of family and experimental context on cognition in anxious children. *Journal of Abnormal Child Psychology, 29,* 585–596.

Siegel, D. J., & Hartzell, M. (2003). *Parenting from the inside out: How a deeper self-understanding can help you raise children who thrive.* New York: Penguin Putnam.

Southam-Gerow, M. A., Kendall, P. C., & Weersing, V. R. (2001). Examining outcome variability: Correlates of treatment response in a child and adolescent anxiety clinic. *Journal of Clinical Child Psychology, 30,* 422–436.

Spencer, E. D., DuPont, R. L. & DuPont, C. M. (2003). *The anxiety cure for kids: A guide for parents.* Hoboken, NJ: Wiley.

Wehrenberg, M., & Prinz, S. M. (2007). *The anxious brain: The neurobiological basis of anxiety disorders and how to effectively treat them.* New York: Norton.

Wolpe, J. (1984). Deconditioning and ad hoc uses of relaxation: An overview. *Journal of Behavior Therapy and Experimental Psychiatry, 15,* 299–304.

7

USE OF PLAY IN CHILD–PARENT PSYCHOTHERAPY WITH PRESCHOOLERS TRAUMATIZED BY DOMESTIC VIOLENCE

MANUELA A. DIAZ AND ALICIA F. LIEBERMAN

When parents perpetrate violence against each other, their child, or other family members, they change in the child's perception of them from sources of comfort and security to bearers of danger and fear as they scream in anger and plead in pain. Amid this chaos, young children are developmentally predisposed to give meaning to the physical and emotional turmoil that result from this violence. This meaning is profoundly shaped by the child's normative developmental themes and anxieties, which in the first 5 years of life include fear of abandonment, fear of losing the parents' love, fear of body damage, and fear of not meeting social standards of goodness (S. Freud, 1926/1959). The effort to find meaning is vividly manifested in children's play because play is children's developmentally appropriate vehicle to process, communicate, regulate, make sense of, and reconstruct their experience of everyday life and its attendant fears, wishes, and fantasies in a form that allows them to tolerate affectively charged material.

Play has long had a central role in individual child psychotherapy because it enables the therapist to witness and assist in the processes of reality testing, affect modulation, and meaning making that promote the child's emotional health (Erikson, 1950; Schaefer & O'Connor, 1983; Slade & Wolf, 1994). Play is also an integral component of relationship-based interventions such as child–parent psychotherapy (CPP) because playing together enables the parent and child to dispel taboos and create a joint narrative that provides an age-appropriate frame to facilitate coping with traumatizing situations such as domestic violence (Lieberman & Van Horn, 2005, 2008).

In this chapter, we describe CPP in the treatment of young children exposed specifically to domestic violence in the form of violence involving the parents. Although domestic violence overlaps with child abuse and other forms of family violence (Edleson, 1999; Kitzmann, Gaylord, Holt, & Kenny, 2003), it deserves specific focus as a traumatic stressor with distinct negative repercussions for children's mental health (Scheeringa & Zeanah, 1995). The chapter is divided into four sections. The first section provides a conceptual framework for understanding the transactional processes between trauma exposure and quality of attachment. The second section details how child–parent play can serve to restore a sense of safety to the child–parent relationship as a vehicle to promoting healthier development. The third section consists of a clinical case presentation to illustrate the implementation of CPP play-based interventions. The final section frames the chapter in the context of empirical findings supporting the efficacy of CPP as a model of intervention.

IMPACT OF DOMESTIC VIOLENCE EXPOSURE ON YOUNG CHILDREN

Each year, up to 20% of children in the United States are exposed to domestic violence, with profound consequences for their developmental course and emotional well-being (Carlson, 2000). This exposure may take a number of forms, including visual witnessing; overhearing; intervening; or experiencing sequelae of the violence that include parental separation, injury, and/or depression (Fantuzzo & Mohr, 1999; Wolak & Finkelhor, 1998). Children younger than age 5 tend to be disproportionately represented in households with domestic violence, making this segment of the population the most vulnerable to the adverse effects of exposure (Fantuzzo, Boruch, Beriama, Atkins, & Marcus, 1997).

Witnessing domestic violence often leaves young children in a state of physical vulnerability and emotional disarray. Early childhood is a rapidly evolving developmental stage in which transactional exchanges between the child and different components of the interpersonal environment exert a major influence on the child's development. Repeated exposure to domestic violence in the early years can cause serious disruptions in children's physical, cognitive, and socioemotional functioning (Osofsky, 1999; Rossman, 2001) as well as alterations in children's neurobiology (Cohen, Perel, DeBellis,

Friedman, & Putnam, 2002; Pynoos, Steinberg, Ornitz, & Goenjian, 1997). Young witnesses to domestic violence tend to show heightened irritability and emotional distress, sleep disturbances, regressed behavior in toileting and language, and fears of being alone (Osofsky, 1999, 2003). Early exposure to domestic violence is also linked to increased externalizing and internalizing behavior problems, including aggression, anxiety, and depression (Fantuzzo & Mohr, 1999; Margolin & Gordis, 2000). As noted earlier, violence between the parents overlaps significantly with child maltreatment (Edleson, 1999; Kitzmann, Gaylord, Holt, & Kenny, 2003), particularly in a high-stress family context (Margolin & Gordis, 2003). The 1st year of life has the highest rate of parental maltreatment, and child fatalities resulting from physical abuse and neglect are found primarily in children younger than age 4 (U.S. Department of Health and Human Services, Administration on Children, Youth and Families, 2008).

TRAUMA AND ATTACHMENT

The complementary nature of findings based on attachment theory and the trauma literature is relevant to psychotherapy with young children exposed to domestic violence. Attachment theory establishes a conceptual context for examining the role of early relationships in child mental health, and the literature on trauma provides evidence of the behavioral and physiological responses to perceived danger. The intersection of attachment and trauma theories offers a framework for understanding the deleterious effects of domestic violence exposure on young children and provides the guiding principles for empirically validated treatment interventions (Lieberman, 2004; Lieberman & Amaya-Jackson, 2005).

Attachment in the early years is defined as the affectional tie between a mother and a child with the primary evolutionary purpose of ensuring the child's survival (Ainsworth, 1969; Bowlby, 1969/1982). Children's attachment system encompasses specific safety-seeking behaviors that complement parents' own biological predisposition to ensure the protection and survival of their offspring (Lieberman & Van Horn, 2008). The young child depends on sensitive and consistent caregiving to promote healthy development. Prolonged exposure to domestic violence can lead to the disruption of the child's attachment system as well as to the parents' capacity to protect and rescue the child from danger. When a child feels unsafe because of parental unavailability, inconsistent care, or fear-instilling behavior, the necessary conditions for early mental health are hindered, severely altering children's emotional reliance on their caregivers (Lieberman & Van Horn, 2008; Main & Hesse, 1990).

Play and Early Trauma

Play, described as "the royal road to the child's conscious and unconscious inner world" (Bettelheim, 1987, p. 167), is used by young children as a medium to build bridges between their external reality and their inner world. Play is typically disrupted by the experience of traumatic events such as exposure to violence. Following a traumatic event, young children may present many of the characteristics of an acute posttraumatic stress response, including intense negative emotions and accelerated physiological arousal (Pynoos, 1990; Pynoos, Steinberg, & Piacentini, 1999; van der Kolk, 2003). Symptoms of traumatic stress include repeated reexperiencing of the traumatic event, emotional numbing, loss of developmental milestones, avoidance, and increased arousal (Zero to Three/National Center for Clinical Infant Programs, 2005). If severe enough, these symptoms can prevent children from effectively processing traumatic experiences in their play. Rather than recounting and elaborating symbolically on their recollections of the traumatic event, young children may engage in repetitive posttraumatic play, described as a rigid, compulsive reenactment of traumatic events that tends to exacerbate rather than relieve anxiety (Terr, 1983, 1991). Traumatized children may show poor attention, concentration difficulties, and increased physical activity that interfere with their ability to focus and become engrossed in play. Loss of developmental milestones may be manifested in developmentally delayed play skills and inability to engage in symbolic play.

Play can become a primary source of opportunities for therapeutic intervention in the early years because children use play to repeat an anxiety-provoking situation, change its outcome, or avoid it altogether by choosing a different play theme. Through self-directed play, children can process strong feelings and internal conflicts arising from exposure to traumatic events, including feeling threatened by their attachment figures. Symbolic play provides children with the structure to facilitate the free exploration of feelings in a contained and safe environment. The role of the parent in supporting children's symbolic play is pivotal in the recovery of young children exposed to domestic violence because the parent can acknowledge with the child the reality of frightening events that are often not spoken about or addressed in daily life. When these events are recognized as real and their emotional impact is appreciated and acknowledged, parents learn to empathize with the child's feelings of terror and mistrust and can repair the ruptures in the quality of the child–parent relationship by providing corrective attachment experiences that increase safety and rebuild the child's trust.

The therapist has a pivotal role in guiding and facilitating the process of restoring safety in the child–parent relationship following the child's exposure to domestic violence. Parents who are victims of domestic violence are often depressed, emotionally unavailable, and unresponsive to their children's needs (Osofsky, 1999, 2003). They may feel distressed and helpless if they feel that they have failed in their parental role of providing safety and protection. In these conditions, they need the therapist's active intervention to gain a sense of self-efficacy in parenting.

Child–Parent Psychotherapy as Trauma-Focused Treatment

CPP is an empirically supported, manualized, relationship-based intervention designed to treat children younger than age 6 who show emotional and other developmental disturbances as the result of traumatic events, adverse environmental conditions, or psychosocial risk factors (Lieberman & Van Horn, 2005, 2008). Treatment takes place in joint sessions with the child and the parent or primary caregiver. CPP is described in *"Don't Hit My Mommy!"*: *A Manual for Child–Parent Psychotherapy for Young Witnesses of Family Violence* (Lieberman & Van Horn, 2005), which describes specific intervention modalities, including the use of play as well as unstructured developmental guidance, insight-oriented interpretation, addressing traumatic reminders, the retrieval and creation of benevolent memories to generate hope, crisis intervention, and assistance with problems of living (Lieberman & Van Horn, 2005, 2008). The focus of clinical attention is the emotional quality of the child–parent relationship and the unique contributions of each partner to the affective tone of the parent–child interactions. CPP has been effectively used with young witnesses of domestic violence, where the focus is on helping the parent cocreate with the child a play and verbal narrative of the violence with the goal of promoting safety, restoring trust, and repairing disordered mutual attributions and interactional patterns between parent and child (Lieberman, Ghosh Ippen, & Van Horn, 2006; Lieberman, Van Horn, & Ghosh Ippen, 2005).

CPP uses a multitheoretical, integrative approach to maximize health-promoting opportunities in young children and their caregivers. Anchored in attachment and psychodynamic theories, it shares key goals with other trauma treatments, including (a) supporting a return to normal development, (b) fostering an increased capacity to respond realistically to threat, (c) maintaining regular levels of affective arousal, (d) reestablishing trust in bodily sensations, (e) restoring reciprocity in intimate relationships, (f) normalizing the traumatic response, (g) encouraging a differentiation between reliving and remembering the trauma, and (h) placing the traumatic experience in perspective (Lieberman & Van Horn, 2005; Marmar, Foy, Kagan, & Pynoos, 1993).

Play between the child and the parent is a key CPP therapeutic modality. Traditional psychoanalytical approaches to child psychotherapy have long emphasized the therapist's function in construing the meaning of children's play and using verbal interpretation to bring unacceptable conflicts and desires into consciousness as a way of making them amenable to adaptive integration

(Benedict, 2006; Bromfield, 2003; Esman, 1984; A. Freud, 1936/1966; Klein, 1932). Psychoanalytic play therapy has been expanded to include the idea of "simply playing," a noninterpretative, child–therapist collaborative endeavor in which the therapist provides a safe space that enables the child to play spontaneously to build psychological structures and make meaning of his or her experience (Slade, 1994). CPP expands even further on this approach by promoting play between the child and the parent as the preferred avenue toward lasting improvement in the child. The CPP therapist encourages the parent to participate in the child's play and serves as a translator of the function and meaning of the child's play for the parent as well as for the child (Van Horn & Lieberman, 2006).

The CPP clinician chooses toys on the basis of information collected during the assessment phase, always bearing in mind the child's developmental stage and the treatment goals. These include toys that may evoke the trauma to facilitate the child's construction of a play narrative that will give meaning to his or her experience; toys that allow the child to enact developmentally appropriate themes, such as daily caregiving routines; and toys that allow the child to engage in age-appropriate skill building, such as stacking blocks and drawing materials. The focus on free play enables the child to take the lead in determining which toys are most relevant at any given time.

When the child engages in posttraumatic play that increases anxiety, the therapist comments on the meaning of play as a way of remembering the traumatic event and helps the child and the parent to differentiate between reliving and remembering by articulating the safety of the present moment. The variety of play themes reflects the multiple facets of the child's inner life as well as changing needs in the course of treatment. The parent witnesses and participates in the child's play, learning to understand its meaning as a reflection of the child's experience. Through shared play, the child–parent dyad becomes progressively more adept at expressing the range of feelings associated with the trauma and coconstructing a trauma narrative that validates and supports both of their experiences. The progress of treatment can be assessed by shifts from a preponderance of traumatic play and preoccupation with themes of danger, aggression, and fear to increasing engagement with developmentally appropriate activities and interests and greater spontaneous intimacy and joy in the child–parent interaction. The clinical example that follows illustrates the uses of play in CPP.

A CLINICAL EXAMPLE

The following case example describes the implementation of CPP with a child–mother dyad suffering from the sequelae of domestic violence. We focus on four interrelated clinical issues: (a) the mother's inability to join the child in play as a result of her hyperarousal in response to the play themes; (b) the child's quickly alternating feelings of love, anger, and fear about her father; (c) the mother's ambivalence toward the child and difficulty accepting the child's positive feelings for her father; and (d) the progress in treatment of the child's and mother's ability to relate to each other and engage in physical closeness.

Presenting Problem

Camila was 4 and a half years old when she was referred for treatment by a preschool mental health consultant because of her aggressive behavior toward her peers. During the initial referral phone call, her mother, Rose, said that Camila's troubling behavior ranged from screaming tantrums to verbal and physical aggression toward others, including her mother. Rose told the therapist that whenever Camila got upset with her, she tried to hit her and told her, "I'm going to beat you up like my dad did; I'm going to kill you." Camila also called her mother "ugly" or "stupid" whenever Rose did not comply with her requests. In a sad voice, Rose stated that she had been close to losing her temper and hitting Camila but had resolved to use "long time-outs" instead, which at times consisted of leaving Camila in her room for hours. She disclosed recent involvement of child protective services in the family because of the father's alleged physical abuse of Camila and substantiated exposure of the child to domestic violence. Rose stated that she was hesitant about bringing "such a young child" to psychotherapy, but was very worried that Camila would get expelled from preschool if she continued misbehaving and felt that psychotherapy for the child was her only option.

Initial Assessment

The initial assessment started with three weekly meetings with Rose to gather relevant background information and discuss at length her concerns about Camila. These meetings were followed by two additional sessions to assess the effect of trauma exposure on the functioning of the mother–child dyad. At the conclusion of the assessment, the clinician met with Rose to provide feedback on the assessment results and discuss the treatment plan.

Individual Meetings With the Mother

The therapist obtained information about Rose's ethnicity and her cultural beliefs and attitudes about parenting and child-rearing practices, including how she viewed children's play. Rose proudly told the therapist that she was a first-generation Latina of Central American descent and described how her parents came to the United States in search of a better future. She was fully bilingual in English and Spanish and maintained close ties to her cultural heritage. Rose stressed her desire to pass this legacy on to Camila. The therapist, also a Latina, used this opportunity to validate Rose's wish to transmit valuable aspects of her culture to her daughter. Regarding play therapy, Rose stated that play was "an activity only for children" and added that she rarely engaged in play with Camila unless the child needed help with the play equipment at the park; for example, she would push Camila on the swing.

During the assessment sessions, Rose described an extensive history of domestic violence, which began soon after she married her boyfriend of 3 months at the age of 22. The physical violence increased when Rose became pregnant and worsened after Camila's birth. On repeated occasions, Camila watched in horror as her intoxicated father kicked and punched Rose in the face and stomach and threatened to kill her with a kitchen knife. The beatings often left Rose with bruises and an aching body, but she did not seek medical attention or any other services. When Camila was 2 years old, her father, following a drinking binge, struck Rose over the head with a beer bottle and repeatedly hit her head against the wall and kitchen table until she passed out. When Rose regained consciousness, she found her husband gone and Camila asleep under the bed.

Rose reported that Camila had cried inconsolably since she was an infant when she witnessed her father's violence. As the child started to walk, she placed herself between her parents and screamed at the top of her lungs, "Papa, Mama, no!" Rose stated that as a young toddler, Camila needed "a lot of attention" after these episodes, explaining, "Camila wanted to be rocked and carried all the time like a baby; it was too much for me. There were times when I couldn't even get out of bed." Rose also said that Camila became more "independent" as she grew older. For example, when Camila was 2 years old, she once asked Rose for her bottle after a violent episode, but Rose did not respond because she was in bed with a severe headache and aching body. Later, Rose found Camila drinking out of the milk carton, which she had managed to take out of the refrigerator on her own.

As she listened to Rose, the clinician noticed that she spoke of Camila as though she were a much older child. Rose was convinced, for example, that Camila understood why she and her mother were no longer living with her father although Rose had never explained it to her. Rose was also quite impatient with her child's behavior. She said with frustration in her voice, "I can't understand why Camila is worse now that we are no longer living with her father. Camila is just a difficult child; she inherited her father's temper!"

Camila witnessed the last episode of her father's violence against her mother when she was 4 years old. Camila's father accused Rose of having been unfaithful with one of her coworkers while he was away on a trip. He hit Rose with his belt on her body and face, kicked her in the head while she was on the ground, and threatened to kill her if he ever saw her talking to another man or if she left him. Rose vividly recalled how Camila "stood there and just watched" as the violence unfolded. She resented the child's failure to take action to defend her and assumed that the child took her father's side in this conflict. Fearing for her life, Rose phoned a girlfriend the following day while her husband was at work, and the friend drove Rose and Camila to a domestic violence shelter where they were still living 6 months later at the time of the referral. It is noteworthy that in spite of her ambivalence toward Camila, Rose took her to the shelter instead of leaving her with her father. At the shelter, Rose was helped to make a police report, and her husband was arrested and charged with assault and battery. Rose obtained a permanent restraining order and told the therapist that neither she nor Camila had had any contact with him since then. Rose denied any physical abuse against Camila but reported that Camila's father made derogatory comments to the child, called her names, and threatened to send her to live with distant relatives whenever she misbehaved.

During the assessment, the clinician collected information about Rose's childhood trauma history and assessed her level of symptomatology to anticipate possible triggers during the child–mother dyadic sessions. In addition to the domestic violence she had experienced during the previous 6 years, Rose described growing up in a chaotic family environment and witnessing extreme incidents of domestic violence between her own parents, both of whom had histories of alcoholism. Her parents used harsh punishment to discipline her, and Rose vividly narrated several incidents of being hit with belts and household objects. She also recalled that at age 9 she had to take care of not only her mother but also her younger siblings because her mother was "too drunk" to attend to them. Rose became tearful while recounting these events in her life. It was clear from these reports that there was a strong intergenerational component in Camila's experience of domestic violence and that Rose's own trauma history as a child would play a major role in the child's treatment. Given that maladaptive parent–child interactions often arise from unresolved experiences of parental trauma, the clinician viewed Rose's perceptions of and mothering behavior toward Camila as influenced by Rose's intrapsychic conflicts involving her own parental figures—that is, "ghosts in the nursery" (Fraiberg, 1975, p. 387). The clinician hypothesized that through the process of parenting Camila and the construction of a coherent joint trauma narrative, Rose would have opportunities for personal growth and development as well as to recover from the effects of trauma.

Child–Mother Assessment Sessions

The second phase of the intake assessment included sessions with the child and the child–mother dyad. The therapist administered the Wechsler Preschool and Primary Scale of Intelligence—Third Edition (Wechsler,

2002) to assess Camila's cognitive, motor, and language development, followed by a play session between mother and child that included free play, semistructured activities, and a brief separation–reunion episode. Camila's full-scale IQ was below average, with verbal IQ significantly lower than performance IQ.

Throughout all of these activities, Camila displayed restlessness and hypervigilance and avoided eye contact. During the cognitive testing, she gave up when unable to successfully complete a task after the first attempt and needed constant reassurance from the therapist, particularly during the administration of the verbal items. She was easily startled by noises in the hallway outside the playroom but remained physically distant from her mother. When Camila became clearly distressed, Rose did not help her and at times worsened the situation with threats such as "Do you want to go back to live with your father? Is that what you want? I'm going to send you there if you continue to misbehave." It is noteworthy that these threats echoed the father's earlier threats that he would send the child away to live with relatives if she misbehaved.

Rose's expectation that Camila act like a much older child was apparent in frequent comments such as "You are big girl; you shouldn't need help building a tall tower with those blocks" and "That puzzle is too easy for you; it should only take you a few minutes to put together." Toward the end of one of the assessment sessions, Rose described an incident in which Camila had asked her to leave their bedroom because Camila wanted to be alone in the room while coloring in her coloring book. Although this request had hurt Rose's feelings, Rose said that she left the room because "that's what Camila wanted; Camila clearly did not want to be around me." Rose's comments about Camila's behavior problems at school also contained many negative attributions, such as "Camila is just like her father; she is mean and manipulative like him." Camila showed no distress when separated from her mother, and after reunion displayed minimal changes in her behavior and affective state.

Feedback Session

At the conclusion of the assessment, the therapist met with Rose individually to provide feedback. She started by validating Rose's concerns about Camila's behavior problems and then discussed the specific findings of the assessment. She explained that Camila had been exposed to multiple severe traumatic events at a very young age, and this exposure might be linked to Camila's behavioral problems and delays in language and cognitive performance. In recommending psychotherapy, the therapist reminded Rose that treatment would require active participation on her part, including engaging in play with Camila. The therapist used this opportunity to address the Latino cultural value of *respeto* (respect) in interpersonal relationships—defined as deference to older people and authority figures—explaining that the treatment would focus on different aspects of Camila's behavior, including her tendency to hit and use insulting language with her mother. The therapist described treatment as a trusting collaboration between Rose and the therapist with the goal of helping Rose facilitate Camila's recovery. In describing the value of child–parent play during treatment, the therapist also explained that playing between parents and children was very common in many cultures and not considered a sign of disrespect but rather a form of trust from the child to the parent. She added that she would not consider it impolite if Rose and her daughter did not fully pay attention to her while they were engaged in play during the sessions. The therapist also highlighted the importance of telling Camila the reasons for treatment, including speaking candidly about the violence that the child had witnessed. She acknowledged that it might be difficult initially for both mother and child to speak about these events. Rose nodded in agreement and said, "Whatever you think would be helpful; it is fine with me." Finally, the therapist raised the topic of Rose's own trauma history and told her that she was also experiencing symptoms of traumatic stress and depression. Rose seemed receptive to this information and accepted the therapist's offer of a referral to individual therapy in a community agency.

Starting Treatment: Setting the Stage for Play

For the first session, the therapist chose toys that could evoke Camila's experiences of violence while also giving her opportunities to seek a reprieve from becoming overly aroused by traumatic triggers. The toys included a doll-house, a family doll set, a fairy-tale doll set with three characters (a prince, a princess, and a knight holding a sword), kitchen toys (dishes, utensils, and food), a baby doll, nursing bottles, a doctor's kit, telephones, puppets, a police car, an ambulance, a large family car, and different sets of animal families. The clinician anticipated that characters such as the prince and the sword-wielding knight would evoke in Camila the conflicting feelings she was experiencing about her own father, who was not only the perpetrator of the violence but also the bearer of love and affection. As therapy unfolded, these characters proved to be an effective means of helping Camila symbolically reveal the polarity of feelings inundating her inner world, a polarity that was contributing to her emotional distance from her mother as a protective figure.

Child–Mother Dyadic Sessions

Rose and Camila attended 62 weekly joint mother–child sessions following the assessment feedback. The therapist had five individual meetings with Rose to address maternal clinical issues surfacing in the sessions that directly impacted mother–child relationship functioning. Rose and Camila were living in a shelter when treatment began, and Rose preferred that sessions be conducted at the clinic. At Rose's request, we continued to meet at the clinic after they left the shelter.

Initial Dyadic Sessions

Camila and Rose arrived 20 minutes early to their first appointment. Rose quickly walked ahead of her daughter and entered the playroom, leaving Camila behind. After settling in the room, Rose began calling out Camila's name while the therapist stood by the door, encouraging the child to join her. Camila seemed frightened by the simultaneous arrival of other people to the clinic and began to walk cautiously toward the playroom while avoiding eye contact with the therapist. Her eyes widened as she took a visual inventory of the toys on the floor, but she sat down on the carpet and leaned against her mother's chair without approaching the toys. Rose told the therapist that this behavior was typical and went on to emphasize Camila's noncompliance and defiance toward adults. The therapist acknowledged Rose's frustration and then turned to Camila, explaining in a sympathetic tone of voice, "This is the first time you are here in this room. You've seen me only twice. You still don't know me well. . . . This place is all new to you." Without attending to the therapist's efforts to offer support to the child, Rose proceeded to describe her frustrations about having to deal with what she called "the preschool teachers' weekly complaints about Camila." The therapist sympathized with Rose's feelings and then asked whether she could explain to Camila, who was still leaning against the chair, why they were coming for treatment. Rose looked hesitant but seemed to remember the agreements made during the feedback session and nodded her head in agreement. The therapist told Camila about her mother's description of the "scary fights" the child had witnessed between her parents, giving some specific examples. She then added, "Camila, you saw your father get very angry and hurt your mother. A lot of children get frightened when they see these scary fights between their parents." The therapist also spoke about the many feelings—anger, fear, longing, and sadness—that children and mothers feel when there are fights at home and the father is no longer living with them. Camila, with a big forced smile on her face, nodded her head and looked away. Rose seemed annoyed and angrily told Camila, "Sit up and listen to what the doctor is saying." The therapist commented that these were very difficult things for both of them to hear and talk about and added,

> Your mother is very worried about you and wants to help you. I am a doctor that helps children and their parents with their strong feelings. Here we can simply play, or, if you like, we can talk about how you are feeling and the scary things that you saw at home.

Camila looked down, nervously fidgeting with her hands. Although as the session progressed she engaged in short periods of solitary play, her play was disorganized and repetitive, and no meaningful themes emerged. She spent time arranging the furniture in the dollhouse but she never asked for help, although at times she displayed frustration when she could not make some of the furniture stand. Rose, for her part, seemed to be engulfed in her concerns about Camila's "problematic behavior" and throughout the session remained seated in the adult chair with her back to Camila while talking about the many troublesome incidents involving Camila that had transpired over the past few months. The therapist believed that Rose's constant criticism of Camila was a serious impediment to the child's freedom to engage in imaginative play.

The following sessions gave further evidence of the lack of trust and reciprocity between mother and child. Rose reported that Camila had a stomach virus over the weekend and was still not fully recovered. The therapist told Camila, "Your mother is telling me that you were sick and still not feeling well." Looking tired and pale, Camila nodded and continued exploring the dollhouse. Rose commented that Camila never told her when she was feeling sick or hungry, and this made it very difficult to care for her. The therapist used this opportunity to start exploring this pattern and suggested a connection between Camila's behavior and the traumatic events that mother and child had endured during the past years, saying,

> You told me about times when you could not respond to Camila when she asked for your help because you were too sore and weak to move. Perhaps she learned to fend by herself from an early age and does not want to bother you.

Rose responded that she felt unsure whether Camila could remember these past events but seemed open to hearing the therapist talk about their past experience. Later sessions continued to include conversations about the impact on Camila of living in a family environment where her needs were not consistently met and her parents were, at times, either frightening or unavailable. In one of these conversations, the therapist commented that in the past it had been very difficult for Rose to attend to Camila after a beating that left her hurting and scared and alluded specifically to the incident with the milk. She then commented that it might be hard for Rose to now try to change this pattern. Rose nodded tearfully, saying, "It still affects me when I remember that day and that particular incident. I just couldn't get out of bed." Turning to Camila, the therapist explained that her mother was sad and tearful because she wished she had felt better that day so she could have given the milk to her. With a tense facial expression, Camila looked at Rose and then quickly went back to exploring the dollhouse. The child was giving clear signals that she needed to process this information slowly and cautiously.

Starting with the 10th dyadic session, Camila consistently began using the same toys, which included the dollhouse, doll furniture, and the family and fairy-tale doll sets. By the 12th session, Camila began showing her feelings through rich and imaginative play that conveyed sadness and grief about the loss of her father as well as fear about the violence she had witnessed. Camila tended not to include Rose in her play. Rose limited herself to watching Camila play while sitting on her chair without approaching the child in spite of the therapist's encouragement.

A Turning Point

At the 14th session, Rose arrived as in previous sessions with the urge to provide every detail of the incidents that had transpired during Camila's "very difficult week." Camila, however, had a look of excitement in her face as she looked at the toys. The therapist commented on Camila's excitement while also sympathizing with the mother's concerns and invited Rose to join her and the child in play. For the first time, Rose agreed to sit on the carpet with Camila but continued to remain an observer of Camila's play. As before, this turned out to be no obstacle for Camila, who quickly began to arrange the furniture in each of the rooms of the dollhouse. She meticulously placed the two beds and the largest closet in one of the bedrooms. She grabbed the knight doll and whispered with a tone of urgency, "Everyone needs to hide now! Hurry, hurry, they need to hide from the bad man, now!" She placed the princess, prince, and two baby dolls under the bed and covered them with the blankets. The therapist whispered, "What is happening?" and the child replied, "They are all hiding . . . hiding from the bad man." Rose watched quietly. Camila added, "The bad man is being mean . . . mean to them" and with a gruff, deep voice said, "I'm going to beat you all up. You are being bad, bad! Stupid, you bitch . . . I'm going to kill you all!" Camila, holding the knight doll, began hitting the other dolls with the sword while giving voice to them by saying, "Don't hit us, mean bad man, don't hit us, please, no, no, nooo."

The therapist said with a tone of concern,

> The bad man is hitting the dolls; no wonder they are so scared of him. They are scared of the bad man because he is being very mean to them. He is hitting them . . . yelling at them . . . using mean, hurtful words. . . . He is very scary.

Camila replied in a deep voice, "He is going to kill all of them." At this point, Rose, with tears in her eyes, began recounting an incident in which Camila had hid under the bed after hearing her father yelling before becoming physically violent toward Rose. Looking at Camila, who at this point had stopped her play and was looking at her mother with a blank stare, the therapist told Camila that her mother became very upset and sad when she remembered those scary times. The therapist then asked Camila if the same thing also happened to her. Camila paused for a few seconds, looked down at the floor, and then resumed her play. First, she moved all the dolls except the princess out of the room and then placed the knight on the same bed as the princess. The therapist asked Camila what was happening now. Camila replied, "He is being nice, and giving mommy kisses and hugs." The therapist used this as an opportunity to talk about Camila's conflicting feelings, commenting, "Sometimes the bad man can be nice and loving but there are other times when he can be very scary, especially when he gets mad. This is so confusing!" The therapist then asked whether this description reminded Camila of her own father because he sometimes hugged her and kissed her but was also very scary when he hit her mother. Camila slowly nodded her head and proceeded to put the baby dolls on the swing. After about 5 minutes, she started exploring the other toys on the floor. Rose once again became tearful while she talked about how her happiness with Camila's father had only lasted for a few months and pondered on all the harm he had done to her during the past years. She was able to recall only one loving interaction during the initial stages of the relationship as well as some of the fights that Camila had witnessed between them. While looking at her mother, Camila grabbed the doctor's kit, sat next to the therapist, and began checking the therapist's vital signs. She then asked the therapist to do the same thing with Rose. When the therapist finished checking Rose, Camila came close to her mother, who correctly understood Camila's unspoken request and began checking the child's heart with the toy stethoscope. This play continued throughout the remainder of the session. During this session, Rose also recalled her own exposure to domestic violence when she was a little girl. She talked about how she remembered being very scared when her own father used to hit her mother and said that she did not want her daughter to "go through the same thing again." The therapist concluded the session by providing examples of how things were different at home compared with how they were when they lived with Camila's father. She said that now there were no more "scary fights" and no more screaming, and she described the steps that Rose had taken to keep them safe.

Promising Changes, Difficult Interactions

During the ensuing sessions, Camila began to show her desire for physical and emotional intimacy with her mother. She smiled anxiously and leaned on her mother whenever Rose talked about difficult interactions they had during the week or about the past violence. Rose, however, did not seem ready yet to show physical affection to Camila and seemed unable to help Camila calm herself when she became upset. Rose seemed uncomfortable with Camila's attempts at physical contact and gently pushed her away while telling her, "Camila, sit up and listen to what we are saying. You need to be polite!" Physical interactions between mother and child were still tainted by awkwardness and misattunement. During these sessions, the therapist sympathetically acknowledged Camila's response to remembering difficult times while also affirming Rose's culturally acceptable wish for her daughter to be well mannered in paying attention and responding to adult requests. The therapist also provided psychoeducation about the effects of trauma on young children and unstructured developmental guidance centered around developmentally appropriate expectations for Camila.

Changes in Life Circumstances

As the therapy moved into the midtreatment phase, significant changes in the mother's and child's circumstances prompted a shift in Camila's play. Rose and Camila moved into a transitional housing program. Rose started working part time in retail while attending school half time. She enrolled Camila in a new preschool closer to where she worked and began a friendship with Joseph, one of the preschool teachers, that later became a courtship. During this period, Camila's play continued to be rich and creative, revealing her enthusiasm for making sense of these changes as well as demonstrating her longing for a paternal figure who could provide safety and reassurance.

In one session during this treatment phase, Camila greeted the therapist with a big smile as she quickly entered the room with her mother right behind her, sat down, requested that her mother join her on the floor, and began taking out the dolls from the basket. While holding the prince doll, Camilla said, "I'm going to be the prince." She then turned to Rose and said, "You are going to be the princess," and gave her the princess doll. Camila looked at the therapist and said, "You'll be the baby." She went on to say, "The prince is happy today; he wants to dance and play in the castle. He is having a party because it's his birthday. We have many guests." She proceeded to bring the other dolls from the basket and began arranging them around these characters. Camila then asked her mother and the therapist to join in the activities the prince had planned for his birthday. She then enacted how she felt in the presence of the prince, whom she called Joseph—the male figure in her life, representing the father she was yearning to have. Just like the real-life Joseph, the prince liked playing with her, danced with her and her mother, bought Camila and her mother presents, and gave Camila undivided attention. Rose, with some hesitation, was able to participate in Camila's play. Rose correctly understood that the prince represented the real-life Joseph. During a later follow-up telephone conversation with the therapist, Rose revealed that she was not interested in having a romantic relationship with Joseph but also acknowledged how much Camila liked him.

A few weeks later, Rose revealed with excitement that she had met "a very nice guy" 2 weeks earlier while picking up Camila from her preschool. William, a single father of two, had just begun to work as a substitute teacher at Camila's preschool. Rose added, "For some reason, Camila is not too fond of him." During the following weeks, Camila was able to use her play to process her feelings of anger and jealousy toward William, who was now pursuing her mother romantically.

In one of these sessions while Rose and Camila were arranging the furniture together in the dollhouse, Camila told her mother that she wanted to play only with the prince and princess. She added that the princess and prince were going away on a trip and asked her mother to help her put them inside the large family car. Rose grabbed another male doll and placed it inside the car, saying that she wanted more people to go on the trip. Camila, with an angry expression on her face, grabbed the male doll, threw it out of the car, and asked her mother not to do it anymore. Rose insisted, asking Camila, "Why wouldn't such a nice guy go with the prince and princess on a trip?" Camila replied, "Because he misbehaved" and proceeded to run over the male doll with the car before departing for "a very long trip." Rose, who seemed surprised by Camila's reaction, said, "Poor little man; he just wanted to go away on a trip with them." Camila replied, "No. He is not going this time!" While observing their different affective experiences in reaction to the play outcome, the therapist said,

> It seems like the prince and princess are going alone on a trip. The poor little man has to stay. That must be hard for him because he really wanted to go with them. I wonder what he has done?

Camila smiled as her eyes widened, and her play shifted back to joyful exchanges between the prince and princess. In a later session, Camila suggested preparing an elaborate meal for the family and asked Rose to place the dolls around the table. As soon as Rose grabbed a male doll other than the prince, Camila put it back on the basket and said firmly, "But Mama, I just want the prince, the princess, and the girl doll at the table. Please!"

Sensing that these mother–child exchanges represented a real-life impasse between mother and child, the therapist suggested an individual collateral session with Rose to talk about the progress of treatment and find out how things were going with her personally. Rose reported that she had observed improvements in Camila's symptoms and went on to discuss the strong physical attraction she was feeling toward William and her feelings of friendship for but lack of romantic interest in Joseph, who continued to court her assiduously. She said that she would like to remarry and give Camila a family and viewed William as a prospective partner. In a worried tone of voice, Rose told the therapist that "Camila always had a temper tantrum" whenever she spoke with William. She added with a sigh that she herself "forgot about everything" when she was with him. In contrast, she got upset and embarrassed when Camila told everyone at the preschool that Joseph was her "papa." The therapist validated Rose's feelings for William and then commented that it might be very difficult for Camila to feel excluded from attention whenever Rose talked to William.

This led to a conversation in which Rose and the therapist discussed the possibility that William's presence might remind Camila of times when she needed Rose's attention but was not able to get it and of the anxiety that this might provoke in her, especially if she felt that she was going to lose her mother's love. The therapist and Rose went on to discuss how to help Camila during the sessions as she used her play to express these feelings. The clinician hypothesized that Camila's clear preference for Joseph was also fueled by her age-appropriate competitiveness with her mother for the attention of a father figure who was also an idealized love object. Joseph was able to divide his attention evenly between Rose and Camila; William, however, only had eyes for Rose. The therapist chose not to bring up this angle of the situation with the mother because she thought that Rose was not in a position to understand and accept Camila's competitiveness with her.

During the next sessions, Camila was given the space in her play to openly express her longing for a father like Joseph, who was loving and caring toward her and her mother. As the sessions progressed, Camila allowed the inclusion of another male character in her play but only if she chose who the male doll would be, and she always made sure to choose the most physically unattractive of the male dolls.

Rose's hopes for a relationship with William did not materialize because of William's lack of interest in having a committed relationship. Initially heartbroken, Rose was able to process her feelings of sadness and disillusionment during two collateral sessions with the therapist. During these sessions, Rose gained greater insight into her feelings and their connection to her early relationships. She also decided to continue cultivating a friendship with Joseph, who became a very important source of instrumental and emotional support for both Rose and Camila.

Another Turning Point

The 30th session marked another turning point in treatment. Rose started the session by reporting that Camila's behavior had shifted dramatically, and she was now clingy; showed strong separation anxiety; needed more supervision; was "misbehaving even more than before"; and did not let Rose do anything alone, not even go to the bathroom. She also described an incident in which they were waiting in line to order at a restaurant when Camila smilingly told her mother that her father was right behind them. Rose said that when she turned around, she saw a man who looked very much like Camila's father. She became so scared that the man could indeed be him that she decided to leave the restaurant immediately and became very angry at Camila for "lying." The therapist acknowledged Rose's feelings and helped her process her intense physical response to this triggering event. She then looked at Camila and asked how the child felt when she thought she saw her father at the restaurant. Camila responded with a big smile that she had been happy but that she wanted to leave the restaurant and go home with her mother. This response provided the therapist with an opening to talk about Camila's ambivalent feelings toward her father. The therapist said, "You want to see your dad, but you are also scared of him." Rose commented that she thought Camila had called her attention to the man to scare her and that she had not realized that Camila could also be afraid of seeing her father. During the rest of the session, Camila played with nurturing toys and made an elaborate meal for Rose and the therapist. Responding to Rose's concern that there might be an acute worsening of Camila's behavior problems, the therapist provided psychoeducation about a pattern that is common in young children and consists of a worsening of symptoms before there is sustained improvement.

Elaboration of the Themes of Violence and Danger

During the next 10 sessions, Camila requested greater involvement from Rose and included the therapist less in her play. The characters and themes revolved around both her own recollections of the violence she witnessed between her parents and the difficult interactions that transpired between her and her mother during the week. When Rose asked Camila what was happening in her play, the child responded, "Everybody is hurting each other; they are all hiding from the bad man [the knight]." Through her play, Camila expressed intense feelings of anger and fear toward both her father and her mother. This rich imaginative play at times became disrupted by Camila's increased arousal and stressful environmental triggers, such as loud noises or an occasional ambulance siren. During this phase of treatment, Rose became more responsive and attentive to what Camila did during the sessions.

Consolidation and Improvement: Late Treatment and Termination

By the 50th therapy session, Rose reported a decrease in Camila's symptoms and improvement in all areas of concern. During this phase, Rose consistently began showing behaviors depicting an understanding of Camila's experience. She actively supported Camila's expression of feelings about her father in the sessions and outside of therapy. Rose reported that Camila had begun asking for her father and about the reasons for his being absent from her life, saying, for example, "How come he is not looking for me?" "Does he have another baby?" "Is he going to call me?" With the support of Rose and the therapist, Camila talked openly during the sessions about her worries about and her feelings toward her absent father. The quality of the dyadic play between mother and child also shifted markedly. Whenever Camila's play became chaotic or disorganized, Rose used words and supportive action to provide clarity and organization, putting Camila's feelings into words and helping them create meaningful and coherent stories.

In one of these sessions, Camila decided to play with the ambulance and the fairy-tale dolls. Camila grabbed the knight doll (whom she named "Richie", her father's nickname) and began to run over it again and again with the family car. She then asked Rose to help her take "wounded Richie" to the hospital in the ambulance for "the nurse [Rose] to help him feel better." Rose narrated,

> Richie needs help because he got badly hurt. When people get hurt, they need to get help so they can feel better. That's why we have to take Richie to the hospital so the nurse can take care of him.

In a later session, Camila asked Rose to be the knight and asked her to rescue the "mommy princess" and her baby from being run over by a car. Throughout this play, Rose gave eloquent voice to the characters' feelings and also allowed Camila to tell a story about each particular situation and how the characters were feeling.

At this point in treatment, the therapist had become an observer of the play and interactions between child and mother. As the weeks progressed, Rose described several incidents in which she was able to help Camila regulate her affect. When Camila had a bad dream about a "scary black cat," Rose made up a song to "scare away" the scary black cat. Rose also allowed Camila to put a picture of herself and her father on her nightstand. She was better able to validate Camila's feelings and help her with her conflicting feelings toward her father. While anticipating the termination of CPP, Rose also began individual therapy to address her own trauma history.

Conclusions

The damaging influence of exposure to domestic violence on the attachment system was hypothesized to be at the root of Camila's symptomatic behavior. When Camila came to treatment, she showed a range of symptoms emblematic of a young child whose developmental needs and expectations of being consistently cared for and protected by her primary caregivers were not met. Camila relied on maladaptive patterns of self-protection by becoming aggressive when frightened, a response that her mother misinterpreted as a characterological predisposition inherited from her violent father.

The different elements of CPP's conceptual frame allowed Camila to process, freed from unrealistic maternal expectations and the constraints of reality, the severe violence she had witnessed between her parents as well as the pain of her father's loss and her wish for a happier future with a loving new father. Age-appropriate developmental themes not directly associated with the violence she had witnessed became an increasingly central focus of treatment. Play served as a bridge to communicate a range of experiences to Camila's mother. Rose was initially unable to tolerate Camila's feelings and observed from a safe distance. During this treatment phase, the therapist supported Rose in understanding the ways in which Camila's play reflected her inner struggles as she remembered the incidents of violence. Once Rose became conscious of the damaging effects of trauma exposure on Camila's development, she was able to recognize that Camila's symptoms reflected the consequences of the trauma and became more responsive to Camila's needs. The shift in Rose's and Camila's affective experience increased the range and richness of developmentally appropriate themes and led to an overall improvement in the child–parent relationship. As treatment progressed, Camila and Rose had more intimate and reciprocal exchanges and were better able to negotiate and resolve the conflict inherent in daily living. Rose became more adept at helping Camila regulate her affect, especially when Camila became aroused by memories of the trauma or sad about her father's absence from her life. Rose, indeed, became an anchor for Camila's affective experience and an active participant in her journey to recovery.

EMPIRICAL SUPPORT FOR CHILD–PARENT PSYCHOTHERAPY

The improvement in Camila and in her relationship with her mother is not an isolated clinical phenomenon but has been demonstrated systematically in many children and mother–child dyads receiving CPP. CPP has been empirically tested and implemented as an ecologically valid and culturally relevant intervention. Before its adaptation to the treatment of traumatized children and their caregivers, CPP was found to be efficacious in improving the quality of the mother–child relationship and child developmental outcomes, specifically the socioemotional functioning in a sample of anxiously attached toddlers of low-income immigrant mothers (Lieberman, Weston, & Pawl, 1991) and of toddlers with depressed mothers (Cicchetti, Toth, & Rogosch, 1999). A more recent randomized controlled trial provided evidence of CPP's efficacy in the treatment of preschoolers exposed to domestic violence (Lieberman et al., 2005). Compared with their control group counterparts, CPP treatment participants showed a significant reduction in child behavioral problems and in maternal and child posttraumatic stress disorder symptomatology at 1-year follow-up (Lieberman et al., 2005); these improvements were sustained 6 months after the termination of treatment (Lieberman et al., 2006). Further evidence for the empirical validation of CPP has been obtained from randomized trials with maltreated toddlers (Cicchetti, Rogosch, & Toth, 2006; Toth, Rogosch, & Cicchetti, in press) and preschoolers (Toth, Maughan, Manly, Spagnola, & Cicchetti, 2002), in which it was found that CPP treatment participants showed significant improvement in rates of secure attachment and the quality of children's parental representations compared with control groups receiving treatment as usual.

It is worth noting that the body of research documenting CPP efficacy has been conducted with children in families with a high prevalence of low-income, high-adversity circumstances and a high proportion of minority groups. There is a broad range of research directions that remain to be pursued. For example, assessing the efficacy of different lengths of treatment for samples suffering from single trauma versus cumulative, chronic trauma can lead to a more judicious selection of cost-effective treatment tailored to the specific needs being addressed. The extension of CPP to new samples, including pregnant women and fathers who perpetrate domestic violence, is another important area that awaits further investigation.

SUMMARY AND DISCUSSION

Witnessing domestic violence is a major threat to young children's overall health, often derailing them from normal developmental pathways. Because play is a self-regulatory mechanism that organizes children's inner self-experience, it serves as a natural conduit for children to manifest their inner struggles as they attempt to bring meaning to their experience of witnessing parental violence. CPP is a relationship-based therapeutic modality that incorporates play as a viable medium for helping young children and their caregivers process traumatic events and recover from their effects. The clinical case presented in this chapter elucidated the implementation of CPP with a mother–child dyad experiencing the sequelae of domestic violence exposure. We described ways in which the parent is reestablished as the anchoring system for the child's emotional experience, which in turn restores and improves the child–parent relationship.

REFERENCES

Ainsworth, M. D. (1969). Object relations, dependency, and attachment: A theoretical review of the infant–mother relationship. *Child Development, 40,* 969–1025.

Benedict, H. E. (2006). Object relations play therapy: Applications to attachment problems and relational trauma. In C. E. Schaefer & H. G. Kaduson (Eds.), *Con-*

temporary play therapy: Theory, research, and practice (pp. 3–27). New York: Guilford Press.

Bettelheim, B. (1987). *A good enough parent: A book on child-rearing*. New York: Random House.

Bowlby, J. (1982). *Attachment and loss: Vol. 1. Attachment* (2nd ed.). New York: Basic Books. (Original work published 1969)

Bromfield, R. N. (2003). Psychoanalytic play therapy. In C. E. Schaefer (Ed.), *Foundations of play therapy* (pp. 1–13). Hoboken, NJ: Wiley.

Carlson, B. E. (2000). Children exposed to intimate partner violence: Research findings and implications for intervention. *Trauma, Violence, and Abuse, 1*, 321–342.

Cicchetti, D., Rogosch, F. A., & Toth, S. L. (2006). Fostering secure attachment in infants in maltreatment families through preventive interventions. *Development and Psychopathology, 18*, 623–649.

Cicchetti, D., Toth, S. L., & Rogosch, F. A. (1999). The efficacy of toddler–parent psychotherapy to increase attachment security in offspring of depressed mothers. *Attachment and Human Development, 1*, 34–36.

Cohen, J. A., Perel, J. M., DeBellis, M. D., Friedman, M. J., & Putnam, F. W. (2002). Treating traumatized children: Clinical implications of the psychobiology of PTSD. *Trauma, Violence, and Abuse 3*, 91–108.

Edleson, J. L. (1999). The overlap between child maltreatment and woman battering. *Violence Against Women, 5*, 134–154.

Erikson, E. H. (1950). *Childhood and society*. New York: Norton.

Esman, A. (1983). Psychoanalytic play therapy. In C. Schaefer & K. O'Connor (Eds.), *Handbook of play therapy* (pp. 11–20). New York: Wiley/Interscience.

Fantuzzo, J. W., Boruch, R., Beriama, A., Atkins, M., & Marcus, S. (1997). Domestic violence and children: Prevalence and risk in five major U.S. cities. *Journal of the American Academy of Child & Adolescent Psychiatry, 36*, 116–122.

Fantuzzo, J. W., & Mohr, W. K. (1999). Prevalence and effects of child exposure to domestic violence. *Future of Children, 9*, 21–32.

Fraiberg, S. H., Adelson, E., & Shapiro, V. (1975). Ghosts in the nursery: A psychoanalytic approach to the problems of impaired infant-mother relationships. *Journal of the American Academy of Child Psychiatry and Adolescent Psychiatry, 14*, 387–422.

Freud, A. (1966). The ego and the mechanisms of defense. *The writings of Anna Freud* (Vol. 2). New York: International Universities Press. (Original work published 1936)

Freud, S. (1959). Inhibitions, symptoms and anxiety. In J. Strachey (Ed. & Trans.), *The standard edition of the complete psychological works of Sigmund Freud* (Vol. 20, pp. 87–156). London: Hogarth Press. (Original work published 1926)

Kitzmann, K., Gaylord, N., Holt, A., & Kenny, E. (2003). Child witnesses to domestic violence: A meta-analytic review. *Journal of Consulting and Clinical Psychology, 71*, 339–352.

Klein, M. (1932). *The psychoanalysis of children*. London: Hogarth Press.

Lieberman, A. F. (2004). Traumatic stress and quality of attachment: Reality and internalization in disorders of infant mental health. *Infant Mental Health Journal, 25*, 336–351.

Lieberman, A. F., & Amaya-Jackson, L. (2005). Reciprocal influences of attachment and trauma: Using a dual lens in the assessment and treatment of infants, toddlers, and preschoolers. In L. J. Berlin, Y. Ziv, L. Amaya-Jackson, & M. T. Greenberg (Eds.), *Enhancing early attachments: Theory, intervention, and policy* (pp. 100–124). New York: Guilford Press.

Lieberman, A. F., Ghosh Ippen, C., & Van Horn, P. (2006). Child–parent psychotherapy: 6-month follow-up of a randomized control trial. *Journal of the American Academy of Child & Adolescent Psychiatry, 45*, 913–918.

Lieberman, A. F., & Van Horn, P. (2005). *"Don't hit my mommy!": A manual of child–parent psychotherapy for young witnesses of family violence*. Washington, DC: Zero to Three Press.

Lieberman, A. F., & Van Horn, P. (2008). *Psychotherapy with infants and young children: Repairing the effect of stress and trauma on early attachment*. New York: Guilford Press.

Lieberman, A. F., Van Horn, P., & Ghosh Ippen, C. (2005). Toward evidence-based treatment: Child–parent psychotherapy with preschoolers exposed to marital violence. *Journal of the American Academy of Child & Adolescent Psychiatry, 44*, 1241–1248.

Lieberman, A. F., Weston, D. R., & Pawl, J. H. (1991). Preventive intervention and outcome with anxiously attached dyads. *Child Development, 62*, 199–209.

Main, M., & Hesse, E. (1990). Parents' unresolved traumatic experiences are related to infant disorganized attachment status: Is frightened and/or frightening parental behavior the linking mechanism? In M. T. Greenberg, D. Cicchetti, & E. M. Cummings (Eds.), *Attachment in the preschool years: Theory, research, and intervention* (pp. 161–182). Chicago: University of Chicago Press.

Margolin, G., & Gordis, E. B. (2000). The effects of family and community violence on children. *Annual Review of Psychology, 51*, 445–479.

Margolin, G., & Gordis, E. B. (2003). Co-occurrence between marital aggression and parents' child abuse potential: The impact of cumulative stress. *Violence and Victims, 18*, 243–258.

Marmar, C. R., Foy, D., Kagan, B., & Pynoos, R. S. (1993). An integrated approach for treating post-traumatic stress. In J. M. Oldham, M. B. Riba, & A. Tasman (Eds.), *American Psychiatric Association review of psychiatry* (Vol. 12, pp. 239–272). Washington, DC: American Psychiatric Publishing.

Osofsky, J. D. (1999). The impact of violence on children. *Future of Children, 9,* 33–49.

Osofsky, J. D. (2003). Prevalence of children's exposure to domestic violence and child maltreatment: Implications for prevention and intervention. *Clinical Child and Family Psychology Review, 6,* 161–170.

Pynoos, R. S. (1990). Posttraumatic stress disorder in children and adolescents. In B. D. Garfinkel, G. A. Carlson, & E. B. Weller (Eds.), *Psychiatric disorders in children and adolescents* (pp. 48–63). Philadelphia: Saunders.

Pynoos, R. S., Steinberg, A. M., Ornitz, E. M., & Goenjian, A. K. (1997). Issues in the developmental neurobiology of traumatic stress. In R. Yehuda & A. C. McFarlane (Eds.), *Annals of the New York Academy of Sciences: Vol. 821. Psychobiology of posttraumatic stress disorder* (pp. 176–193). New York: New York Academy of Sciences.

Pynoos, R. S., Steinberg, A. M., & Piacentini, J. C. (1999). A developmental psychopathology model of childhood traumatic stress and intersection with anxiety disorders. *Biological Psychiatry, 46,* 1542–1554.

Rossman, B. B. R. (2001). Longer term effects of children's exposure to domestic violence. In S. A. Graham-Bermann & J. L. Edleson (Eds.), *Domestic violence in the lives of children: The future of research, intervention, and social policy* (pp. 35–66). Washington, DC: American Psychological Association.

Schaefer, C., & O'Connor, K. (Eds.). (1983). *Handbook of play therapy.* New York: Wiley.

Scheeringa, M. S., & Zeanah, C. H. (1995). Symptom expression and trauma variables in children under 48 months of age. *Infant Mental Health Journal, 16,* 259–270.

Slade, A. (1994). Making meaning and making believe: Their role in the clinical process. In A. Slade & D. Wolf (Eds.), *Children at play: Clinical and developmental approaches to meaning and representation* (pp. 81–107). New York: Oxford University Press.

Slade, A., & Wolf, D. (Eds.). (1994). *Children at play: Clinical and developmental approaches to meaning and representation.* New York: Oxford University Press.

Terr, L. (1983). Chowchilla revisited: The effects of psychic trauma four years after a school-bus kidnapping. *American Journal of Psychiatry, 140,* 1543–1550.

Terr, L. (1991). Childhood traumas: An outline and overview. *American Journal of Psychiatry, 148*(1), 10–20.

Toth, S. L., Maughan, A., Manly, J. T., Spagnola, M., & Cicchetti, D. (2002). The relative efficacy of two interventions in altering maltreated preschool children's representation models: Implications for attachment theory. *Development and Psychopathology, 14,* 877–908.

Toth, S. L., Rogosch, F. A., & Cicchetti, D. (in press). Toddler–parent psychotherapy reorganizes attachment in young offspring of mothers with major depressive disorder. *Journal of Consulting and Clinical Psychology.*

U.S. Department of Health and Human Services, Administration on Children, Youth and Families. (2008). *Child maltreatment 2006.* Washington, DC: U.S. Government Printing Office.

van der Kolk, B. A. (2003). The neurobiology of childhood trauma and abuse. *Child and Adolescent Clinics of North America, 12,* 293–317.

Van Horn, P., & Lieberman, A. F. (2006). Play in child–parent psychotherapy with traumatized preschoolers. In J. L. Luby (Ed.), *Handbook of preschool mental health: Development, disorders, and treatment* (pp. 372–387). New York: Guilford Press.

Wechsler, D. (2002). *WPPSI-III administration and scoring manual.* San Antonio, TX: Psychological Corporation.

Wolak, J., & Finkelhor, D. (1998). Children exposed to partner violence. In J. L. Jasinski & L. M. Williams (Eds.), *Partner violence: A comprehensive review of 20 years of research* (pp. 73–112). Thousand Oaks, CA: Sage.

Zero to Three/National Center for Clinical Infant Programs. (2005). *Diagnostic classification of mental health and developmental disorders of infancy and early childhood* (Rev. ed.). Washington, DC: Author.

8

COGNITIVE–BEHAVIORAL PLAY THERAPY FOR PRESCHOOLERS: INTEGRATING PLAY AND COGNITIVE–BEHAVIORAL INTERVENTIONS

SUSAN M. KNELL AND MEENA DASARI

Cognitive–behavioral play therapy (CBPT) is a developmentally sensitive adaptation of cognitive therapy (Beck, 1964, 1976) and behavioral techniques (Bandura, 1977; Wolpe, 1982) designed specifically for young children (ages 3–8 years). It is based on the integration of theories related to cognitive therapy, behavioral modification, emotional development, and psychopathology as well as on interventions derived from these theories. Behind cognitive therapy (CT) is the idea that how people view the world in large measure determines how they behave and feel and how they understand life situations. According to Beck (1967, 1972, 1976), a person's emotional experiences are determined by cognitions that have developed in part from earlier life experiences. Cognitive–behavioral therapy (CBT) builds on CT principles and includes additional techniques focusing on changing behavior through the use of reinforcement, role playing, and modeling. CBT was developed as a structured, focused approach to help individuals make changes in their behavior by changing the thoughts and perceptions underlying it. Over the past 50 years, CT and CBT have been applied to increasingly broader populations, with more developmentally appropriate adaptations of CT for use with younger populations (Emery, Bedrosian, & Garber, 1983; Kendall & Braswell,1985).

CBPT was introduced into the psychotherapy literature in the 1990s and was developed by incorporating cognitive and behavioral interventions within a play therapy paradigm. Through the use of play, therapy can be communicated indirectly (Knell, 1993a, 1993b, 1994, 1998, 1999, 2000, 2009; Knell & Dasari, 2006, 2009). Before the development of CBPT, most play therapy techniques were based on either psychodynamic or client-centered theories. With both of these earlier theoretical approaches, play therapy was unstructured and guided by the child. CBPT provided a novel theoretical approach to child psychotherapy in that the most significant differences between CBPT and other play therapies are its structure, psychoeducational components, and goal-directed and collaborative approaches (i.e., guided by both child and therapist). For example, toys can be used to model cognitive strategies such as countering maladaptive beliefs and making positive self-statements. In fact, most of CBPT is delivered in a developmentally sensitive way by modeling interventions through play materials.

Although some believed that CT could not be adapted for very young children, previous research has demonstrated effective use of CBPT. Numerous descriptions of the theory and applications of CBPT have been published in the literature (Knell, 1993a, 1993b, 1994, 1997, 1999, 2000, 2003; Knell & Beck, 2000; Knell & Dasari, 2006; Knell & Moore, 1990; Knell & Ruma, 1996, 2003). These writings include case examples describing the successful use of CBPT with children with selective mutism (Knell, 1993b), separation anxiety (Knell, 1999), anxiety disorders (Knell, 2000; Knell & Dasari, 2006), phobias (Knell, 1993a; Knell & Dasari, 2009), and histories of sexual abuse (Knell & Ruma, 1996, 2003; Ruma, 1993). CBPT has also been used with children who have sleep problems (Knell, 2000) or encopresis (Knell, 1993a; Knell & Moore, 1990), who are acting out (Knell, 2000), and who are experiencing life events or traumas such as parental divorce (Knell, 1993a; Knell & Dasari, in press). A number of writings include more specific and detailed descriptions of the application of CBPT, including transcribed therapy sessions (Knell, 1993b) and commentary about specific clinical decision making (Knell, 1993b, 1997).

In this chapter, we address the developmental issues that arise with CBPT for young children and outline the treatment approach, guided by both theory and research. We then use a discussion of CBPT for toileting issues to illustrate the implementation of techniques for a 5-year-old girl who refused to use the toilet.

DEVELOPMENTAL ISSUES

Developmental concerns are at the forefront of issues regarding the appropriateness of CBT with young children. In the preoperational stage, a child's egocentrism, concrete thought processes, and seemingly irrational thinking would seem to preclude the kind of cognitive abilities necessary to participate in CT. Cognitive distortions in very young children may be developmentally appropriate, yet maladaptive. In most cases, children incorporate life experience into their thinking and, with the help of everyday parent–child discourse, are able to integrate this learning into more adaptive thought ("My dad was very sick. He died because he was sick and couldn't get better"). Given the nature of thought at this age, maladaptive thoughts may be developmentally appropriate, although problematic.

In some cases, no meaning is attached to a specific event; however, there may be an absence of adaptive beliefs that might facilitate coping. In these instances, the child might benefit from learning more functional, adaptive self-statements to facilitate coping. These more positive self-statements are not meant to replace maladaptive thoughts but to boost more adaptive thinking and behavior. For example, a young child may have difficulty coping with parental divorce. Maladaptive beliefs (e.g., "Dad is divorcing us, not Mom") may not be present or may not be expressed verbally. A child who learns more adaptive, positive coping statements such as "Mom and Dad don't get along, but they both still love me" may learn a more realistic, positive outlook on the family situation. Such statements can replace maladaptive beliefs (either spoken or felt, but not verbalized) or be a new cognition replacing either neutral or nonexistent beliefs.

ADAPTING COGNITIVE THERAPY FOR USE WITH CHILDREN

CBT interventions often rely on fairly sophisticated cognitive abilities, such as abstract thinking and hypothesis testing, as well as collaborative empiricism. Because most young children have difficulty distinguishing between illogical, irrational thoughts and more logical, rational ones, such complex, verbally based interventions are likely to be ineffective. However, there is ample evidence to suggest that young children's ability to understand complex problems may be enhanced by specific techniques. Clinicians and researchers alike have noted that children's ability to understand complex problems can be improved by specific approaches, such as using more concrete examples, fewer open-ended questions, and visual cues (e.g., Bierman, 1983). Rather than assuming that children cannot benefit from CT, it makes sense to consider ways to make interventions more developmentally appropriate and accessible to this young population.

Knell (1993a, 1993b, 1994, 1997, 1998) proposed that CT could be modified for use with young children if presented in a way that was highly accessible to children. In finding more developmentally appropriate methods of intervention, the therapist should capitalize on the child's strengths rather than his or her weaknesses. More experiential interventions that incorporate play and deemphasize cognitive and verbal skills are indicated. Drawing on research (Bandura, 1969; Meichenbaum, 1971) suggesting that coping models are more effective than mastery models in facilitating behavior change, play materials can be used to present coping models to children. For example, models such as puppets, stuffed animals, books, and other toys can be used to model cognitive strategies. The coping model (e.g., a puppet) can make mistakes and model learning from these mistakes so that the child is then observing the model in its efforts to learn more appropriate behaviors. With a coping model approach to CT, the model (e.g., a puppet) can verbalize problem-solving skills or solutions to problems that parallel the child's own difficulties with the hope that the child will internalize the coping statements. For instance, when working with a child who has a dog phobia, a puppet might say aloud, "I am scared, but I know the dog won't hurt me" while approaching a toy dog.

One important area for intervention is encouraging and facilitating language to describe experiences and emotions. Despite dramatic growth in vocabulary during the early preschool years, the child's descriptive vocabulary for emotions is still often quite limited. In addition to words to describe feelings, young children often benefit from help in matching their behaviors and feelings and learning to express feelings in more adaptive, language-based ways. For example, rather than expressing frustration and anger through aggression, a child can be taught to understand that he or she is angry and can express that feeling in words rather than behavior. In doing so, the child may benefit from a sense of control over emotions. Also, the child is likely to receive support and certainly more positive feedback from the adults around him or her.

For children, play is a developmentally appropriate and natural means of communication. Children can use toys and play as their words—the tool through which they communicate and articulate feelings and emotions. The therapist's ability to be flexible, reduce focus on verbalizations, and increase use of experiential approaches can contribute to the successful adaptation of CT with young children (Knell & Dasari, 2006; Knell & Ruma, 1996, 2003). Adaptations to younger populations have changed the methods through which CT is delivered, but not the theoretical underpinnings of the approach. Finding ways to deliver CT without an emphasis on language that might be too complex for a young child represents one of the challenges faced in the development of CBPT.

CBPT places a strong emphasis on the child's involvement in treatment and on a framework for the child's participation by addressing issues of control, mastery, and responsibility for one's own behavior change. CBPT's cognitive components may help children become active participants in change and gain mastery over problems. For example, by guiding children in identifying and modifying potentially maladaptive beliefs, they may experience a sense of personal understanding and empowerment. Integrating cognitive and behavioral interventions may offer effects of the combined properties of all approaches, which might not otherwise be available (Knell, 1993a). In addition, the use of play therapy as a medium is likely to be highly engaging and fun for children.

COGNITIVE–BEHAVIORAL PLAY INTERVENTION PROCEDURES

CBPT procedures are developed with respect to each child's presenting diagnosis. The therapist implements the procedures in treatment stages, so that the child typically is guided through the four stages that have been described as *introductory–orientation, assessment, middle,* and *termination*.

Introductory–Orientation Stage

The child often is introduced to the notion of play therapy by the parents after they have met with the CBPT therapist. During that initial interview, one of the therapist's tasks is to help parents understand how best to prepare the child for his or her first session. The therapist should spend some time discussing the most developmentally appropriate explanation for the child. Books such as *A Child's First Book About Play Therapy* (Nemiroff & Annunziato, 1990) can be recommended to the parent as a helpful adjunct to their discussion with the child.

It is important to orient and to prepare both the child and the parents for CBPT. Typically, the parents and therapist will meet together, without the child present, so that the therapist can complete a clinical interview to gather history and background information. Gathering data from parent rating scales may be involved, especially as a way to compare the child's feelings and behaviors with normative data. The initial parent session usually involves (a) an agreement on presenting problem or diagnosis (i.e., depression, eating problems) and treatment goals, (b) psychoeducation, and (c) a plan for preparing the child for therapy. Psychoeducation related to the child's presenting problems, or related to either child therapy or parent involvement, is usually included. During this initial session, the therapist usually helps the parents formulate the best way to explain therapy to the child. By choosing their words carefully, the parents can be honest, straightforward, noncritical, nonthreatening, and developmentally appropriate. Parents should be guided to normalize the experience of seeing a therapist and to highlight both child and therapist strengths. For example, talking with the child about his or her ability to talk with adults might help the child feel more comfortable with the therapist, as would explaining how nice the therapist is or what fun toys the therapist has. Here is a sample statement that the therapist can use to help coach the parents:

> We are concerned about how you are feeling. We know that you are sad about a lot of things. We went to talk to someone about it. She is a "feelings" doctor. She talks and plays with kids who have lots of different feelings. We met her, and she is very nice and has a fun room where you will talk and play. Next time we go, you will go with us and have a turn talking and playing with her.

Clearly, the most important aspect of preparation is gearing the parents' comments to their specific child rather than providing a blanket, one-size-fits-all explanation.

Establishing goals is an important part of CBPT. The CBPT therapist works with the child and family to set goals and help the child work toward these goals. Movement toward the goal is assessed on an ongoing basis. Whereas goals and movement toward goals are counter to the basic philosophy of more traditional play therapies, such as client-centered play therapy (see Axline, 1947; Landreth, 2002), they are an integral part of CBPT. The CBPT therapist's selection of a direction may still be child led, based on the child's initiative or on knowledge of the child's situation as understood from the parent interview or other source. However, in CBPT the therapist may introduce themes and provide direction on the basis of knowledge obtained from a parent or teacher and not necessarily directly from the child. For example, the CBPT therapist may purposefully and systematically have a puppet behave in a certain way and verbalize issues that the child reportedly exhibits. The puppet can also articulate goals in a way that is accessible and rewarding to the child (e.g., "Wow, I can't wait until I feel brave enough to walk into school alone!")

Assessment Stage

After preparation for CBPT, the assessment begins. Ultimately, the therapist is trying to better understand the context of the presenting problems, get clarity about diagnostic issues, and develop a treatment plan. Often assessments are most thorough if they use a combination of assessment methods to estimate the child's developmental level of cognitive, emotional, social, and problem-solving skills. These assessments include any combination of the following: clinical interview or parent report, child self-report, therapist behavioral observations, and school evaluations. In general, the purpose of the assessment is to determine whether the child's skills are similar to those of same-age peers (Knell & Dasari, 2006). The therapist can supplement this information with behavioral observations of the child's ability to express and regulate emotions in a therapeutic setting. Understanding children's pretend play ability is important in determining whether CPBT is an appropriate intervention for a child. Research has shown that play therapy is more effective for children who already have good pretend play skills (Russ, 2004). CBPT can be useful even with children with developmental delays because the intervention can be adapted to individual needs. Treatment can be flexible and individualized and rely on more play and fewer verbalization.

More structured play assessments may be used in addition to other assessment methods. A number of such assessment measures, described in Gitlin-Weiner, Sandgrund, and Schaefer (2000), include scales for assessing therapeutic play, tapping both affective and thematic characteristics of play. Projective techniques, with their long history in the assessment literature, might not seem compatible with more cognitive–behavioral approaches. A puppet sentence completion task is one developmentally sensitive projective assessment measure appropriate for use in CBPT assessment with young children (Knell, 1992, 1993a, Knell & Beck, 2000).

Middle Stage

During the middle stage of CBPT, the therapist has developed a treatment plan, and the therapy begins to focus on increasing the child's self-control and sense of accomplishment and learning more adaptive responses to deal with specific situations. Depending on the presenting problem or problems, the therapist will have a wide array of cognitive and behavioral interventions from which to chose. These are considered carefully, with as much specificity as possible between the intervention and the child's specific problems or concerns. Much of the actual therapy and the use of cognitive–behavioral interventions takes place during this middle stage. Generalization and relapse prevention are incorporated into the middle stages of therapy so that the child can learn to use new skills across a broad range of settings and begin to develop skills that will enhance the chances of setbacks after therapy is completed.

Structured Versus Unstructured Play

The process of change is considered to take place in both the structured and the unstructured components of the sessions (Knell, 1993a, 1999). For CBPT to be effective, it should provide structured, goal-directed activities as well as unstructured time, during which the child brings spontaneous material to the session. The balance of spontaneously generated and more structured activities is a delicate one in CBPT. Through unstructured play, the therapist can gain a sense of the child's thoughts and perceptions by observing the child's spontaneous behavior and verbalizations. Unstructured, spontaneously generated information is critical to the treatment; without it, the therapist would lose a rich source of clinical information. However, structured, goal-directed activities are important for working on problem solving and teaching more adaptive behaviors. Thus, when therapy is completely unstructured and nondirective, it is not possible to provide the psychoeducational aspects of therapy.

It is usually helpful to structure the therapy sessions by using several puppets or toys with a variety of problems. Two or three puppets are chosen. The therapist names them (or if the child is willing, the child helps the therapist give them names) . Finally, the therapist identifies the puppets' problems. At least one of the puppets should have a problem that closely matches the child's problem (e.g., "This puppet gets angry when his dad drops him off at mom's house. Sometimes, he hits and kicks, because he doesn't want his dad to leave").

Methods

Most cognitive–behavioral interventions with children of all ages include some form of modeling. This is particularly true of CBPT, in which modeling is a critical component of the play. In CBPT, modeling is used to demonstrate adaptive coping skills to the child, with a toy, book, or puppet demonstrating the behavior that the therapist wants the child to learn.

Another method of delivering CBPT is through role playing, in which the child practices skills with the therapist. This method is often more effective with school-age children, although role playing can in itself be delivered through modeling. For example, the models can role-play, and the child can observe and learn from watching the models.

Interventions

CBPT interventions can be categorized as either behavioral or cognitive. Although behavioral approaches have often been implemented via a significant adult, they can be used directly with the child in therapy. In either case, the therapist tries to identify factors that reinforce and maintain problematic behaviors so that they can be altered. Behavioral methods usually involve an alteration in activity, whereas cognitive methods deal with changes in thinking. Because maladaptive thoughts lead to maladaptive behavior, changes in thinking should produce changes in behavior. Through cognitive interventions, children learn to identify maladaptive thoughts, replace them with more adaptive ones, and ultimately change maladaptive behaviors. Because of the verbal nature of cognitive interventions, CBPT relies on modeling, and more developmental adaptations, to deliver these interventions in more child-friendly ways. In general, research has suggested that the combination of cognitive and behavioral interventions are effective in helping children cope with difficult events and emotions (for reviews, see Compton et al., 2004; Velting,

Setzer, & Albano, 2004). For a more comprehensive discussion of how behavioral and cognitive techniques can be integrated into play therapy, see Knell & Dasari (2009).

CBPT is developed by integrating empirically supported behavioral and cognitive techniques into play therapy. These techniques are adapted to the developmental level of the child's cognitive, emotional, and social skills. There is no specific formula for deciding on which interventions to use in CBPT, beyond integrating evidence-based practice into the treatment. Any of a vast number of empirically supported techniques from the CBT literature can be incorporated into the play and used to help children build skills.

Play Materials

Numerous authors have written extensively about the use of materials in play therapy. Axline (1947) listed guidelines for play materials, a list that is still commonly quoted and used. In the CBPT literature, play materials are a critical component of therapy, with both child and therapist choosing appropriate materials either collaboratively or independently. The playroom is well stocked with a wide array of toys and play materials, and at times an individual child's presenting problems may require an object not typically found in the playroom. Typically found objects are art supplies, puppets, dolls, dollhouses, books, and various toys. There are times when a specific toy may be needed to treat a particular child. At times, play materials that are available can be adapted to meet these specific needs. At other times, a specific toy may need to be brought in to the playroom because the child cannot pretend or be flexible in the use of already existing toys. An example of this would be a child who has toileting issues. The child might be able to use a plastic bucket as a pretend toilet, or even a toy toilet that comes with the furniture in a dollhouse. However, it might be necessary to bring in an actual child's potty seat or to use a real toilet in the bathroom.

Play Therapy Room Setup

A number of authors have written extensively about setting up the play therapy room (Giorano, Landreth, & Jones, 2005; Landreth, 2002; O'Connor, 1991). For CBPT, toys are (a) visible and easily accessible to the child and (b) kept in the same place so that the child knows where they are from one session to the next. If the child is working on a project or has papers (e.g., pictures, individual, self-created book), it is important that the therapist and the child have a safe, consistent place in which to keep these materials. A locked drawer or other place is recommended so that the child knows that his or her confidentiality is being respected.

Termination Stage

During the termination stage, which is the fourth stage, the child and family are prepared for the end of therapy. Specific procedures relating to generalization and response prevention are implemented and usually involve role plays in sessions and practice tasks outside of sessions. In addition, as the treatment nears an end, the child deals with the reality of termination as well as with feelings about ending treatment.

Braswell and Kendall (1988) noted that children often made gains in CBT but failed to generalize and maintain these gains after the completion of therapy. More recently, attention to the need for the therapist to help the child generalize what is learned in therapy to other settings such as home and school has grown. Because adults often play important roles in a child's life, their attitudes and behavior toward the child can influence such generalization of adaptive skills learned in therapy. For example, if parents, teachers, day care providers, and others support and reinforce the child's new adaptive skills, these skills are more likely to be used in other settings. Thus, therapy should be designed to promote and facilitate generalization rather than assuming it will occur naturally.

The therapist can promote generalization directly through several methods. One is by creating play scenarios with settings and people similar to those in the child's life. Also, the significant adults in the child's life should be involved in treatment (e.g., trained to use appropriate reinforcement of adaptive behaviors and extinction of maladaptive ones) and be taught ways to help the child practice adaptive skills at home (e.g., not interrupting another child during a play date). Cognitive–behavioral interventions that promote self-control of behavior will help the child generalize, so that his or her behavior is not completely driven by others.

Relapse prevention is another important component of CBT and involves both consolidating cognitive and behavioral techniques and decreasing reliance on the therapist (Velting et al., 2004). Therapists should work to highlight the key techniques that were effective in allowing the child to overcome difficulties. In CBPT, this can be done by making a book of "lessons learned." The therapist can encourage both the parents and the child to review the book if and when the problem resurfaces.

Although setbacks are part of learning any new skill, children and parents should be helped to understand how they can cope when such setbacks occur. Treatment should take the possibility of setbacks into account and address this issue directly, thereby preparing both the child and the parents for what to expect and what to do in certain situations that might arise. High-risk situations are identified as things that might present a threat to the child's sense of control and ability to manage.

Ideally, it is recommended that therapy termination be a gradual process so that preparation for completion of therapy takes place over several sessions. The child should be prepared for the concrete reality of termination (e.g., "You will only be coming in for two more sessions and then we will be saying goodbye") and for the feelings that may accompany the end of treatment. It is common for children to have conflicting feelings about the end of treatment. The therapist may address such feelings directly (e.g., "It seems like you may be a little sad that we won't be meeting anymore") or indirectly (e.g., "Some kids tell me that they feel sad when they stop coming to therapy"). Some children may benefit from hearing the therapist model an appropriate emotion related to the end of therapy (e.g., "I will miss seeing you, but I will feel happy knowing that you are doing so well"). The CBPT therapist can confirm for the child that he or she is important and that it is okay to have feelings about termination (e.g., "I will miss you too"; "The puppets will miss you, but we're all happy to know you are doing so well").

Younger children often benefit from some type of concrete representation of the end of treatment (e.g., a construction-paper chain with each link representing a therapy session until the last one). Older children may understand a calendar marked with the final therapy sessions. These concrete reminders may also provide visual aids that help the child talk about affect related to the end of therapy. Some children are also helped by a concrete transitional object, such as the therapist's business card (with name and phone number) or a picture the child draws for the therapist that he or she sees is being kept in a special place in the therapist's office.

Often the final sessions are tapered, so that the therapist may meet with the child biweekly or monthly for a period of time. These intermittent appointments may serve to communicate to the child that she or he can manage without the therapist. This is often supplemented with positive reinforcement from the therapist regarding how well the child is doing between sessions. Sometimes, these appointments are scheduled over a period of time as part of the phasing out. Other times, they are intermittently scheduled with a particular event in mind (e.g., the beginning of the school year, a family move, parent remarriage). For example, a child who is doing well but who has some concerns about starting at a new school may be seen intermittently until after she or he has begun in the new setting.

It is important for the child to understand the end of therapy as a positive event rather than as a negative one. The therapist should identify and praise the child's accomplishments in therapy (e.g., working hard, talking about difficult feelings). If the child feels that bad behavior or problems will prompt a return to therapy, the child may act out to see the therapist again. In addition, the therapist should normalize the experience of saying goodbye to significant relationships by talking about examples in the child's life (e.g., friends at the end of camp, teachers at the end of the school year). Reassurances and suggestions for keeping in touch can be helpful. Children often like to hear that the parents will keep in touch with the therapist or that the child can send the therapist a picture or card. Describing an open-door policy—particularly that it is acceptable to return to see the therapist even if things are good—may help the child understand that the therapist still cares, even if the child is not coming in regularly.

Finally, a termination party or celebration, scheduled for the final session, provides a concrete bridge between therapy and termination. It can be useful to involve the child in specific plans for the celebration. The main purpose of this event is to highlight the positive gains made in therapy, emphasizing the child's self-control and mastery of self-help skills. It is appropriate to provide the child with a small, symbolic token of these gains (e.g., a certificate or a small puppet like one that helped the child most in treatment.)

EMPIRICAL SUPPORT

CBPT is a developmentally based, integrated model of psychotherapy for young children that is solidly grounded in data. (Chambless, 1993; Chambless et al., 1996). It incorporates empirically supported techniques such as modeling. Research has suggested that learning through modeling is an effective way to acquire, strengthen, or weaken behaviors and thus is an efficient and effective way to acquire behaviors and skills (Bandura, 1977). Other well-documented interventions, such as systematic desensitization, are used in CBPT (Wolpe, 1982).

More specifically, CBT techniques have been shown to be effective for children, adolescents, and adults with a variety of mental health disorders. These include but are not limited to depression, anxiety, obsessive–compulsive disorder, posttraumatic stress disorder, eating issues, and relationship problems (Monrow, 2005). However, the efficacy of adaptations of CT for young children (i.e., ages 3–8) is inconclusive and has not yet been demonstrated. In a review of current research, Grave and Blissett (2004) concluded their research-based summary by stating that "young children can demonstrate the cognitive capacity to benefit from creatively delivered forms of CBT" (p. 417). The authors found that children younger than age 11 can benefit from current CBT adapted from the adult literature, but their symptoms are less likely to improve after CBT than those of children older than age 11. Grave and Blisset's work strongly suggests that current CBT techniques—as used with older children—need to be modified to be more effective with younger children. This finding is consistent with the focus of CBPT.

Only recently has the question of CBPT's efficacy been subjected to empirical study. Pearson (2007) found that teachers reported significantly higher hope, higher social competence, and fewer anxiety–withdrawal symptoms for preschoolers in a cognitive–behavioral play intervention group than for those in a matched play control group. The children in the cognitive–behavioral play intervention group were seen individually for three sessions incorporating cognitive–behavioral interventions, although this was not technically CBPT. However, this study was the first to empirically support CBPT interventions. Although no clinical trials exist, there are many case studies with outcome measures that support CBPT's effectiveness (e.g., Knell, 1993a, 1999; Knell & Dasari, 2009). More empirical work will be needed on the road to establishing CBPT's efficacy.

CBPT is an approach that allows the therapist to combine empirically supported cognitive–behavioral techniques within a play paradigm. CBPT is applicable to a broad range of behavioral problems. A comprehensive overview of appropriate populations for CBPT is beyond the scope of this chapter; however, one group of children who might benefit from CBPT are those with toileting issues. Children with toileting issues often have specific issues with control, as well as with mastery of a significant developmental task. CBPT may provide them with a sense of active participation in their treatment. Here we present a brief description of the use of CBPT with toileting issues, followed by a case example that highlights this approach with a child who refused to use the toilet in a developmentally appropriate way.

COGNITIVE–BEHAVIORAL PLAY THERAPY WITH TOILETING ISSUES

Inappropriate, inadequate, or aversive toileting experiences are often considered to explain toileting problems and encopresis in young children who do not present with any concomitant psychopathology. Although many toileting problems resolve in time, more serious issues can result in *encopresis,* which refers to the repeated defecation in developmentally inappropriate places (e.g., clothing, floor) that is either involuntary or intentional. Prevalence studies of encopresis are rare and often outdated. A recent study in the Netherlands ($N = 13,111$) found a 4.1% incidence rate of encopresis in 5- to 6-year-old children (van der Wal, Benninga, & Hirasing, 2005). More common than the diagnosis of encopresis is the prevalence of intense fears associated with toileting. Although typical in toddlers (ages 18 months–3 years), these fears can continue in older preschool-age children. For example, fears of falling in or being flushed down the toilet or having painful eliminations associated with sitting on the toilet can carry over into children who, by chronological age, should be toilet trained. A toilet phobia may exist when such fears persist and interfere with the child's ability to eliminate in the toilet.

In some instances, inappropriate or coercive toilet training methods may be the basis of the child's fears. The child may have been punished or ridiculed for accidents when a resistance or phobia around the toilet develops. Often, children have had a painful or frightening bowel movement related to constipation that they then associate with any subsequent toilet use. It is difficult for such children to understand that their previous experience may not be repeated each time they eliminate in the toilet. A retrospective study (Fishman, Rappaport, Cousineau, & Nurko, 2002) found that constipation accounted for 35% of cases of encopresis. In fact, further findings have suggested that fear of the toilet is more common in *primary encopresis* (present from birth) than in *secondary encopresis* (occurring after a period of fecal continence). Research has suggested that such fears associated with the toilet may play a significant role in children who do not develop age-appropriate toilet use.

Literature on the treatment of encopresis is similarly sparse. McGrath, Mellon, and Murphy (2000) reviewed empirical research examining behavioral and medical treatments for constipation and fecal incontinence. No well-established interventions emerged from this study; however, behavioral interventions were considered probably efficacious.

Issues of control and self-management are often evident in children with elimination problems. Because children are often entering a more negative stage (e.g., "the terrible 2s") when parents begin toilet training, power struggles around appropriate toilet use can ensue. Toileting also allows the child an opportunity to gain mastery over a significant developmental task. For children presenting with toileting issues, CBPT may provide an opportunity for control and mastery, particularly in helping the child want to change. The child's involvement in treatment, as opposed to a parent-implemented behavioral program, may be part of increasing the treatment's success.

Case Illustration

Julia was a 5-year-old girl with a fear of using the toilet. Julia attained developmental milestones early, walking at 10 months and speaking in long sentences at 18 months. She was receptively bilingual (understanding both English and Spanish, but speaking only English). She did well in her preschool program and was scheduled to start kindergarten in the fall. Her mother described Julia as a typically developing child, with the exception of her lack of toilet use, although strong willed, very active, and sometimes oppositional.

Julia began to use training pants at age 2 and a half because she would sit on the toilet only to urinate. When Julia felt the need, she would change from her underwear to training pants and defecate behind a closed bathroom door. She had reportedly only used the toilet once for defecation. Her mother reported one incident of constipation around age 4, in which Julia was taken to the emergency room because of impaction. Although the intervention was painful and Julia screamed and cried, she did use the toilet for defecation one time after the hospital visit. Her mother reported that she had tried many things to get Julia to use the toilet but had not been successful. When therapy began, Julia had used the toilet for defecation only these two times.

Julia was seen 10 times in individual CBPT over the course of 3 months, with the parents seen periodically. At the initial child assessment session, Julia's play skills were observed to be age appropriate. Julia noted that she was scared of monsters in the toilet and the sound of the toilet flushing. At this session, a bear who was afraid of using the toilet was introduced to Julia. The therapist and Julia went together to the bathroom, where the therapist had Julia stand outside the bathroom door as the therapist flushed the toilet. Julia agreed to move closer and closer to the door, moving forward at her own pace as she stated that she was not afraid of the noise as it became slightly louder. Once back in the play therapy room, the therapist and Julia drew pictures of Julia on the toilet and making bowel movements, with the therapist stating positive self-statements and writing them on the pictures ("I can poop in the potty"; "It feels really good to poop in the potty"). At this point, Julia suggested that she and the therapist take the bear to the bathroom to show him that the noise really was not too loud. Moving back to the bathroom, Julia excitedly showed the bear the toilet as the therapist flushed it, and both explained to the bear that the noise was not too loud. The therapist also gave the bear stickers for trying, and others to be put away for when either the bear or Julia used the toilet for defecating. Julia eagerly said she would use the toilet so she could get the stickers.

At the second appointment, Julia told the bear that she used the toilet to poop and inquired about the bear's use of the toilet and whether he got stickers. During this session, the therapist and Julia played out the bear using the toilet, in the guise of a plastic bucket, with a clay bowel movement. The therapist and Julia praised the bear for his efforts. Julia told the bear proudly that she was not afraid of the flushing noise, taking the bear and the therapist to the bathroom to show them. During this session, she also sat on the toilet to urinate, saying spontaneously that she was not afraid to defecate, but later acknowledging that she really was.

Check-ins with the mother were done at the end of each session throughout treatment. Between the first and second appointments, Julia accidentally produced some fecal liquid in the toilet when she was sitting down to urinate. The parents, who felt that this was accidental, did not reinforce her efforts or allow her to have the stickers. When told about this, the therapist encouraged the parents to provide positive reinforcement for such situations even if they were not purposeful because they were opportunities for rewards and labeled praise for toilet use. By the third appointment, the mother noted that Julia was showing more interest in toileting and books and videos about toileting, in which she had shown little interest before.

At the third session, the therapist continued to have the bear express fear of using the toilet, with Julia trying to talk him out of his fear. Julia continued to tell the bear that she was not afraid anymore, but the therapist reframed this for her, stating that she probably was still afraid but that it was okay. Julia acknowledged that she was still afraid of monsters. She repeatedly showed the bear how to sit on the toilet, pretending to defecate (making grunting noises) and saying positive self-statements. When using the real toilet, the therapist had the bear defecate pretend balls of toilet paper, talking about how this was "pretend poop".

Julia and the therapist wrote a book for the bear about getting on the toilet, pooping, feeling good, and eventually having a goodbye party for his training pants. Julia and her mother took the book home to read in between sessions. Julia enjoyed illustrating the text that had been written down by the therapist:

> Once upon a time there was a bear who had a toilet and pooped in it with fake clay. He was so scared and he was thinking to poop, and then he did. Then he did. He wanted to. If he wanted to, he couldn't do it because he was so scared. He wanted some candy so Julia can share it with him and she gave him some. Julia gave him candy. He did poop in the toilet forever! He didn't use pull-ups ever again! He had a bye-bye pull-ups party. He helped his friend Julia. Julia wasn't scared anymore. Julia said, "Bye-bye monsters!" Julia said, "I can poop on the toilet. Yeah!" Julia said, "Bye bye-bye pull-ups." Everyone poops. Julia is happy. Everyone poops in the toilet. The End.

Over the next few sessions, Julia and the therapist read the book, adding to it and continuing to add illustrations. Several puppets were introduced who had other fears and who interacted with the bear, sharing discussion about their fears, while the therapist modeled positive self-statements. At the fifth session, Julia's mother noted that Julia had used the toilet one time to defecate, for which parents were very positive and reinforcing. At this point, Julia's verbalizations about the toilet turned more negative; she stated that she did not want to use the toilet, that she would if she wanted to, and that she needed her training pants for defecation. However, she continued to show the bear how to sit on the toilet and engaged positively in the play around toileting. Julia agreed to pick a date for her "bye-bye pull-ups" party, with the bear and therapist providing a lot of positive reinforcement.

In a parents-only session, Julia's mother described her concerns about Julia not being ready to abandon her training pants. The therapist provided encouragement and review of the progress that Julia had made to date. Further discussion stressed the importance of avoiding impaction, with the mother giving Julia a fiber supplement as prescribed by her pediatrician. Also, Julia's mother was aware that once the training pants were taken away, she should not give them back. If an alternative was needed, Julia could be given a newspaper to put on the floor for defecating. The parents expressed concern about moving ahead but were encouraged and coached in being neutral, but firm and in not arguing with Julia but rather stating clearly what the expectations were. Julia, her parents, and the therapist together reviewed plans for the party, with assignments for who would bring what. Related to the significance of the party, Julia told her parents, "I will have to use the toilet to poop after the party."

Subsequent play therapy sessions continued to reinforce positive self-statements for using the toilet as well as planning for the party. A construction-paper chain was made for Julia and her parents, with a link to pull off for each day leading up to the "bye-bye pull-ups" party. The parents reported that Julia happily pulled off a link every day until the night before the party, when she stated that she was not ready and refused to pull off the last link. However, at the party, the bear, therapist, Julia, and her parents decorated the room and served refreshments. The bear was particularly encouraging and playful with Julia as she got ready to throw out what was left of the package of training paints. Julia was cooperative, reviewing the list and the signs for her bathroom at home, and proudly accepted the certificate given to her stating that she had thrown away her training pants.

According to her parents, the day after the party, Julia tried several times to use the toilet and then did so successfully, defecating in the toilet. She and her mom left a message for the therapist that evening, stating that she had pooped in the toilet and everyone was very happy. In a report about 1 week later, Julia's mother indicated that Julia continued to use the toilet as often as two to three times per day for defecation. Her mother also reported that Julia then became much more agreeable and more compliant and that generally, "her personality changed."

Discussion

This case describes a 5-year-old preschooler who presented with a fear of using the toilet for defecation. The history included constipation, painful toileting, impaction, and a traumatic emergency room visit. A comprehensive CBPT approach was taken, using a number of cognitive–behavioral interventions, including contingency management, systematic desensitization, bibliotherapy, and positive self-statements. All were presented through a coping model, with a bear puppet modeling positive steps toward appropriate toilet use. The bear's efforts were yoked to the child's so that a healthy competition could exist between them, with the child striving to use the toilet and get beyond her fears in the same way in which the bear did. Throughout the treatment, a very playful, engaging atmosphere was created. This likely helped engage the child in the treatment and motivated her to take her own steps toward toilet use. For example, when going to the bathroom, the therapist and child would walk quickly, "so that the bear didn't have an accident," or in encouraging the bear, the therapist would add enthusiasm and excitement to her statements.

The interventions were combined in such a way as to be more successful as well as more fun for the child. Systematic desensitization, particularly around the fear of the toilet, was always combined with positive reinforcement, often in the form of labeled praise as well as stickers. The therapist handled issues of fear (e.g., of the monsters) carefully. On the one hand, it was important to accept the child's fear and not minimize or belittle her. On the other hand, to help the child move forward and past the fear, it was important to acknowledge it to provide support for the child's uncertainty ("It's okay to be afraid"), and to provide some ways to get beyond the fear. These means were provided in the form of modeling through the bear and the book and through positive reinforcement from therapist and parents. In allowing the child to help the bear, the child was also put in the role of modeling for the bear, which was a positive, motivating role for her.

The issue of "being ready" for a task such as toileting when the lack of appropriate toileting had gone on for so long is complicated. If one took the stance of waiting until the child was ready all on her own, it might have been a much lengthier process and the child might have been stuck in a developmental rut, unable to move beyond her fears and lack of readiness. However, if the therapist had pushed the child too soon, termination and beginning toileting might have been unsuccessful. This is a delicate balance, a clinical decision that must be made on the basis of the therapist's perception of the child's progress of getting past the fears and readiness to do something that has been frightening and aversive.

Despite the parents' attempts before therapy began, their efforts to be more positive had at times turned negative. Although they interacted well with Julia, her continued refusal to use the toilet was frustrating to them. Their frustrations were compounded by the ways in which she became oppositional, particularly related to toileting. This is not unusual or surprising, given how aversive it can be for parents to have an older child who is still using training pants. Some of the work with the parents was to help them be more positive and to rewarding efforts toward appropriate toileting. This was particularly critical when they were not positive after the possibly accidental but nonetheless important toilet use that took place during treatment. The therapist guided them in thinking more of the child's efforts as closer and closer approximations of the ultimate goal rather than waiting for the perfect toileting use before being positive with her.

CONCLUSION AND FUTURE DIRECTIONS

CBPT is designed specifically for young children ages 3 to 8 and emphasizes the child's participation in therapy. It addresses issues of control, mastery, and responsibility for changing one's own behavior. The child is helped to become an active participant in change (Knell, 1993a). By presenting developmentally appropriate interventions, the therapist helps the child benefit from a type of therapy that might otherwise be inaccessible. A wide array of cognitive and behavioral interventions can be incorporated into play therapy, and its use with a wide range of presenting problems is emerging. CBPT provides structured, goal-directed activities while allowing the child to bring spontaneous material to the session. The balance of spontaneously generated and more structured activities is a delicate one, although both are critical to the success of CBPT. Without the spontaneous material, a rich source of clinical information would be lost. Similarly, if the structure and direction of CBPT were not present, it would be impossible to help the child develop more adaptive coping skills. There is reason to believe that children who need to learn more adaptive coping skills, or whose direct involvement in treatment is important, would be ideal candidates for CBPT.

Given the nature of toileting issues in preschool children, the use of such a treatment approach is logical. As opposed to a parent-implemented behavioral approach, CBPT allows the child to have a significant role in the change process. Moreover, the therapist learns firsthand of the child's perceptions and, as in the case example here, fears (e.g., monsters in the toilet). In addition to the behavioral piece, the therapist can work with the child's maladaptive cognitive thoughts in preparing him or her to move on to more appropriate toilet use.

REFERENCES

Axline, V. (1947). *Play therapy*. New York: Houghton-Mifflin.

Bandura, A. (1969). *Principles of behavior modification*. New York: Holt, Rinehart & Winston.

Bandura, A. (1977). *Social learning theory*. Englewood Cliffs, NJ: Prentice Hall.

Beck, A. T. (1964). Thinking and depression: Part 2. Theory and therapy. *Archives of General Psychiatry, 10*, 561–571.

Beck , A. T. (1967). *Depression: Clinical, experimental, and theoretical aspects*. New York: Harper & Row.

Beck, A. T. (1972). *Depression: Causes and treatment*. Philadelphia: University of Pennsylvania Press.

Beck, A. T. (1976). *Cognitive therapy and the emotional disorders*. New York: International Universities Press.

Bierman, K. L. (1983). Cognitive development and clinical interviews with children. In B. B. Lahey & A. Kazdin (Eds.), *Advances in clinical child psychology* (Vol. 6, pp. 217–250). New York: Plenum Press.

Braswell, L., & Kendall, P. C. (1988). Cognitive–behavioral methods with children. In K. S. Dobson (Ed.), *Handbook of cognitive behavioral therapy* (pp 167–213). New York Guilford Press.

Chambless, D. L. (1993). *Task Force on Promotion and Dissemination of Psychological Procedures: A report adopted by the Division 12 board—October 1993*. Retrieved June 3, 2009, from http://www.apa.org/divisions/div12/est/chamble2.pdf

Chambless, D. L. Sanderson, W. C., Shoham, V., Bennett Johnson, S., Pope, K. S., Crits-Christoph, P., et al. (1996). An update on empirically validated therapies. *Clinical Psychologist, 49*, 5–18.

Compton, S. N., March, J. S., Brent, D., Albano, A. M., Weersing, V. R., & Curry, J. (2004). Cognitive–behavioral psychotherapy for anxiety and depressive disorders in children and adolescents: An evidence-based medicine review. *Journal of the American Academy of Child & Adolescent Psychiatry, 43*, 930–959.

Emery, G., Bedrosian, R., & Garber, J. (1983). Cognitive therapy with depressed children and adolescents. In D. P. Cantwell & G. A. Carlson (Eds.), *Affective disorders in childhood and adolescence—An update* (pp 445–471). New York: Spectrum.

Fishman, L., Rappaport, L., Cousineau, D., & Nurko, S. (2002). Early constipation and toilet training in children with encopresis. *Journal of Pediatric Gastroenterology and Nutrition, 34*, 385–388.

Giorano, M., Landreth, G., & Jones, L. (2005). *A practical handbook for building the play therapy relationship*. Northvale, NJ: Jason Aronson.

Gitlin-Weiner, K., Sandgrund, A., & Schaefer, C. (2000). *Play diagnosis and assessment* (2nd ed.). New York: Wiley.

Grave, J., & Blissett, J. (2004). Is cognitive behavior therapy developmentally appropriate for young children? A critical review of the evidence. *Clinical Psychology Review, 24*, 399–420.

Kendall, P.C., & Braswell, L. (1985). *Cognitive–behavioral therapy for impulsive children*. New York: Guilford Press.

Knell, S. M. (1992). *Puppet sentence completion task*. Unpublished manuscript.

Knell, S. M. (1993a). *Cognitive–behavioral play therapy*. Northvale, NJ: Jason Aronson.

Knell, S. M. (1993b). To show and not tell: Cognitive–behavioral play therapy in the treatment of elective mutism. In T. Kottman & C. Schaefer (Eds.), *Play therapy in action: A casebook for practitioners* (pp. 169–208). Northvale, NJ: Jason Aronson.

Knell, S. M. (1994). Cognitive–behavioral play therapy. In K. O'Connor & C. Schaefer (Eds.), *Handbook of play therapy: Vol. 2. Advances and innovations* (pp. 111–142). New York: Wiley.

Knell, S. M. (1997). Cognitive–behavioral play therapy. In K. O'Connor & L. Mages (Eds.), *Play therapy theory and practice: A comparative presentation* (pp. 79–99). New York: Wiley.

Knell, S. M. (1998). Cognitive–behavioral play therapy. *Journal of Clinical Child Psychology, 27*, 28–33.

Knell, S. M. (1999). Cognitive behavioral play therapy. In S.W. Russ & T. Ollendick (Eds.), *Handbook of psychotherapies with children and families* (pp. 385–404). New York: Plenum Press.

Knell, S. M. (2000). Cognitive–behavioral play therapy with children with fears and phobias. In H. G. Kaduson & C. E. Schaefer (Eds.), *Short term therapies with children* (pp. 3–27). New York: Guilford Press.

Knell, S. M. (2003). Cognitive–behavioral play therapy. In C. E. Schaefer (Ed.), *Foundations of play therapy* (pp. 175–191). New York: Wiley.

Knell, S. M. (2009). Cognitive behavioral play therapy: Theory and applications. In A. Drewes (Ed.), *Effectively blending play therapy and cognitive behavioral therapy: A convergent approach* (pp. 117–133). New York: Wiley

Knell, S. M., & Beck, K. W. (2000). Puppet sentence completion task. In K Gitlin-Weiner, A. Sandgrund, & C.E. Schaefer (Eds.), *Play diagnosis and assessment* (2nd ed., pp. 704–721). New York: Wiley.

Knell, S. M., & Dasari, M. (2006). Cognitive–behavioral play therapy for children with anxiety and phobias. In H. G. Kaduson & C. E. Schaefer (Ed.), *Short term therapies with children* (2nd ed., pp. 22–50). New York: Guilford Press.

Knell, S. M., & Dasari, M. (2009). CBPT: Implementing and integrating CBPT into clinical practice. In A. Drewes (Ed.), *Effectively blending play therapy and cognitive behavioral therapy: A convergent approach* (pp. 321–352). New York: Wiley.

Knell, S. M., & Moore, D. J. (1990). Cognitive–behavioral play therapy in the treatment of encopresis. *Journal of Clinical Child Psychology, 19*, 55–60.

Knell, S. M., & Ruma, C. D. (1996). Play therapy with a sexually abused child. In M. Reinecke, F. M. Dattilio, & A. Freeman (Eds.), *Cognitive therapy with children and adolescents: A casebook for clinical practice* (pp. 367–393). New York: Guilford Press.

Knell, S. M., & Ruma, C. D. (2003). Play therapy with a sexually abused child. In M. A. Reinecke, F. M. Dattilio, & A. Freeman (Eds.) *Cognitive therapy with children and adolescents: A casebook for clinical practice* (2nd ed., pp. 338–368). New York: Guilford Press.

Landreth, G. (2002). *Play therapy: The art of the relationship* (2nd ed.). New York: Routledge.

McGrath, M. L., Mellon, M. W., & Murphy, L. (2000). Empirically supported treatments in pediatric psychology: Constipation and encopresis. *Journal of Pediatric Psychology, 25*, 225–254.

Meichenbaum, D. (1971). Examination of model characteristics in reducing avoidance behavior. *Journal of Personality and Social Psychology, 17*, 298–307.

Monrow, P. J. (2005). Literature review of current uses and applications of cognitive behavioral therapy. *Dissertation Abstracts International, 66*(1), 588B.

Nemiroff, M. A., & Annunziato, J. (1990). *A child's first book about play therapy.* Washington, DC: American Psychological Association.

O'Connor, K. (1991). *The play therapy primer.* New York: Wiley.

Pearson, B. (2007). *Effects of a cognitive behavioral play intervention on children's hope and school adjustment.* Unpublished doctoral dissertation, Case Western Reserve University, Cleveland, OH.

Ruma, C. (1993). Cognitive–behavioral play therapy with sexually abused children. In S. M. Knell (Ed.), *Cognitive–behavioral play therapy* (pp. 199–230). Hillsdale, NJ: Jason Aronson.

Russ, S. W. (2004). *Play in child development and psychotherapy: Toward empirically supported practice.* Mahwah, NJ: Erlbaum.

van der Wal, M. F., Benninga, M. A., & Hirasing, R. A. (2005). The prevalence of encopresis in a multicultural population. *Journal of Pediatric Gastroenterology and Nutrition, 40,* 345–348.

Velting, O., Setzer, J., & Albano, A. (2004). Update on and advances in assessment and cognitive–behavioral treatment of anxiety disorders in children and adolescents. *Professional Psychology: Research and Practice, 35,* 42–54.

Wolpe, J. (1982). *The practice of behavior therapy* (3rd ed.). New York: Pergamon Press.

III

PLAY INTERVENTIONS FOR EXTERNALIZING DISORDERS

9

THE ROLE OF SOCIODRAMATIC PLAY IN PROMOTING SELF-REGULATION

KATHERINE A. GIOIA AND RENÉE M. TOBIN

Issues of self-regulation are pervasive in the psychological research and treatment literatures. In the past several decades, basic and applied research in this area have grown significantly (Eisenberg, 2002; see Tobin & Graziano, 2006, for a review of empirical self-regulation research). More recently, efforts have been made to link the basic research literature on self-regulation to improvements in the delivery of interventions, particularly those targeting preschool children (Tobin, Sansosti, & McIntyre, 2007). In this chapter, we begin by defining self-regulation and reviewing the typical developmental course of these processes. Building on this literature, we then discuss the relation between sociodramatic play and the development of self-regulation. We conclude with a discussion of the roles of therapists, parents, and teachers in promoting self-regulation in children and demonstrate the play therapist's role with a case illustration.

We thank W. Joel Schneider and Laura E. Berk for helpful suggestions and comments.

WHAT IS SELF-REGULATION?

Self-regulation is a broad set of processes that are the building blocks of positive development. The development of self-regulation includes mastering such skills as impulse control, self-control, self-management, self-direction, and independence (Bronson, 2000). Self-regulation is

> the ability to comply with a request, to initiate and cease activities according to situational demands, to modulate the intensity, frequency, and duration of verbal and motor acts in social and educational settings, to postpone acting upon a desired object or goal, and to generate socially approved behavior in the absence of external monitors. (Kopp, 1982, pp. 199–200).

Self-regulation has also been defined as "an array of complex mental capacities that includes impulse and emotion control, self-guidance of thought and behavior, planning, self-reliance, and socially responsible behavior" (Berk, Mann, & Ogan, 2006, p. 74). The development of self-regulatory behaviors sets the stage for children's positive development in school, at home, and with peers.

WHY IS SELF-REGULATION IMPORTANT?

The development of self-regulatory behaviors assists children in monitoring their own thoughts, behaviors, and emotions using more internal control (Bronson, 2000). Children who are well self-regulated are more likely to have better long-term outcomes. Specifically, self-regulatory behaviors assist children in developing goal-directed behavior and planning and organizational skills (Bronson, 2000). These executive functions become increasingly important for high academic performance. Past research has indicated that self-regulation is related to better adaptation to the classroom (Shields et al., 2001) and later academic performance (Gumora & Arsenio, 2002).

Children who are well self-regulated are also able to maintain appropriate behavior and tend to have positive interactions with others. Children who are well self-regulated are more likely to comply with adult demands and are able to control their behaviors when given a particular command (Bronson, 2000). Moreover, because children who are well self-regulated are more likely to control their emotions and behavior, they are likely to have increased social competence in preschool and are less likely to be rejected by peers (Denham et al., 2003; Eisenberg et al., 1997).

In contrast, approximately 10% to 15% of preschool children engage in problem behaviors that are likely to be attributed to poor self-regulation (Campbell, 1995; Cornely & Bromet, 1986; Earls, 1980), and these children are commonly referred for intervention services. Deficits in self-regulation are central to a broad range of mental health disorders including attention-deficit/hyperactivity disorder, oppositional defiant disorder, conduct disorder, mood disorders, anxiety disorders, and other childhood disorders. These findings suggest that fostering self-regulation skills may be profitable, particularly at a young age. Development of these processes may be facilitated through play interventions and other play-based interpersonal treatments such as parent and teacher training.

DEVELOPMENTAL ISSUES

Self-regulation processes improve gradually throughout development, beginning as early as infancy. In the Kopp (1982) model, self-regulation is described as an evolving process with five phases. The first developmental phase occurs in infants' first 2 to 3 months. During these months, infants begin regulating their neurophysiological functions such as arousal states, reflex movements, and self-soothing behaviors such as thumb sucking (Kopp, 1982). By the end of the first 3 months, infants tend to master one critical self-regulatory skill, wake cycles. During the second developmental phase, 3-month-olds to 1-year-olds begin to regulate their sensorimotor states such as adapting behavior on the basis of environmental stimuli (Kopp, 1982). Infants in the second phase focus on adapting their behaviors such as holding, reaching, and playing. These behaviors are modulated on the basis of interaction with environmental stimuli such as a parent's gaze or contact. During the third developmental phase, 12- to 18-month-olds begin to develop control of both behavioral and cognitive systems (Kopp, 1982). Within behavioral systems, these children become aware of social demands and adapt their behavior and emotions accordingly. According to Kopp, control over cognitive systems such as intentionality and awareness of action also occur during this stage. Together, the development of these systems enables young children to control their behaviors and actions on the basis of a parent's demand (e.g., "Don't touch!") or a past learning experience.

During the last developmental phases of self-regulation, young children begin developing self-control and self-regulation (Kopp, 1982). During the fourth stage, which occurs around 24 months, young children begin to develop self-control. The behavioral and cognitive systems continue to develop, assisting children in the ability to comply and use delay of gratification in response to adult demands. By 36 months, children who are beginning to master the fifth stage begin to use self-control and adapt their behaviors depending on situational demands. During this stage, children's regulatory abilities are much more flexible and typically generalize to new settings and situations. Young children who have mastered the five phases of self-regulation tend to display self-control and compliance when engaging in a variety of behaviors such as playing, eating, dressing, spending time with adults or peers, and behaving independently (Kopp, 1982).

INFLUENCE OF MAKE-BELIEVE PLAY ON DEVELOPMENT OF SELF-REGULATION

Play provides repeated opportunities for children to acquire skills in self-regulation. One developmentally important form of play is *make-believe* play, also known as *symbolic* or *dramatic* play (Smilansky & Shefatya, 1990; Wolfgang, Mackender, & Wolfgang, 1981). In make-believe play, children express their thoughts and feelings through the use of objects, materials, and gestures. With the support and encouragement of parents, children show the very beginnings of pretending in the middle of the 2nd year. Around age 2, young children engage in make-believe play by pretending to talk on the phone or eat with objects (Wolfgang et al., 1981). As shown in Figure 9.1, at the same time developmentally, children also begin to initiate self-regulation skills, although the foundation for the development of these skills is set in infancy.

As discussed previously, at around 24 months children's behavioral and cognitive systems continue to develop, assisting with their ability to meet adult demands. In terms of play, children between the ages of 2 and 3 years also begin to engage in make-believe play by substituting similar and dissimilar objects for real objects. Children's *sociodramatic* play, or collaborative make-believe play with others, is present by the 2nd year, although it is more often achieved with a *scaffolding* adult (i.e., an adult who selectively provides support when children are engaging in tasks within their zone of proximal development and remains unobtrusive when children are fully capable of completing the task independently) than with a peer. In fact, by age 3 children's interest in make-believe play is in part the result of adults' ability to make play an exciting and interesting learning experience (Haight & Miller, 1993). Around 36 months, adults' scaffolding attempts transfer to make-believe play interactions with same-age peers. By age 3, children tend to focus on engaging in make-believe play during parallel play and associative play interactions with same-age peers (Wolfgang et al., 1981). It becomes increasingly important for children who are playing with same-aged peers to engage in self-regulatory behaviors such as self-control and regulation of emotions and behaviors so that they can get along with these other children.

Self-Regulation Development

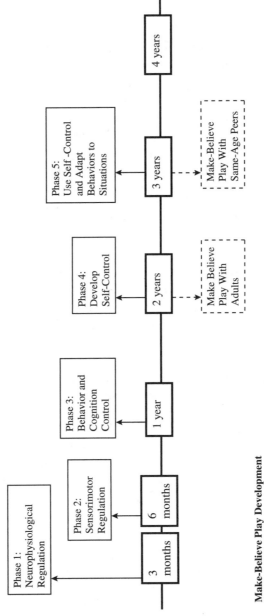

Make-Believe Play Development

Figure 9.1. Children begin to initiate self-regulation skills (top, data from Kopp, 1982) at the same time that they develop make-believe play patterns (bottom, data from Wolfgang, Mackender, & Wolfgang, 1981).

BASIC RATIONALE AND THEORY

Theorists agree that play provides children with opportunities to develop socially and emotionally. Erikson (1950) described play as opportunities for children to practice, experience, and test out different social roles. By setting up situations such as school or the doctor's office, children can begin to become proficient in the demands and roles expected of them. Piaget (1936/1951) described play as a developmental progression from reflexive behaviors to symbolic play. Play, then, provides children with opportunities to develop schemas and symbols for objects. As children further their cognitive development, play provides an opportunity to use environmental objects as symbols for children's own schemas such as falling asleep and eating dinner.

Vygotsky (1930–1935/1978) also viewed play as a core process in children's development. Vygotsky posited that specific types of play are particularly effective at facilitating the development of regulatory skills within an adult–child relationship. He noted that sociodramatic play promotes the development of self-regulation. Smilansky (1968) proposed six required elements for play to be considered sociodramatic. First, sociodramatic play requires that children pretend to be a certain role by imitating the person or thing using language. Second, in imitating the role, children who engage in sociodramatic play use materials or toys that are substituted for a real object. Third, children use language to substitute for their actions. For example, rather than pretending to watch a movie, a child might say, "OK, we're watching a movie." Fourth, sociodramatic play requires that children engage in the role for at least 10 minutes. Fifth, within the play theme, children must be engaged with at least two other children who also have roles. Finally, within sociodramatic play, children must be communicating verbally to one another. Make-believe play differs from sociodramatic play in that it does not require the last two essential elements, and this form of play is consistent with what play therapists often provide when intervening (Smilansky & Shefatya, 1990).

According to Vygotsky (1930–1935/1978), there are distinctive features of make-believe play that contribute to children's development. First, make-believe play allows children to create separate internal ideas from external words, gestures, and objects. This enables children to use their ideas and thoughts to control their own behavior and impulses. Second, make-believe play provides opportunities for children to practice rule-based behavior. In other words, children practice following social rules that are typically expected in their own family and community experiences. Together, these unique features of make-believe play allow children to strengthen their internal socialization and adhere to external demands of behaving in socially appropriate ways (Berk, 2001). Vygotsky theorized that make-believe play provides children with opportunities to develop emotional regulation and socially responsible behavior (Vygotsky, 1930–1935/1978). Together, the development of these areas contributes to self-regulatory skill building and is the core of many play therapy approaches.

PLAY INTERVENTION PROCEDURES

Because make-believe play occurs within the home, school, and other contexts, parents, teachers, and therapists can play an important role in shaping children's make-believe play. When children engage in make-believe play, their play is guided by their own observations of appropriate adult social behavior and speech. A central tenet of Vygotsky's (1930–1935/1978) theory is children's experiences in their zone of proximal development. A task within a child's zone of proximal development is a task that the child could not ordinarily accomplish alone, but can complete with appropriate adult support (Berk et al., 2006). When facilitating children's social or academic learning, adults play a role in challenging children's learning while simultaneously supporting it. Two key components of the zone of proximal development are intersubjectivity and scaffolding. *Intersubjectivity* refers to shared understandings between two people that stem from empathic mindfulness of the other's experiences and perspectives (Berk et al., 2006). Adults capable of relationships characterized by such intersubjectivity are in the position to provide scaffolding for children. Adults can use scaffolding and intersubjectivity to promote self-regulation when engaging in make-believe play with their children. Together, adult support, scaffolding, and intersubjectivity increase the likelihood of successful practice of social norms, autonomous functioning, and impulse control when children engage in challenging play.

Because adult support and scaffolding can play a vital role in the facilitation of children's self-regulation, there are several recommendations play therapists can follow. For example, one of the greatest resources an adult can provide is his or her time. It is recommended that adults take time out of their week to engage in make-believe play with children in need of self-regulatory skill building. During play, adults such as therapists who engage in joint play with children can serve multiple functions, including teaching, enlivening daily routines, defusing conflict, expressing emotion, regulating emotion, influencing another's social behavior, and having fun (Berk, 2001). When jointly interacting in make-believe play, these adults can teach children social norms, life skills, and prosocial behavior (Berk, 2001). For example, if a child is pretending that a doll is hurt and crying, the therapist can take another doll and show the child's doll empathy by asking if it is all right and comforting it.

Play therapists can use make-believe play to facilitate children's development of prosocial behaviors and, eventually, their social competence with peers. The development of self-regulation contributes to the development of children's socially responsible behavior (Berk et al., 2006). In one study of preschool children's behavior, conducted in the fall and spring of the academic year, Elias and Berk (2002) examined the relation the children's complexity of sociodramatic play and their degree of self-regulation as measured by independent clean-up behaviors in the spring. The researchers found no evidence of a significant relation between complex sociodramatic play and attentiveness during circle time.

Make-believe play also contributes to the development of emotional self-regulation, a key process that facilitates children's social competence (Eisenberg & Fabes, 1992). Eisenberg et al. (1997) defined *emotion regulation* as "the ability to inhibit, enhance, maintain, and modulate emotional arousal to accomplish one's goals" (p. 642). The regulation of emotions assists children in using problem-focused coping when they are engaged in an emotionally arousing situation. Past research has found that children who engage in optimal levels of emotion regulation are also more likely to have higher social competence, social skills, and popularity as assessed through sociometric status (Eisenberg et al., 1993, 1997). Theorists, including psychoanalysts, have believed that make-believe play provides children with opportunities to regulate their emotions (Bretherton & Beeghly, 1989; Fein, 1989). Specifically, make-believe play is likely to result in conflict with other children and other emotionally arousing situations. Therefore, make-believe play in home, school, and therapeutic contexts creates opportunities for children to learn skills such as emotional expression, emotion management, conflict resolution, and other problem-solving strategies.

To facilitate these activities, therapists can also be gatekeepers to the physical context of play. They can control play environments by providing appropriate play materials and arranging the environment to encourage make-believe play consistent with a structured play therapy approach (Bronson, 2000). For instance, play materials should be placed at children's level so they can prepare to play independently. Play therapists can arrange the environment so that each spot has a relevant, designated activity. These can include dress-up, house, blocks, art, quiet area, and computer. Within each of these areas, play therapists can discuss expectations and rules with children. These rules should explain how to use, share, and put away materials. By arranging the environment, children learn to take initiative, plan, and make choices about their own behavior, all of which contribute to their development of self-regulation (Bronson, 2000).

Zahn-Waxler and colleagues (Robinson, Zahn-Waxler, & Emde, 1994; Zahn-Waxler, Radke-Yarrow, & King 1979) examined another aspect of adult–child relationships that influences the development of self-regulation processes. Specifically, they examined parental behaviors within the context of play that are associated with children's development of prosocial behavior. Findings from this line of research offer several ways for parents to promote their children's social and emotional development. These recommendations, although directed toward parents, can also be used by play therapists and other adults. First, adults who provide children with clear rules are more likely to foster prosocial behavior. For example, adults who provide children with rules such as "We don't hit people" are more likely to see them engage in prosocial behavior across settings than those who say "Don't do that" or "Stop." Second, when providing rules and expectations, adults should convey these messages with emotional intensity. When these rules are conveyed with conviction, children are more likely to understand the rules of prosocial behavior. Third, adults who attribute children's prosocial behavior to their prosocial nature are more likely to motivate children to engage in socially responsible behavior. For example, children feel good when they are told they are "kind" or "helpful." Children then internalize these statements and begin to take the initiative to be kind and helpful in social situations, particularly when the connection between their behavior and these attributes is made clear. Next, adults who model prosocial and altruistic behavior are more likely to have children who behave in a similar manner. Just from seeing these behaviors modeled, children learn a great deal about social rules and responsibilities. Finally, adults who are warm and responsive to children's needs and emotions are likely to motivate children to do the same for others. The environmental climate that adults create sets the stage for children's prosocial behavior. Sociodramatic play provides repeated opportunities for adults to engage in these five behaviors that assist children's development of prosocial and socially responsible behavior. Furthermore, these methods can be used to facilitate these processes within a play therapy relationship.

EMPIRICALLY SUPPORTED PLAY INTERVENTION

For children who are struggling to develop adaptive social and emotional skills, previous research has supported the role of play as a therapeutic treatment (see Reddy, Files-Hall, & Schaefer, 2005). In the context of play therapy, the therapist's role is to develop rapport with the child, encourage the child's self-exploration, and conceptualize the child's behavior (Schaefer, 1993; Webb, 1999). The therapist provides toys and other objects to act as a child's words. The communicative exchange, then, is represented in the child's and therapist's play (Landreth, 2002). In doing so, play therapy provides children with opportunities to learn new skills, cope with difficult stressors, and address emotions while being supported emotionally by a therapist (Clark, 2007). Schaefer (1993) recommended that play therapists use a prescriptive approach, specifically, that play therapists individualize play therapy on the basis of each child's symptoms.

Play therapy is an empirically validated intervention for children with various backgrounds and experiences (see Reddy et al., 2005). For example, research has supported the use of play therapy for children who have experienced extreme stress, including witnessing domestic violence (Kot & Tyndall-Lind, 2005). Play therapists working with children exposed to domestic violence often use the core elements of sociodramatic play, including imagination and the use of materials to substitute for real objects. Therapists use play materials as a means of communication. For example, a child coping with domestic violence may be provided with a dollhouse, whereas a child coping with a medical illness may be provided with a doctor's kit. By providing specific objects related to the stressor, therapists set the stage for children to develop self-regulatory skills through self-direction and imaginal coping by supporting and scaffolding their play (Clark, 2007). These methods are in line with the promotion of self-regulatory abilities seen in nondisordered populations.

Similarly, play therapy has also been empirically validated for children with externalizing symptoms such as attention deficits, aggression, and other behavior problems (Crenshaw & Mordock, 2005; Drewes, 2001; Reddy et al., 2005). Children who have deficits in attention and self-control typically act impulsively and tend not to think before they act. Therapists working with children with externalizing problems also use key elements of sociodramatic play, including the use of language to substitute for behaviors and the use of materials to substitute for real objects. By communicating with the therapist through sociodramatic play, children begin to practice self-regulatory behaviors such as developing plans and expressing their thoughts and ideas. Play therapy also provides an opportunity for therapists to assist in managing children's aggression and anger (Crenshaw & Mordock, 2005; Drewes, 2001). Certain toys used in sociodramatic play, such as balls or clay, can be used with children to assist their emotion regulation of anger and aggression. Using particular sociodramatic materials and methods, the play therapist's role is to teach children to regulate their anger and learn other techniques to solve problems in ways that do not involve aggression. Progress occurs not because of the use of punishment, but because of the play therapist's unconditional assistance and support.

Parent–child interaction therapy (Eyberg & Calzada, 1998; Hembree-Kigin & McNeil, 1995; see chap. 10 of this volume) is another empirically supported play therapy technique used to assist with children's development of self-regulatory skills. Parent–child interaction therapy is structured to teach parents effective parenting techniques while also teaching children prosocial behaviors such as sharing, taking turns, and complying with adult requests (Herschell & McNeil, 2005). Working with children and parents, play therapists use elements of sociodramatic play, including practicing the new roles by using imitation. With the play therapist's assistance and coaching, parents practice using effective parenting strategies while playing with their children, including forms of sociodramatic play. Eventually, parents transfer skills to the home setting. Children also use play materials to imitate and practice new prosocial behaviors and social responsibilities. The goal of parent–child interaction therapy, then, is for the therapist to use play as an outlet for teaching parents and children new behaviors and ways of interacting.

Another type of play therapy, *child-centered* play therapy, focuses on providing the child with a safe environment that encourages the development of self-regulation. Specifically, play allows children to release and/or reduce undesirable emotions (Axline, 1969; Clark, 2007). Play therapists use elements of sociodramatic play such as imagination to provide children with opportunities to reenact situations and express their emotions in a safe environment. In child-centered play therapy, children have control and guide the session, but only within the therapist's limits. Specifically, the therapist sets up rules and then allows the child to explore within those limits. This approach enables the child to practice taking initiative and being in control of his or her behavior, which assists the child in learning socially responsible behavior. The goals of child-centered therapy are to provide opportunities for children to develop self-regulation by communicating their thoughts, to learn and express their emotions, and to learn self-control.

CASE ILLUSTRATION

At the time of treatment, Mike was a 4-year-old boy with self-regulation difficulties, particularly in dealing with his negative emotions and aggression. Mike had two older siblings and lived in a single-family household. His mother reported that he was often defiant, disobeying her commands frequently and even slapping her when upset. She also stated that she could not leave him alone with his siblings or other neighborhood children because he often engaged in physical fights with them when playing.

Mike attended a full-day classroom at a day treatment facility with 12 other children between the ages of 3 and 5. Mike's classroom teacher expressed concern about his aggressive behaviors. She described Mike as impulsive and inattentive, reactive and angry, and aggressive toward his teachers and peers. When playing inside, Mike was unable to appropriately attend to and transition from activity areas in the room appropriately. He ran around the room, knocked down other children and materials, and was unable to keep his voice at an "inside" level. When playing outside, Mike was unable to share basketballs and other toys with his classmates. Instead, he frequently had tantrums when it was not his turn, stole toys from other children, and hits and kicked when he lost privileges or toys.

On the basis of the empirical literature, Mike was an ideal candidate for an intervention focused on make-believe play therapy. Given Mike's impulsive behaviors and inattention, it was clear that he had difficulty regulating his thoughts and behaviors. He also has difficulties with regulating his emotions, judging by his emotional reactivity and aggressive behaviors. In this case, the therapist's role was to facilitate Mike's development of self-regulation and emotion regulation.

Using sociodramatic play, the play therapist targeted self-regulatory behaviors using a structured play therapy room that had multiple centers including a block area, an art area, a kitchen area, and a truck or train area. Throughout 10-minute sessions, the therapist used imitation as a means of developing Mike's self-regulatory behaviors. For example, the play therapist used a dollhouse and people figurines to describe appropriate ways to transition from activities and model how to plan and control behaviors. The play therapist also used other aspects of make-believe play such as substituting language for actions. The therapist elicited Mike's thoughts and described his behaviors to scaffold his development of self-regulation. By modeling and describing new ways of behaving, the therapist was able to target areas of self-regulation, including self-control, attentional control, and delay of gratification.

To target emotion regulation, a play therapist also used a Lego structure and child figurines. To facilitate Mike's development of emotion regulation, the play therapist used make-believe situations that drew on his imagination to assist in the teaching of appropriate social behaviors. In this case, the therapist used a figure that resembled Mike, other figures that resembled his classmates, and small toys such as a toy computer or toy basketball. Within the play setting, the figures played out social situations such as sharing toys and joining in activities. The therapist's role was to model appropriate prosocial behaviors such as sharing, compromising, and communicating with peers and adults. The therapist also elicited Mike's imitation and practice of prosocial behaviors. Once Mike developed social awareness and knowledge, the play therapist moved from make-believe play to the use of sociodramatic play to assist Mike. Thus, at least two other children joined Mike in communicating and playing with one another. In this case, Mike practiced these prosocial behaviors with same-age peers either in the play therapy setting or in his classroom.

EXTENDING TO THE HOME AND TO THE CLASSROOM

Beyond the play therapy context, research on sociodramatic play also has implications for improving children's functioning at home and at school. Play therapists can serve an important role as consultants to both teachers and parents in promoting self-regulatory behaviors in young children through the use of make-believe play.

Parents can use make-believe play to enliven daily routines such as cleaning and other household chores (Berk, 2001). Converting everyday tasks such as preparing a meal into a joint make-believe play interaction may facilitate positive development by providing the child with an opportunity to develop new skills, engage in creative activities, and deepen the parent–child bond while simultaneously completing a household task. For example, while cleaning up a child's room, an adult may pretend to be in a race to see who will be the winner of the fastest cleaner award. Adults can also use make-believe play to defuse conflicts between parent and child by increasing the likelihood of child compliance. Make-believe play also provides parents and therapists with an outlet to provide examples of different emotional expressions within a safe environment. For instance, children often pretend to be hurt or scared when playing, and this may create an opportunity for an adult to explain the child's feelings in a comforting and safe environment. Finally, adults who engage in make-believe play create opportunities to have fun, laugh, and enjoy spending time with their children.

Teachers can also use playtime as an opportunity to scaffold their students' development of self-regulatory abilities. For instance, teachers can incorporate opportunities to engage in make-believe play into their daily lesson plans. Wolfgang et al. (1981) provided several play activities based on the types of play, including sociodramatic play. Activities that assist with children's development of self-regulation include acting with puppets, being in a parade or a fashion show, pretending to work at a restaurant or a grocery store, or acting out favorite bedtime stories. Together, these activities will assist children in language development, prosocial behavior, and abstract thought while they learn about their thoughts, feelings, and actions (Wolfgang et al., 1981). In terms of intervention, play therapists engage in similar sociodramatic play behaviors that likely facilitate the development of these processes.

Findings from the sociodramatic play literature also inform educational practices for young children. Berk (2001) suggested indicators of high-quality preschools that are likely to assist children's development of self-regulation and other adaptive abilities. First, the classroom environment is divided into separate learning areas (e.g., science, math, books, art). Throughout the day, children are provided with a daily schedule that allows for ample time to engage in multiple activities. Second, within the daily schedule, children are provided with opportunities to choose their own activity and learn through their own experiences. Teachers should encourage initiative and allow children to individualize their learning. Third, the teachers provide a climate that is supportive, facilitates learning, and conveys that each child is valued. In this context, the teachers also interact positively with each child to facilitate not only the child's learning, but also his or her prosocial behavior. Next, teachers promote parent interaction with the classroom and students. Teachers encourage parents to visit the classroom to observe or volunteer time and keep consistent and frequent communication a priority. Finally, for preschoolers the group size is kept at a maximum of 20 students, with one teacher for every 10 children. These are simple techniques teachers can use to encourage children's development of prosocial behaviors and self-regulation, and therapists may serve as consultants in implementing them.

Parents, teachers, and therapists can also support children's development of self-regulation by being gatekeepers to children's play practice with peers. As discussed earlier, at around ages 3 to 5 children's opportunities for play with same-age peers greatly increase. Children engage in elaborate make-believe play, assigning roles and working together toward common goals. Past research has indicated that unless disagreements or conflicts ensue, parents, teachers, and other adults tend to disengage from preschoolers' peer interactions (Berk, 2001; Howes & Clemente, 1994). Moreover, when parents and teachers do take action, it is typically to tell the children to stop, separate, or wait (Berk, 2001; File, 1993). Parents, teachers, and other adults are instead encouraged to take both a preventive and a mediator role in children's play. Before games and activities occur, adults should encourage children to set their own rules and agree to the activity. Should conflicts arise, parents, teachers, and therapists can then assist the children in problem solving. First, adults may assist the children in emotion regulation by asking them to calm down by taking a deep breath. A scaffolding adult may then encourage the children to identify their feelings and what they would like to see happen. Then, parents, teachers, and other adults can help the children problem solve to accommodate all of their desires (Berk, 2001). Adults should take the opportunity to let the children take initiative in problem solving, but provide support and suggestions on the basis of each child's social skills.

According to Berk (2001), parents, teachers, and other adults can follow three suggestions when mediating the child's social interactions with same-age peers. First, parents and teachers should mediate and intervene as early as possible. Second, adults should consider the child's social developmental level when addressing the current conflict. For instance, when a conflict arises, parents and teachers, perhaps in consultation with a therapist, should recall past situations that may have been similar and what skills they can provide the child to develop that particular social skill. Finally, parents and teachers should use the least restrictive intervention strategies to maintain the child's independence and social responsibility. Therapists may help parents and teachers to identify the child's social goal and how much adult assistance the child needs to acquire the goal.

CONCLUSION AND FUTURE DIRECTIONS

Play therapists routinely rely on sociodramatic play approaches in their clinical work. Although not traditionally identified as main components of play therapy, elements of sociodramatic play are central to play therapy interventions. In this chapter, we have reviewed several ways in which play therapists currently engage in sociodramatic play to facilitate the development of self-regulation in preschool children. We also have highlighted new roles for play therapists as models for and consultants to teachers and parents in facilitating these self-regulatory behaviors in preschool children. Although serving as a consultant is not a traditional role for play therapists, doing so may increase the effectiveness of their individual therapy efforts over time by providing children with opportunities to generalize their skills to other settings. Thus, we provide details for applying sociodramatic approaches across settings, including the play therapy context, home, and school.

Sociodramatic play therapy literature would benefit from future research focused on determining the specific elements of sociodramatic play that facilitate the development of self-regulation processes. For example, it is unclear which or how many of the six elements of sociodramatic play are related to improvements in self-regulation, particularly as they are executed in a play therapy context. Future research may examine these relations by implementing each of the six independently and systematically and observing changes in self-regulatory behaviors over time. Previous research has indicated that play therapy is effective for treating various populations and behaviors and more focused investigation would assist in identifying the most promising elements and methods for intervention.

REFERENCES

Axline, V. M. (1969). *Play therapy*. New York: Ballantine Books.

Berk, L. E. (2001). *Awakening children's minds: How parents and teachers can make a difference*. New York: Oxford University Press.

Berk, L. E., Mann, T. D., & Ogan, A. T. (2006). Make-believe play: Wellspring for the development of self-regulation. In D. G. Singer, R. Golinkoff, & K. Hirsh-Pasek

(Eds.), *Play = learning: How play motivates and enhances children's cognitive and social–emotional growth* (pp. 74–100). New York: Oxford University Press.

Bretherton, I., & Beeghly, M. (1989). Pretense: Acting "as if." In J. J. Lockman & N. L. Hazen (Eds.), *Action in social context: Perspectives on early development* (pp. 239–271). New York: Plenum Press.

Bronson, M. B. (2000). *Self-regulation in early childhood: Nature and nurture.* New York: Guilford Press.

Campbell, S. B. (1995). Behavior problems in preschool children: A review of recent research. *Journal of Child Psychology and Psychiatry, 36,* 113–149.

Clark, C. D. (2007). Therapeutic advantages of play. In A. Göncü & S. Gaskins (Eds.), *Play and development: Evolutionary, sociocultural, and functional perspectives* (pp. 275–293). Mahwah, NJ: Erlbaum.

Cornely, P., & Bromet, E. J. (1986). Prevalence of behavior problems in 3-year-old children living near Three Mile Island: A comparative analysis. *Journal of Child Psychology and Psychiatry, 27,* 489–498.

Crenshaw, D. A., & Mordock, J. B. (2005). *A handbook of play therapy with aggressive children.* Lanham, MD: Jason Aronson.

Denham, S. A., Blair, K. A., DeMulder, E., Levitas, J., Sawyer, K., Auerbach-Major, S., & Queenan, P. (2003). Preschool emotional competence: Pathway to social competence. *Child Development, 74,* 238–256.

Drewes, A. A. (2001). The possibilities and challenges in using play therapy in schools. In A. Drewes, L. J. Carey, & C. E. Schaefer (Eds.), *School-based play therapy* (pp. 105–122). New York: Wiley.

Earls, F. (1980). The prevalence of behavior problems in 3-year-old children. *Archives of General Psychiatry, 37,* 1153–1159.

Eisenberg, N. (2002). Emotion-related regulation and its relation to quality of social functioning. In W. Hartup & R. A. Weinberg (Eds.), *Child psychology in retrospect and prospect: In celebration of the 75th anniversary of the Institute of Child Development* (pp. 133–171). Mahwah, NJ: Erlbaum.

Eisenberg, N., & Fabes, R. A. (1992). Emotion, regulation, and the development of social competence. In M. S. Clark (Ed.), *Review of personality and social psychology: Vol. 14. Emotion and behavior* (pp. 119–150). Newbury Park, CA: Sage.

Eisenberg, N., Fabes, R. A., Bernzweig, J., Karbon, M., Poulin, R., & Hanish, L. (1993). The relations of emotionality and regulation to preschoolers' social skills and sociometric status. *Child Development, 64,* 1418–1438.

Eisenberg, N., Fabes, R. A., Shepard, S. A., Murphy, B. C., Guthrie, I. K., Jones, S., et al. (1997). Contemporaneous and longitudinal prediction of children's social functioning from regulation and emotionality. *Child Development, 68,* 642–664.

Elias, C. L., & Berk, L. E. (2002). Self-regulation in young children: Is there a role for sociodramatic play? *Early Childhood Research Quarterly, 162,* 1–23.

Erikson, E. H. (1950). *Childhood and society.* New York: Norton.

Eyberg, S. M., & Calzada, E. (1998). *Parent–child interaction therapy: Procedures manual*. Unpublished manuscript, University of Florida, Gainesville.

Fein, G. G. (1989). Mind, meaning, and affect: Proposals for a theory of pretense. *Developmental Review, 9,* 345–363.

File, N. (1993). The teacher as guide of children's competence with peers. *Child and Youth Care Quarterly, 22,* 351–360.

Gumora, G., & Arsenio, W. F. (2002). Emotionality, emotion regulation, and school performance in middle school children. *Journal of School Psychology, 40,* 395–413.

Haight, W. L., & Miller, P. J. (1993). *Pretending at home: Early development in a sociocultural context*. Albany, NY: SUNY Press.

Hembree-Kigin, T. L., & McNeil, C. B. (1995). *Parent–child interaction therapy*. New York: Plenum Press.

Herschell, A. M., & McNeil, C. B. (2005). Parent–child interaction therapy for children experiencing externalizing behavior problems. In L. A. Reddy, T. M. Files-Hall, & C. E. Schaefer (Eds.), *Empirically based play interventions for children* (pp. 169–190). Washington, DC: American Psychological Association.

Howes, C., & Clemente, D. (1994). Adult socialization of children's play in child care. In H. Goelman (Ed.), *Children's play in day care settings* (pp. 20–36). Albany, NY: SUNY Press.

Kopp, C. B. (1982). Antecedents of self-regulation: A developmental perspective. *Developmental Psychology, 18,* 199–214.

Kot, S., & Tyndall-Lind, A. (2005). Intensive play therapy with child witnesses of domestic violence. In L. A. Reddy, T. M. Files-Hall, & C. E. Schaefer (Eds.), *Empirically based play interventions for children* (pp. 31–49). Washington, DC: American Psychological Association.

Landreth, G. L. (2002). *Play therapy: The art of the relationship*. London: Taylor & Francis.

Piaget, J. (1951). *Play, dreams, and imitation in childhood*. New York: Norton. (Original work published 1936)

Reddy, L. A., Files-Hall, T. M., & Schaefer, C. E. (2005). *Empirically based play interventions for children*. Washington, DC: American Psychological Association.

Robinson, J. L., Zahn-Waxler, C., & Emde, R. N. (1994). Patterns of development in early empathic behavior: Environmental and child constitutional influences. *Social Development, 3,* 125–145

Schaefer, C. E. (1993). *The therapeutic powers of play*. Northvale, NJ: Jason Aronson.

Shields, A., Dickstein, S., Seifer, R., Giusti, L., Magee, K. D., & Spritz, B. (2001). Emotional competence and early school adjustment: A study of preschoolers at risk. *Early Education & Development, 12,* 73–96.

Smilansky, S. (1968). *The effects of socio-dramatic play on disadvantaged preschool children*. New York: Wiley.

Smilansky, S., & Shefatya, L. (1990). *Facilitating play: A medium for promoting cognitive, socio-emotional and academic development in young children.* Gaithersburg, MD: Psychosocial & Educational Publications.

Tobin, R. M., & Graziano, W. G. (2006). Development of regulatory processes through adolescence: A review of recent empirical studies. In D. Mroczek & T. Little (Eds.), *Handbook of personality development* (pp. 263–283). Mahwah, NJ: Erlbaum.

Tobin, R. M., Sansosti, F. J., & McIntyre, L. L. (2007). Developing emotional competence in preschoolers: A review of regulation research and recommendations for practice. *California School Psychologist, 12,* 105–118.

Vygotsky, L. S. (1978). *Mind in society: The development of higher mental processes* (M. Cole, V. John-Steimer, S. Scribner, & E. Souberman, Eds. & Trans.). Cambridge, MA: Harvard University Press. (Original work published 1930–1935)

Webb, N. B. (1999). *Play therapy with children in crisis.* New York: Guilford Press.

Wolfgang, C. H., Mackender, B., &Wolfgang, M. E. (1981). *Growing and learning through play: Activities for preschool and kindergarten children.* Columbus, OH: McGraw-Hill.

Zahn-Waxler, C., Radke-Yarrow, M., & King, R. A. (1979). Child rearing and children's prosocial initiations towards victims of distress. *Child Development, 50,* 319–330.

10

PARENT–CHILD INTERACTION THERAPY

CORISSA L. CALLAHAN, MONICA L. STEVENS, AND SHEILA EYBERG

Parent–child interaction therapy (PCIT) is an evidence-based treatment for disruptive behavior in young children that targets maladaptive interaction patterns in the parent–child relationship. Parents first learn a child-directed interaction (CDI) in which they follow the child's lead using play therapy skills. In CDI, parents learn to provide positive attention to the child and the child's ideas and activities, as long as they are acceptable; the positive attention maintains and models positive play behaviors and increases the quality and warmth of the parent–child interaction. The CDI phase of PCIT provides the foundation for implementing the parent-directed interaction (PDI) phase. In PDI, parents learn to lead the child's activity with clearly communicated directions and to follow through consistently to improve child compliance and decrease child behavior problems. In PCIT, parents practice the interactions with their child while the therapist coaches them from an observation room via "bug-in-the-ear" transmission, enabling parents to learn the skills quickly and accurately with therapist support.

In this chapter, we describe the conceptual rationale underlying PCIT, present a step-by-step description of the therapeutic procedures used in each phase of treatment, illustrate the application of PCIT with a young child diagnosed with oppositional defiant disorder, and provide an overview of research findings demonstrating PCIT outcomes with several child and family populations. We conclude the chapter with suggestions for future directions in the application of PCIT.

BASIC RATIONALE AND THEORY

PCIT is based on Baumrind's (1966, 1991) developmental theory of parenting styles and corresponding research demonstrating that an authoritative parenting style, consisting of nurturance, clear communication, and firm control, produces optimal child mental health outcomes. In CDI, parents learn skills to follow the child's lead in play using differential social attention, providing positive attention to prosocial child behaviors (Boggs & Eyberg, 2008) and ignoring negative behavior. The goal of this phase is to strengthen the parent–child attachment in preparation for the PDI phase of treatment.

In the PDI phase, parents learn to lead their child's behavior with clear directions and consistent follow-through to reduce child noncompliance and other negative behaviors not extinguished by the application of CDI skills alone. PDI reverses the coercive patterns that develop in interactions between parents and disruptive children when parents attempt to lead. As described by Patterson (1982), this cycle begins when negative child behavior in response to parental commands is reinforced by negative parental attention. This coercive cycle continues when the parent, in response to the child's escalating negative behavior, eventually withdraws the original command, thereby reinforcing the negative behavior. The parent is also reinforced for withdrawing the command because the child temporarily stops the negative behavior. The PDI procedure interrupts this cycle by teaching parents to give clear commands that are followed by consistent consequences, either praise and positive attention when the child obeys or time out from positive reinforcement when the child disobeys. Over time, the positive interactions become progressively more reinforcing to both parent and child, which increases prosocial child behavior and positive parenting skills (Hood & Eyberg, 2003).

DEVELOPMENTAL ISSUES

The preschool years are a time of incredible growth and development for children. Although many young children exhibit noncompliant, aggressive, and highly active behaviors during the course of normal development, studies have suggested that parents of young children with disruptive behavior problems have less knowledge of early child development and less effective child management skills than other parents (Rickard, Graziano, & Forehand, 1984). By supplementing parenting skills training with education about preschoolers' cognitive, social, and emotional development, PCIT therapists have opportunities to help align parents' expectations of their child's behavior with their child's actual abilities and to help parents promote their child's healthy development.

In relation to cognitive development, for example, many preschoolers have limited attention spans (Flavell & Miller, 1998); PCIT therapists teach parents to hold their children's attention during CDI by coaching them to use behavior descriptions at a high rate, thereby reinforcing the immediate play behavior ("You're putting on a blue block, and now a red, and a white"). Therapists can then point out to parents that through repeated trials they have been able to increase their child's attention span. Therapists can explain how, with continued practice, children learn to maintain their attention to tasks on their own. PCIT therapists also teach parents to maintain their children's attention during PDI by coaching parents to use clear, direct commands to redirect children when they are off task ("Now put another red block on the wall").

Young children also have limited memory strategies. Many parents believe their preschoolers "purposely" forget what they are told to do. In PCIT, parents learn to give children directions to do only one thing at a time. Therapists then have the opportunity in coaching to point out how well the child listens to age-appropriate directions. PCIT therapists also clarify children's cognitive abilities to understand adult reasoning. Parents learn how to use reasons effectively to help children learn. During PDI, they practice giving their child age-appropriate reasons before giving a command ("The house needs to be neat for Grandma's visit. Please put your coat in the closet") and again after their child obeys ("Thank you for putting it away. The house will look nice when Grandma visits").

PCIT therapists also guide parents in supporting and encouraging their child's social development. During CDI, therapists coach parents to model and reinforce prosocial behaviors such as sharing and turn taking in tasks and games. Therapists also coach parents to model turn taking in parent–child conversation. During PDI, parents may teach polite behaviors very directly, for example, by telling the child to say "please" or "thank you" and then praising that behavior ("That was a very nice way of asking me to help. When you say 'please' it makes me want to help you").

Children begin understanding their and others' emotions during the preschool years, and they gain increasing ability to regulate their emotions. PCIT therapists encourage parents to describe children's emotions during play and to label their own emotions when appropriate. For example, a parent might be encouraged to say to the child, "Thank you for sharing the red blocks with me. It makes me happy when you share your toys and play nicely!" As disruptive children learn to express negative feeling in words instead of actions, parents are coached to acknowledge the change and express their pleasure in their child's new skills ("I know you are upset that the train isn't here today, but I'm very proud that you used your words to tell me. You are getting to be such a big boy. I will ask them if we can use the train next time we come.")

PLAY INTERVENTION PROCEDURES

PCIT is a unique play-based intervention. The parent and child are treated together, and the dyad is the focus of treatment. Assessment is a key component of PCIT, occurring before and after treatment to measure treatment success, as well as within each session to pace treatment according to each family's individual progress. Before initiating treatment, an intake assessment is scheduled to obtain information about the child's history and current functioning at home and preschool, the relationships within the family, the parents' discipline and child management procedures, and any services the family has previously obtained for the child. In this interview, the therapist describes PCIT and the demands of this treatment, seeks to understand and clarify the parents' expectations for treatment, and works to resolve potential barriers to treatment participation.

Following the clinical interview, parents complete the Eyberg Child Behavior Inventory (ECBI; Eyberg & Pincus, 1999), a baseline measure of the frequency of child disruptive behavior, and each parent is observed interacting with the child in three standard situations using the Dyadic Parent–Child Interaction Coding System (Eyberg, Nelson, Duke, & Boggs, 2005). These observations provide baseline measures of parenting skills and difficult child behaviors that will be targeted in treatment. Both the ECBI and the relevant Dyadic Parent–Child Interaction Coding System measures are collected weekly during treatment to assess progress in parent skill acquisition and to track child behavior change. If the child is experiencing difficulty in preschool, the child's teacher may complete a teacher rating scale of disruptive behavior (the Sutter-Eyberg Student Behavior Inventory; Eyberg & Pincus, 1999).

Each phase of treatment, CDI and PDI, begins with one *teach session* with the parents alone in which the therapist demonstrates the individual skills of the interaction, role-plays the skills with the parents, and describes the emotional and behavioral effects of each skill on the child. Therapists also discuss with parents the importance of practicing the skills with the child at home 5 minutes every day. All subsequent sessions in each phase of PCIT are called *coach sessions*. In these sessions, the parent and child practice the CDI or PDI together in the playroom while the therapist observes and coaches the parent from an observation room.

Child-Directed Interaction

CDI is the initial focus of treatment because it increases the warmth of parent–child interaction, strengthens parent–child attachment, and decreases the readiness to anger of both parent and child. The basic rule for the parent in CDI is to follow the child's lead, and each of the individual CDI skills serves to facilitate this rule. The CDI skills involve making statements that give positive attention to acceptable child behaviors (the "do skills") and avoiding statements that lead or provide attention to unacceptable behaviors (the "don't skills"). In the CDI teach session, the therapist defines each skill and its specific effect on the child and facilitates parents' learning by engaging them in discussion and role-play of the skills. The CDI do skills are referred to as the PRIDE skills—praise, reflection, imitation, description, and enthusiasm.

Do Skills

Labeled praise is a compliment directed to the child that specifically labels what the child did that was positive. Praise increases the likelihood that the child will repeat the praised behavior. Praise also serves to improve self-esteem and add warmth to the interaction. Therapists can assist parents in learning this skill by stating several praise stems (e.g., "I like how you _____," "Thank you so much for _____") and having parents finish the sentences with positive opposites of problem behaviors their child exhibits. For example, the parent of a hyperactive child might wish to praise calm behavior using such statements as "I like how you stayed in your chair while you colored that house." During coaching, therapists encourage parents to search for positive opposites, and they point out changes in child behaviors that parents have praised. The coach's praise of the parent similarly increases the parent's use of purposeful labeled praise and serves to increase the parent's self-efficacy.

Reflection is a statement that repeats or paraphrases the child's verbalizations. This skill is effective in rewarding the child for appropriate talk and showing the child that the parent is actively attending to him or her. Reflections are also beneficial to speech and language development because of the parent's ability to restate child verbalizations correctly. For example, if a child said, "I don't got anymore of those ones," the parent might reflect, "That's right—you don't have any more blue blocks." Reflections should not change the meaning of a child's verbalization but can model correct vocabulary, grammar, and pronunciation for the child.

Imitation involves attending to the child's appropriate play by engaging in similar play and mirroring the child's activity and level of enthusiasm. Imitation expresses interest and approval of the child's activity and leads to child imitation of the parent's behaviors (Roberts, 1981). For parents who do not typically play with their child or who are unsure of how to play, imitation helps them know what to do and helps them match their play to the child's developmental level. Children with oppositional behavior may initially be resistant to cooperative play in which a parent might add parts to the child's construction or draw on the child's picture. In these cases, parents begin with parallel play, engaging in similar play right next to the child. As therapy progresses and the child becomes more receptive, the therapist guides the parent gradually toward cooperative play.

Behavior descriptions describe specifically what the child is doing (e.g., "You're putting the blue blocks on top"). They describe the child's immediately ongoing behavior rather than past behavior or suggestions for future behavior. Behavior descriptions are another way for parents to express approval of their child's activities. Through their coaching, therapists help parents learn to focus descriptions on behaviors that they want to increase. For example, parents can encourage persistence in children with low frustration tolerance by describing effortful behaviors ("You are working hard to fit the block in that space").

Enthusiasm is a quality of genuine involvement that expresses enjoyment in the parent–child interaction. This aspect of CDI comes naturally to some parents, but others may need to be reminded that expressing enthusiasm adds warmth and positivity to the interaction. To help increase parental enthusiasm, therapists model enthusiasm in their voice as they coach, and they praise successive approximations of parental enthusiasm. When parents express enthusiasm in the play, therapists are alert to point out the positive response of the child.

Don't Skills

Parents are also taught not to use commands, questions, or criticisms during the CDI. Therapists explain that both commands and questions have important functions in parent–child communication but that during daily CDI, these behaviors should be avoided because they are leading, rather than following, behaviors and the parent must follow the child's lead during CDI. Commands are clearly leading—they tell the child to do something. Questions lead the conversation and request an answer from the child. Questions can also inadvertently express disapproval of the child's behavior. Criticism leads by suggesting that the child stop or change current behavior. Criticism also lowers child self-esteem and lessens the positivity and warmth of the interaction that CDI is designed to create.

Active Ignoring

A key component of CDI is the use of *active ignoring* of negative child behavior in conjunction with use of the PRIDE skills to reinforce positive child behavior. Active ignoring decreases mild negative attention-seeking behaviors, such as yelling, sassing, or whining. Parents learn to remove their attention completely when their child engages in negative behavior and to reengage quickly when the negative behavior stops. When parents first use an active ignore, the therapist coaches the parent to explain to the child that they will not play with the child unless the child plays nicely. After this explanation is given, the therapist then coaches the parent to ignore each time a negative behavior occurs and helps the parent continue to ignore the behavior by providing nonstop comments of support. As soon as the child engages in any non-negative behavior, the therapist immediately coaches the parent to praise that behavior. The contrast in the parents' response to child's positive versus negative behaviors has the effect of rapidly changing the child's behavior in the session, which provides an important demonstration to parents of their ability to shape their child's behavior with their attention during CDI. Parents are assigned to practice the CDI skills at home with their child for 5 minutes each day; these CDI home sessions are labeled *special time* to the child. The remaining treatment sessions in this first phase of PCIT are coaching sessions that include the child.

Child-Directed Interaction Coach Sessions

The coach sessions begin with a 5- to 10-minute check-in when the therapist and parents review the CDI homework and the child's behavior during the previous week. The therapist then has the parent begin practicing the CDI with the child while the therapist codes the interaction from an observation room. By coding, or tallying, the frequency of the parents' skills during a 5-minute observation, the therapist can assess progress made since the previous session and can determine which skills to focus on during coaching. When coaching the CDI, therapists initially focus on following the parent's lead, just as the parent follows the child's lead in the CDI. One of the most effective kinds of coaching statements is a short, labeled praise following the parent's use of a CDI skill, such as "Great reflection!" or "Excellent behavior to praise." Coaching in CDI becomes a bit more directive after one or two coach sessions, when parents are comfortable with the procedure. For example, a therapist might suggest that the parent praise a particular behavior, such as "You could praise him for sharing with you," to help parents notice cooperative positive opposite behaviors.

Parents continue in the CDI phase of treatment until they have mastered the CDI skills, as indicated by the data coded in the 5-minute observation at the start of the session. The CDI mastery criteria consist of 10 behavior descriptions, 10 reflections, and 10 labeled praises with no more than three of the don't skills (questions, commands, or criticisms) during the 5-minute interval. Once parents have met the CDI mastery criteria, they are ready to begin the second phase of treatment.

Parent-Directed Interaction

The PDI phase of treatment also begins with a parents-only PDI teach session in which the specific skills of the interaction are described, the rationale for each step is discussed, and the interaction is role-played with the parents. Therapists begin by explaining that parents will continue to spend 5 minutes of CDI special time daily with their child and will practice the PDI initially in daily play situations as well. Unlike with CDI, however, PDI homework progresses in gradual steps from initial practice during play to a procedure used only when it is necessary to obtain the child's compliance.

Effective Commands

The first skill that parents learn in the PDI teach session is to give effective commands. Therapists describe eight rules for effective commands. The first rule is to make the command direct—not to state it as a question or a choice for the child to make. The PDI commands are also stated positively—telling the child what to do rather than what not to do. Positive commands give the child a clear understanding of the exact behavior expected. The third rule of effective commands is that only one command is given at a time. Effective commands also specify the exact behavior the child is to perform and call for behavior the child is capable of doing. The commands must be given in a polite and respectful tone, which helps compliance generalize to other settings such as school. Finally, commands must be explained, either before they are given or after they are obeyed but not in between ("I want to play with the crayons now. Please hand me the crayon box."). This final rule is important because it allows children to hear the reason but prevents the reason from reinforcing dawdling or other negative behavior that might occur after a command.

Figure 10.1 presents a diagram detailing the steps of the PDI procedure from initial command to the final labeled praise for child compliance. The procedure provides specific statements for use at each step, which provides consistency in behavior management and simplifies the process for both parent and child.

After the Command

During the PDI teach session, therapists ask parents to predict how their child might respond at each step so the discussion can be tailored to the child's specific behavioral issues. Compliance is defined as obeying or clearly beginning to obey within 5 seconds of the command. After a command, parents are instructed to count silently to 5 and to say nothing during this time unless their child complies. When the child obeys, parents immediately give their child an enthusiastic labeled praise. If the child does not obey within

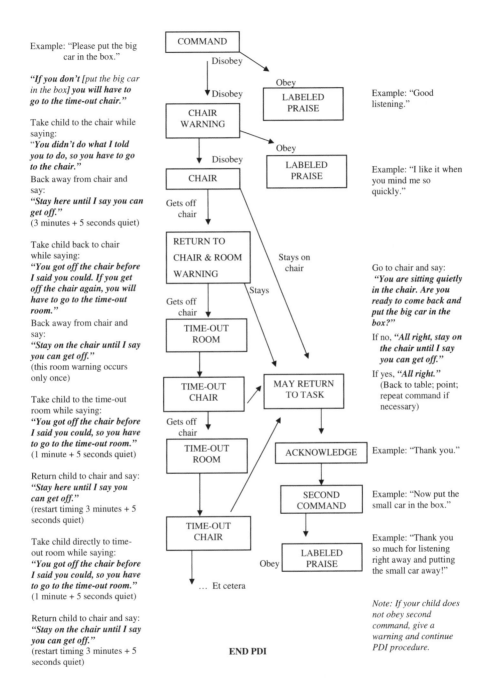

Example: "Please put the big car in the box."

"If you don't [put the big car in the box] you will have to go to the time-out chair."

Take child to the chair while saying:
"You didn't do what I told you to do, so you have to go to the chair."
Back away from chair and say:
"Stay here until I say you can get off."
(3 minutes + 5 seconds quiet)

Take child back to chair while saying:
"You got off the chair before I said you could. If you get off the chair again, you will have to go to the time-out room."
Back away from chair and say:
"Stay on the chair until I say you can get off."
(this room warning occurs only once)

Take child to the time-out room while saying:
"You got off the chair before I said you could, so you have to go to the time-out room."
(1 minute + 5 seconds quiet)

Return child to chair and say:
"Stay here until I say you can get off."
(restart timing 3 minutes + 5 seconds quiet)

Take child directly to time-out room while saying:
"You got off the chair before I said you could, so you have to go to the time-out room."
(1 minute + 5 seconds quiet)

Return child to chair and say:
"Stay on the chair until I say you can get off."
(restart timing 3 minutes + 5 seconds quiet)

COMMAND

Disobey

Obey

Disobey

Obey

LABELED PRAISE

Example: "Good listening."

CHAIR WARNING

Disobey

Obey

LABELED PRAISE

Example: "I like it when you mind me so quickly."

CHAIR

Gets off chair

RETURN TO CHAIR & ROOM WARNING

Stays on chair

Stays

Gets off chair

TIME-OUT ROOM

TIME-OUT CHAIR

MAY RETURN TO TASK

Go to chair and say:
"You are sitting quietly in the chair. Are you ready to come back and put the big car in the box?"

If no, *"All right, stay on the chair until I say you can get off."*

If yes, *"All right."*
(Back to table; point; repeat command if necessary)

Gets off chair

TIME-OUT ROOM

ACKNOWLEDGE

Example: "Thank you."

TIME-OUT CHAIR

SECOND COMMAND

Example: "Now put the small car in the box."

Obey

LABELED PRAISE

Example: "Thank you so much for listening right away and putting the small car away!"

... Et cetera

Note: If your child does not obey second command, give a warning and continue PDI procedure.

END PDI

Figure 10.1. Time-out diagram. PDI = parent-directed intervention.

5 seconds, however, parents give a warning, using the same phrase each time (see Figure 10.1).

After their warning, parents again remain silent until the child obeys or until 5 seconds have elapsed without compliance. If the child obeys, the parent gives a labeled praise. If the child does not comply within 5 seconds, the parent takes the child quickly to the time-out chair while explaining the reason for time-out in the fewest words possible. This reason (see Figure 10.1) is stated each time the child goes to the chair for disobeying a warning.

In discussing the time-out chair, the therapist explains the importance of saying only the scripted statement while taking the child to the chair and demonstrates calm and safe ways to escort or carry the child if needed. Therapists also teach methods the parents might use to keep themselves calm during this procedure.

Each time the parents leave their child on the time-out chair, they remind the child to stay on the chair until he or she is given permission to get off. Time-out on the chair lasts for 3 minutes plus a final 5 seconds during which the child is quiet on the chair. The child is not told that time-out is 3 minutes because most preschoolers have a poor concept of time, and these extra words are not necessary. As soon as the 3 minutes are up, the therapist cues the parent to count silently to 5 if the child is quiet. If the child is not quiet, the therapist begins counting for the parent each time there is a silence, until a 5-second period of quiet has been achieved. Therapists explain the importance of ignoring all of the child's attention-seeking behaviors on the chair. The final 5 seconds of quiet prevents the child from learning that some disruptive behavior just before time-out ended was causal. After 3 minutes plus 5 seconds of quiet, the parent states that the child has been quiet on the chair and asks whether the child is ready to come back and obey the original command.

If the child indicates willingness to obey the command, the parent leads the child back to the task. If the child does not indicate willingness to obey, the 3 minutes plus 5 seconds on the chair begins again. Once the child has agreed to obey the command and returns to the task, it is likely the child will obey. When the child obeys, the parent acknowledges the compliance and immediately gives another very similar command. The child is again likely to obey, at which point the parent gives enthusiastic labeled praise for minding so quickly and moves back into CDI. These final steps not only reward compliance but also concretely demonstrate for the child the difference between timely compliance and disobedience.

Time-Out Room

The time-out room is a back-up procedure for children who do not stay on the time-out chair as instructed. It provides a physical-barrier time-out until the child learns to stay on the chair during time-out. Children quickly learn that getting off the chair without permission leads only to a different time-out that does not permit escape and that they must still complete a chair time-out before being allowed to obey the original command and return to play. On average, disruptive children go to the time-out room twice before learning to stay on the chair.

When selecting a time-out room in the clinic or in the child's home, the main requirement is a physical barrier that prevents the child from receiving attention from the parent, such as being chased, and that prevents access to toys or similar reinforcement. Many clinics build dedicated time-out rooms adjoining the playroom, which are typically small (perhaps around 5 feet × 5 feet), well-lit, empty rooms with a high doorknob to prevent escape or with Dutch doors that can be fastened from the outside. The clinic time-out room could also be another nearby clinic room emptied of items that could be damaged. With regular doors, it is important to have a window or ceiling video monitor into the room. At home, the most common time-out room is the child's bedroom, child-proofed for safety and with toys removed during the 1st or 2nd week of PDI homework when a back-up room may be needed.

When a child gets off the time-out chair without permission, the parent gives one warning that the child will go to the time-out room if he or she get off the chair again without permission. After that point, when a child gets off the chair without permission, the parent directs the child to the room while giving the reason (see Figure 10.1). The child stays in the room for 1 minute plus 5 seconds of quiet. Then the parent brings the child back to the time-out chair, and the procedure continues until the child obeys the original and second command and the parent and child return to CDI.

Parent-Directed Interaction Coach Sessions

After the PDI teach session, parents do not practice the PDI with their children until the first PDI coach session. This allows parents to be coached the first time they practice PDI with their child. The structure of the PDI coach sessions is similar to that of the CDI coach sessions.

At the first PDI coach session, the interaction is not coded at the start of the session. Rather, this session begins immediately with coaching to ensure that the procedure is followed precisely the first few times the child experiences the PDI. Coaching in PDI is initially highly directive. Parents have become comfortable with coaching during the CDI phase of treatment, and at this point they trust the therapist's direction. Knowing they have therapist support when they first practice the PDI with their child is reassuring to parents. Therapists help parents correct mistakes, and they verbalize the next steps of the PDI. As parents become confident with the procedure in later sessions, therapist coaching becomes less directive. Therapists may then focus on reinforcing parent skills and fine tuning their timing and selection of positive opposite commands to target remaining child problems.

House Rules

House rules are introduced in the PDI phase of treatment after the child no longer requires time-outs to obey running commands. House rules serve as standing commands in the household—they are always in effect, so parents need not restate the command before it is enforced. House rules are used primarily to deal with unpredictable destructive or aggressive behaviors that have no immediate positive opposite command that can be effectively used. Parents first explain a house rule to their child at a neutral time and then for awhile they label the targeted behavior for the child when it occurs until they are certain the child understands what behavior is encompassed by the house rule. For example, parents might target "hurting the cat," and for 2 days point out each time it occurs ("That is hurting the cat") until they are certain the child understands what "hurting" includes. Once the rule is in place, the child is sent immediately to the time-out chair whenever the house rule is broken. When the 3 minutes plus 5 seconds on the chair is completed, the parent says simply, "Time-out is over now. Remember not to hurt the cat."

In addition to house rules, two other variations of the PCIT procedures may be introduced in the final few PDI sessions if problems remain with the child's behavior in public situations (e.g., in the grocery store) or during sibling interactions. These procedures, which parents can learn quickly at this point in treatment, are optional and depend on the family's needs (see Eyberg & Child Study Lab, 1999).

Criteria for Treatment Completion

PDI mastery criteria are met when, in the coded observation of PDI at the start of a session, at least 75% of parent commands are positive, direct commands with at least 75% correct follow-through—labeled praise following compliance or a time-out warning following noncompliance. If a command requires a warning, the PDI procedure must be followed through correctly until the original command is obeyed.

PCIT continues until three completion criteria are met: (a) The parents demonstrate mastery of the PCIT skills (both CDI and PDI skills); (b) the child's behavior is rated on the ECBI within 0.5 standard deviation of the normative mean (raw score ≤ 114 on the ECBI Intensity Scale); and (c) the parents indicate confidence in their ability to manage their child's behavior on their own. The average length of treatment is 14 sessions.

EMPIRICAL SUPPORT

Positive parent and child outcomes of PCIT have been demonstrated in several randomized controlled trials (Bagner & Eyberg, 2007; Chaffin et al., 2004; Nixon, Sweeny, Erickson, & Touyz, 2003; Schuhmann, Foote, Eyberg, Boggs, & Algina, 1998), and long-term follow-up studies have found maintenance of parent and child gains up to 6 years (Boggs et al., 2004; Eyberg et al., 2001; Hood & Eyberg, 2003). Effects of treatment have demonstrated generalizability to the child's classroom behavior (Funderburk et al., 1998; McNeil, Eyberg, Eisenstadt, Newcomb, & Funderburk, 1991) and to untreated siblings of the target child (Brestan, Eyberg, Boggs, & Algina, 1997)

Recent studies have reported on PCIT's effectiveness for treating children with related disorders such as attention-deficit/hyperactivity disorder (Matos, Torres, Santiago, Jurado, & Rodriguez, 2006) as well as internalizing disorders such as separation anxiety disorder (Chase & Eyberg, 2008; Pincus, Santucci, Ehrenreich, & Eyberg, 2008). Successful outcomes have been reported with families from diverse cultural groups including Mexican American families (McCabe & Lau, in press), Puerto Rican families (Matos et al., 2006), Norwegian families (Bjørseth & Wormdal, 2005), Australian families (Nixon et al., 2003; Phillips, Morgan, Cawthorne, & Barnett, 2008), and Chinese families (Leung, Tsang, Heung, & Yiu, 2009). Positive outcomes in pediatric primary care (Harwood, O'Brien, Carter, & Eyberg, 2008) and with children born prematurely (Bagner, Sheinkopf, Miller-Loncar, Vohr, & Lester, 2008) have also been reported when PCIT has been used as a preventive intervention.

CASE ILLUSTRATION

Casey is a 4-year-old girl who was referred to the clinic by her pediatrician after two unsuccessful medication trials for treatment of hyperactive, disruptive behavior at home and in preschool. Casey's mother, Ms. Brown, is a single mother who works full time as a waitress. Casey has never known her father, and there are no other children in the family.

During the clinical interview, Ms. Brown appeared fatigued and was near tears much of the time. She reported that Casey's teacher had threatened to remove Casey from the school if Ms. Brown failed to do something about her behavior. Casey was becoming increasingly aggressive with peers and defiant with her teacher. Ms. Brown was also concerned that Casey would have difficulty in kindergarten the following year if her school behavior did not improve.

Following the interview, Ms. Brown completed the Child Behavior Checklist (Achenbach, 1991) to help the therapist obtain a broad picture of

Casey's behavior in multiple domains and the ECBI (Eyberg & Pincus, 1999) to obtain a baseline measure of Casey's disruptive behaviors at home. Ms. Brown brought to the interview a copy of the Sutter-Eyberg Student Behavior Inventory (Eyberg & Pincus, 1999), a measure of oppositional behavior and attentional difficulties at school Rayfield, Eyberg, & Foote, 1998), that had been completed by Casey's teacher.

The interactions between Casey and her mother were observed and coded during three standard laboratory situations (child-led play, parent-led play, and clean-up) using the Dyadic Parent–Child Interaction Coding System. In the child-led play situation, Ms. Brown spoke very little but watched Casey play with foam blocks, building towers and aggressively knocking them down. When Ms. Brown tried to join the play by asking Casey about her buildings and suggesting that she bring the blocks to the table, Casey ignored her. During the parent-led play, Ms. Brown tried to get Casey to color pictures with her at the table, but Casey said she would color later, when she finished playing blocks. Casey then moved to the jungle animals and continued refusing to color at the table. When Ms. Brown was instructed to tell Casey it was time to leave and she had to put the toys away by herself, Ms. Brown repeatedly asked Casey to clean up. Casey first just ignored her mother, but as Ms. Brown insisted, Casey escalated from whining to yelling "no" to throwing the rubber animals across the room. Ms. Brown finally began putting the toys away herself without saying anything to her daughter. Casey then ran to the toy box and pulled out the blocks while screaming that she wanted to play longer.

The assessment information indicated that PCIT would be an appropriate treatment for Casey and Ms. Brown. During the CDI teach session, Ms. Brown remained enthusiastic about getting help for Casey's behavior but expressed concern about having time to practice at home. The therapist listened empathically as Ms. Brown described her hectic schedule and helped her develop a homework plan she felt was feasible. The therapist then asked Ms. Brown to elaborate her plan, including the room and the toys they would use and the different schedules they would follow for weekdays and weekends. The therapist gave Ms. Brown a homework sheet to mark her 5-minute practice each day and asked her to bring it back the following week.

During the first CDI coach session, Ms. Brown reported that practicing CDI with Casey was harder than she expected, especially refraining from asking questions, and she appeared anxious about being observed. The therapist acknowledged that using the CDI skills would be a major change in how she typically talked to Casey, which is why these skills take several weeks to learn. The therapist also told her that most parents struggle with questions but that she, the therapist, would help through coaching. The therapist observed the play for 5 minutes to assess Ms. Brown's skills and noted that although Ms. Brown still asked many questions she had notably increased the praise she gave to Casey. The following is an excerpt from coaching in this first coaching session.

Casey is holding her doll and quickly searching through a box of play food.

Ms. Brown: What're you looking for? You're looking for the baby's food, aren't you?

The therapist ignores Ms. Brown's questions and waits for a CDI skill before starting to coach.

Ms. Brown: It's nice you found the bottle for baby.

Therapist: Excellent labeled praise. You told her exactly what you liked.

By waiting until Ms. Brown used a CDI skill, the therapist was able to begin to build Ms. Brown's confidence and help lessen her anxiety.

Ms. Brown: Are you. . . . It's nice you're feeding the baby.

Therapist: Wow. You caught the question and made it a praise.

Ms. Brown: You're giving her lots of milk.

Therapist: Great behavior description! You didn't even *start* a question that time.

As Ms. Brown realized that she was improving her skills, she became less anxious, and she increased her praise even more. Using labeled praises for Casey's behavior enabled Ms. Brown to increase Casey's attention to one task. At the beginning of the session, Casey was going from toy to toy, but over the course of the session, Casey played with each toy a little longer. Near the end of the first CDI coach session, the therapist pointed out to Ms. Brown how much longer Casey was playing with a single game, coloring, than she had earlier in the session. Mrs. Brown praised Casey for finishing her picture.

Ms. Brown's skills and self-confidence in giving praise and describing Casey's behavior were noticeably stronger in the second CDI coach session, although she continued to have difficulty with questions, especially when trying to give reflections. Questions remained high in the initial observation at the third CDI coach session. The therapist asked Ms. Brown whether she would find it helpful if the therapist pointed out the questions when they occurred, so that Ms. Brown might become more aware of them and could turn them into statements. Ms. Brown indicated she would like to try that. With Ms. Brown's permission, and with her increased confidence and comfort with coaching, the therapist focused on reducing questions and became slightly more directive in her coaching in this session.

Casey:	I made a flower!
Ms. Brown:	You drew a flower? [*voice inflection rises slightly*]
Therapist:	[*gently*] Oops. Make it a statement.
Ms. Brown:	You *did* draw a flower. A big red flower!
Therapist:	Perfect statement. Those were great reflections!
Casey:	I made a stem on it, too.
Therapist:	Try another reflection.
Ms. Brown:	You made a stem? . . . You made a stem.
Therapist:	Good reflection! Good catching the question and making a statement.
Ms. Brown:	I like your nice straight stem on the flower.
Therapist:	Excellent labeled praise.

By the end of coaching in the third CDI coach session, Casey was talking much more during the play. The therapist explained to Ms. Brown that her reflections had led to Casey's increased sharing of her ideas. She also commented on how much both of them seemed to enjoy this CDI time together.

Ms. Brown's ECBI ratings of Casey's behavior had declined gradually each week in CDI, and by the fifth CDI coach session she described Casey as much less defiant and sassy during transitions or when asked to help pick up her things. She also described Casey as more calm and less wired. Ms. Brown reported that Casey's teacher had commented on her increased cooperation with the other children and noted that Casey had not caused trouble for quite some time. Ms. Brown laughed while thinking about her earlier statement that she might not have time for special time: "Now Casey won't let me forget!" Ms. Brown described Casey's special time as very special for her as well and described it as allowing them to bond in a different way: "We really do have fun together, and I think I get her more now." Ms. Brown met mastery criteria in the sixth CDI coach session.

In the final CDI coach session, the therapist noted several changes in the quality of the mother–child interaction since the initial session. Ms. Brown seemed more relaxed and spontaneous in her play with Casey, and the two talked and laughed together while they played. Casey now remained next to her mother, engaged in a single game throughout their interaction, and even praised her mother twice during the final CDI session. Still, Ms. Brown was eager to begin the PDI to address Casey's dawdling and reluctance to finish tasks, particularly at times they were in a hurry.

During the PDI teach session, Ms. Brown was motivated and positive while the therapist discussed the general goals of PDI and the rules for effective commands, although she expressed concern that Casey would get upset if she used commands that direct. Ms. Brown also expressed hesitancy about the time-out procedure. Ms. Brown said she had tried a time-out chair in the past and it did not work because Casey rarely stayed on the chair. The therapist recalled from the clinical interview that Ms. Brown had described the time-out routine as stressful for both of them and had described frequently reassuring Casey that time-out would be over soon. Ms. Brown had admitted trying to avoid time-out because Casey cried and alternated between apologies and spiteful comments, both of which made Ms. Brown feel guilty.

The therapist explained that the time-out procedure in PCIT is different in several important ways from the procedure she had used. First, she noted that Casey's anger and defiance had decreased markedly during CDI, which would likely mean Casey would be more responsive now to time-out from the positive reinforcement of her mother's attention. The therapist also noted that it is natural for children to test the limits when first in time-out, but she assured Ms. Brown that consistency was the key for Casey to learn PDI quickly. The therapist gave Ms. Brown the PDI handout (Figure 10.1) to review every day so she would feel more confident of the steps during the first practice at the first PDI coach session. She emphasized that Ms. Brown should not attempt the time-out procedure at home until after they practiced in session, explaining that it was important for everything to go just right at the beginning.

In the first PDI coach session, the therapist introduced Casey to the new procedure. The therapist demonstrated the steps of PDI using a large stuffed animal named Mr. Bear. Casey scolded Mr. Bear for not minding and giggled when he went to the chair. She told the therapist that she did not like that chair and was ready to play with her mother. The therapist acknowledged that Casey liked to play with her mother, but if she had to go to the chair, it would be very important for her to stay on the chair quietly until her mother told her she could get off. The therapist also reminded Casey that as long as she minded her mother, they could keep playing and having fun. After a few minutes of CDI coaching, the following exchange took place:

Therapist:	You and Casey are engaged in a very warm interaction. Now, think of a simple, direct command that you can give to Casey, and when you are ready, go ahead and give the command to Casey.
Ms. Brown:	Honey . . . honey, will you hand me that block?
Therapist:	Whoops. Say, "Please hand me the red block."
Ms. Brown:	[*to therapist*] Sorry! [*to Casey*] Hand me the red block, please, Casey.
Casey:	But Mommy, I need it for this tower!
Therapist:	Good direct command. One, two, three, four . . . .

Casey throws the block to her mother.

> Ms. Brown: [to therapist] Do I praise that? [to Casey] Thank you, Casey.

> Therapist: Great staying calm. Good praise, but label it: "Thanks for giving me the block."

> Ms. Brown: Thank you for giving me the block.

> Therapist: Good labeled praise. We'll ignore that throwing right now and just return to CDI. For the next command, we'll tell her to give you something *gently.*

> Ms. Brown: Now you're putting the blue block on top of my red block!

> Therapist: Wonderful jumping right back into CDI. We'll stay in CDI for half a minute now, and then we'll use the "gently" command.

The therapist continues to praise mother's CDI skills for 30 seconds.

> Therapist: OK, tell her to hand you something *gently.*

> Ms. Brown: Please put the green block in my hand gently.

> Therapist: Perfect direct command.

Casey hesitates at first but then places block in Ms. Brown's hand softly.

> Therapist: Now big labeled praise for minding!

> Ms. Brown: Thank you for listening to me right away, sweetie!

> Therapist: Wonderful labeled praise! Now back to CDI, and you can explain why you like it when she listens.

By the third PDI coach session, Ms. Brown knew all of the steps of the PDI procedure and demonstrated no hesitation in using them. Casey had been sent to the time-out chair twice in the first PDI coach session but had not had to go to the time-out chair in the second PDI coach session or in this session. In the third PDI coach session, Ms. Brown needed to use only one warning, which Casey obeyed quickly. Because Ms. Brown had been consistent in using direct commands since beginning PDI, Casey's behavior had never escalated to throwing toys or other aggressive behaviors in response to directions. At home, Casey was increasingly more compliant to her mother's commands, and Ms. Brown said the home had become "so much more peaceful."

The homework sheets reflected the positive change reported by Ms. Brown. The week after the first PDI coach session, Casey was taken to the chair several times and to the back-up room twice. After the first week of PDI practice at home, Casey no longer got off the time-out chair without permission, and time-outs became less frequent. Time-out warnings also decreased each week. The therapist compared the improvements Ms. Brown reported with her ratings on the ECBI, which she had graphed each week for their review. The graph reflected a continued decline in problem behaviors. The therapist and Ms. Brown identified remaining problem areas and discussed useful positive opposite commands that Ms. Brown could use at home to reduce these behaviors.

During the fourth PDI coach session, the therapist and Ms. Brown discussed house rules. Although most often used for aggressive or destructive behaviors, Casey was no longer playing aggressively at home. However, Ms. Brown was concerned about Casey's running in the house and jumping on the furniture. She had tried praising the positive opposite behaviors (walking in the house, keeping her feet off the furniture) daily, but it did not seem to have an effect when Casey was what her mother described as "wound up." Ms. Brown was eager to implement house rules to address these behaviors. She chose to start with jumping on the furniture, which included jumping on the living room sofa and on Casey's bed. The therapist and Ms. Brown made the following plan: For 2 days after the session, Ms. Brown would label this behavior for Casey so that Casey would clearly understand the scope of the new house rule. On the 3rd day, Ms. Brown would explain to Casey that it had been hard for Casey to remember not to jump on the furniture, so to help her remember the rule, she would have to go to time-out any time she jumped on the furniture until she learned to obey the rule.

At the next session, Casey was eager to tell the therapist that she did not jump on the furniture any more. Both the therapist and her mother praised her for being such a fast learner and working hard to obey the house rule. The therapist and Ms. Brown conferred briefly, and then together they told Casey that there was only one other house rule that she needed to learn. They explained the "no running in the house" rule. Ms. Brown and Casey then began playing with the toys while the therapist coded their behaviors in the CDI and PDI. Ms. Brown demonstrated skills mastery criteria in both situations, and Casey obeyed all the commands she was given during the observation. The therapist coached Ms. Brown for just a few minutes in CDI and quickly scored the ECBI, which was now within the normal range. The therapist returned to the playroom and asked Ms. Brown about Casey's behavior at school, commenting that Ms. Brown had not mentioned that recently. Ms. Brown looked surprised and then said, "I had almost forgotten that school had been a problem. Casey's teacher hasn't sent home notes for at least 3 weeks." The therapist also asked about Casey's behavior with her mother in public. Ms. Brown described shopping at the mall with Casey earlier in the week without problems, even when they stopped in the mall restaurant for lunch.

The therapist gave Ms. Brown a handout about handling misbehavior in public but noted that Casey seemed to be cooperating very well both at home and in public. They looked at the graph of Casey's ECBI scores, and the therapist noted to Ms. Brown that she was now rating Casey's behavior as typical of most 4-year-olds. The therapist again praised Ms. Brown's CDI and PDI skills, stated that she had worked hard in PCIT, and asked about her feelings of readiness to graduate. Ms. Brown said that when the therapist originally mentioned graduation last week, she could not have imagined managing on her own, but after thinking about it all week, she had decided that maybe she could. However, she expressed concern that the changes might not last. The therapist assured Ms. Brown that she and Casey did not have to end treatment until Ms. Brown felt ready. The therapist suggested waiting 3 or 4 weeks before their next session so Ms. Brown could see how she did on her own. She gave Ms. Brown a Sutter-Eyberg Student Behavior Inventory for the teacher to complete, so that she could bring it back to the last session and they could be sure things at school were on track. Ms. Brown looked relieved about having a "check-up" session and stated that it was an excellent plan. An appointment was made for 4 weeks later, and the therapist told Ms. Brown she could call if an earlier appointment was needed, although her parenting skills and confidence would likely continue to increase as time elapsed. She gave Casey a blue ribbon that read "Good Behavior" and told her she had done a wonderful job of learning to get along with her mom and her friends at school. She told Casey and Ms. Brown together to be sure to have special time every day forever. About 1 week prior to the scheduled "booster" session, Ms. Brown called the therapist to cancel the appointment because "things were just going so smoothly."

CONCLUSION AND FUTURE DIRECTIONS

PCIT is a theoretically grounded, evidence-based treatment for young children with disruptive behavior. The goal of PCIT is to teach parents skills that reflect both the nurturance and the limits required for healthy child development. The initial phase of treatment enhances the parent–child attachment relationship and is the foundation for the second phase in which parents learn to give clear, age-appropriate directions with consistent follow-through. Progress through PCIT is guided by parent skill acquisition and child behavior change, both of which are monitored weekly during treatment to enable the therapist to tailor treatment to the family's needs.

Effective dissemination of PCIT from academic settings to community-based settings is a priority for PCIT researchers. The skills required of PCIT therapists, including the coding and coaching of parent–child interactions, are complex and require extensive training and practice to master. Preliminary research examining alternative methods for training community providers has suggested that simply reading the treatment manual is not sufficient (Herschell et al., 2008), but much more research is needed to identify the necessary and sufficient components of training for effective treatment delivery. Effective dissemination of PCIT to the community also requires examination of the extent to which treatment can be streamlined, without losing its effectiveness, to meet different levels of need. For example, the feasibility of a bibliotherapy format and an abbreviated group treatment format for preventive intervention in pediatric primary care was recently examined with promising results (Harwood, O'Brien, Carter, & Eyberg, 2008). Further study of innovative adaptations of PCIT for children and families with different needs may lead to effective services for a greater number of families.

REFERENCES

Achenbach, T. M. (1991). *Integrative guide for the 1991 CBCL/4-18, YSR, and TRF profiles*. Burlington: University of Vermont, Department of Psychiatry.

Bagner, D. M., & Eyberg, S. M. (2007). Parent–child interaction therapy for disruptive behavior in children with mental retardation: A randomized controlled trial. *Journal of Clinical Child and Adolescent Psychology, 36*, 418–429.

Bagner, D. M., Sheinkopf, S. J., Miller-Loncar, C., Vohr, B. R., & Lester, B. M. (2008, October). *A randomized treatment trial for externalizing behavior problems in children born premature: Interim findings*. Poster presented at the Kansas Conference on Child Health Psychology, Lawrence, KS.

Baumrind, D. (1966). Effects of authoritative parental control on child behavior. *Child Development, 37*, 887–907.

Baumrind, D. (1991). The influence of parenting style on adolescent competence and substance use. *Journal of Early Adolescence, 11*, 56–95.

Bjørseth, Å., & Wormdal, A. K. (2005). Med terapeuten påøret [Parent child interaction therapy]. *Tidsskrift for Norsk Psykologforening, 42*, 693–699.

Boggs, S. R., & Eyberg, S. M. (2008). Positive attention. In W. O'Donohue & J. D. Fisher (Eds.), *Cognitive behavior therapy: Applying empirically supported techniques in your practice* (2nd ed., pp. 396–401). New York: Wiley.

Boggs, S. R., Eyberg, S. M., Edwards, D., Rayfield, A., Jacobs, J., Bagner, D., & Hood, K. (2004). Outcomes of parent–child interaction therapy: A comparison of dropouts and treatment completers one to three years after treatment. *Child & Family Behavior Therapy, 26*, 1–22.

Brestan, E. V., Eyberg, S. M., Boggs, S. R., & Algina, J. (1997). Parent–child interaction therapy: Parent perceptions of untreated siblings. *Child & Family Behavior Therapy, 19*, 13–28.

Chaffin, M., Silovsky, J. F., Funderburk, B., Valle, L. A., Brestan, E. V., Balachova, T., et al. (2004). Parent–child interaction therapy with physically abusive parents: Efficacy for reducing future abuse reports. *Journal of Consulting and Clinical Psychology, 72*, 500–510.

Chase, R. M., & Eyberg, S. M. (2008). Clinical presentation and treatment outcome for children with comorbid externalizing and internalizing symptoms. *Journal of Anxiety Disorders, 22,* 273–282.

Eisenstadt, T. H., Eyberg, S., McNeil, C. B., Newcomb, K., & Funderburk, B. (1993). Parent–child interaction therapy with behavior problem children: Relative effectiveness of two stages and overall treatment outcome. *Journal of Clinical Child Psychology, 22,* 42–51.

Eyberg, S. M., & Child Study Lab. (1999). *Parent–child interaction therapy: Integrity checklists and materials.* Retrieved December 1, 2008 http://www.pcit.org

Eyberg, S. M., Funderburk, B. W., Hembree-Kigin, T. L., McNeil, C. B., Querido, J. G., & Hood, K. (2001). Parent–child interaction therapy with behavior problem children: One and two year maintenance of treatment effects in the family. *Child & Family Behavior Therapy, 23,* 1–20.

Eyberg, S. M., Nelson, M. M., Duke, M., & Boggs, S. R. (2005). Manual for the Dyadic Parent–Child Interaction Coding System (3rd ed.). Retrieved April 23, 2006, from http://pcit.phhp.ufl.edu/DPICSfiles/DPICS%20Draft%203.03.pdf

Eyberg, S. M., & Pincus, D. (1999). Eyberg Child Behavior Inventory & Sutter-Eyberg Student Behavior Inventory: Professional manual. Odessa, FL: Psychological Assessment Resources.

Flavell, J. H., & Miller, P. H. (1998). Social cognition. In D. Kuhn & R. S. Siegler (Eds.) & W. Damon (Series Ed.), *Handbook of child psychology: Vol. 2. Cognition, perception, and language* (5th ed., pp. 851–898). New York: Wiley.

Funderburk, B. W., Eyberg, S. M., Newcomb, K., McNeil, C., Hembree-Kigin, T., & Capage, L. (1998). Parent–child interaction therapy with behavior problem children: Maintenance of treatment effects in the school setting. *Child & Family Behavior Therapy, 20,* 17–38.

Harwood, M.D., O'Brien, K. A., Carter, C., & Eyberg, S. M. (2008, April). *Early identification and intervention for disruptive behavior in primary care: A randomized controlled trial.* Poster presented at the Child Health Psychology Conference, Miami, Florida.

Hood, K., & Eyberg, S. M. (2003). Outcomes of parent–child interaction therapy: Mothers' reports on maintenance three to six years after treatment. *Journal of Clinical Child and Adolescent Psychology, 32,* 419–429.

Leung, C., Tsang, S., Heung, K., & Yiu, I. (2009). Effectiveness of parent child interaction therapy (PCIT) in Hong Kong. *Research on Social Work Practice, 19,* 304–313.

Matos, M., Torres, R., Santiago, R., Jurado, M., & Rodriguez, I. (2006). Adaptation of parent–child interaction therapy for Puerto Rican families: A preliminary study. *Family Process, 45,* 205–222.

McCabe, K. M., & Lau, A. (in press). Parent–child interactions among Mexican-American parents and preschoolers: Do clinic-referred families differ from nonreferred families? *Behavior Therapy.*

McNeil, C., Eyberg, S., Eisenstadt, T., Newcomb, K., & Funderburk, B. (1991). Parent–child interaction therapy with behavior problem children: Generalization of treatment effects to the school setting. *Journal of Clinical Child Psychology, 20,* 140–151.

Nixon, R. D. V., Sweeny, L., Erickson, D. B., & Touyz, S. W. (2003). Parent–child interaction therapy: A comparison of standard and abbreviated treatments for oppositional defiant preschoolers. *Journal of Consulting and Clinical Psychology, 71,* 251–260.

Patterson, G. R. (1982). *Coercive family process.* Eugene, OR: Castalia.

Phillips, J., Morgan, S., Cawthorne, K., & Barnett, B. (2008). Pilot evaluation of parent–child interaction therapy delivered in an Australian community early childhood clinic setting. *Australian and New Zealand Journal of Psychiatry, 42,* 712–719.

Pincus, D. B., Santucci, L. C., Ehrenreich, J., & Eyberg, S. M. (2008). The implementation of modified parent–child interaction therapy for youth with separation anxiety disorder. *Cognitive and Behavioral Practice,15,* 118–125.

Rayfield, A. R., Eyberg, S. M., & Foote, R. (1998). Teacher rating of conduct problem behavior: The Sutter–Eyberg Student Behavior Inventory Revised. *Educational and Psychological Measurement, 58,* 88–98.

Rickard, K., Graziano, W. G., & Forehand, R. (1984). Parental expectations and childhood deviancy in clinic-referred and non-clinic children. *Journal of Clinical Child Psychology, 13,* 179–186.

Roberts, M. C. (1981). Toward a reconceptualization of reciprocal imitation phenomenon: Two experiments. *Journal of Research in Personality, 15,* 447–459.

Schuhmann, E. M., Foote, R., Eyberg, S. M., Boggs, S., & Algina, J. (1998). Parent–child interaction therapy: Interim report of a randomized trial with short-term maintenance. *Journal of Clinical Child Psychology, 27,* 34–45.

11

JUNGIAN SANDPLAY THERAPY FOR PRESCHOOLERS WITH DISRUPTIVE BEHAVIOR PROBLEMS

ERIC J. GREEN AND KRISTI GIBBS

The conflict can only be resolved through the symbol. (Jung, 1943, p. 191)

In this chapter, we look at the usefulness of sand therapy with preschool children diagnosed with disruptive behavior disorders, including attention-deficit/hyperactivity disorder and oppositional defiant disorder. First, we provide a brief overview of the theory behind and depth of symbolic meaning in conducting sand therapy with young children. Next, we review the current literature on developmental issues related to young children's disordered behaviors to provide a context for mental health clinicians working with this special population. Following this, we describe several sand techniques in detail. Last, we present a case study from Eric J. Green's clinical practice that illustrates the concepts contained in this chapter on honoring the depth and meaning of sandplay while assisting a young child with significant behavior problems. The goal is to uncover symbols in preschool children's play that may lead to a healthy integration of the conflicting behaviors and motivations behind those behaviors.

BASIC RATIONALE AND THEORY

Jungian sandplay originated in the 1950s when Jung asked Swiss psychotherapist Dora Kalff to study sandplay under Margaret Lowenfeld in London. In the 1920s, Lowenfeld (1979) developed a therapeutic method for preschool children to communicate their feelings and thoughts, symbolically, by playing in sand. Through the use of sand trays, sand, and sand miniatures, Lowenfeld discovered that children communicated conscious and unconscious thoughts in less threatening ways than by directly verbalizing them to an adult. Lowenfeld created the *world technique*, a therapeutic intervention in which children used sand figurines in a sand tray to construct a world.

In 1962, Kalff built on Lowenfeld's work and termed the intervention *sandplay* while at a conference of Jungian analysts in California (Steinhardt, 2000). Kalff's (1980) sandplay was rooted in Jung's belief that the psyche can be activated to move toward wholeness and healing and that individuation occurs in the sand process through the *temenos*, or free and protected space. *Protected space* refers to the way in which the therapist listens, observes, and serves nonjudgmentally as a psychological container for the emotional content that becomes activated by the sand therapy process (Green, 2008; McNulty, 2007). The counselor provides the free and protected space in which a creation in the sand may symbolize the inner drama and healing potential of the child's psyche. The therapeutic space is referred to in the literature by multiple names, including *secured–symbolizing field* (Goodheart, 1980), *transitional play space* (Winnicott, 1971), and *third area* or *area of experience* (Gordon, 1993). Activating the self-healing force in a child's psyche to resolve psychosocial struggles may occur within the safety of the space where unconscious forces are free to reproduce, as is inherent in sandplay.

The therapeutic rationale for sandplay is that children reproduce symbolic scenes of their immediate experience and link opposites from their inner and outer worlds. Through the concretization of unconscious experiences, children's psyches are able to make meaningful links and develop mastery over difficult feelings. Moreover, it is what children experience for themselves that is therapeutic in sandplay (Bradway & McCoard, 1997; De Domenico, 1994), not the therapist's analysis of the symbols contained within the scene. The emerging worlds in the tray illustrate the child's unconscious conflicts as sandplay provides an opportunity for both symbolic and realistic grounding to occur. Moreover, sandplay permits children to express their archetypal and intrapersonal worlds, connects them to everyday reality, and creates a communication between the conscious and unconscious minds through which psychogenic healing occurs (Boik & Goodwin, 2000; Carey, 1999; Green & Connolly, 2009; Weinrib, 1980).

Edinger (1992) described the four central archetypes found in sandplay: (a) Great Mother, which is the feminine principle, or *anima;* (b) Spiritual Father, which is the masculine principle, or *animus;* (c) Transformation, which is the journey, descent into darkness, death, rebirth, and redemption; and (d) the central archetype, the Self, which is wholeness, depicted as a circle. The Self is the organizing archetype of unity and represents the totality of the individual to which the ego is subordinated (Steinhardt, 2000). In sandplay, Jungian play therapists believe the Self is depicted in the sand tray, as the center of the child's psychic existence.

Themes or symbols emerge out of children's sandplay. These themes are typically fluid, serving as guides for further exploration when assisting a child within the therapeutic context. Steinhardt (2000) listed meanings of symbols in sandplay. These meanings were meant to be guideposts or generalities for the therapist, not static definitions, because symbols and their meanings differ among individuals. All symbols in sandplay should be carefully viewed in the context of the individual child and the meaning the child ascribes to them. Steinhardt described the following symbols that may appear in sandplay:

- a hole scooped out of the sand could symbolize a cave, a womb, a volcano, or an entrance into the collective unconscious;
- a mound in the sand or a mountain could symbolize the body of the Earth Mother, a container of warmth;
- drawing lines in the sand could be seen as a life path, a demarcation of territory, or a new path to follow;
- a tunnel or bridge could symbolize communication between where one is and where one wants to go or has been;
- passages downward could symbolize burying something hideous to the conscious—the shadow; and
- resurrection of buried objects may symbolize repressed emotions being released or exposed.

One of the most common sand tray activities in which children engage is the burying of objects (Steinhardt, 2000). Children enjoy burying small objects in the sand tray, just as they enjoy burying objects in sand while playing on a beach. Sometimes children will ask their counselor to find the object hidden in the sand tray. Jungian-oriented counselors could view this request in several different ways. First, children's search into the sand's depth could symbolize the belief that their inner world could be unearthed with the therapist's help. Second, children's request for the therapist to locate hidden objects in the sand tray may be viewed as the children's revealing something that had been unclear or scary and that can now be revealed and tolerated without judgment. Third, the burial of an object could symbolize children's longing for self-acceptance or parental approval, buried deep within their unconscious longings and tacit desires. Or the child could be simply be having fun burying objects in the sand with no deeper subtext involved.

Contemporary authors have cited several therapeutic benefits resulting from children engaging in sandplay therapy to reduce disordered behaviors (Allan, 1988; Allan & Berry, 2002; Boik & Goodwin, 2000; Carey 1999, 2006; Green & Connolly, 2009; Green & Ironside, 2004; McNulty, 2007; Shih, Kao, & Wang, 2006). From a Jungian perspective, sandplay is the physical embodiment of active imagination. It frees creativity, perceptions, inner feelings, and memories as the child transports unconscious thoughts and feelings from the interior to the exterior realm of consciousness directly to the sand tray. Second, many children view sandplay as a natural form of expression, and they are readily attracted to it. Although some children are reticent to engage in certain play activities (i.e., some children are resistant to art activities because they do not believe that they are good artists), they tend to respond positively to sandplay because they feel free to create with less self-criticism or constraint (Green & Christensen, 2006). Third, sandplay is a technique that facilitates a sense of mastery of difficult feelings and conflicted thoughts. Moreover, because sandplay involves nonverbal expression, it engenders a necessary therapeutic distance from distressing or traumatic events for children, including the engagement in disordered or disruptive behaviors.

Sandplay is distinguished from other forms of therapy because it permits children to create a world that provides concrete images of their inner thoughts and feelings because the symbols and sand miniatures serve as a common language. Also, sandplay provides a unique kinesthetic quality because the extremely tactile experience of manipulating sand can be a therapeutic encounter. Touching and playing in the sand may produce a calming effect in anxious or disruptive preschool children (Shih et al., 2006). From a Jungian perspective, the primary therapeutic benefit of sandplay involves the autonomous and regenerative healing power of the child's psyche, which activates and produces symbols that are witnessed without judgment by a caring therapist. Kalff (1980) emphasized that the transformative experience of creating a world in the sand contains the healing. Sandplay facilitates healing and transformation in young children by releasing conflicts from the unconscious in symbolic form and by supporting a healthy reordering of psychological contents (Turner, 2005).

Finally, sandplay therapists believe that children's creative expressions in the sand exemplify a cathartic release of their current distress, pathology, grief, hope, or all of these. Moreover, sandplay shows the means by which children are coping with emotional pain and wounding. By expressing their psychogenic pain in the sand tray, children participate in an emotional catharsis, which may release repressed hostilities and rage associated with unconscious conflicts at the root of disruptive behaviors. "Each sandtray in the process may be seen as part of a series of successive attempts to cope with past and current wounds or as a step in the ongoing journey towards individuation or, almost necessarily, both" (Bradway & McCoard, 1997, p. 49). Catharsis is facilitated by the witnessing of the child's sand scenes by a nonevaluative, caring, trusted adult.

DEVELOPMENTAL ISSUES

According to Powell, Dunlap, and Fox (2006), 10% to 20% of preschool children present the following behaviors at home and/or day care: impulsivity, hyperactivity, oppositionality, and aggression. Approximately half of preschoolers continue to display these behaviors over time (Williford & Shelton, 2008). Some of these preschoolers' disruptive behaviors will continue to escalate in chronicity and impairment, often resulting in a *Diagnostic and Statistical Manual of Mental Disorders* (4th ed.; American Psychiatric Association, 1994) diagnosis of attention-deficit/hyperactivity disorder, oppositional defiant disorder, or conduct disorder. Once established, disruptive behaviors become strikingly stable over time and are resistant to treatment (Hinshaw &Anderson, 1996). Thus, it is prudent for caretakers and clinicians to intervene at an early age while the child is still developmentally susceptible and responsive to behavioral changes (Keenan & Shaw, 1994; Riviere, 2006).

Parenting Styles

When assessing the developmental context of aggressive behavior problems, it is critical to examine the preschool period because most disruptive behaviors begin during this developmental epoch (Davenport & Bourgeois, 2008; Williford & Shelton, 2008). Negative parenting and an inconsistent home environment are the primary variables that facilitate the continuation of disruptive behaviors. According to Davenport and Bourgeois (2008), negative parenting characteristics (e.g., harsh discipline, inconsistent and ineffective discipline, and negative attributions) have consistently been found to predict the development and maintenance of behavior problems in children. Preschool-age children bereft of early positive parenting (e.g., warmth, support, secure attachment) may be more susceptible to acquiring and maintaining aggressive behavior problems throughout childhood.

A significant predictor of children's externalizing and problematic behaviors is parents' use of harsh and punitive discipline (e.g., scolding, spanking, restraining, verbally threatening, grabbing; Davenport & Bourgeois, 2008; Stormshak, Bierman, McMahon, & Lengua, 2000). The component of harsh discipline that seems to affect children most adversely is if their parents' discipline is perceived as including extreme condescension, humiliation, or contempt. Parents who rely on physically aggressive discipline to gain control of their children are more likely to have children who engage in more severe forms of aggressive behavior. According to Davenport and Bourgeois, the obstreperous child's personality interacts with the parents' discipline style in a way that elicits ineffective and inconsistent discipline:

> Over time, these problem behaviors of the child are reinforced when they are effective in preventing discipline, resulting in decreased monitoring of the child by primary caregivers and increasingly negative behaviors by the child within most interpersonal relationships, including those with teachers and peers. (p. 6)

Caretaker Attachments

Attachments between children and their caretakers are another dominant developmental factor in preschoolers' disordered behaviors (Chorpita, Becker, & Daleiden, 2007; Davenport & Bourgeois, 2008). Children whose emotional and physical needs are taken care of consistently and in a timely way by a nurturing caretaker typically develop a *secure attachment*. These children tend to view their world as stable, predictable, comforting, and safe. Because of these distinctive perceptions, they are less prone to defensiveness or emotional–behavioral reactivity (i.e., screaming or hitting violently) when faced with adversity. Pettit, Laird, Bates, and Dodge (1997) found that secure attachments in early childhood predicted reduced levels of disruptive behavior in preschool children.

Insecure attachments, in which children's needs are inconsistently met by a caretaker and are characterized by avoidant or disorganized style, are linked to the development of behavioral problems, including aggression (Allan, 1988; Carey, 1999; Davenport & Bourgeois, 2008). Insecure attachments often lead to aggressive behavior problems because of their negative impact on children's nascent perceptions of the world as either stable and secure or unstable and insecure. Children with insecure attachments to their caretakers typically perceive the world as threatening and other people as untrustworthy and unreliable. Depending on many contextual factors, these perceptions may lead to a primarily defensive orientation within interpersonal interactions, with aggressive behaviors operating to maintain a position of power and invulnerability. Insecure attachments lead to affect dysregulation, including frequent child temper tantrums, whining, stubbornness, and noncompliance, which make up the oppositional, defiant spectrum of behaviors.

From a Jungian perspective, insecure attachments engender children's ego defenses to rely heavily on primitive structures that create breaks in the *ego–Self axis* (Knox, 2003), the mediation between the child's inner and outer worlds.

With the introjection of the not-good-enough-parent imago, the child may perceive the world as hostile and unreliable. With this insecure attachment come feelings of debasement and the child's internalizing perceptions of being not good enough. Because of the nascent cognitive functioning of the psyche in early childhood, rigid ego defenses develop to protect the fragile ego, which create a psychopathology of defensive splitting of the Self from the ego for preservation in extraordinary stress or trauma. A significant component of this defensive splitting is manifested behaviorally through disruptive behaviors that serve to temporarily reduce overwhelming anxiety and feelings of alienation.

PLAY INTERVENTION PROCEDURES

Jungian sandplay with disruptive children typically involves the therapist's giving the child choice in the sand tray, with no direction or guidance, and with little to no processing (resolving) afterward (Preston-Dillon, 2007). Therapists permit children to draw, depict, or form whatever world they wish. The therapist may say,

> Create a sand world. Anything you'd like. There's no right or wrong way to do this. It's completely up to you. After you finish, we may talk a little about your sand world. I'll be quiet while you play unless you want to talk. It's up to you.

As is common in sandplay with very young children (ages 3–5), they will typically engage the therapist in verbal commentary while creating their scene. Some children will even ask their therapists to play with them in the sand. If this occurs, it is wise for the therapist to ask the child what the child would have the therapist do, specifically. Some children become annoyed with this nondirective stance and may reiterate, "Just play with me!" To meet the aggressive child's developmental needs within the sandplay trajectory and not disrupt the transference, therapists need to be able to shift between nondirective and directive modalities. After children complete their sand worlds, therapists might inquire about the sand world's name or title. Then, therapists may ask, "If you were in this world, what would you feel like?" Last, therapists may probe children further by asking how they felt while forming the world. Sample questions for processing sandplay worlds could include "What were you feeling when you dug that hole?" and "If this symbol [or object or person] were talking, what would it be saying or feeling?"

A therapist may use Jungian sandplay techniques to facilitate containment of the child's affect in the sand tray. Additionally, some children will ask the therapist to devise a new game or activity for sandplay, which should signify to the therapist a specific need for emotional containment. *Create your mandala* is a semidirective technique used to facilitate sandplay therapy with disruptive preschool children (Green, 2008). This experiential activity encourages children to produce unconscious psychic material within the therapeutic container. By making hidden, unconscious fantasies, dreams, and desires tangible or conscious, children's psyches begin the therapeutic process of bridging the unconscious to the conscious, and vice versa, which promotes emotional health.

Using the create-your-mandala technique, the Jungian play therapist first asks the child to spend a couple of minutes relaxing. With the child in a comfortable seated position with eyes closed, the therapist leads the child through a guided imagery technique, assisting him or her in releasing any frustrations or anxieties accumulated throughout the school day by means of deep breathing. Children who engage in disruptive behaviors also tend to present with features of anxiety. Therefore, the therapist may ask the child whether he or she would like to manipulate Play-Doh or clay as an anxiety-releasing technique while deeply breathing. After a couple of minutes, the therapist asks the child to draw a large circle in the sand tray. The child is then instructed to depict, draw, or create a world within the circle. Once the child finishes, the therapist and the child contemplate the images in silence for a few seconds.

Next, the therapist may process the sandplay mandala with the child using a phenomenological, or individual, perspective. Jung (2008) believed the mandala, or an object (perhaps a circle) with an image contained within it, represents unity or wholeness. From a Jungian perspective, unity or wholeness is commensurate with psychological healthiness, because Jung believed a reconciliation of opposites has occurred in the individual (*individuation*). In individuation, the child functions outside of the constraints of the ego, operating from the true center of being—the autonomous Self. Jungians believe that a mandala in sand depiction may be representative of the child's rich, interior life (Kalff, 1980).

After the therapist facilitates the child's concretization of the unconscious, the child then progresses toward wholeness through *ego-based reliability* (depending on the ego to differentiate emotional polarities uncovered from within). The salubrious transformation a child experiences through sandplay occurs within the warm, caring therapeutic relationship and the experiencing of the sand scene, not necessarily through specific sand techniques or elegant therapeutic interpretations. Therefore, Jungians honor the process and depth of sandplay by attending to the child's individuality with complete acceptance and do not focus on providing the child with clever interpretations.

A second Jungian sandplay technique is *fairy tales in the sand* (FTS). FTS identifies archetypal manifestations in the child through fantasy imagery and fairy-tale depictions (Green, 2009). The FTS process begins with the therapist reading a fairy tale to the child. When working with children with behavior problems, it is important for the therapist to allow the child to choose the fairy tale. Jungians believe the Self leads the child in the right direction for healing. The therapist may bring 8 to 10 preselected fairy tales with a variety of themes commensurate with the child's current psychosocial struggles. After the child selects a fairy tale, the therapist reads it and asks the child to identify a particularly important component of it—an image, a theme, a plot, or a character. After the child has identified a portion of the fairy tale, the child depicts the image or feeling associated with that symbol in the sand. The therapist silently observes while the child creates a world in the sand.

After the child finishes the fairy-tale sand creation, the therapist processes the creation with the child by asking questions similar to those listed earlier, such as "If you could give a title to this sand world, what would it be?" "If you were inside this sand world, how would you feel?" and "If you could change anything about this sand world, what would you change and how would it be different?" FTS allows the child—through active imagination—to identify with myths and inherent archetypal realities that may provide numinous (spiritual) transmutation. Specifically, children consciously connect to meaningful myths and mythical figures in fairy tales that closely encapsulate their personal struggles or genesis of their psychic–emotional crisis. As with the draw-your-mandala technique, FTS facilitates healing through a trusting, caring relationship with a therapist within which children identify with, express, and connect to the myth and symbols they are living out. Once children become aware of these, they are sometimes able to more accurately form effective coping mechanisms to understand and transform pain and suffering. Jung (1943) discussed psychotherapy as a time when the patient comes to terms with understanding during suffering and ultimately finding acceptance through sorrow.

EMPIRICAL SUPPORT

A significant number of child referrals in mental health settings involve problems with externalizing or disruptive behaviors, including oppositional, defiant, aggressive, or delinquent behaviors (Garland, Hawley, Brookman-Frazee, & Hurlburt, 2008). Recent research, including meta-analyses and extensive literature reviews, have reported the effectiveness of such interventions as play therapy in decreasing externalizing behavior problems in young children (Bratton, Ray, Rhine, & Jones, 2005; Davenport & Bourgeois, 2008; Hoagwood et al., 2008; Stormshak et al., 2000; Williford & Shelton, 2008). Commonalities are present across many different evidence-based models, including the importance of (a) facilitating functional parent–child interactions, (b) implementing behavioral strategies, and (c) providing mental health consultation with teachers. Training parents to properly use positive and negative reinforcement with their child is often an important component of evidence-based parent training programs.

In addition, Garland et al. (2008) found multiple psychosocial intervention protocols that demonstrate efficacy for preschool children with disruptive behavior problems: behaviorally oriented parent training, parent–child interaction therapy, parent management training, and cognitive–behaviorally oriented skills training (e.g., anger coping therapy and problem-solving skills training). Other empirically based practices associated with decreasing disruptive behavior disorders in preschool children are therapeutic limit setting, time-out, ignoring, parent praise, problem solving, parent psychoeducation, and tangible rewards (Chorpita et al., 2007).

In a search of the current literature, we located no empirical support for or quantitative research regarding the effectiveness of sandplay with preschool children exhibiting behavior problems. This search included a review of all of the major article contributions to the *Journal of Sandplay Therapy* since its inception. However, play therapy has generally been found to be effective in reducing children's externalizing behaviors (Bratton et al., 2005; Davenport & Bourgeois, 2008), and sandplay is one play therapy medium. As mentioned earlier, a large amount of qualitative and anecdotal data support the use of sand therapy with children with disruptive behavior problems. This area is one needing empirical study, which we address in the concluding section.

Because no current empirical support for Jungian sandplay with preschool children exists, it is prudent for clinicians who use this treatment modality to be cognizant of the current empirically based data on this special population. A clinician using Jungian sandplay with children who exhibit disruptive behaviors may choose to incorporate filial therapy, use interventions from the behavioral paradigm, provide psychoeducation to parents, and offer mental health consultation on evidence-based interventions to teachers. Green (2008) wrote about the role of the Jungian play therapist as incorporating current, empirically based interventions and offering children interdisciplinary services. These services begin with weekly individual play sessions and include filial sessions every 3 weeks or so and consistent mental health consultations with significant adults in the child's life, including teachers and staff from the educational setting. The following case study describes the use of Jungian sandplay with a 5-year-old child with disruptive behavior problems.

CASE ILLUSTRATION

Anthony, a 5-year-old, was referred to counseling by the headmistress at the preschool he was attending. On the day of the referral, Gema, Anthony's mother, was asked to retrieve her son from his preschool. According to the headmistress, Anthony was being highly disobedient and wanted to play aggressively with other children instead of completing his school tasks. Because of his disruptive behavior, he was not permitted to return to the school until he met with a child psychotherapist and a pediatrician.

Because of the child's young age, Anthony's mother was referred to a play therapist. After the initial intake with Gema, the play therapist consulted with a variety of significant adults in Anthony's life to formulate a clinical picture and procure an accurate diagnosis. In Eric J. Green's opinion, labels and diagnoses are only important in that they incorporate evidence-based practices and maintain accountability to patients when working with third-party payers. After procuring the necessary releases of confidential information, the play therapist consulted with the headmistress, who provided the following biographical information about Anthony. She stated that Anthony had been born and raised in a highly dysfunctional family and that his father was often verbally and physically abusive toward Gema. She said that Anthony had lived in several shelters and presented a socially deviant temperament because of inconsistencies in his home life. She also mentioned that Gema occasionally spanked Anthony and that teachers at Anthony's previous preschool spanked him as well because of his disobedient behaviors. She said that he was defiant, hit and punched children, threatened children with violence, used inappropriate language, spat on children, shoved other children, and lacked empathy.

As part of the cognitive–behavioral intake, the therapist uncovered the following information about Anthony from his mother, his mother's boyfriend, his grandparents, and his teachers. Anthony witnessed domestic violence at a very young age, perhaps as early as 6 months old, according to his mother. Anthony's father engaged in regular drinking binges, had low self-esteem, lacked empathy for others, was highly aggressive, stole jewelry and valuables out of people's homes to make extra income, lacked friendships, and regularly vandalized and damaged other people's property. He regularly physically abused his wife while Anthony watched. When he was 4 years old, Anthony made the following comment to Gema after witnessing his father beating her with a leather belt: "I want to die 'cause no one loves me."

Gema moved out of her home with her son to escape the domestic violence and precarious situation she believed her son was in with her abusive and alcoholic husband. Consequently, both she and Anthony moved among 12 different shelters, halfway houses, cities, and schools before Anthony was 5 years old. Many of the caretakers in Anthony's life commented on his anger, rage, and disruptive behaviors, citing incidences of Anthony's not following household or school rules, repetitively arguing or reasoning, propensity to challenge authority figures, talking excessively at inappropriate times, frequent interruptions, difficulty waiting his turn, and impulsivity. His mother and grandparents noted that he displayed the following traits with chronicity: stubbornness, hyperdistractibility, overactivity, and aggressiveness. In the 6 months before his referral, Anthony had developed the following new temperaments: suspicious cautiousness, frequent temper outbursts, impulsiveness, and violence. A multidisciplinary team consisting of a pediatrician, neurologist, psychiatrist, and play therapist diagnosed Anthony with oppositional defiant disorder and attention-deficit/hyperactivity disorder, combined type.

Case Conceptualization

From a Jungian perspective, when an unbearable level of anxiety devastates the child's susceptible ego, as in the case of Anthony's witnessing his mother being verbally abused and physically beaten or when his mother was physically aggressive with him, *deintegration* (loss of a stable ego) occurs that threatens to annihilate the child's personality (Green, 2008, 2009; Jung, 1964). Kalsched (1996) theorized that to prevent this eradication, an archetypal self-care system comes to the child's rescue—an antiquated apparatus that creates a defensive splitting to encapsulate the child's fragile personal spirit in safety by expelling it to the unconscious. The child's psychic defense against unendurable pain sends an archetypal *daimon*, or an image from the self-care system, to help the child detach from the vast anxiety (Green, 2008, 2009). Children like Anthony who exhibit severe externalizing behavior problems often have a disconnect from the Self to their ego's stability in managing the external world. Specifically, children with aggressive and disruptive behavior problems may have particularly deprived links between their inner and outer worlds because of the deterioration of their good-enough parental introjects (i.e., the images and feelings associated with those images of the good mother or good father archetypes that provide safety). Anthony's good-enough parent image dissolved when he watched his father persistently and savagely abuse his mother and when she physically disciplined him.

As implied by the quote Gema provided from Anthony regarding wanting to die and feeling unloved, young children who witness chronic domestic violence or who are on the receiving end of corporal punishment may feel rejected at a profoundly deep, primal level because they personalize the attacks and wonder, "What's wrong with me? Why am I not OK?" Anthony developed aggressive and disruptive behaviors to (a) mediate the immense anxiety he experienced from witnessing domestic violence and receiving harsh physical discipline; (b) seek attention from significant caretakers, whether positive or negative, to recover from his feelings of being not good enough; (c) cope with, in a primal or rudimentary way, his feelings of intense sadness, dejection, and uprootedness resulting from his and his mother's frequent moves; and (d) model his parents' behaviors of coping with extreme stress.

Treatment Goals

Helping Anthony recover his good-enough parent imago so that his creative capacities are reestablished would involve the augmentation of the link between the unconscious and the conscious (Allan, 1988; Green, 2008; Jung, 1964). In Jungian sandplay, this entails increasing Anthony's ego strength and its capacity to explore emotional polarities (e.g., hatred–forgiveness, desolation–connectedness, and terror–safety) arising within the safety of the sand tray projections. Jungian play therapy penetrates deep psychic mechanisms by exploring emotional polarities or complexes, and sandplay allows for the release of rage associated with the painful and shadowy aspects of these emotional polarities. Once the child's psyche has the opportunity to become cognizant of and release the indefatigable feelings of suffering through sandplay, breaks in the defensive wall of the ego may emerge that stimulate self-healing.

The sandplay treatment goals with Anthony included (a) building an emotionally safe, trusting, therapeutic alliance in which he could self-nurture and internalize a positive, good-enough parental imago; (b) allowing for the expression of complicated emotions through representational and tangible channels and regulating or achieving mastery over these difficult emotions; (c) giving his rage a voice in the playroom and therapeutically carrying that rage so that it can be altered; (d) conducting filial sessions[1] with Gema every 2 to 3 weeks to provide different ways of interacting with her son that would decrease disruptive behaviors; and (d) collaborating with Anthony's preschool teacher and school counselor to provide regular mental health consultations through e-mail or telephone on evidence-based interventions to reduce disordered behaviors. Also, we should note that Anthony was placed on two different psychotropic medications on the basis of psychodiagnostic tests and medical evaluation by his neurologist, pediatrician, play therapist, and psychiatrist: Risperdal (risperidone), an atypical antipsychotic, and Concerta (methylphenidate), a stimulant.

Treatment

At the initial session, Anthony appeared to be a jovial, energetic child who smiled frequently and seemed genuinely curious about the world. The therapist stated, "In here, you can play with all of the toys in most of the ways you want." From the very beginning of play therapy, Anthony seemed to be seeking a place or social relationship that would be stable. Perhaps Anthony felt safe

---

[1]*Filial therapy* is a process through which a therapist trains the caretaker in child-centered play therapy principles so that the caretaker ultimately conducts 30 minutes of special play time weekly with the child.

and protected within the *temenos* of the playroom, a place where he was told that he would not be judged, a place where he would find 45 minutes of peace each week outside the tumultuous external reality he was experiencing. The therapist commented,

> I've spoken to your mom, as she's told you, and I know that things have been difficult lately. I'm not sure how things will work out, as sometimes things don't always end happy, but I do know that I will be here with you.

After this admission, Anthony elicited a smile from the therapist and began his exploratory play.

During the first few sessions, Anthony engaged in exploratory play by examining the dollhouse, art supplies, sand tray, puppet house and puppets, sand figurines, and costumes in the drawers underneath the sand tray. His presentation indicated that he was coping with an extraordinary amount of anxiety because he would intermittently stop playing and bite his nails nervously. Afterward, he would smile and then frenetically shift to a different toy. He also had difficulty sitting still, staying focused on one task, and remembering things he had done in previous sessions. Strengths observed in his first few assessment sessions included his infectious energy and exuberance for life, his uncanny ability to listen and respond accordingly (when he wanted to), and his advanced verbal and reasoning skills. After manipulating the sand figurines and sand tray during the first three sessions, in the fourth session he asked the therapist, "What do kids do with this? Should I build a sand castle?" The therapist responded,

> In here, you can decide that. Some children create worlds in the sand. Maybe they place those figures [*pointing to the sand figures*] in the sand however they want and tell a story or show something. I usually call it *sandplay*.

Anthony immediately began building his world, and this led to the inception of the sandplay process.

At Anthony's first sandplay session, as well as in Sessions 4 to 8, he repeatedly, chaotically tossed figures over his head and into the sand tray (see Figure 11.1), peering at the therapist and laughing playfully while he did this. There was a joy in him while he created these worlds, with figures piled on top of each other in a disorganized pattern with no discernable configuration. Chaos, usually characterized by a child's dumping several toys into the sand tray, not necessarily with form or foundation, may be symbolic of the child's ego being overwhelmed by distressing emotions (Allan, 1988).

The therapist interpreted Anthony's sandplay as a mirroring of his emotional landscape, which was fraught with confusion, distraction, and destruction. As the play therapist observed these initial sand worlds of chaos, he

Figure 11.1. Sand world of chaos.

empathized with Anthony's play and the affect he demonstrated while playing. The therapist felt a predominant sense of powerlessness and decimation in viewing Anthony's sand worlds once they were completed. This insight added to the clinical picture and gave the therapist important affective information on which to rely when making interpretations. During Session 8, after Anthony made another sand world of chaos, the therapist provided an interpretation after it was complete:

> Anthony, when I watched you build this world, I felt like if I would be in it, it would be very scary. Nothing seems to go together or make much sense. I would probably hide underneath there [*pointing to a bridge*] to feel safe.

It is interesting that Anthony replied, "Aw, if you felt scared, I would take care of you. Nothing bad would happen to you here." In this exchange, components of Anthony's good-enough parental projections were transferred to the therapist.

In Sessions 9 to 10, Anthony's sand worlds contained pandemonium, but the chaos was more organized and had structure. The Self had begun the process of *constellating* (forming). For instance, Anthony began creating a world with army men and epic battles with two red dragons. The army men were lined up, shooting the dragons. The dragons would breathe fire and incinerate a majority of the army. However, the story never contained a definitive ending; after the destruction, Anthony would throw different sand figurines into the sand tray and laugh mischievously. The therapist asked, "What happened after the dragons destroyed the army?" Anthony replied, "I don't know," and continued tossing sand figurines into the sand tray. Here, his ego may have been coming to terms with the shadowy sides of his destructive temperament. Because it was so overwhelming, he discontinued the flow of the play to protect his ego. However, the therapist viewed this as progress because Anthony was beginning to tell his story symbolically through the sand scene. The therapist was accepting of Anthony and his emotional pain.

During the first 3 months of play therapy, the therapist conducted frequent mental health consultations with Anthony's teacher and school counselor. With the teacher, these consultations consisted primarily of cognitive–behavioral interventions she could implement to reduce disordered behaviors, and it also contained a bit of psychoeducation on oppositional defiant disorder and attention-deficit/hyperactivity disorder. With the school counselor, the play therapist coordinated services for Anthony to receive weekly problem-solving skills training in group counseling with male peers. Also, Gema participated in filial sessions every 2 to 3 weeks in which she learned child-centered skills. Infusing evidence-based interventions, the therapist augmented the traditional filial therapy paradigm with behaviorally oriented parent training. This included therapeutic limit setting, time-out, ignoring, parent praise, problem solving, psychoeducation, and implementing tangible rewards (Chorpita et al., 2007).

During the week of Session 9, the therapist received this summary of Anthony's social progress from his preschool teacher during a consultation:

- showed care and concern for other's well-being,
- took responsibility for rules of the classroom,
- initiated consequences when he did not follow classroom rules,
- became liked by his male peers,
- enjoyed being the teacher's helper,
- greeted students every morning,
- told the teacher when he was upset or needed to talk,
- took his behavioral contract seriously,
- responded to warnings when given options, and
- decreased aggressiveness.

In Sessions 11 to 16, Gema and Anthony's grandparents began commenting on the positive behavioral changes Anthony was exhibiting. However,

Anthony's grandmother brought to the therapist's attention that Anthony had been drawing some disturbing, dark images of monsters and talked about pain and death. The therapist empathically responded and mentioned that sometimes when children are exorcising their demons in the playroom, darkness from the bottom of their psyches bubbles to the surface like crude oil from a well. This process, also called "the blackening" by alchemists (Moore, 2008), was tangibly represented by Anthony's raw material appearing in charred form. Just as alchemists burned elements and metals to ash to make gold, Anthony safely explored his inner darkness with the facilitation of a supportive therapist so that his self-healing (i.e., gold) could activate.

Anthony continued the theme of epic battles, except the battles became organized. The dragons continued to dominate the scenes, except the size of the army was augmented. The army men were delineated in military lineups with precision: The front lines contained cannons and the back rows of army men carried rifles for sniper fire. In the middle of the ferocious battle scene was a small bridge (see Figure 11.2). Bridges may represent a child's transitional space, or connection, between the inner and outer worlds (Bradway & McCoard, 1997). After Anthony finished one of his epic battle scenes in Session 15, he

Figure 11.2. Anthony's epic battle.

commented (in a loud voice), "The army men are tired of fighting and just want the dragons to leave them alone." The therapist, staying at the child's feeling level and within the metaphor, responded, "It sounds like the army is very brave but tired of fighting everyday. Is there anything they could do to make the dragons leave them alone?"

Anthony thought about the therapist's question for a few seconds, then grabbed a green-colored jewel from the sand figures and placed it in the middle of the curve of the bridge. With a look of amazement (as though this was the first time he realized something could prevent the dragons from coming into the world), Anthony uttered in a triumphant tone, "This could do it. This is a magic jewel that makes the dragons sleep. And as long as the army keeps it on the bridge, the dragons will stay away." He became noticeably calm, and his affect regulated. The therapist reflected back the feeling and content:

> The world looks like it's finally at peace. Like maybe the army men are relieved because they aren't fighting the dragons all the time, even though everyone already knows that they are fearless. I noticed how the army can be brave warriors yet want peace. They have two opposite feelings at the same time, and that gives them strength and courage.

Anthony replied, "I know. They are brave like me." Here, Anthony depicts his self-healing archetype as a green stone. Also, the army men were green in color, and he chose green construction paper for several art activities. According to Allan (1988), the color green may point to an escape from overwhelming anxiety, such when the green stone prohibited the destructive dragons from fighting with the army. Allan went on to say that green may represent "a sense of controlled behavior, a return to an untroubled nature" (p. 147).

During the time of Sessions 17 to 20, Anthony began to exhibit marked improvements in behavior at home and at school. His mother, Gema, commented that he listened to directions at home, was less argumentative, was able to express his feelings when he was mad without hitting anything, and had not been in trouble at school for several weeks. During these sessions, the therapist introduced the create-your-mandala and FTS activities for containment purposes. Anthony's Self began to constellate the good-enough-parent imagoes and presented a shift in archetypal motifs in sandplay from destruction–decay to nurturance–compassion.

Termination

After 8 months of coordinated multidisciplinary services, including weekly play therapy sessions, Anthony demonstrated behavioral improvement and a cessation of many of the disruptive behaviors he had presented with at the inception of play therapy. To mark the occasion as celebratory, the therapist held a "good-bye celebration," and cookies and punch were provided. For the first 30 minutes, Anthony and his therapist reviewed the past 8 months together in play and the good decisions Anthony was making. Anthony asked, "Are you proud of me?" The therapist smiled and responded,

> What matters most is what you think. I, along with your family, care about you and whether or not you make good or bad choices. I am so pleased with all of the effort you have made into getting along with others. You did that!

Anthony responded, "OK. But are you proud of me for not being a bad boy anymore? That's what I wanna know!" The therapist responded in a gentle, caring tone,

> You never were a bad boy. It's just that sometimes you made bad choices. And everyone does that sometimes, including me. What I've learned about you is that you deeply care for those around you and are working hard to show them without hurting them. You've been very brave to try to make things different or better for you and your family.

After hearing this encouragement, Anthony grinned. During the last 15 minutes, the therapist invited Gema to join the good-bye celebration. The psychotherapy ended on a positive note of transitioning out of the safety and security of the playroom to the outer world where Anthony had discovered the inner strength and familial and community support to resolve some of his emotional and behavioral difficulties.

CONCLUSION AND FUTURE DIRECTIONS

As a result of the interdisciplinary team of mental health, medical, and educational professionals coordinating and collaborating on services, Anthony's behavioral interventions and psychotherapy were systemically linked. Not only was play therapy and sandplay used as part of the treatment modality, but evidence-based and evidence-informed practices were used, including cognitive–behavioral management strategies, filial therapy, and mental health consultations with significant adults in the child's home and in his educational environment. Anthony was kinesthetically compelled to the soft white sand in the sand tray from the first few play sessions. He became a sandplay enthusiast, consistently returning to this activity weekly with little to no direction. Jungian sandplay was listed in his treatment protocol as one of the play therapy interventions used to help him communicate and express his worries and difficult feelings.

Because of the nature of Jungian child psychotherapy and sandplay, Anthony was able to safely communicate his inner world of turmoil to the therapist. The therapist provided little to no interpretations but instead witnessed and contained the images in the sand worlds. Part of the Jungian play therapist's role when working with children is to carry some of their psychological poison so that they can be relieved of their psychic burdens and begin the integration of opposites. In the sandplay, Anthony conveyed his most hideous feelings of abandonment and emotional anguish brought about by the many assaults to his fragile ego as an infant and toddler. Eventually, he discovered the green stone, or self-healing archetype, representing his own inner reserves that transformed the disruption and aggression into solace and healing.

Because of the scarcity of empirical data to support sandplay with children with disruptive behavior disorders, investigations regarding its effectiveness with young children are needed. Future research should include a controlled, empirical study of the effectiveness of sand therapy with children diagnosed with disruptive behavior disorders.

REFERENCES

Allan, J. (1988). *Inscapes of the child's world*. Dallas, TX: Spring.

Allan, J., & Berry, P. (2002). Sand play. In C. E. Schaefer & D. M. Cangelosi (Eds.), *Play therapy techniques* (pp. 161–168). Northvale, NJ: Jason Aronson.

American Psychiatric Association. (1994). *Diagnostic and statistical manual of mental disorders* (4th ed.). Washington, DC: Author.

Boik, B. L., & Goodwin, E. A. (2000). *Sandplay therapy*. New York: Norton.

Bradway, K., & McCoard, B. (1997). *Sandplay: Silent workshop of the psyche*. New York: Routledge.

Bratton, S. C., Ray, D., Rhine, T., & Jones, L. (2005). The efficacy of play therapy with children: A meta-analytic review of treatment outcomes. *Professional Psychology: Research and Practice, 36,* 376–390.

Carey, L. (1999). *Sandplay therapy with children and families*. Northvale, NJ: Jason Aronson.

Carey, L. (2006). *Expressive and creative arts methods for trauma survivors*. London: Jessica Kingsley.

Chorpita, B. F., Becker, K. D., & Daleiden, E. L. (2007). Understanding the common elements of evidence-based practice: Misconceptions and clinical examples. *Journal of the American Academy of Child & Adolescent Psychiatry, 46,* 647–652.

Davenport, B., & Bourgeois, N. M. (2008). Play, aggression, the preschool child, and the family: A review of literature to guide empirically informed play therapy with aggressive preschool children. *International Journal of Play Therapy, 17,* 2–23.

De Domenico, G. (1994). Jungian play therapy techniques. In K. J. O'Connor & C. E. Schaefer (Eds.), *Handbook of play therapy: Advances and Innovations* (2nd ed., pp. 253–282). New York: Wiley.

Edinger, E. (1992). *Ego and archetype*. Boston: Shambhala.

Garland, A. F., Hawley, K. M., Brookman-Frazee, L., & Hurlburt, M. S. (2008). Identifying common elements of evidence-based psychosocial treatments for children's disruptive behavior problems. *Journal of the American Academy of Child & Adolescent Psychiatry, 47*, 505–514.

Goodheart, W. (1980). [Review of the books *The listening process, The therapeutic environment, Technique and transition, Intrapsychic and interpersonal dimensions of treatment: A clinical dialogue, Collected papers on schizophrenia and related subjects* and *Countertransference and related subjects: Selected papers*]. *San Francisco Jung Institute Library Journal, 1*, 2–39.

Gordon, R. (1993). *Bridges: Metaphor for psychic processes*. London: Karnac.

Green, E. J. (2008). Re-envisioning Jungian analytical play therapy with child sexual assault survivors. *International Journal of Play Therapy, 17*, 102–121.

Green, E. J. (2009). Jungian analytical play therapy. In K. O'Connor & L. Braverman (Eds.), *Play therapy theory and practice: A comparative presentation* (2nd ed., pp. 83–122). Hoboken, NJ: Wiley.

Green, E. J., & Christensen, T. M. (2006). Elementary school children's perceptions of play therapy in school settings. *International Journal of Play Therapy, 15*, 65–85.

Green, E. J., & Connolly, M. (2009). Jungian family sandplay with bereaved children: Implications for play therapists. *International Journal of Play Therapy, 18*, 84–98.

Green, E. J., & Ironside, D. (2004). Archetypes, symbols, and Jungian sandplay: An innovative approach to school counseling. *Counselor's Classroom*. Retrieved September 22, 2007, from http://www.guidancechannel.com

Hinshaw, S. P., & Anderson, C. A. (1996). Conduct and oppositional defiant disorders. In E. Mash & R. Barkley (Eds.), *Child psychopathology* (pp. 113–154). New York: Guilford Press.

Hoagwood, K. E., Olin, S. S., Kerker, B. D., Kratochwill, T. R., Crowe, M., & Saka, N. (2008). Empirically based school interventions targeted at academic and mental health functioning. *Journal of Emotional and Behavioral Disorders, 15*, 66–92.

Jung, C. G. (1943). Psychotherapy and a philosophy of life. In H. Read, M. Fordham, & G. Adler (Eds.), *The collected works of C. G. Jung* (Vol. 2). Princeton, NJ: Princeton University Press.

Jung, C. G. (1964). *Man and his symbols*. Garden City, NY: Doubleday.

Jung, C. G. (2008). *Children's dreams: Notes from the seminar given in 1936–1940*. Princeton, NJ: Princeton University Press.

Kalff, D. (1980). *Sandplay: A psychotherapeutic approach to the psyche*. Boston: Sigo Press.

Kalsched, D. (1996). *The inner world of trauma: Archetypal defenses of the personal spirit*. New York: Routledge.

Keenan, K., & Shaw, D. S. (1994). The development of aggression in toddlers: A study of low-income families. *Journal of Abnormal Child Psychology, 22,* 53–77.

Knox, J. (2003). *Archetype, attachment, analysis: Jungian psychology and the emergent mind.* New York: Brunner-Routledge.

Lowenfeld, M. (1979). *The world technique.* Boston: Allen & Unwin.

McNulty, W. (2007). Superheroes and sandplay: Using the archetype through the healing journey. In L. C. Rubin (Ed.), *Using superheroes in counseling and play therapy* (pp. 69–89). New York: Springer.

Moore, T. (2008). *A life at work: The joy of discovering what you were born to do.* New York: Broadway Books.

Pettit, G. S., Laird, R. D., Bates, J. E., & Dodge, K. E. (1997). Patterns of after school care in middle childhood: Risk factors and developmental outcomes. *Merrill Palmer Quarterly, 43,* 515–538.

Powell, D., Dunlap, G., & Fox, L. (2006). Prevention and intervention for the challenging behaviors of toddlers and preschoolers. *Infants and Young Children, 19,* 25–35.

Preston-Dillon, D. (2007). *Sand therapy: An introduction* (Association for Play Therapy audio course). Unpublished manuscript.

Riviere, S. (2006). Short term play therapy for children with disruptive behavior disorders. In H. G. Kaduson & C. E. Schaefer (Eds.), *Short-term play therapy for children* (2nd ed., pp. 31–70). New York: Guilford Press.

Shih, Y. L., Kao, S. S., & Wang, W. H. (2006). The process study of the sandplay therapy on oppositional defiant disorder. *Chinese Annual Report of Guidance and Counseling, 19,* 41–72.

Steinhardt, L. (2000). *Foundation and form in Jungian sandplay.* Philadelphia: Jessica Kingsley.

Stormshak, E. A., Bierman, K. L., McMahon, R. J., & Lengua, L. J. (2000). Parenting practices and child disruptive behavior problems in early elementary school. *Journal of Clinical Child Psychology, 29,* 17–29.

Turner, B. A. (2005). *The handbook of sandplay therapy.* Cloverdale, CA: Temenos Press.

Weinrib, E. (1983). *Images of the self.* Boston: Sigo Press.

Williford, A. P., & Shelton, T. L. (2008). Using mental health consultation to decrease disruptive behaviors in preschoolers: Adapting an empirically-supported intervention. *Journal of Child Psychology and Psychiatry, 49,* 191–200.

Winnicott, D. (1971). *Playing and reality.* New York: Basic Books.

12

PARENTS, TEACHERS, AND THERAPISTS USING CHILD-DIRECTED PLAY THERAPY AND COACHING SKILLS TO PROMOTE CHILDREN'S SOCIAL AND EMOTIONAL COMPETENCE AND BUILD POSITIVE RELATIONSHIPS

CAROLYN WEBSTER-STRATTON AND M. JAMILA REID

If left untreated, early-onset conduct problems (e.g., high rates of aggression, noncompliance, oppositional behaviors, emotional dysregulation) place children at high risk of recurring social and emotional problems, underachievement, school dropout, and eventual delinquency (Loeber et al., 1993). The development of emotional self-regulation and social competence in the early years plays a critical role in shaping the ways in which children think, learn, react to challenges, and develop relationships throughout their lives (Raver & Knitzer, 2002). Thus, early intervention efforts designed to assist parents, teachers, and child therapists to promote children's optimal social and emotional competencies and reduce behavior problems can help lay a positive foundation and put children on a trajectory for future success.

The Incredible Years (IY): Parents, Teachers, and Children Training Series is a set of three separate but interlocking evidence-based programs designed to prevent and treat conduct problems and promote social and emotional competence in young children (Webster-Stratton, 2005). First is the IY Parent Training Program, which consists of three basic programs, one for parents of babies and toddlers (ages 6 weeks to 3 years), one for parents of children in the early childhood years (ages 3–6 years), and one for school-age children (ages 6–12 years). The length of these programs varies from 12 to 20 two-hour

245

sessions offered weekly to groups of 8 to 12 parents. The primary goals of these programs are to strengthen parent–child attachment and nurturing and caring relationships, increase positive discipline (rules, predictable routines, effective limit setting), and decrease critical or harsh parenting (consequences, problem solving). The foundation of the program is parents' investment in continual use of play and coaching strategies with their children throughout the program. Through child-directed play interactions, parents strengthen their relationships with their children and learn to coach them in ways that promote their social, emotional, and academic growth.

The second program is the IY Teacher Training Program, a 6-day training program for teachers of students ages 3 to 8. This training is offered monthly to groups of 10 to 15 teachers, who complete classroom assignments between trainings. Some individual teacher consultation is provided, as needed, for children with specific behavior problems. The goal of the training is to promote positive teacher classroom management skills and nurturing relationships with students, including training in social, emotional, academic, and persistence coaching as well as praise and encouragement during child-directed play interactions, circle times, small group work times, and unstructured play times.

The third program is the IY Child Training Program (also known as the Dina Dinosaur curriculum), which is a 20-week treatment program offered in 2-hour sessions to groups of six children with conduct or social problems or attention-deficit/hyperactivity disorder (ADHD). A prevention and therapeutic classroom version of the dinosaur curriculum is also available for teachers to use in 40 to 60 lesson plans offered two to three times a week. Topics include teaching children how to play with other children, including learning social skills (turn taking, waiting, asking, sharing, helping) as well as ways to talk with peers, express their feelings, solve problems, and manage anger. Material is taught to the children during circle time, small-group activities, and free play. Therapists use child-directed play and coaching throughout the session to enhance children's social, emotional, and academic goals. Large puppets are also incorporated into the learning and play interactions to provide another teaching and relationship-building tool to use with the children.

All three programs (parent, teacher, and child) rely heavily on performance training methods and group support, including presentation of video vignettes and observational learning through modeling, assigned home and classroom practice activities, and live feedback and coaching from trained group leaders and other participants. For further information and description of these programs, please see Webster-Stratton (1999) and Webster-Stratton and Reid (in press).

Each of these three separate parent, teacher, and child programs has been researched in numerous randomized control group trials by the developer Carolyn Webster-Stratton as well as by independent investigators and has been shown to improve parent–child, teacher–student, and peer interactions and to be effective in reducing children's conduct problems and promoting social and emotional competence and school readiness (for research reviews, see Webster-Stratton et al., 2001; Webster-Stratton & Reid, in press). These interventions have been evaluated as treatment programs by therapists in mental health clinics for children with early-onset conduct problems, ADHD, and internalizing problems (Beauchaine, Webster-Stratton, & Reid, 2005; Webster-Stratton & Herman, 2008) as well as evaluated as selective and indicated prevention programs in Head Start and schools with socioeconomically disadvantaged families and higher risk children (Webster-Stratton, 1998).

Prevention and treatment studies demonstrating the added impact of combining the IY parent program with the teacher classroom management program and/or with the child Dina Dinosaur program have shown that these teacher and child programs significantly enhance the outcomes for children in terms of peer relationship improvements, school readiness outcomes, and reduction of aggressive behaviors in the classroom (Webster-Stratton & Hammond, 1997; Webster-Stratton, Reid, & Hammond, 2004). In our prevention studies, the highest risk children were reported to make the greatest improvements, but generally all the children in the classroom showed improved social competence and school readiness (Reid, Webster-Stratton, & Hammond, 2007; Webster-Stratton, Reid, & Stoolmiller, 2008). In treatment studies, conditions combining parent, teacher, and child programs showed the most sustained effects for child outcomes at 2-year follow-up assessments (Webster-Stratton et al., 2004).

One of the key therapeutic aspects of all three of these interventions is training for parents, teachers, and therapists in child-directed play interactions using academic, persistence, social, and emotional coaching skills. At least half of all the content and time spent training in each of these programs is focused on therapeutic play interactions and specific coaching skills. These play interaction skills form the foundation for building children's relationships with their parents, teachers, and peers. It is noteworthy that our programs have only been evaluated as a complete intervention that includes the play interaction coaching skills in combination with the limit setting and positive discipline components. In fact, no research has been done that evaluates shorter versions of the program, using either the play and coaching skills or the limit-setting sections separately. It is our belief that teaching the play interaction, relationship building, and coaching components before training in the discipline components is essential to the therapeutic behavior change model, and we do not recommend shortening or using the discipline parts of the programs in isolation from the child-directed play training. It is noteworthy that parent–child interaction therapy, which was developed by Sheila Eyberg and which also emphasizes both the child-directed play and the discipline components and has theoretically compatible origins to the

IY program, has also had very positive outcomes in randomized trials (Eyberg et al., 2001; Funderburk et al., 1998).

In this chapter, we focus primarily on describing the child-directed play interaction and coaching sections of each of the three IY programs, describing their rationale, theories, and practical uses and how we adjust our approaches to meet the particular developmental needs of each child and family. More information on the full program, including the praise, incentives, discipline, and problem-solving sections, can be found in other chapters and articles (Webster-Stratton, 2006; Webster-Stratton & Herbert, 1994). See Figure 12.1.

THEORETICAL UNDERPINNINGS

The use of child-directed play and coaching strategies with children draws from underlying social learning theory, modeling, and relational theories such as attachment and psychodynamic theories. In addition, extensive

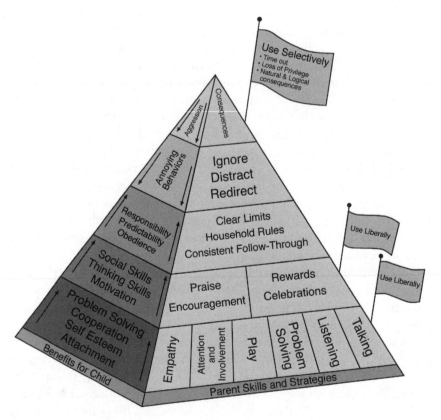

Figure 12.1. Parenting pyramid. Copyright by C. Webster-Stratton.

research regarding children's social, emotional, and cognitive development has provided our interventions with a framework of empirically based models of normal and pathological child development.

Contributions From Social Learning Theory

Our child training philosophy has its roots in applied behavior analysis, models of operant behavior (Baer, Wolf, & Risely, 1968), and cognitive social learning theory (Bandura, 1989). A key assumption is that children's behaviors are learned from their interactions with significant people in their lives, particularly their parents, teachers, and peers. Child problem behaviors—be they internalizing problems, such as fears and anxieties, or externalizing problems, such as defiance and aggression—are believed to be maintained by environmental reinforcers. The focus of training from this perspective is on changing maladaptive child behaviors by changing the environmental contingencies that maintain them. For example, in the case of an internalizing problem such as a social phobia or separation anxiety, research has suggested that family interactions play a role in the development and maintenance of these fears (Kendall, 1993); parents may inadvertently reward anxious behavior by their attention, remove aversive stimuli by permitting a child to stay home from school, or both (King, Hamilton, & Ollendick, 1988). In this example, parents would learn to use child-directed play and social coaching skills with the goal of promoting a secure parent–child relationship, building their child's self-confidence, encouraging and giving attention to brave behavior, and improving positive peer interactions. In addition, they learn the importance of avoiding giving undue attention to their child's fears and avoidant responses and coaching their child successfully so that he or she attends school. This conceptualization is also useful and relevant for externalizing conduct problems. Research has demonstrated that when parents or teachers interact with aggressive children, they may engage in practices that promote aggressive behavior (through attention and compliance to child coercive strategies) and suppress prosocial behavior (by ignoring or even providing aversive consequences; Hinshaw & Anderson, 1996; Patterson, Reid, & Dishion, 1992). Through child-directed play and social and emotional coaching, parents, teachers, and therapists learn how to give attention to and coach prosocial behaviors while ignoring the inappropriate behaviors. (This is described in more detail later in the case illustrations.)

Social learning theory (Bandura, 1977) posits that children learn a behavior not only by experiencing its direct consequences but also by observing similar behavior and its consequences. Research supporting this modeling theory has shown that children with high levels of fears and anxieties are more likely than nonfearful children to have anxious or fearful parents (Kendall,

1992). Studies have also shown that aggressive children are more likely than nonaggressive children to have parents who use aggressive discipline or who are antisocial themselves (Patterson & Capaldi, 1991). Our program incorporates modeling theory by emphasizing the importance of parents', teachers', and therapists' modeling appropriate social interactions, emotional regulation, and appropriate expression of emotions for their children.

In accordance with a social learning model, then, each of the three IY intervention programs is aimed at helping parents, teachers, and therapists identify and isolate children's prosocial (or appropriate) and maladaptive (or inappropriate) behaviors and change the reinforcement contingencies by reinforcing positive behavior and instituting brief consequences for negative behavior. From this perspective, the purpose of the child-directed and coached play approaches is to alter the interactions so that parents, teachers, and therapists are modeling social skills and emotional regulation in their interactions with the children as well as prompting, coaching, and reinforcing their social and self-regulatory behavior whenever it occurs. Methods of teaching parents, teachers, and children are also based on social learning theory using video modeling, role play practice and rehearsal, weekly practice activities, and direct reinforcement (social and tangible) given to parents and teachers and children for their achievements.

Contributions From Relational Theories

The IY programs also draw from relational approaches of attachment and psychoanalytic theory because of their central concern with emotion, affective processes, and the quality of relationships. Social learning and behavioral theory suggest that a more positive child relationship will occur when parents and teachers use child-directed and coaching skills with children because their use of attention and praise makes them more reinforcing. However, we believe that using child-directed play and coaching strategies with children influences the affective and relational aspects of adult–child interactions as separate from behavioral management. Within a relational focus as espoused by Axline (1969), child-directed play is seen as a way to promote positive parenting and adult–child bonding or attachment and is a goal in itself. Developmental psychology has demonstrated a strong relationship between parental nurturance (and positive limit setting) and positive child outcomes (Baumrind, 1995). Thus, the IY programs emphasize the importance of parents', teachers', and therapists' increased expression and communication of positive affect, including love, affection, acceptance, enjoyment, and empathy during their play interactions. Another therapy component that grows out of relational theory is training parents, teachers, and therapists to label, encourage, and respond to children's expression of emotions, including a focus on teaching adults and children to process and manage strong emotions. This renewed interest in affective processes reflects a growing recognition that a parent's or teacher's emotional expression and self-regulation ability are likely to affect the quality of children's emotional expression, which in turn affects the quality of their social relationships and ability to self-regulate in the face of conflict.

PLAY INTERACTION AND COACHING SKILLS

In this section, we describe how the IY programs use various types of play and develop coaching skills for adults.

Child-Directed Play

The IY: Parents, Teachers, and Children programs start by building a foundation of positive adult–child relationships through child-directed play interactions together. This style of interacting during play means that parents, teachers, and therapists avoid giving unnecessary commands or corrections or asking questions during play. Instead, these adults follow children's lead and ideas, enter into their imaginary and pretend world with them, express their joy and playfulness with them, and help them feel special by being an appreciative audience to their play. Parents, teachers, and child therapists are helped to understand the value of this focused attention and encouragement during play times for promoting children's self-confidence, self-esteem, and security in their relationships and for encouraging their creativity and independence (Webster-Stratton, 1999). Because one of the major developmental tasks for preschool children is to become more autonomous and to develop an individual sense of self, parents come understand how time spent playing with their children in child-directed ways is valuable in helping their children feel more securely attached to them. This secure relationship eventually leads to fewer difficulties separating from parents and easier transitions to preschool. When teachers also use these child-directed play strategies, it helps them to build positive relationships with their students and helps children to feel they are in a safe environment in the classroom. Strong teacher–child bonds set in motion a positive school experience and an environment conducive to learning.

Descriptive Commenting

Parents, teachers, and therapists are taught how to coach children during child-directed play times using descriptive commenting (Hanf & Kling,

1973). *Descriptive commenting* is a running commentary during play describing the children's behaviors and activities. It often sounds like a sports announcer's play-by-play description of a game. It includes describing children's actions as well as the objects they are playing with and their positions. This form of descriptive commenting not only indicates to the child how focused the parent, teacher, or therapist is on what she or he is doing but is also an invaluable teaching tool. It bathes the child in language, providing the child with direct important verbal information about his or her behavior or objects that she or he is touching. It also provides positive attention to (and reinforcement of) whatever aspect of play on which the commenting is focused. Thus, descriptive commenting can be delivered strategically and tailored to meet a number of academic, social, and other behavioral goals according to children's needs and developmental levels. Children in Level 1 play are still in parallel play. Children in Level 2 play are beginning to be interested in other children but lack the social skills to initiate and sustain these interactions on their own. Children in Level 3 play have progressed to some sustained interactions with other children but still need coaching to maintain these interactions in a positive way and to solve interpersonal peer issues during the play. (See Tables 12.1–12.3 for more information.)

Academic Coaching

In academic coaching, parents and teachers focus their comments on academic skills, including the names of objects, shapes, colors, sizes, number, textures, and position (e.g., *on, under, inside, beside, next to*). For example, when the parent or teacher says, "You have three yellow rectangles on top of the red fire truck," the child is learning about shape, colors, and number and the language to describe these concepts.

Persistence Coaching

Persistence coaching is when the parent, teacher, or therapist comments on the child's cognitive and behavioral state while she or he is playing. For example, a teacher interacting with a student working on a project will comment on the child's being focused, concentrating well, trying hard, or persisting and staying patient even though the activity is difficult. Recognizing the child's internal state of mind as well as the physical behaviors that go along with that state is especially important for children who are inattentive, easily frustrated, impulsive, or hyperactive. Labeling the times a child is focused and persisting patiently with a difficult task enables the child to recognize that internal state, what it feels like, and put a word to it.

TABLE 12.1
Parent–Child Social Coaching: Child Developmental Level 1

Social and friendship skills	Example
Parent models	
Sharing	"I'm going to be your friend and share my car with you."
Offering to help	"If you want, I can help you with that by holding the bottom while you put another on top."
Waiting	"I can use my waiting muscles and wait until you're finished using that."
Suggesting	"Could we build something together?"
Complimenting	"You are so smart in figuring out how to put that together."
Behavior to feelings	"You shared with me. That is so friendly and makes me feel happy."
	"You helped me figure out how to do that. I feel proud that you could show me that."
Parent prompts	
Self-talk	"Hmm, I really wish I could find another piece to fit here."
	"Hmm, I'm not sure I know how to put this together."
Asking for help	"Can you help me find another round piece?"
	"Can you share one of your cars with me?"
Parent response	
Praise child when she or he shares or helps.	"That was so helpful and friendly to share with me."
Ignore or model acceptance when child does not share or help.	Continue to use descriptive commenting.
	"I can keep trying to find that round piece." (model persistence)
	"I can wait until you're finished playing with the cars." (model waiting)
	"I know it is hard to give up that car, so I will wait to have a turn later."
Puppet or action-figure models	
Entering play	"Can I play with you?"
	"That looks like fun. Can I do that with you?"
Being socially friendly	"I'm being friendly. I'd like to play with you."
Ignoring aggression	"I want to play with a friendly person. I think I will find somebody else to play with."

Note. Parent–child play: Parents can use social coaching in one-on-one interactions with their children to help them learn social skills and emotional language before they begin to play with peers. A great deal of children's learning will occur by modeling and by the parents' descriptive commenting, which will enhance the children's language skills as well as help them recognize their social skills.

This attention and coaching help the child stick with the task longer than he or she might have otherwise, but it also helps the child learn an important life message. That is, the child learns that it is normal to find it hard to learn a new skill, but that with patience and persistence he or she will be able to eventually accomplish the task.

TABLE 12.2
Parent–Child Social Coaching: Child Developmental Level 2

Social and friendship skills	Examples
Parent coaches	
Asking for what they want	"You can ask your friend for what you want by saying, 'Please can I have the crayon?'"
Asking for help	"You can ask your friend for help by saying, 'Can you help me?'"
Asking a friend to wait	"You can tell your friend you are not ready to share yet."
	If your child responds to your prompt by using his or her words to repeat what you said, praise this polite asking or friendly helping.
Parent prompts	
Noticing other child	"Wow, look what a big tower your friend is building." "You are both using green markers."
Initiating interaction with other child	"Your friend is looking for small green pieces. Can you find some for him?"
	"Your friend has no cars, and you have eight cars. He looks unhappy. Can you share one of your cars with your friend?"
Giving child a compliment	"Wow! You can tell your friend his tower is cool."
	If your child does repeat this, you can praise him or her for a friendly compliment.
	If child does not respond, continue descriptive commenting.
Parent praises	
Behavior to feelings	"You shared with your friend, that is so friendly and makes her feel happy."
	"You helped your friend figure out how to do that; she looks very pleased with your help."
Playing together	"Your friend is enjoying playing these Legos with you. You look like you are having fun with your friend. You are both very friendly."
Puppet or action figure models	
Sharing or helping	"Wow! Do you see the tower that Nancy is building?"
	"Can either of you help me find a red block to make this truck?"
	"Could I help you build that house?"
	"Do you think we could ask Freddy if he'll share his train?"

Note. Children in parallel play: Young children start out playing with other children by sitting next to them and engaging in parallel play. In the beginning, they do not initiate interactions with other children or seem to notice that they are even there. They may not talk to them or offer an idea or interact with them in any way. Parents can help promote peer play by prompting their children to use social skills or to notice their friends' activities or moods. Providing children with the actual words for interactions or modeling social behaviors will be important because children may not yet have these skills in their repertoire.

TABLE 12.3
Child–Peer Social Coaching: Child Developmental Level 3

Parent-coached skills	Example
Social and friendship skills	
Asking in a friendly voice (polite, quiet)	"You asked your friend so politely for what you wanted and he gave it to you; you are good friends."
Giving help to friend	"You helped your friend find what she was looking for. You are both working together and helping each other like a team."
Sharing or trading	"That's so friendly. You shared your blocks with your friend. Then she traded with you and gave you her car."
Asking to enter play	"You asked kindly to play and they seemed happy to have you join in."
Giving a compliment	"You gave a compliment to her; that is very friendly."
Agreeing with or giving a suggestion	"You accepted your friend's suggestion. That is so cooperative."
Self-regulatory skills	
Listening to what a peer says	"Wow, you really listened to your friend's request and followed his suggestion. That is really friendly."
Waiting patiently	"You waited and asked first if you could use that. That shows you have really strong waiting muscles."
Taking turns	"You are taking turns. That's what good friends do for each other."
Staying calm	"You were disappointed when she wouldn't let you play with her, but you stayed calm and asked someone else to play. That is really brave."
Problem solving	"You both weren't sure how to make that fit together, but you worked together and figured that out—you are both good problem solvers."
Empathy	
Behavior to feelings	"You shared with your friend; that is so friendly and makes her feel happy."
	"You saw that she was frustrated and helped her put that together. That is very thoughtful to think of your friend's feelings."
	"You were both frustrated with that but you stayed calm and kept trying and finally figured it out. That is real teamwork."
	"You were afraid to ask her to play with you, but you were brave and asked her, and she seemed really pleased that you did."
Apology and forgiveness	"That was an accident. Do you think you can say you're sorry?" or "Your friend seems really sorry he did that. Can you forgive him?"

Note. Children who initiate play: Young children move from parallel play to play in which they are initiating interactions with each other. They are motivated to make friends and interested in other children. Depending on their temperament, impulsivity, attention span, and knowledge of social skills, their interactions may be cooperative or at times conflictual. Parents can help promote social skills during peer play by prompting and coaching them to use skills or by praising and giving attention to social skills.

Emotion Coaching

A second major developmental task for young children is the development of emotional self-regulation skills such as the recognition and expression of emotions, the ability to wait and accept limits, the development of empathy, and self-control over aggression. Emotion coaching by parents, teachers, and therapists helps children with this because once children have words to express their feelings, it is easier for them to self-regulate. *Emotion coaching* is when parents or teachers label children's emotions during play, including times when they are happy, confident, surprised, curious, proud, excited, frustrated, sad, lonely, tense, or angry. Labeling these feelings when children experience them helps children link a word to a feeling state, which helps them develop a vocabulary for recognizing and expressing emotions. Once children are emotionally literate, they will be able to express their feelings to others and more easily regulate their emotional responses. In addition, they will begin to recognize emotions in others—the first step toward empathy.

Parents, teachers, and therapists are encouraged to give more attention to positive emotions than to negative emotions. However, when children do exhibit negative emotions such as anger or fearfulness, the adult playing with them will coach them by pairing the negative emotion with the positive coping response. For example, a teacher might say to a child whose tower is knocked over, "You look frustrated about that, but you are staying calm and trying to solve the problem," or to a fearful child, "I could tell that you felt shy about asking her to play; it was really brave of you to try it!" In this way, the teacher validates the angry or shy feeling without giving it too much attention and also expresses faith that the child will be able to cope with the positive opposite feeling to produce a positive outcome. This may even preempt an escalation of an angry tantrum.

Following is a case example demonstrating the ways in which academic, persistence, and emotion coaching are used to meet a particular child's goals. In all the case examples included in this chapter, parents were in the IY 20-week parenting group and their children were in the IY 20-week small-group social and emotional skills training (treatment model). School consultation was also provided for teachers. In this way, the child's and family's goals were worked on by parents, therapists, and teachers.

Case Example: Tony

Tony is a 4-year-old boy with developmental and speech delays. At the onset of therapy, he was difficult to understand and had limited ability to express his needs verbally. He exhibited considerable oppositional behavior and frequent temper tantrums, often at times when he was unable to find the words to express his wishes or needs. He quickly became frustrated with tasks or games and moved rapidly from one activity to another, often in a some-what destructive whirlwind. When asked questions, Tony would often shut down and refuse to respond, even to questions for which he may have had the words to answer.

One important aspect of Tony's treatment plan was academic descriptive commenting to provide words that would help increase his vocabulary and confidence in using language. Tony's mother (at home) and therapist (in the child group) each worked to surround Tony in language that would provide him with words for objects that he commonly used. At the same time, they worked hard to limit their questions to Tony so that he would not feel pressured to have to provide verbal information, for example,

> Wow, Tony is rolling that train up the hill. Now his train is going under the track. Tony has a long track, and he is adding, one, two, three pieces to it. Now the track is even longer. He's pushing that blue engine around the corner.

Tony seemed to enjoy the use of this language and would often look up with interest as his therapist was commenting. Occasionally, he would even hold up a particular toy for her to identify and would then resume his play. He also began to imitate some of the descriptive commenting and label some of the objects on his own. In this way, his vocabulary began to increase, and he seemed more confident in his ability to communicate verbally.

Persistence and emotion coaching were also an important part of Tony's treatment plan. To gradually increase the amount of time that Tony spent on a given activity, Tony's mother and therapist worked hard to identify times when Tony was focused, calm, working hard, working carefully, and sticking with an activity. Tony's attention span was immediately longer whenever descriptive commenting was used, most likely because he enjoyed the attention and wanted it to continue. This provided many opportunities to comment on his persistence. Because Tony was also easily dysregulated and quick to get angry, attention was given to times when he was calm, regulated, and content. When Tony started to become angry, his feelings were labeled, and the therapist would then predict that he would be able to stay calm and try again. (If he tantrumed, he was ignored.) Tony gradually began to label his own emotions ("I frustrated!" or "I happy") and to use simple calm-down techniques when he was dysregulated (e.g., taking deep breaths).

One-on-One Social Coaching

A third major developmental task for young children is the development of social and friendship skills that include beginning to share, help others, initiate conversations, listen, and cooperate. *Social coaching* involves playing with children in a way that models, prompts, and reinforces these skills. The first step in social coaching is for the teacher, parent, or therapist to model and label appropriate social skills whenever they occur in the child. For example, a teacher or parent might model social skills by saying, "I'm going to be your friend and share my truck with you." Next, the teacher can prompt a social behavior by asking for the child's help in finding something or asking the child for a turn. If the child does share or help, then the teacher responds to this behavior by describing it and praising, for example, "Thank you! You found the blue Duplo I was looking for. That was so helpful. You are a good friend!" However, if the child does not share or help when prompted by the teacher, parent, or therapist, the adult models waiting and being respectful by saying, "I guess you are not ready to share, I am going to wait for a turn and do something else right now." Through modeling, prompting, and scaffolding social skills with social coaching and praise during one-on-one play times with parents or teachers or therapists, children learn positive play social interactions.

Case Example: Tony

Tony's social skills were also extremely delayed, and his play was most often parallel (see Table 12.1). At times when he came into contact with other children during play, he screamed or had a tantrum because he believed that they were going to take away his toys. If another child had a toy that he wanted, he would grab, hit, or scream in an attempt to get the toy for himself. Social coaching was integral to Tony's treatment plan. Because he had extreme difficulty playing near other children, the therapists began using social coaching in their individual play with Tony. The therapists would model and label skills for him. If they saw that he was interested in something they were holding, they would say, "Tony, I'd like to share this block with you." After Tony became used to the idea that adults would share with him, the therapists began to prompt him to use words to ask when he wanted something, for example, "Tony, I see that you want this train. You can say, 'Please can I have the train?'" At first, they did not ask Tony to reciprocate because the idea of giving up something he was holding was so difficult for him. However, they involved Tony in simple turn-taking activities, for example,

> Tony, would you like to help me build a tower? I'll wait while you put the first piece on. Wow! Now you're waiting while I add a piece. You and I are sharing these blocks and are really taking turns!

Peer Social Coaching

Next parents, teachers, and therapists learn to do social coaching with several children playing together at the same time. This time the adult prompts, models, and describes the social skills that occur between the children. For example, they comment on times the children share, wait, take turns, say thank you, help each other, ask before grabbing a toy, and give a friendly suggestion. They also facilitate interactions between children by providing words for a child to use to ask for something she or he wants or by praising a child who is waiting when another child is not ready to share.

Individual or *peer social coaching* strengthens children's friendships and makes it clear what the desired social skills are. However, it is important to assess children's developmental readiness for social play with peers. Children who are primarily engaged in parallel play and who do not initiate play with peers or seem very interested in peers will benefit from individual practice with an adult before entering into situations with a peer (see Table 12.1). Then, when they do play with peers, intense scaffolding by adults will be necessary for them to be successful. Children who are interested in playing and motivated to play with other children but who lack the impulse control or skill to do so successfully will also benefit from individual coaching because an adult can patiently help a child to practice and fine tune social skills (see Table 12.2). Then, when playing with peers, the adult can continue to prompt and praise social behaviors as they happen. For example, the teacher might say, "You shared with Mary. That was so friendly! Look at how happy your friend seems now." Helping children make the connection between their positive social behavior and another child's feelings is important for them in developing peer relationships. See Tables 12.1 through 12.3 for descriptions of how this coaching differs depending on the child's developmental level of play.

METHODS FOR TEACHING AND COACHING NEW SKILLS

In IY treatment groups for the child training program (Dina Dinosaur curriculum), therapists combine child-directed play and social coaching with direct instruction in new skills (Webster-Stratton & Reid, 2005). This process involves three steps:

1. Children watch video vignettes of children playing with peers in friendly ways with a variety of toys (blocks, make believe, puzzles, art projects, etc.) and in a variety of settings (playground, classroom). While children are watching these video vignettes, the therapists enhance the modeling effect by pausing the video scenes to prompt and cue the children to notice how the children on the video scenes wait, take turns, share, and are friendly.

2. After the video scene is shown, each child practices and rehearses the play skill modeled in the video scene with one of the puppets and is reinforced by the therapist for this practice.

3. Next, children are paired with another child to play while the therapist prompts, coaches, and reinforces them for using these friendly play behaviors. Once the child is doing well with one peer, a second peer may be added to the play interactions. Therapists also use emotion coaching to help children learn to self-regulate when they are getting overly excited. They model and prompt ways to calm down, such as taking deep breaths, practicing positive self-talk, and thinking of happy and calm images in their minds.

ADAPTING CHILD-DIRECTED PLAY TO MEET CHILDREN'S DEVELOPMENTAL AND BEHAVIORAL NEEDS

Adults need to adapt child-directed play to meet children's needs. This section describes how caregivers can use such adaptation to deal with several different types of child behavior.

Children With Oppositional Behavior

Children with conduct problems are difficult because they are noncompliant and oppositional to adult's requests. When adults cannot get children to do what they want, they cannot socialize or teach them new behaviors. Sometimes parents, teachers, and other caregivers respond to this defiant behavior by criticizing, yelling, or hitting children to try to make them comply. Sometimes the intensity of a child's response causes adults to give in to children's demands. This results in inconsistent responses or a lack of follow through with discipline. These unpredictable responses lead to children feeling insecure in their relationships. In addition, hitting or yelling at a child models aggressive behavior and gives the child's oppositional behavior powerful emotional attention, thereby reinforcing its occurrence.

Child-directed play can be used with oppositional and noncompliant children to model compliance with children's ideas and requests as long as they are behaving appropriately. This gives the children some legitimate opportunities to exercise control and to observe their parent or teacher being compliant and respectful. Child-directed play with an oppositional child helps promote a more positive attachment or relationship between the child and the adult. Often parents or teachers of such children feel angry with them because of their disruptive behavior, and they have experienced very few positive times together. These play times will begin to build up the positive bank account in the relationship between the parent and child. When this bank account of positive feelings is full, then discipline is more likely to be effective.

Children who are oppositional with adults are usually aggressive with peers and have few friends. Other children do not like to play with them because they are uncooperative, bossy, and likely to criticize their ideas and suggestions. These negative responses and rejection by peers further compound the oppositional child's problems, reinforcing his or her negative reputation. The resulting social isolation results in even fewer opportunities to make friends, low self-esteem, and loneliness. Social coaching can be used with oppositional children to help them use appropriate friendship skills with peers. The teacher may comment on how the target child is sharing, being a good team member in play, or helping another. The teacher can also help the oppositional child to use coping strategies when he or she is frustrated, which will help the child solve peer problems in a more positive way. This teacher praise for the target child in the classroom not only reinforces the appropriate social behavior for the child with behavior difficulties but also helps to change his or her negative reputation with peers. As the teacher comments on the target child's friendly behaviors and points out how he or she is working hard to help or share with others, peers will begin to see the child as more friendly.

Case Example: Dylan

Dylan, age 5, is a child with oppositional defiant disorder. At the onset of therapy, he was noncompliant with approximately 90% of parent or teacher requests; he had multiple tantrums each day, at home and at school; and his parents felt as though they were held hostage to his behavior. He was aggressive with adults and peers. He was extremely volatile and easily irritated and had dramatic mood swings during which he became enraged with very little provocation or warning. Teachers and parents reported that they walked on eggshells around Dylan because they were afraid of his extreme reactions. His parents alternated among using punishment, nagging, and bribes to try to get his cooperation and found themselves structuring their whole lives around his behaviors and moods. Dylan's parents reported that they had begun to resent the negative impact that he was having on their family, their relationship, and their younger daughter. Although they loved their son very much, they felt as though they no longer enjoyed him.

Because almost all adult–child interactions with Dylan involved a power struggle and because his negative behaviors had placed such great strain on the parent–child relationship, the first goal of therapy was to use child-directed play to begin to change the dynamic of this relationship. Dylan's parents were encouraged to experiment with play sessions where they sat back and let Dylan orchestrate the play. Their job was to be an appreciative audience, follow his lead, and not make demands or even ask questions as long as he was appropriate. Using this style of play with Dylan was intended to give him some power in the relationship in an appropriate setting, to show him that his parents valued him, and to give his parents a time when they could just enjoy his creativity and playfulness without feeling as though they had to make him behave in a certain way. At first, Dylan's parents reported that he rejected even their attempts to play with him. They were encouraged to be persistent and to make regular attempts each day to engage with him in this way. Gradually, Dylan became used to these interactions, first tolerating them, and then looking forward to this time with his parents. Dylan began to invite his parents into his play and seemed excited that they were willing to play on his terms. Although much of Dylan's behavior outside of the play sessions continued to be negative and challenging, his parents reported that he seemed calmer after play sessions and that they had moments of feeling connected and appreciative of his strengths.

Children With Attention-Deficit/Hyperactivity Disorder

Children with attention-deficit disorder with or without hyperactivity also have difficulty playing with peers and making friends (Coie, Dodge, & Kupersmidt, 1990). Because of their impulsivity and distractibility, it is hard for them to wait for a turn when playing or to concentrate long enough to complete a puzzle or game or building project. They are more likely to grab things away from another child or to disrupt a carefully built tower or puzzle because of their activity level and lack of patience. In fact, research has shown these children are significantly delayed in their play skills and social skills (Barkley, 1996; Webster-Stratton & Lindsay, 1999). For example, a 6-year-old with ADHD plays more like a 4-year-old and has difficulty focusing on a play activity for more than a few minutes, sharing with peers, or even being aware of a peer's requests for help, suggestions, or feelings. Such children are more likely to be engaged in solitary or parallel play (Table 12.1). Other typically developing 6-year-olds will find such children annoying to play with, so these inattentive children frequently experience peer rejection—a problem that further compounds their social difficulties and their self-esteem. Persistence coaching is key to helping children with ADHD sustain focus or attention for longer periods of time, emotion coaching is crucial in teaching them to regulate strong emotions, and social coaching helps to build their friendship skills. These coached play interactions not only enhance children's skills but also have the added advantage of helping parents and teachers understand and accept the developmental, temperament, and biological differences in these children such as variation in their distractibility, impulsiveness, and hyperactivity. Previous research has also shown that teaching children how to play games that are developmentally appropriate has been effective in successfully treating children with ADHD as well as those with conduct problems (Reddy, Spencer, Hall, & Rubel, 2001; Reddy et al., 2005).

Case Example: Kevin

Kevin is a 6-year-old boy with ADHD. He was adopted at birth by a single mother, Julie, and has a younger sibling who is also impulsive. At home, Julie is able to manage Kevin's behavior in most areas by being very consistent and also adjusting her expectations to match his developmental level. Her biggest area of concern at home is Kevin's behavior with his brother. The two boys play together much of the time but are in constant conflict. At school and with his peers, Kevin has much more difficulty. Kevin is eager to please adults, but he is not able to wait for the teacher's attention, blurts out answers, has trouble sitting still in class, and is very easily drawn into others' off-task behavior. With friends, Kevin is eager to play and has many friendly social skills in his repertoire. He knows how to share, ask, trade, and even make suggestions and negotiate with friends (Table 12.3). However, he has difficulty sustaining play because of his impulsivity. For example, he inadvertently messes up the play with expansive body movements, has difficulty waiting for a turn, impulsively grabs toys, and sometimes cannot maintain attention long enough to listen and respond to peers' ideas. He is also occasionally aggressive, usually in reaction to something another child says or does.

For Kevin, the first emphasis during child-directed play was on persistence and emotion regulation. Kevin's mother and therapists used focused coaching to comment when they saw Kevin being persistent, calm, or patient with an activity. For example, they learned to say such things as "You are really concentrating and working hard on that puzzle; you just keep trying and are going to figure it out." Emphasis was placed on helping Kevin become aware of the state of his body, particularly at times when he was moving slowly and calmly: "Wow! Your body is so slow and calm right now. You're able to stack all those blocks so high because you are moving so carefully!" "I can see that you are really thinking about where your body is moving, and you are being careful to step over that railroad track." Kevin's teachers and therapists extended this commenting to times when he was engaged in academic tasks (circle time and seat work): "Kevin, I see that you are sitting patiently in your spot on the carpet! You are waiting so patiently." "Kevin, I know that you want a turn to talk. I'm proud of you for waiting till I call on you." "I think that you're frustrated with that math problem, but you are staying so focused and you are trying to figure it out."

Persistence, social, and emotional coaching were also used with Kevin's peers and sibling. The key in these situations was to monitor carefully and notice when Kevin was beginning to become dysregulated. At these moments, Kevin's therapists, teacher, and mother would intervene with reminders of how his body could stay calm: "Kevin, I see that you want to use that toy too. I think you can stop your body and take a deep breath." Then they would provide Kevin with words to use to facilitate the interaction: "Can you ask Bill if you can borrow it?" Kevin was very responsive to this type of coaching. Because he already had many of the skills in his repertoire, these simple prompts were enough to keep his play on track. In addition, emphasis was placed on describing times when he was waiting, listening to a friend, playing calmly, and keeping his body slow and careful. Kevin continued to be quite impulsive and needed much structure in his school and play environments. However, with this coaching his behaviors at school and with peers and his brother became more controlled and manageable. After a time, Kevin's therapists, teachers, and mother were able to make their verbal reminders briefer, and he was able to respond to some nonverbal cues as a trigger for exerting impulse control in challenging situations.

Children With Attachment Problems

Children with conduct problems, ADHD, or both may also have ambivalent or avoidant attachment patterns with their biological, foster, or adoptive parents for a variety of reasons (Bakermans-Kranenburg, Van IJzendoorn, & Juffer, 2003). Insecure attachment may develop because children have experienced abandonment, neglect, death of a parent, trauma, or physical abuse during their early childhood years. It may also occur because parents' or caregivers' responses have been unpredictable, inconsistent, harsh, neglectful, and dismissive of children's emotional needs. Children who have experienced such stressful, inconsistent, and non-nurturing parenting learn not to trust the world or their relationships with others. Their insecure attachment, in turn, affects how they process information, solve problems, and behave with others. For example, children with insecure attachment may be angry with adults and oppositional, suspicious, or rejecting of caregiver nurturing. Children may also experience sadness, anxiety, and withdrawal. In some cases, these feelings have been ignored or invalidated by caregivers, and consequently children may not be able to label or discuss their feelings easily and may not believe that it is safe to share these feelings with others. Children may have an insatiable need for adult attention and be resentful and clingy whenever adult attention is given to someone other than themselves. Still other children with insecure attachment may be frightened of adults and become emotionally absent or disassociated as a way of escaping their fears. Children's attachment classifications are not permanent and may become more secure if parent and other adult relationships become more predictable and consistent, sensitive to their cues, calming and nurturing when they are distressed, and accepting of their emotions (Van IJzendoorn, Juffer, & Duyvesteyn, 1998).

Case Example: Michelle

Michelle is a 4-year-old girl who lives with her single mother. Michelle's father left when she was 2 years old, and Michelle's mother is clinically depressed. She tries to meet Michelle's needs, and there are times when she lavishes attention on Michelle. However, she treats Michelle like a peer, engaging in activities that are age inappropriate (e.g., makeovers, adult music, watching adult movies, sharing personal aspects of her adult life). At other times, she does not have the energy to engage with Michelle at all. She may go to bed in the afternoon and leave Michelle to entertain herself, eat dinner, and go to bed alone. Michelle's mother is also erratic in her discipline, sometimes letting Michelle do whatever she wants and at other times yelling or sending her to her room for long periods of time. At times, she has threatened to send Michelle to her father, believing that she is an unfit mother. At the onset of treatment, Michelle had difficulty separating from her mother at the beginning of each Dina Dinosaur small-group therapy session, and she was then clingy and almost inappropriately attached to the two child group therapists whom she had just met. At times she was withdrawn and sad, and at other times she seemed angry, defiant, oppositional, and noncompliant. She was interested in other children and seemed to want to make friends, but was easily jealous of any attention that other children were getting from the therapists. She had little sense of appropriate physical boundaries and hugged and kissed therapists and other children without tuning in to their responses. She was often pouty or weepy when she did not get her way.

Therapy for this family involved using the parent group to help Michelle's mother provide regular and predictable child-directed play times during which she consistently gave Michelle positive attention, consistent responses, and positive emotional coaching. The goal of providing this predictable, undivided, focused attention was to help Michelle feel valued, respected, and more secure in her relationship with her mother. Michelle's mother was also encouraged to let Michelle be a child and to follow her daughter's lead in imaginary play. This allowed Michelle's mother to develop empathy and learn to appreciate Michelle's ideas, feelings, and fears and the point of view of a 4-year-old. It also provided a new and more age-appropriate way for Michelle and her mother to interact. As Michelle's mother continued these parent group sessions, her confidence in her skills as a parent began to increase. She was helped to develop more positive self-talk and to learn how to provide herself with some pleasurable activities. She reported that for the first time in her life, she believed that she had good things to offer Michelle. Although she still struggled with her own depression and with Michelle's behavior, she felt more hopeful about her ability to cope.

Therapists also played with Michelle in ways that would model healthy relationships. Using puppets, therapists modeled setting boundaries on physical touch by teaching Michelle how to ask before hugging or touching someone else. They paid little attention to Michelle's sulky or pouty behavior but continued to encourage her to engage in activities with other children. For example, if Michelle was sulking, no direct attempts were made to cajole her out of her mood. Rather, therapists might say, "John, I'm really enjoying working on this art project with you. I bet that when Michelle is ready to join us, she'll have some great ideas about what we should add to our drawing. She's a great artist." Puppets were an important part of Michelle's treatment plan. She seemed much more willing to share feelings and experiences with the puppets than directly with the therapists. Through puppet play, Michelle also began to establish close and healthy relationships with the therapists. Therapists also showed Michelle that they would continue to be positive and engage with her, even after she had rejected their attention or been oppositional. This attention was always given strategically so that Michelle received little attention when her behaviors were negative, but was quickly reinforced as soon as she was neutral or positive. Gradually, Michelle began to seem happier and more secure in the group.

Children With Internalizing Problems Such as Anxiety and Depression

In our studies of young children with conduct problems, we have found that more than 30% of the children are also comorbid for internalizing problems (generalized anxiety disorder, social or school phobia, separation anxiety disorder, obsessive–compulsive disorder, or depression; Beauchaine et al., 2005). Our research using the IY parent program has shown not only changes in externalizing problems but also significant changes in internalizing problems (Webster-Stratton & Herman, 2008). Young children may not recognize these feelings or be able to talk about them with others. Consequently, their anxieties may be expressed in a variety of symptoms including crying, clinging behavior, stomachaches, headaches, irritability, and withdrawal. Depressed children may misbehave or even express their sadness in the form of aggressive behavior and angry talk in their interactions with others.

The goal of treatment is to help parents and teachers understand how they can help children manage their distress by teaching them social skills, problem solving, and emotional vocabulary so that they can recognize and cope successfully with their uncomfortable feelings. Child-directed play and social coaching can help to meet these goals by strengthening children's positive relationships and teaching them the emotion language they need to express their feelings. It can also increase children's feelings of self-confidence and provide them with coping skills to manage their strong feelings.

A focus on social, emotion, and problem-solving coaching during play interactions is important for children with anxious or depressed affect. Very often these children have received a lot of adult concern and recognition around their fearful and sad behaviors. Although it is important to ensure that children have the vocabulary and awareness to recognize and discuss these feelings, these negative feelings should be cues for them to implement anxiety management and coping strategies. These coping strategies will be both behavioral (e.g., find a friend, take a deep breath, find something fun to do, use a muscle relaxation strategy, give yourself a reward for trying) and cognitive (e.g., stop the negative self-talk, think of a happy or relaxing thought, give yourself a compliment, tell yourself that you can change your feelings, change anxious self-talk to a coping thought). The emphasis should be on the power that children have to make themselves feel better. Children who are socially phobic or are just fearful of interactions with other children need help in making friends and knowing how to enter into play or to play cooperatively with another child.

Case Example: Michelle

As noted earlier, Michelle exhibited both externalizing and internalizing behaviors. Her internalizing behaviors included separation anxiety and depressed affect. Child-directed play sessions included emotion coaching to help Michelle identify and cope with a variety of different feelings. Care was taken not to dwell on her expression of sad or anxious feelings but rather to identify those feelings and then provide her with a coping strategy, for example, "I'm glad you told me you're sad. I wonder what activity you could choose to make yourself feel better." In addition, therapists looked for opportunities to praise and give Michelle attention and affection when she was happy, brave, calm, or relaxed (e.g., "Wow! I'm so impressed with you. You are so brave to come to group all by yourself, and you even look very calm! You must be so proud of yourself to be able to do that. Can I give you a hug?"). As Michelle learned that she could cope with her anxious and sad feelings, she seemed to have increased self-confidence and did not need to seek as much adult reassurance to regulate these feelings. Michelle's mother also encouraged these behaviors in her play sessions at home. Because Michelle's mother also struggled with depressed mood, she was encouraged to use modeling and positive self-talk to let Michelle know her own coping strategies (e.g., "You know, I was feeling a little sad this morning, so I decided to go for a walk, and now I'm feeling better"). She was also encouraged to label her positive feelings out loud (e.g., "I'm feeling excited today because after school you and I will go get hot chocolate") and to avoid depressive talk with her daughter.

Michelle was also sometimes reluctant to initiate play with other children and held back, watching, rather than join in their play. She seemed fearful of rejection and unsure of how to involve herself in the game. In the child dinosaur group, social coaching was used to provide Michelle with the scaffolding to feel more confident in her peer interactions. Therapists began by labeling friendly behaviors so that Michelle would begin to see other children as friends rather than as threats (e.g., "Michelle, Miguel is asking you to play. He wants to be your friend." "Look, all these friendly kids are having a good time. I bet that they would like to play with you"). Then therapists provided Michelle with modeling, prompting, and support to ask to play and to accept an invitation to play. Initially this was done with puppets, and Michelle was very responsive to these nonthreatening role plays. After she was successful with puppets, she was encouraged to try playing with peers. At first, therapists carefully paired Michelle with other children who were likely to be responsive and positive so that her efforts to interact would be reinforced. Therapists provided prompting and support as she played, continuing to give more attention to positive than to negative emotions (e.g., "I see that you're feeling a little sad right now because Josh is using the toy you want, but I bet you'll be able to find something else to do while you're waiting. Wow! You are waiting so patiently, and it looks like you're having fun with the book that you picked.")

CONCLUSIONS

In this chapter, we highlighted how the IY: Parents, Teachers, and Children programs use child-directed play and four types of coaching during play as integral components in the treatment of child behavior problems. We believe these play interventions are a necessary or key ingredient of the IY program's successful outcomes because they build a more positive and loving relationship between the parent, teacher, therapist, and child and set the foundation for later success with the program's discipline components. We also believe that these play interactions have the additional advantage of teaching children (through modeling and guided practice) key social skills such as how to take turns, wait, share, make a suggestion, give an apology or compliment, share a feeling, or learn to cooperate and compromise. In our case examples, we have shown how important it is that these play interventions be tailored to each child's particular developmental level, target each child's specific goals, and take into account the parents' particular needs and issues.

As with any therapy, there is no "magic moondust," and changing behavior is hard work for parents, teachers, therapists, and children. Progress is often measured in small steps, and parents, teachers, and therapists are counseled to expect setbacks as well as improvements. At any time throughout the program, adults who are working with children are encouraged to go back to child-directed play when they are feeling stuck or frustrated with the progress that the child is making. Reconnecting by strengthening the adult–child relationship is often the key to making progress in difficult areas. A final case example follows.

In the 19th week of therapy, Tony arrived first at the group. He came in the door with a smile on his face and said, "Is my friend Grant here yet? I want to play with him!" He waited eagerly for Grant to arrive, and then said, "Hi, Grant. Do you want to play with me?" For Tony, a child who could not even play near another child at the beginning of the group, this was a huge developmental leap. He had now experienced the concept that playing with another child was fun and rewarding, and he even had the social skills to initiate this interaction. He had successfully moved from parallel play to social interaction. He continued to have difficulty with sustained play because it was hard for him to accept when the play did not go the way he wanted it to. Therefore, new therapy goals were formulated to focus on coaching social and emotional responses to his peers.

There are numerous randomized control group studies using the IY: Parents, Teachers, and Children Training Series with children with conduct problems (e.g., Webster-Stratton et al., 2004), children with internalizing problems (Webster-Stratton & Herman, 2008), and children who are at risk because of socioeconomic disadvantage, parental neglect, and foster care (Hurlburt, Nguyen, Reid, Webster-Stratton, & Zhang, 2008; Hutchings et al., 2007; Linares, Montalto, Li, & Oza, 2006; Miller Brotman et al., 2003; Raver et al., 2008; Webster-Stratton et al., 2008), showing the programs' effectiveness in promoting children's social and emotional competence and more positive relationships with caregivers.

However, the process of behavior change is not well understood and deserves further research. For example, a critical ingredient of all three of these group-based training programs is child-directed play and coaching in supportive group settings; however, to date the IY interventions have been evaluated in their entirety without collecting outcome measures after each stage of therapy. To understand the impact of child-directed play with parents, teachers, and peers in terms of child outcomes, it would be helpful to evaluate outcomes after the first stage of therapy (child-directed play and parent–child relationship building) before moving into the more traditional parent training material (positive management, praise, incentives, limit setting, consequences) and problem solving. Moreover, our research has focused primarily on outcomes related to conduct problems at home and school and to peer relationships. Further research is needed to evaluate how child-directed play affects parent, teacher, or child attachment or bonding. The more we can understand the processes involved in bringing about improvement in children's mental health, the stronger our early intervention efforts will be in stemming the later development of school underachievement, depression, delinquency, and substance abuse. Moreover, it seems clear that the power of group peer support, playful learning methods, and positive relationships is foundational to the success of all the programs, whether they be parent, teacher, or child training.

REFERENCES

Axline, V. (1969). *Play therapy*. New York: Ballantine Books.

Baer, D. M., Wolf, M. M., & Risely, T. R. (1968). Some current dimensions of applied behavior analyses. *Journal of Applied Behavior Analyses, 1,* 91–97.

Bakermans-Kranenburg, M. J., Van IJzendoorn, M. H., & Juffer, F. (2003). Less is more: Meta-analyses of sensitivity and attachment interventions in early childhood. *Psychological Bulletin, 129,* 195–215.

Bandura, A. (1977). *Social learning theory*. Englewood Cliffs, NJ: Prentice-Hall.

Bandura, A. (1989). Regulation of cognitive processes through perceived self-efficacy. *Developmental Psychology, 25,* 729–735.

Barkley, R. A. (1996). Attention deficit/hyperactivity disorder. In E. J. Mash & R. A. Barkley (Eds.), *Child psychopathology* (pp. 63–112). New York: Guilford Press.

Baumrind, D. (1995). Child rearing dimensions relevant to child maltreatment. In D. Baumrind (Ed.), *Child maltreatment and optimal care giving in social contexts* (pp. 55–73). New York: Garland.

Beauchaine, T. P., Webster-Stratton, C., & Reid, M. J. (2005). Mediators, moderators, and predictors of one-year outcomes among children treated for early-onset conduct problems: A latent growth curve analysis. *Journal of Consulting and Clinical Psychology, 73,* 371–388.

Coie, J. D., Dodge, K. A., & Kupersmidt, J. B. (1990). Peer group behavior and social status. In S. R. Asher & J. D. Coie (Eds.), *Peer rejection in childhood* (pp. 17–59). New York: Cambridge University Press.

Eyberg, S. M., Funderburk, B. W., Hembree-Kigin, T. L., McNeil, C. B., Querido, J. G., & Hood, K. K. (2001). Parent–child interaction therapy with behavior problem children: One and two year maintenance of treatment effects in the family. *Child and Family Behavior Therapy, 23,* 1–20.

Funderburk, B. W., Eyberg, S. M., Newcomb, K., McNeil, C. B., Hembree-Kigin, T., & Capage, L. (1998). Parent–child interaction therapy with behavior problem children: Maintenance of treatment effects in the school setting. *Child and Family Behavior Therapy, 20,* 17–38.

Hanf, E., & Kling, J. (1973). *Facilitating parent–child interactions: A two-stage training model*. Portland: University of Oregon Medical School.

Hinshaw, S. P., & Anderson, C. A. (1996). Conduct and oppositional defiant disorders. In E. J. Mash & R. A. Barkley (Eds.), *Child psychopathology* (pp. 113–149). New York: Guilford Press.

Hurlburt, M. S., Nguyen, K., Reid, M. J., Webster-Stratton, C., & Zhang, J. (2008). *Efficacy of Incredible Years group parent program with families in Head Start with a child maltreatment history.* Manuscript submitted for publication.

Hutchings, J., Gardner, F., Bywater, T., Daley, D., Whitaker, C., Jones, K., et al. (2007). Parenting intervention in Sure Start services for children at risk of developing conduct disorder: Pragmatic randomized controlled trial. *British Medical Journal, 334,* 1–7.

Kendall, P. C. (1992). Childhood coping: Avoiding a lifetime of anxiety. *Behavioural Change, 9,* 1–8.

Kendall, P. C. (1993). Cognitive–behavioral therapies with youth: Guiding theory, current status, and emerging developments. *Journal of Consulting and Clinical Psychology, 61,* 235–247.

King, N. J., Hamilton, D. I., & Ollendick, T. H. (1988). *Children's fears and phobias: A behavioral perspective.* Chichester, England: Wiley.

Linares, L. O., Montalto, D., Li, M., & Oza, S. V. (2006). A promising parent intervention in foster care. *Journal of Consulting and Clinical Psychology, 74,* 32–41.

Loeber, R., Wung, P., Keenan, K., Giroux, B., Stouthamer-Loeber, M., Van Kammen, W. B., et al. (1993). Developmental pathways in disruptive child behavior. *Development and Psychopathology, 5,* 103–133.

Miller Brotman, L., Klein, R. G., Kamboukos, D., Brown, E. J., Coard, S. I., & Sosinsky, L. S. (2003). Preventive intervention for urban, low-income preschoolers at familial risk for conduct problems: A randomized pilot study. *Journal of Child Psychology and Psychiatry, 32,* 246–257.

Patterson, G. R., & Capaldi, D. (1991). Antisocial parents: Unskilled and vulnerable. In P. Cowan & M. Hertherington (Eds.), *Family transitions* (pp. 195–218). Hillsdale, NJ: Erlbaum.

Patterson, G., Reid, J., & Dishion, T. (1992). *Antisocial boys: A social interactional approach* (Vol. 4). Eugene, OR: Castalia.

Raver, C. C., Jones, S. M., Li-Grining, C. P., Metzger, M., Champion, K. M., & Sardin, L. (2008). Improving preschool classroom processes: Preliminary findings from a randomized trial implemented in Head Start settings. *Early Childhood Research Quarterly, 23,* 10–26.

Raver, C. C., & Knitzer, J. (2002). *Ready to enter: What research tells policy makers about strategies to promote social and emotional school readiness among three and four year old children.* New York: National Center for Children in Poverty.

Reddy, L. A., Spencer, P., Hall, T. M., & Rubel, D. (2001). Use of developmentally appropriate games in a child group training program for young children with attention-deficit/hyperactivity disorder. In A. A. Drewes, L. J. Carey, & C. E. Schaefer (Eds.), *School-based play therapy* (pp. 256–274). New York: Wiley.

Reddy, L. A., Springer, C., Files-Hall, T. M., Benisz, E. S., Braunstein, D., & Atamanoff, T. (2005). Child ADHD Multimodal Program: An empirically supported intervention for young children with ADHD. In L. A. Reddy,

T. M. Files-Hall & C. E. Schaefer (Eds.), *Empirically based play interventions for children* (pp. 145–167). Washington, DC: American Psychological Association.

Reid, M. J., Webster-Stratton, C., & Hammond, M. (2007). Preventing aggression and improving social, emotional competence: The Incredible Years Parent Training in high-risk elementary schools. *Journal of Clinical Child and Adolescent Psychology, 36,* 605–620.

Van IJzendoorn, M. H., Juffer, F., & Duyvesteyn, M. G. C. (1998). Breaking the intergenerational cycle of insecure attachment: A review of the effects of attachment-based interventions on maternal sensitivity and infant security. *Journal of Child Psychology and Psychiatry, 65,* 98–109.

Webster-Stratton, C. (1998). Preventing conduct problems in Head Start children: Strengthening parenting competencies. *Journal of Consulting and Clinical Psychology, 66,* 715–730.

Webster-Stratton, C. (1999). *How to promote children's social and emotional competence.* London: Sage.

Webster-Stratton, C. (2005). The Incredible Years parents, teachers, and children training series: Early intervention and prevention programs for young children. In P. S. Jensen & E. D. Hibbs (Eds.), *Psychosocial treatments for child and adolescent disorders: Empirically based approaches* (pp. 507–556). Washington, DC: American Psychological Association.

Webster-Stratton, C. (2006). *The Incredible Years: A trouble-shooting guide for parents of children ages 3–8 years.* Seattle: Incredible Years Press.

Webster-Stratton, C., & Hammond, M. (1997). Treating children with early-onset conduct problems: A comparison of child and parent training interventions. *Journal of Consulting and Clinical Psychology, 65,* 93–109.

Webster-Stratton, C., & Herbert, M. (1994). *Troubled families—problem children: Working with parents: A collaborative process.* Chichester, England: Wiley.

Webster-Stratton, C., & Herman, K. (2008). The impact of parent behavior-management training on child depressive symptoms. *Journal of Counseling Psychology, 55,* 473–484.

Webster-Stratton, C., & Lindsay, D. W. (1999). Social competence and early-onset conduct problems: Issues in assessment. *Journal of Child Clinical Psychology, 28,* 25–93.

Webster-Stratton, C., Mihalic, S., Fagan, A., Arnold, D., Taylor, T. K., & Tingley, C. (2001). *Blueprints for violence prevention. Book 11: The Incredible Years—Parent, teacher, and child training series.* Boulder, CO: Center for the Study and Prevention of Violence.

Webster-Stratton, C. H., & Reid, M. J. (2005). Treating conduct problems and strengthening social and emotional competence in young children: The Dina Dinosaur Treatment Program. In M. Epstein, K. Kutash, & A. J. Duchowski (Eds.), *Outcomes for children and youth with emotional and behavioral disorders and their families: Programs and evaluation best practices* (2nd ed., pp. 597–623). Austin, TX: PRO-ED.

Webster-Stratton, C., & Reid, M. J. (in press). The Incredible Years parents, teachers and children training series: A multifaceted treatment approach for young children with conduct problems. In J. Weisz & A. Kazdin (Eds.), *Evidence-based psychotherapies for children and adolescents* (2nd ed.). New York: Guilford Press.

Webster-Stratton, C., Reid, M. J., & Hammond, M. (2004). Treating children with early-onset conduct problems: Intervention outcomes for parent, child, and teacher training. *Journal of Clinical Child and Adolescent Psychology, 33,* 105–124.

Webster-Stratton, C., Reid, M. J., & Stoolmiller, M. (2008). Preventing conduct problems and improving school readiness: Evaluation of the Incredible Years teacher and child training programs in high-risk schools. *Journal of Child Psychology and Psychiatry, 49,* 471–488.

IV

PLAY INTERVENTIONS FOR DEVELOPMENTAL DISORDERS

13

FROM NOVICE TO EXPERT: GUIDING CHILDREN ON THE AUTISM SPECTRUM IN INTEGRATED PLAY GROUPS

DAVID NEUFELD AND PAMELA WOLFBERG

The integrated play group (IPG) model (Wolfberg, 2003, in press) has evolved over 20 years as an outgrowth of close collaboration with professionals and family members of children with autism spectrum disorders (ASD). *ASD* refers here to a broad definition of autism, including classic autism, Asperger's syndrome, and other pervasive developmental disorders, all of which share core characteristics. Hallmarks of autism include impairments in social interaction, communication, and imagination, which are inextricably linked to challenges in play (American Psychiatric Association, 2000). The IPG model was designed in an effort to address these challenges while supporting the social inclusion of children on the autism spectrum with typically developing peers.

Simply put, the IPG model offers a methodology for promoting play and social development within adult-facilitated groups that include both children with ASD (novice players) and typically developing peers (expert players). Under the IPG model, trained adult facilitators (play guides) give varying degrees of support to both novice and expert players to encourage social interaction and facilitate play while incorporating the skills and interests of the children themselves. Rather than teaching discrete play skills whereby children learn to play in a scripted way (e.g., children play restaurant by following a set order of steps and speaking a set sequence of dialogue), IPGs seek to engage children with autism in natural play with peers. The IPG model also differs from other models in that it actively encourages the expert players in the group to engage and draw out the novice players socially. The play guide takes a decreasing role over time, so that ideally the groups almost run themselves, with the facilitator providing overall organization and supervision, stepping in only when necessary to assist.

The IPG model is designed to support children across the entire spectrum of autism. This includes children who exhibit mild to moderate to severe challenges in terms of their social, communication, and play behavior. Because IPGs are tailored to individual children, we set goals relative to each child's unique profile of development and experience. We further expect growth rates to vary from child to child in light of these factors.

Although the IPG model is designed to address a wide range of social, communicative, and play behaviors in children representing diverse developmental levels, for the purposes of this chapter we largely confine our discussion to one aspect of the model. We have chosen to focus primarily on guiding children with ASD in pretend play (particularly sociodramatic or social pretend play) with peers. We have done this for several reasons. First, a typically developing child's ability to engage in social pretend play with peers has been linked to several important aspects of social–emotional development. Specifically, children engaging in social pretend play with peers have demonstrated more positive and less negative affect (Singer & Singer, 1990), a higher proportion of play involving shared focus and high emotional investment (Lorimier, Doyle, & Tessier, 1995), and greater acceptance by peers (Ladd & Coleman, 1993; Ladd, Price, & Hart, 1988, 1990).

Similarly, engagement in dramatic play with peers has been shown to be highly correlated with positive affect, concentration, interaction with others, cooperation with and acceptance by peers, language use, frequency of friendly interactions, and actions taken independently of teachers. Conversely, the results show negative correlations between sociodramatic activity and negative emotions such as anxiety, fear, and sadness, and signs of fatigue (see Smilansky, 1990, for a review of relevant studies).

Finally, the IPG model, because it focuses so strongly on supporting social engagement and mutual enjoyment between children with ASD and their typically developing peers, seems uniquely suited to encouraging the development of social pretend and dramatic play skills in novice players. Thus, although the IPG model is designed for children across the entire spectrum, in this chapter we focus on children who are demonstrating emerging developmental capacities at the higher end of the spectrum (e.g., symbolic thought and role playing).

We begin with a discussion of the basic rationale and theory behind the IPG approach to guiding children's pretend play with peers. We then discuss the developmental issues that affect children on the autism spectrum and how the model specifically addresses these. Next, we address the intervention procedures (the how-to portion of the chapter) and empirical support for the model that has been obtained thus far. We provide a case illustration of IPGs in action and finish by suggesting future directions for research and practice.

BASIC RATIONALE AND THEORY

The IPG model is strongly grounded in theory and research. What follows is a brief discussion of that literature that specifically addresses the effects of pretend and dramatic play on social–emotional development. This literature is at the heart of the IPG model.

Connections Between Pretend Play and Social–Emotional Development

Lev Vygotsky, in his seminal work *Mind in Society* (1978), gave one of the clearest theoretical arguments for play as a contributor to children's social development. He saw play as a way in which a child can try on different social roles in imaginary situations and in so doing construct knowledge of how to operate within the social rules and realities that exist implicitly and explicitly in his universe (p. 94). Vygotsky contended that the social character of play creates a *zone of proximal development* for the child, which he defined as

> the distance between the actual developmental level as determined by independent problem solving and the level of potential development as determined through problem solving under adult guidance or in collaboration with more capable peers. (p. 86)

This suggests that one of the keys for social growth and understanding in any developing child is play-based interaction and that this growth is maximized when a child engages in play with other children (or adults) who have greater tools for comprehending the world.

Singer and Singer (1990) described several studies showing a positive correlation between imaginative play and positive emotions (e.g., joy, eagerness) and a negative correlation between imaginativeness and negative emotions (e.g., anxiety, sadness). One of these studies, carried out by Connolly, Doyle, and Reznick (1988), examined this relationship further by attempting to separate the imaginative component of such play from the social component. Connolly et al. found that children displayed more positive and less negative affect during social pretend play than they did during nonpretend social activities (e.g., putting puzzles together or playing a bowling game). They also found that during social pretend play, children attempted to influence the ongoing social interaction and complied more with other children's directives than they did in nonpretend play.

These results suggest that more than the social component of play, the imaginative component may have the greatest effect on social and emotional development. However, as Lorimier et al. (1995) pointed out, the study compared pretend play with all nonpretend activities, not just playful ones. That is to say, Connolly et al. (1988) looked at children's interactions when they were engaged in pretense with peers versus when they were engaged in anything not considered pretense, whether these nonpretend activities were playful (e.g., building with blocks, pushing a toy car back and forth) or not (e.g., doing a puzzle or a workbook page together).

To make a more direct comparison of pretend and nonpretend play interaction and to examine whether social pretend play provides a specific context for young children to practice social–emotional skills, Lorimier et al. (1995) carried out a study with 24 four- and six-year-old girls, videotaping each participant with a familiar peer for two 30-minute play sessions. They found that the proportion of high-level social coordination was indeed greater in pretend than in nonpretend play. They also found that a higher proportion of social play involving shared focus and a higher average level of emotional investment in play were present in pretend than in nonpretend play. This led them to conclude that social pretense was in fact a vehicle for practice and consolidation of socially mature behavior, a conclusion that seems to substantiate the claims of both Vygotsky (1978) and Connolly et al. (1988).

One final aspect of play that relates to social development is its connections to acceptance by peers. Singer and Singer (1990) reported on a study by Ladd et al. (1988; see also Ladd & Coleman, 1993; Ladd et al., 1990), which looked at how children's behavior in school contributes to their status in the eyes of their peers. They found that "children who played cooperatively with peers at the outset of the school year tended to do so at later points in time, and this disposition was associated with long-term gains in peer acceptance" (p. 70). This notion, combined with Singer and Singer's own findings that imaginative play is correlated with cooperation with peers, led them to conclude that "imaginative play . . . can lead to greater popularity and acceptance by other children" (p. 71).

All of this theory and research presents many compelling reasons to consider pretend play a fundamental part of a young child's social development. Let us turn now to a more specific type of pretend play, known as *dramatic* or *sociodramatic play*.

Connections Between Dramatic–Sociodramatic Play and Social–Emotional Development

Before we begin the next phase of our discussion, it will be helpful to have a working definition of what constitutes dramatic and sociodramatic play.

Defining Dramatic and Sociodramatic Play

According to Smilansky (1990), dramatic play is not the same thing as basic pretend play, which, especially in very early childhood, often consists only of using one object to represent another (e.g., pretending a banana is a telephone) or of feigning behaviors (e.g., pretending to sleep when one is awake or pretending to swim when one is really lying on the carpet). Dramatic play goes beyond basic pretense and into the realm of role playing. As Smilansky (1990) defined it,

> Dramatic play consists of children taking on a role in which they pretend to be someone else. They imitate the person's actions and speech patterns, using real or imagined "props" and drawing on their own firsthand or secondhand experience of the imitated individual in various familiar situations. (p. 19)

She then went on to describe a specific type of dramatic play that she called *sociodramatic play*. Although a child who acts out the role of mommy with a baby doll is engaging in imaginative, or dramatic, play, sociodramatic play occurs "when such activity involves the *cooperation* of at least two children and the play proceeds on the basis of interaction between the players acting out their roles, both verbally and in terms of acts performed" (p. 19). To continue with the earlier example, the mommy–baby play would become sociodramatic when the child conscripted a peer to play the part of the baby or the baby's daddy.

Elements of imagination and make believe often enter into dramatic and sociodramatic play (Smilansky, 1990). One of the ways in which we see this is through imitation. For example, a child engaging in a sociodramatic car trip with a peer may move his or her hands to simulate moving a steering wheel and make noises to represent the sounds of the car (e.g., the engine or the squealing of brakes at a red light). He or she may also speak in character to inhabit the play more fully (e.g., "If you and your sister don't stop fighting, I will stop this car!").

Contributions of Dramatic–Sociodramatic Play to Social–Emotional Development

Smilansky (1990) reported on a great many studies looking at the ways in which dramatic play contributes to social–emotional development in typically developing children. The collective results have shown a high correlation between sociodramatic play and measures of positive affect, concentration, interaction with others, cooperation with and acceptance by peers, language use, frequency of friendly interactions, and actions taken independently of teachers. Conversely, the results have shown negative correlations between sociodramatic activity and negative emotions such as anxiety, fear, sadness, and signs of fatigue. Other studies Smilansky listed (e.g., Burns & Brainerd, 1978; Saltz, Dixon, & Johnson, 1977) have suggested that broader social skills such as empathy and perspective taking could be worked on through the lens of dramatic play. All of these are areas in which children with ASD are notably deficient (Sherratt & Peter, 2002; Wolfberg, 2003, in press), suggesting that drama could prove to be a noteworthy intervention for them (See Variation on a (Dramatic) Theme: Integrated Dramatic Play Groups section for further discussion of this notion).

DEVELOPMENTAL ISSUES

Now that we have presented the theoretical underpinnings of the IPG model, we move to a specific discussion of the model itself and the benefits it can provide for children with ASD. Because some readers may not be familiar with ASD, we begin with a brief overview of the impairments and challenges that are characteristic of the disorder.

Impairments Associated With Autism Spectrum Disorders

The *Diagnostic and Statistical Manual of Mental Disorders* (4th ed., text rev.; American Psychiatric Association, 2000) lists three categories of impairments associated with ASD. They are impairment in reciprocal social interaction (i.e., a lack of spontaneous seeking to share enjoyments and interests with others and a lack of social or emotional reciprocity); impairments in communication (i.e., delay of development of spoken language not compensated for by gesture and a lack of varied, spontaneous make-believe play or social imitative play); and restricted repetitive and stereotyped patterns of behavior, interests, and activities (i.e., apparently inflexible adherence to specific, nonfunctional routines or rituals and stereotyped motor mannerisms such as hand flapping).

These difficulties manifest themselves in a variety of ways. Children with autism have severe deficits in symbolic–imaginative play: They do not typically spontaneously engage in pretend play (Baron-Cohen, 1987; Jarrold, 2003; Jarrold, Boucher, & Smith, 1996; Lewis & Boucher, 1988). The role play (i.e., play in which children take on a role in which they pretend to be someone else) of children with ASD is often stereotypical and repetitive and tends not to involve attributing mental states to inanimate objects (Harris, 1993; Sherratt & Peter, 2002). For example, a child with ASD might repetitively enact feeding a baby with a bottle but would likely not make a statement such as "My dolly is hungry" while engaging in this play. Underlying these problems may be deficiencies in the development of theory of mind (the understanding that other people have mental states, feelings, and intentions) in children with ASD. Research has shown that many children with ASD either completely fail to develop a theory of mind or experience severe delays in doing so. As a result, they have difficulties taking others' perspective and fail theory-of-mind tasks such as false belief and representational change tasks (Baron-Cohen, Leslie, & Frith, 1985; Baron-Cohen, Tager-Flusberg, & Cohen, 1993; Frith & Happé 1999; Leslie, 1987).

Evidence suggests that children with ASD are not devoid of desire for peer interaction but lack the social skills necessary to establish and maintain the connections necessary for play. They often cannot clearly communicate their interests in play, nor can they interpret and respond to peers' social advances (Jordan, 2003; Wolfberg, in press). The ability to read others' social cues is crucial to approaching and entering group play. Children with ASD, however, are often observed pursuing repetitive and stereotyped activities in social isolation rather than the complex, cooperative, pretend-oriented play in which typically developing children engage (Frith, 2003; Wing, Gould, Yeates, & Brierly, 1977). Children with ASD may repeat the same play activity for hours on end (e.g., methodically lining cars up in rows) and often show resistance when a preferred play routine is disrupted. These play patterns stand in stark contrast to the rich play experiences of their typically developing peers, and it follows that children with ASD fail to benefit from the many gains associated with play in typical children (Boucher & Wolfberg, 2003).

Addressing the Developmental Needs of Children With ASD Via the IPG Model

The IPG model uses a series of in-depth assessments to shed light on the set of strengths and challenges specific to a novice player (see Wolfberg, 2003, for examples of the specific measures). After an initial parent interview and observation to help determine a given child's developmental play patterns, communication styles, and play preferences, the play guide uses this information to create detailed play goals, which are tracked over the course of the intervention. There are many domains on which an IPG may focus, but four of the most important are social development, symbolic development, social–communication development, diversity of play interests, and fostering reciprocal relationships with typical peers.

Social development, in the context of an IPG, refers to the players' ability to engage with peers in increasingly advanced ways. Assessments are designed to track goals and progress along a continuum referred to as the *social dimension of play*. For example, throughout the course of an IPG, goals for the children might include a progression from playing in isolation to playing in parallel with others or from play involving a common focus (i.e., engaging in reciprocal exchanges around the same play activity, e.g., taking turns building with blocks) to play involving common goals (i.e., coordinating to attain a common goal or make a product, e.g., carrying out a plan to construct a set of buildings together with blocks).

Symbolic development, in terms of an IPG, refers to the players' ability to help create play scenarios in increasingly advanced ways. Assessments are designed to track goals and progress along a continuum referred to as the *symbolic dimension of play*. For example, an IPG might be designed to help a child progress from not being engaged at all to being engaged in *manipulation–sensory play* (i.e., exploring and manipulating objects or toys, but not in conventional ways, e.g., shaking items or twirling a scarf repetitively). After that, a child might progress to *functional play* (i.e., using objects and toys in the ways in which they are intended, e.g., pushing a car back and forth with a peer) and to *symbolic–pretend play* (e.g., pretending that a banana is a telephone or playing Spider-Man or Harry Potter in a dramatic scene).

Social–communication development in an IPG refers to expanding functions and means of communication. *Communicative functions* are the reasons for which a child communicates (e.g., to ask a peer to play, ask a peer for an object, express protest), and *communicative means* are the ways in which a child goes about communicating (e.g., gestures, vocalization, simple or complex speech). Throughout the course of an IPG, the child learns how to communicate for a larger variety of reasons in a larger variety of ways.

Understanding a novice's play preferences (and finding common ground with the interests of expert peers) is another important part of running an IPG. *Play preferences* refer to what "the child spontaneously chooses for free play given a variety of materials, activities, and themes" (Wolfberg, 2003, p. 124). During an IPG, the child is helped to diversify these interests and to become interested in a greater variety of toys, activities, and themes.

Finally, one of the most important goals of any IPG is to foster reciprocal relationships with typical peers. Over the course of an IPG, it is not uncommon for friendships to form that extend beyond the confines of and last longer than the groups themselves. Integral to the IPG model is the overall goal of enhancing understanding, empathy, and acceptance of children with ASD. IPGs allow this to take place in a natural environment in which mutual interests can be honored and expanded on and true, meaningful friendships can be created.

PLAY INTERVENTION PROCEDURES

We now move to an outline of the specific procedures used in the IPG model. The IPG mission statement provides a useful framework for this discussion.

Integrated Play Groups Mission

The mission of any IPG is "to provide a haven for children with diverse abilities to create genuine play worlds together, where they may reach their social and imaginative potential, as well as have fun and make friends" (Wolfberg, 2003, p. 31). Several key components of the IPG model represented in this mission statement warrant specific mention here.

Children With Diverse Abilities

At the heart of the IPG model is the Vygotskian (1978) idea (described earlier) that when accompanied and guided by a more experienced play partner, children can perform at a level higher than that which they can reach on their own. For example, a young child may recognize the words to a song such as "Twinkle, Twinkle, Little Star," but left to his or her own devices may not know how to sing the words him- or herself. However, if a parent or a more experienced peer starts the child on the path by singing "Twinkle, twinkle, little star, how I wonder what you . . . " and then waits expectantly with a big smile on her or his face, the child may very well finish the song by singing *are*. By doing this, the more experienced partner has created a zone of proximal development (Vygotsky, 1978) and helped the less experienced partner to achieve at a slightly higher level.

The IPG model applies this phenomenon by permeating play with the notion of *guided participation*, which refers to the process through which children develop while actively participating in a culturally valued activity with the guidance, support and challenge of social partners who vary in skill and status (Rogoff, 1990). To further this aim, the IPG model uses groups made up of both children with ASD (novice players) and typically developing children (expert players), with the idea that the children teach and learn from each other.

Creating Genuine Play Worlds

An IPG involves the creation of "genuine play worlds." That is to say, the play in an IPG is neither adult led nor adult driven. Rather, although the play is guided by adults, it genuinely comes from the children themselves. It comes from the unique interests and abilities of both the novice and the expert players and should be natural and unscripted. For example, in an IPG one would not teach children how to play doctor by systematically taking them through a series of predetermined steps (e.g., Step 1, Johnny walks into the office; Step 2, Johnny says, "Hello, Dr. Johnson"; Step 3, Johnny sits down, opens his mouth, and says "Ah") designed to methodically and mechanically teach scripts to be memorized by rote.

Following the IPG model, one might instead give the children a basic idea of the flow of a doctor scenario (perhaps through visual aids or a social story), allowing the children themselves to determine what they say and how they go about seeing the story through. The play should be genuine and joyful, free from excessive adult direction and shaping. As one facilitator put it,

> I direct the kids to direct themselves. . . . I set up opportunities for them to find their *own* way to interact. Rather than saying "you do this," it's like "Okay, how am I going to create this scene so that this happens?" That's what facilitating is, more than being directive. (Neufeld, 2009, p. 25)

Ultimately, the best IPGs are those that almost run themselves, where the adults have little to no direct involvement in the play apart from structuring the group and stepping in when necessary to make sure that everyone is participating and everyone is safe.

Integrated Play Group Structure

So far, we have confined ourselves to a primarily theoretical and philosophical description of IPGs. However, there are several structural elements that need to be in place to maximize the success of a given group.

Small, Stable Groups

IPGs are made up of small groups of novice and expert players that remain constant over time, with no fewer than three and no more than five children in a group. These groups contain a higher ratio of expert to novice players. For example, in a group of five children, an ideal ratio would be three expert players to two novice players (although a four-to-one ratio of expert to novice players would also be acceptable). In a group of three children, a ratio of two expert players to one novice player would be necessary.

Novice players can be children of all abilities on the autism spectrum. They may be nonverbal or verbal, with intensive, moderate, or mild forms of autism, as well as Asperger's syndrome. Expert players are typically developing peers or siblings who demonstrate social competence and an enjoyment of playing with others and who can serve as role models to the novice players in these areas. Groups may be made up of children of similar or different ages, as well as the same or mixed genders. Whenever possible, expert and novice players should be drawn from natural preexisting social networks (e.g., siblings, classmates, family friends).

Groups Tailored to the Individual Child

More important than age, gender, or social network, it is crucial that groups be made up of children who are appropriate play matches for one another. For example, if you have a novice player who reacts poorly to loud noises and high levels of activity, it would not be advisable to put him or her in a group made up entirely of children who are loud and boisterous. Rather, you would look for some quieter, mellow children to strike a balance with the more energetic children. Likewise, you would put children together who have similar play interests or have at the very least the potential to develop similar play interests. For example, it would not make sense to put a child who is nonverbal and who might only be interested in manipulation–sensory play into a group made up entirely of highly verbal children interested only in complex role play. IPGs are intended to be an integral part of a child's education and therapy program, and as such it is especially important that the groups be designed to meet the child's individual needs.

Consistent Schedule

IPGs should be run on a consistent schedule in natural play environments within school, home, therapy, or community settings (e.g., inclusive classrooms, after-school programs, recreation centers, neighborhood parks). That is to say, an IPG should have regular and ongoing meetings in a location that remains constant over time. Typically, groups meet two or more times per week for a period of 30 to 60 minutes each time, over a term of 6 to 9 months.

Predictable Structure

Creating a predictable structure is often very helpful for the novice players in a group. In addition to creating clear expectations and organization for the group, adding predictability may also help to ease transitions and maintain order.

IPGs consist broadly of three different phases: (a) an *opening ritual*, (b) *play* (with guided participation, which we describe momentarily), and (c) a *closing ritual*. The opening ritual is designed to gather all the children into the same space and prepare for play. For very young children, this may be as simple as gathering in a circle, singing a hello song, and reviewing rules before starting play. For older children, it may also involve making a plan for the day's activities. Once the opening ritual is complete, play can begin. Once play is completed (and toys have been put away), the group moves to the closing ritual.

The closing ritual is another time at which all the children gather in the same play space, review the session's events, plan for the next time, and say good-bye. A snack may also be incorporated into the schedule.

For children who benefit from using visual schedules, it is often helpful to create icons that show the flow of an IPG session and to post them somewhere in clear view. This schedule can further break down the phases of the IPG (e.g., within the opening ritual section, one may have one icon for saying hello and another for singing). If it is helpful, at the conclusion of each section a child can remove the appropriate icon and place it an "all-done" pocket at the bottom of the schedule (see Wolfberg, 2003, for more examples of visual schedules in IPGs).

Guided Participation in Play

The notion of guided participation is especially important when designing and running an IPG. IPGs should be run by a trained, expert facilitator. This facilitator (or play guide) should be skilled at engaging children of different abilities in play, bridging gaps between children, and making sure that everyone is included. The play guide should also be skilled at knowing when it is appropriate to be very involved in the play and when it is appropriate to back off and let things happen on their own. The facilitator must know how to regulate his or her amount and type of support to each child's needs. This means *scaffolding* (providing adjustable and temporary support structures to) children's play. When scaffolding play, the guide should build on a child's play initiations by

> systematically adjusting assistance to match or slightly exceed the level at which the child is independently able to engage in play with peers— within the child's "zone of proximal development." The idea of scaffolding is to avoid being so lax that the play falls apart or so intrusive that it ruins the moment. The key is to find that ever so delicate balance of allowing the play to unfold in genuine ways while sustaining engagement. That means knowing when to step in, when to step out and especially when to be quiet. (Wolfberg, 2003, p. 172)

Within the IPG model, there are three levels of support that a play guide can give, depending on the needs of the children in the group. Maximum support involves directing and modeling a play action. For example, in playing a game of hide and seek, a play guide might physically bring a novice player over to a hiding spot and hide with him or her, demonstrating exactly how one plays the game. A guide might also direct a given expert player to take a novice player to a hiding spot with her or him, showing the expert player exactly how to encourage the novice player to participate.

Intermediate support is slightly less directive. It involves using verbal and visual cuing rather than direction and modeling. The guide would not model but would instead cue a player on what to do from afar. To continue with the hide-and-seek example, a play guide using intermediate support would tell a novice player (by word, gesture, or visual aid) to go and hide with an expert player or would cue the expert to take the novice player to a hiding spot.

Minimum support is the least directive of all. It involves standing by and allowing the play to proceed on its own. A play guide using minimum support would remain on the sidelines, stepping in only when necessary to get the play going, resolve conflicts, and make sure the children are safe.

It is important to note that these levels of support are not mutually exclusive, nor do they proceed in a set order. Rather, scaffolding is entirely dependent on the children's needs at any given time. It is conceivable that a guide might use one type of support over the course of an entire session, and it is equally possible that a guide might need to switch among them repeatedly over the course of a single session. A play guide must understand when to use each type of support and how to adjust his or her role depending on the group's needs. This is an important component of the training process, and it is key to the overall success of an IPG.

Variation on a (Dramatic) Theme: Integrated Dramatic Play Groups

The principles of IPGs are easily adaptable to new variations. One such variation is the creation of integrated dramatic play groups (IDPGs), which take the principles of IPGs and apply them to a group focused on dramatic play, semistructured improvisation, and simple scripted dramatic scenes. Drama, with its reliance on narrative, action, and character, can provide a structured way for children with ASD to take on and try out new social roles or to explore the world from another person's point of view, something that they typically have difficulty doing (Peter, 2003).

Following Wright (2006), each IDPG session consists of a warm-up period (in which the play guide leads drama exercises and games designed to facilitate group activity and awareness), a period of semistructured group dramatic play or improvisation with the materials at hand (in which one child per session chooses a story he or she would like to play out [e.g., the story of Aladdin], costumes and props are chosen, and short scenes are improvised with the help of the play guide), and a cool-down, reflective period to talk as a group about what occurred during the session (e.g., how the scenes went, problems that might have come up, feelings that might have been hurt).

By encouraging such skills as imagination, social exploration, and taking the perspective of different characters and people, IDPGs may be successful in increasing the ability of novice players to initiate interactions with peers, to acknowledge the initiations of others, and to stay engaged with peers over an extended period of time. Many other variations on the IPG model are possible as well. Among those currently being field tested are groups specifically devoted to sensory integration, art, filmmaking, and other special interests.

EMPIRICAL SUPPORT

To date, several studies have evaluated the IPG model (Gonsier-Gerdin, 1993; Lantz, Nelson, & Loftin, 2004; Mikaelan, 2003; O'Connor, 1999; Richard & Goupil, 2005; Wolfberg, 1988, 1995, 2009; Wolfberg & Schuler, 1992, 1993; Yang, Wolfberg, Wu, & Hwu, 2003; Zercher, Hunt, Schuler & Webster, 2001). These studies have looked at children of a variety of ages (3–11 years) involved in IPGs across a variety of locations ranging from school (O'Connor, 1999; Wolfberg, 1988, 1995, 2009; Wolfberg & Schuler, 1992, 1993) to home (Mikaelan, 2003) to community settings (Zercher et al., 2001). Most of the studies were carried out in urban areas in the United States, but others were performed in rural areas of the United States (Lantz, Nelson, & Loftin, 2004) and in Canada (Richard & Goupil, 2005) and Taiwan (Yang et al., 2003). Many of the studies included social validation components that assessed parent perception of the impact of the IPG programs on their children with autism (Lantz et al., 2004; Mikaelan, 2003; Wolfberg & Schuler, 1993; Yang et al., 2003; Zercher et al., 2001). Building on this research base, a long-term research project has been initiated that pairs two large-group studies to examine children with autism and typically developing peers participating in IPGs (Wolfberg, Turiel, & DeWitt, 2008).

Taken as a whole, the group of studies thus far have obtained impressive results. Over the course of their IPG programs, novice players demonstrated decreases in stereotyped, isolated play and increases in eye contact, watching, and imitating of peers. They displayed greater levels of social initiation and responsiveness, increases in symbolic play levels and communication, and greater diversity of spontaneous play interests. Their ability to engage in socially coordinated play (i.e., parallel and common goal play) increased as well. Furthermore, these skills were maintained when adult support was withdrawn, and preliminary evidence (based on observational and social validation data) was obtained that demonstrates that the new skills generalized beyond the IPG itself to school, home, and community settings.

It is important to note that the expert players involved in these studies benefited from their IPG experiences as well (Gonsier-Gerdin, 1993; Wolfberg, 1995, 2009; Yang et al., 2003). On the basis of observations and interviews with play guides and peers, it was reported that the expert players developed greater sensitivity, tolerance, and acceptance of the novice players' individual differences. They spoke of a sense of responsibility as well as an understanding of how to include the less skilled players by adapting to their different interests and styles of communication. Finally, they reported having fun and developing mutual friendships with novice players that extended beyond the play group setting to after-school activities in the home and community.

CASE ILLUSTRATION

Now that we have described the theoretical background, structure, and empirical support for the IPG model, we present a case illustration from an integrated dramatic play group. This illustration will solidify the ideas we have been discussing and demonstrate the power of the model.

Integrated Dramatic Play Group

Every IDPG begins with the collection of baseline data. Accordingly, we begin our illustration with a description of one novice player's baseline phase by describing Aaron.

Baseline: Week 1

Aaron has a diagnosis of high-functioning autism. He has brown hair and eyes that sparkle with either joy or mischief, depending on the moment. He is highly verbal and likes to talk mostly about movies, video games, and Pokémon. When asked a question that he does not feel like answering, Aaron will say, "I don't want to talk about that" or "I don't want to tell you." He will also revert to talking about his own interests without signaling. For example, during snack on the first day of his IPG, out of nowhere, he declares that he does not like to do homework. He does not ask anyone about homework or indicate in any way that he wants to talk about homework. This sometimes makes it difficult for both adults and peers to follow his train of thought.

Aaron can be happy and cooperative, and he can also be irritable, distractible, and distracting. He occasionally needs to be coaxed into taking part in activities and needs to be reminded several times a session not to turn the lights off and on, especially on days when he is particularly agitated, as he is on the first day of his IPG. On that day, he keeps running into corners and covering his eyes while vocalizing loudly, banging pots, and refusing to look at people or listen to what they have to say. He plays mostly in isolation, spending large amounts of time twirling a scarf around and around without looking at anyone or interacting at all. To help Aaron and the other novice players organize themselves, I decide to implement a predictable schedule with a few structured activities (drama games, free play, then short improvisational scenes).

Week 4

As we are planning our day during the opening ritual, one of the expert players (Duncan) suggests that everyone play Spider-Man. Aaron loves the movie, and likes the idea. However, both Aaron and Duncan want to play Spider-Man. We negotiate for a little bit, and eventually it is decided that because it was Duncan's idea, he gets to be Spider-Man. Aaron decides that he will play Venom instead (Spider-Man's archenemy in the third film, whose main weapons are claws. Aaron uses forks to represent them.)

Because this particular IPG is drama based, we decide to do several short scenes. Each scene involves an expert and a novice player, and the other children watch. Then it is their turn. For the Spider-Man–Venom scene, because both boys really like roughhousing, I (David Neufeld) suggest that Venom attack Spider-Man (safely, of course). After I say "Go," Aaron sneaks out from under the table to do so. The boys chase each other around the table, Duncan pretending to shoot webs and Aaron trying to poke Duncan with his claws. They circle round and round, with Duncan saying "pssh, pssh" every time he shoots a web and Aaron laughing and vocalizing, narrating about attacking him or getting him (e.g., "I'm getting you, Spider-Man! I got you!"). They do not speak to each other directly.

After the fight has gone on for a minute or 2, I say that when I count to five, Spider-Man will wrap Venom up in his webs and win. It works okay, except that Aaron keeps on attacking after I have counted. Duncan tries to wrap Aaron up again, and Aaron still does not realize that he should lose at that point (or does realize it, and simply does not want to lose at all). After the third time, Duncan gently tackles Aaron, wrapping him up in the process. I stop the scene, and we applaud. Both boys look as though they have just had a lot of fun. Even when no dialogue is actually exchanged, these boys are interacting. This is a step in the right direction, although it took a fair amount of structuring and prompting to move Aaron along.

Week 5

However, the next week, we are able to build on Aaron's creation of the Venom character in a more spontaneous way. During free play, the other novice player in the group (Samantha) starts playing with a toy phone. Aaron tries to take it away, so I suggest that he take the other one and call her instead. This works. Samantha says she wants to call Spider-Man, and Aaron says he wants to call Venom. They start out speaking separately to their parties, but somewhere along the line, Samantha starts speaking to Venom instead of Spider-Man. Aaron seizes the opportunity and, without prompting, begins to grump into the phone in a monsterish kind of voice, playing Venom again. When we move into some circle activities, Aaron's spontaneous cooperation continues. Samantha momentarily leaves the group to go to the bathroom, and Aaron tells us we should wait for her before beginning (we do). We play a game called Pass the Clap, in which the children turn to each other, make eye contact, and clap simultaneously. In the past, it has been difficult to get Aaron to attend to this game and even more difficult to get him to clap together with the other kids. Today, though, Aaron spontaneously (i.e., without reminders or prompting) turns to people to clap with them, and although he sometimes claps too fast and wants to lead people instead of clapping simultaneously, it is easy to slow him down and get him to match them.

Week 7

Aaron and Duncan are building a fort with toy bricks, and because Aaron has progressed to the point where he needs only minimal support, I stand by. However, when a little disagreement arises about how to build the fort, Aaron gets frustrated and knocks over a brick on purpose. I jump in, have him pick it up, and then ask Duncan how he feels about the fact that Aaron just did that. "I don't like that, Aaron. Please don't knock the bricks down," Duncan says. We talk about that, and Aaron agrees to stop knocking the bricks over. They begin to cooperate. As building continues, Aaron accidentally knocks some bricks over. This time, however, as soon as he does so, he says, "I made a mistake," acknowledging what has happened and that it was an accident. Go Aaron! I pretend to call him up on the phone: "Hello, wall repair? Is that you? A wall has fallen down! We need you!" Aaron says "No," refusing to come, but he says it with a smile, and then comes and helps anyway when I ask again. The wall breaks a few times, and each time it happens I call Aaron the Wall Repairman to come fix it. He comes every time.

Week 8

Today we are doing a scene from *Aladdin*, in which Aladdin (or in our case today, Jasmine; nobody wanted to play Aladdin) finds the magic lamp in the Cave of Wonders and rubs it, causing the genie to come out. Aaron has been engaged in a disagreement about how to build the cave (something of a pattern with him). He is upset. He starts saying he does not want to be in the play and starts flipping the lights on and off, frustrating me a little bit. However, Duncan (who will be playing the genie) comes up with a great idea about how to include him: "I know how Aaron can be in the play! He can turn the lights off when I pop out of the lamp!" This is a great idea. In fact, I wish I had thought of it! I swear, these kids often teach me more than I teach them. Duncan also wants to make the cave break apart when Samantha (who is playing Jasmine) rubs the lamp, to "booby trap" the cave, like in the movie.

This is also a great idea. Aaron likes the idea of flashing the lights when the genie comes out.

We do the scene. Duncan mistakenly pops out of the lamp when I say "Action!" but I remind him that he has to wait until Jasmine rubs the lamp. He laughs, embarrassed at his mistake, and hides again. Aaron waits patiently by the light switch. Samantha as Jasmine finds the lamp. She rubs it. Duncan as the genie pops out, smashes the cave, and makes the blocks fly everywhere. Aaron flashes the lights. Awesome. The genie tells Jasmine she can make a wish. Jasmine wishes to marry Prince Aladdin. Scene.

The second scene involves Jasmine (still played by Samantha) and Jafar (played by Aaron). The plan is for Jafar to ask Jasmine whom she wants to marry. When Jasmine says "Aladdin," Jafar will say "No!" and Jasmine will yell at him. That's the plan, anyway. Here is what actually happens:

> *Jafar:* Who do you want to marry?
>
> *Jasmine:* Prince Aladdin!
>
> *Jafar:* Okay, I'll marry you! [*hugs Jasmine*]

I have no idea if Aaron forgot the story, forgot who he was playing, or what. But it is ridiculously cute and totally awesome, so we decide to change the story and have Jasmine marry Jafar. Aaron and all the kids are happy. They joyfully take their bows, and we say our goodbyes. They did some great play work today.

Discussion

Several important features of the IPG model are made explicit in the case illustration. First and foremost, the notion of guided participation (which has its roots in the Vygotskian [1978] idea of the zone of proximal development, in which an adult or more experienced peer helps a child to perform just above his or her usual level of play) weaves itself throughout. For example, in Week 4 the facilitator steps in to help the boys (especially Aaron, the novice player) negotiate who will play Spider-Man and who will play Venom in the following scene. A few minutes later, he helps bring the "fight" (which could have gone on indefinitely) to a satisfactory resolution by saying that when he counts to five, Spider-Man will wrap up Venom and win the day. In Week 7, he steps in to help mediate a conflict in which Aaron intentionally knocks down the wall that Duncan is building. In this way, he helps bring the interaction back on track and allows the boys to figure out how they can best cooperate with each other, something they were having difficulty doing on their own. Once they are cooperating, and Aaron knocks the blocks down again (by accident, this time, which he acknowledges by saying "I made a mistake"), the facilitator is able to use it. He picks up the phone and calls for wall repair, and the play continues in a richer way than before.

Another important feature of the model that is made explicit in this description is the idea that the play and sensory needs of all the children should be taken into account. In Week 8, the play guide expresses frustration with the fact that Aaron is continually turning the lights on and off and is refusing to join the scene. He cannot figure out how to get Aaron to cooperate. However, an expert player (Duncan) provides a perfect way to incorporate Aaron's desire to flick the light switch: He suggests that Aaron provide the visual effects for the genie's escape from the lamp. Aaron agrees and decides to take part in the scene after all. Duncan's idea works perfectly and is an excellent demonstration of how to smoothly incorporate an idiosyncratic behavior of a novice player into a context in which the behavior is not only normalized but celebrated for the added dimension it brings to the play.

CONCLUSION AND FUTURE DIRECTIONS

IPGs, with their unique structure, ability to include more highly skilled peers in play, and naturalistic approach to drawing out interaction, language, and excitement from novice players, can be very beneficial for children on the autism spectrum. The high level of training and various levels of support that are at the heart of the model allow for a great deal of flexibility in play and make the model appropriate for children of all skill levels, language abilities, and interests. By pairing novice players with peers who can help them to achieve at a higher level than they would be capable of on their own, IPGs provide an excellent way to maximize each child's social and play development while forming friendships, following their individual interests, and having a great deal of fun.

The research that exists thus far supports this. As previously discussed, novice players involved in IPGs demonstrate a decrease in isolated play and increases in eye contact, watching, imitating, social initiation, and social responsiveness. They also exhibit increases in symbolic play levels, communication, and diversity of play interests (Gonsier-Gerdin, 1992; Lantz et al., 2004; Mikaelan, 2003; O'Connor, 1999; Richard & Goupil, 2005; Wolfberg, 1988, 1995, 2009; Wolfberg & Schuler, 1992, 1993; Yang et al., 2003; Zercher et al., 2001). Expert players develop greater sensitivity, tolerance, and acceptance of novice players' individual differences and also report having fun and developing mutual friendships with them (Gonsier-Gerdin, 1992; Wolfberg, 1995, 2009; Yang et al., 2003).

As exciting as these findings are, it is important to note one significant limitation. By and large, the studies described here were carried out with small sample sizes. This is mostly because autism is a low-incidence disability composed of a highly diverse population, making it difficult to find a large number of participants who can be matched in comparable ways (National Research Council, 2001). The largest number of participants represented in the experiments we have described was a sample made up of 10 groups of 3 to 5 children each (O'Connor, 1999). Although this makes it difficult to draw large generalizations from the individual studies, the aggregate data nonetheless suggest that the IPG model has enormous potential as a therapeutic intervention for children with autism and can provide many important benefits to both the novice and the expert players who are involved in them. Larger scale investigations are needed to solidify this potential and to show that the benefits acquired during an IPG remain over time. To that end, a large randomized control trial of the model that incorporates a longer term follow-up has been designed and is now in the piloting stage.

In addition, more research is needed to demonstrate that when applied to special interest groups such as drama, art, and filmmaking or to groups made up of older children, teenagers, and young adults, the guiding principles of IPGs maintain their effectiveness. Initial field testing of such models has been promising, but empirical examination is needed to complement these groups' initial anecdotal success. The satisfactory completion of this kind of research would allow the benefits of the IGP model to reach a larger variety of children and adults and would further solidify its standing as an evidence-based best-practice intervention for individuals on the autism spectrum.

REFERENCES

American Psychiatric Association. (2000). *Diagnostic and statistical manual of mental disorders* (4th ed., text rev.). Washington, DC: Author.

Baron-Cohen, S. (1987). Autism and symbolic play. *British Journal of Developmental Psychology, 5*, 139–148.

Baron-Cohen, S., Leslie, A. M., & Frith, U. (1985). Does the autistic child have a "theory of mind"? *Cognition, 21*, 37–46.

Baron-Cohen, S., Tager-Flusberg, H., & Cohen, D. J. (Eds.). (1993). *Understanding other minds: Perspectives from autism*. Oxford, England: Oxford University Press.

Boucher, J., & Wolfberg, P. J. (Eds.). (2003) Editorial. *Autism: The International Journal of Research and Practice, 7*, 339–346.

Burns, S. M., & Brainerd, C. J. (1978). Effects of constructive and dramatic play on perspective taking in very young children. *Developmental Psychology, 15*, 512–521.

Connolly, J., Doyle, A.-B., & Reznick, E. (1988). Social pretend play and social competence in preschoolers. *Journal of Applied Developmental Psychology, 9*, 301–314.

Frith, U. (2003). *Autism: Explaining the enigma* (2nd ed.). Malden, MA: Blackwell.

Frith, U., & Happé, F. (1999). Theory of mind and self-consciousness: What is it like to be autistic? *Mind & Language, 14*, 1–22.

Gonsier-Gerdin, J. (1992). *Elementary school children's perspectives on peers with disabilities in the context of Integrated Play Groups: "They're not really disabled, they're like plain kids."* Unpublished manuscript, University of California, Berkeley/San Francisco State University.

Harris, P. (1993). Pretending and planning. In S. Baron-Cohen, H. Tager-Flusberg, & D. J. Cohen (Eds.), *Understanding other minds: Perspectives from autism* (pp. 228–246). Oxford, England: Oxford University Press.

Jarrold, C. (2003). A review of research into pretend play in autism. *Autism: The International Journal of Research and Practice, 7*, 379–390.

Jarrold, C., Boucher, J. & Smith, P. (1996). Generativity deficits in pretend play in autism. *British Journal of Developmental Psychology, 14*, 275–300.

Jordan, R. (2003). Social play and autistic spectrum disorders. *Autism: The International Journal of Research and Practice, 7*, 347–360.

Ladd, G. W., & Coleman, C. C. (1993). Young children's peer relationships: Forms, features, and functions. In B. Spodek (Ed.), *Handbook of research on the education of young children* (pp. 57–76) New York: Macmillan.

Ladd, G. W., Price, J. M., & Hart, C. H. (1988). Predicting preschoolers' peer status from their playground behaviors. *Child Development, 59*, 986–992.

Ladd, G. W, Price, J. M., & Hart, C. H. (1990). Preschoolers' behavioral orientations and patterns of peer control: Predictive of peer status? In S. R. Asher & J. D. Coie (Eds.), *Peer rejection in childhood* (pp. 90–115). New York: Cambridge University Press.

Lantz, J. F., Nelson, J. M. & Loftin, R. L. (2004). Guiding children with autism in play: Applying the integrated play group model in school settings. *Exceptional Children, 37*, 8–14.

Leslie, A. M. (1987). Pretense and representation: The origins of "theory of mind." *Psychological Review, 94*, 412–426.

Lewis, V., & Boucher, J. (1988). Spontaneous, instructed and elicited play in relatively able autistic children. *British Journal of Developmental Psychology, 6*, 325–339.

Lorimier, S. D., Doyle, A.-B., & Tessier, O. (1995). Social coordination during pretend play: Comparisons with nonpretend play and effects on expressive content. *Merrill-Palmer Quarterly, 41*, 497–516.

Mikaelan, B. (2003). *Increasing language through sibling and peer support play*. Unpublished master's thesis, San Francisco State University.

National Research Council. (2001). *Educating children with autism*. Washington, DC: National Academies Press.

Neufeld, D. (2009). *"The easiest hour I ever spent": A qualitative analysis of integrated play groups*. Unpublished position paper submitted to the University of California, Berkeley.

O'Connor, T. (1999). *Teacher perspectives of facilitated play in integrated play groups*. Unpublished master's thesis, San Francisco State University.

Peter, M. (2003). Drama, narrative, and early learning. *British Journal of Special Education, 30*, 21–27.

Richard, V., & Goupil, G. (2005). Application des groupes de jeux integres aupres d'eleves ayant un trouble envahissant du development [Implementation of integrated play groups with PDD students]. *Revue Quebecoise de Psychologie, 26*, 79–103.

Rogoff, B. (1990). *Apprenticeship in thinking*. New York: Oxford University Press.

Saltz, E., Dixon, D., & Johnson, J. (1977). Training disadvantaged preschoolers on various fantasy activities: Effects on cognitive functioning and impulse control. *Child Development, 48*, 367–380.

Sherratt, D., & Peter, M. (2002). *Developing play and drama in children with autistic spectrum disorders*. London: David Fulton.

Singer, D., & Singer, J. (1990). *The house of make-believe: Children's play and the developing imagination*. Cambridge, MA: Harvard University Press.

Smilansky, S. (1990). Sociodramatic play: Its relevance to behavior and achievement in school. In E. Klugman & S. Smilansky (Eds.), *Children's play and learning: Perspectives and policy implications* (pp. 18–42). New York: Teachers College Press

Vygotsky, L. S. (1978). *Mind in society: The development of higher psychological processes*. Cambridge, MA: Harvard University Press.

Wing, L., Gould, J., Yeates, S. R., & Brierly, L. M. (1977). Symbolic play in severely mentally retarded and autistic children. *Journal of Child Psychology and Psychiatry, 18*, 167–178.

Wolfberg, P. J. (1988). *Integrated play groups for children with autism and related disorders*. Unpublished master's field study, San Francisco State University.

Wolfberg, P. J. (1995). Case illustrations of emerging social relations and symbolic activity in children with autism through supported peer play. *Dissertation Abstracts International, 55*, p. 3476.

Wolfberg, P. J. (2003) *Peer play and the autism spectrum: The art of guiding children's socialization and imagination*. Shawnee, KS: Autism Asperger.

Wolfberg, P. J. (2009). *Play and imagination in children with autism* (2nd ed.). New York: Teachers College Press.

Wolfberg, P. J., & Schuler, A. L. (1992). *Integrated play groups project: Final evaluation report* (Contract No. HO86D90016). Washington, DC: U.S. Department of Education, Office of Special Education and Rehabilitative Services.

Wolfberg, P. J., & Schuler, A. L. (1993). Integrated play groups: A model for promoting the social and cognitive dimensions of play in children with autism. *Journal of Autism and Developmental Disorders, 23*, 467–489.

Wolfberg, P., Turiel., E., & DeWitt, M. (2008). *Integrated play groups: Promoting symbolic play, social engagement and communication with peers across settings in children with autism* (Autism Speaks Treatment Grant Proposal, Funded 2008–2011).

Wright, P. R. (2006). Drama education and development of self: Myth or reality? *Social Psychology of Education, 9,* 43–65.

Yang, T., Wolfberg, P. J., Wu, S., & Hwu, P. (2003). Supporting children on the autism spectrum in peer play at home and school: Piloting the integrated play groups model in Taiwan. *Autism: The International Journal of Research and Practice, 7,* 437–453.

Zercher, C., Hunt, P., Schuler, A. L., & Webster, J. (2001). Increasing joint attention, play and language through peer supported play. *Autism: The International Journal of Research and Practice, 5,* 374–398.

14

TEACHING SOCIAL SKILLS TO DEVELOPMENTALLY DELAYED PRESCHOOLERS

JOHNNY L. MATSON AND JILL C. FODSTAD

Children with developmental delays (DD) exhibit slowed acquisition of a multitude of skills across many physical, psychological, and social domains. Discrepancies from normal development can include delayed abilities in turning over, crawling, walking, uttering words, and *joint attention* (sharing one's experience of observing an object or event via nonverbal cues such as eye gaze or pointing) and other problems such as stereotypical behavior (i.e., *sterotypy,* a repetitive or ritualistic movement, posture, or utterance, such as body rocking, hand flapping, or echolalia), failing to orient to sound, sensorimotor deficits, poor visual orientation and attention, aversion to touch, and unnatural posturing (Baranek, 1999). The onset of these problems is typically at a young age, and the more severe the disability, the greater the delays are and the more motor, language, and social behaviors are affected (Matson, Wilkins, & González, 2007). Furthermore, delays in these most important developmental areas are not only inherently problematic but also tend to impede the development of other relevant skills needed for typical skill acquisition. Thus, the presentation of significant developmental delays before age 6 is a commonly referenced benchmark in the literature defining what is considered to be a delay in the normal progression of a child's development (Chang, 2007). As a result, preschool programs and intensive early childhood intervention programs are typically recommended because DD must be intervened with early to ensure that they do not spiral out of control.

It is generally believed that social deficiencies lie at the core of intellectual disability (ID), autism spectrum disorders (ASD; the most common of the DD), and other DD (Matson & Wilkins, 2007). Children with DD evince multiple social problems and difficulties, such as failure to understand social boundaries, how to play reciprocally, how to take turns, how to engage in imaginative play, how to make appropriate eye contact, how to share concern for others, and reciprocal communication. Problems in these areas make it difficult, if not impossible, for the child to begin to engage others and subsequently begin connecting as a social being. Thus, researchers and clinicians have made social skills and social deficiencies the most commonly targeted and studied area for remediation in young children with DD.

Given that a high percentage of children with DD fall into the ID or ASD categories, in this chapter we restrict discussion to those groups. Correctly or not, the literature available on play and social skills focuses almost exclusively on these groups. Having said this, many of these same procedures and problems would also apply to other groups with disability, such as children with severe and disabling physical conditions (e.g., cerebral palsy), chronic illness, and other disabling disorders.

SOCIAL SKILLS AND SOCIAL DEFICIENCIES

Social skills are components of a reciprocal process by which people learn to interact with others (Rehm & Bradley, 2006). These include a wide range of specific behaviors such as eye contact, speech content and volume, social reciprocity, giving compliments, and sharing. All of these behaviors, are interpersonal and interrelated and occur in a socially appropriate context. They must also be appropriate to the setting, the subject matter, and the age and sex of the people who are interacting. As such, these skills are at the same time essential aspects of development and complex (Corsaro & Eder, 1990). Failing to perform or misperforming even one or two aspects of a highly involved social interaction can result in negative responses from others and can impede the possibility of future positive social interactions.

Social behaviors are important for all people, but nowhere is their impact felt more than in children with DD. Social competencies predict school readiness (Carlton & Winsler, 1999), the creation and maintenance of positive relationships with peers (Denham & Burton, 2003), and popularity with other children (Eisenberg, Fabes, Guthrie, & Reiser, 2002), and they serve as predictors of antisocial behavior in adolescence and adulthood (Loeber, Lahey, & Thomas, 1991). These problems become more pronounced with age and take a huge toll on the person with DD, his or her family, and society. Thus, social skills are key building blocks in overall adaptation and adjustment. As noted, children with DD do not simply outgrow these social deficiencies. For those whose social competencies are not remediated, difficulties in adjustment tend to become more entrenched and problematic with time. This makes remediation later in life even more difficult.

Because of early onset and the increasing severity of these behavior problems, preschool programs are considered essential. The goals of the training these programs provide typically include reducing the disability's impact to enhance the likelihood of maximum mainstreaming in regular classrooms and, to the extent possible, eliminating or minimizing the disability long term. The overarching outcome would be to decrease human suffering and minimize financial and social costs to the individual, his or her family, and society (Nelson, McDonnell, Johnson, Crompton, & Nelson, 2007). The primary methods for achieving this goal are early identification and the implementation of psychologically based therapies as early and often as possible.

ASD occurs in approximately 1 per 150 children born every year, and ID occurs in roughly 3 per 100. Even though these prevalence rates are less than 1%, they do not discount the severity of these youngster's social problems or decrease the need for early intervention (Matson & Minshawi, 2006). Furthermore, the disorders overlap considerably. Children with ID or ID and ASD, for example, typically do not develop total independence, even in adulthood (Howlin, 2004). Nonetheless, marked gains are possible even with children with the most severe DD, particularly when intensive behavioral programs are begun by age 2 or 3 (Ben-Itzchak & Zachor, 2007; Matson & Smith, 2008). ASD symptoms appear to be serious as early as age 4, further arguing for early preschool treatments.

DEVELOPMENTAL ISSUES

By definition, children with DD have problems with social skills. Not only are their learning and display of appropriate methods of interaction delayed, but they tend to be qualitatively different from those of typically developing peers. For example, the child with DD may not initiate interactions, even when other social behaviors are reasonably well developed (LeBlanc & Matson, 1995). Therefore, the child may require intervention by knowledgeable professionals to develop the social behaviors other children acquire via the normal course of observation and experience (Rehm & Bradley, 2006). Bolstering this hypothesis are data indicating that although children with disabilities experience learning conditions similar to those of typically developing children, they tend not to learn as well from these experiences.

Thus, children with DD have more poorly developed social relationships (Hogan, Shandra, & Msall, 2007), suggesting that more structure and active involvement are needed to teach the complex rules that constitute reciprocal social interactions.

Repetition and structure appear to be necessary for developing social skills. This point is underscored by the fact that children with DD consistently have fewer opportunities for play and building social skills in other ways than do typically developing children (Missiuna & Pollack, 1991). Learning methods must therefore be used that go above and beyond those that are normal in the course of events and experiences of childhood. Moreover, children with DD may need to practice these skills in a variety of settings and contexts because they have more difficulty generalizing these skills to other situations, settings, or individuals than do typically developing children. For instance, although the typically developing child may be taught a greeting by a parent and can apply this skill to other adults (e.g., grandparents and teachers), the child with DD may need to be shown the greeting and given the opportunity to practice the skill several times with each adult in each setting.

Another focus of intervention has been to determine, from a developmental perspective, discrete behavioral targets about which clinicians and researchers should be particularly concerned. These behaviors have been referred to as *core symptoms*, *behavioral cusps*, or *pivotal behaviors* (Matson & Minshawi, 2006; Rosales-Ruiz & Baer, 1997). These behaviors are the building blocks for appropriate social behavior and are ones that may have consequences beyond the specific behavior that is changed.

RATIONALE FOR TREATMENT

Social behavior deficits (i.e., lack of skills) and excesses (i.e., extreme or abnormal social behaviors such as aggression or the constant need for assurance by caregivers) impede social development and have been a frequent concern of advocates, specialists, and parents. At ages 9 to 12 months, children with DD are often already experiencing difficulties with joint attention, stereotypies, failure to orient to attempts at social engagement by others, poor visual orientation and attention, prompted responses (i.e., responses that occur only after another individual verbally or gesturally indicates the child needs to perform a desired task or behavior) or delayed responses to their name, aversion to physical touch, visual fixation, odd physical posturing, limited or regressed speech and socialization, and poor eye contact (Matson, Wilkins, & Gonzalez, 2007; Watson, Baranek, & DiLavore, 2003). The inescapable conclusion is that the biological and neurodevelopmental variables that play a major role in the development of children result in pervasive deficits in children with DD. Furthermore, without remediation, these problems are likely to persist and even strengthen (Volkmar, Klin, Marans, & Cohen 1996). Many of these behaviors markedly interfere with the child's ability to develop normal play and socialization, which can result in stigmatization, low self-esteem, poorer than expected school performance, lack of popularity, and a host of other problems.

This, then, is the current rationale for intervention as applied to social skills and related play behaviors for children with DD. Play is an aspect of child development that is viewed as a specialized and highly valuable entity in which children learn to engage and be engaged by the world around them. Therefore, ensuring that this aspect of the child's life develops in as normal a fashion as possible is a high priority for intervention. A variety of methods have been tried as interventions to enhance play. We review some of them in the following section.

A common theme of these interventions is the identification of a variety of discrete behaviors for remediation. Emphasis is placed on repetition and one-to-one or small-group efforts because of problems with attention and social reciprocity and on developing specific strengths in self-initiation of play and social behavior. Given that developmental problems accrue for children with DD, these particular intervention goals have the highest relevance.

PLAY INTERVENTION PROCEDURES AND EMPIRICAL SUPPORT

Play is a distinct and unique aspect of childhood. It is developmental in nature and has specific subdomains that are sequential and occur at specific ages for typically developing children. The most rudimentary aspects of play involve solitary pretend activities, mainly involving toys. For typically developing children, the focus of play shifts markedly from solitary to social interactive play between 3 and 4.5 years of age. During this developmental window, children begin to interact socially with others, thereby establishing jointly agreed-on rules and plans (Göncü, 1993). They learn to compromise and take elements from each other's notions of play to develop a uniform approach to the activity, acquire perspective taking, practice taking turns, and develop a number of other adaptive socialization skills that they will use for the remainder of their lives. This social interactive explanation of play generally has been accepted by most theorists in the field (Piaget, 1945; Vygotsky, 1978). Parton (1932) asserted that cooperative play requires commonly agreed-on goals, plans, roles, and divisions of labor. Social interactive play also tends to increase significantly over time (Rubin, Watson, & Jambor, 1978). Underscoring the theme of increased social interaction is the recognition that with advanced age, preschoolers show an increasing ability to move beyond social play to develop complex forms of social interactive activities with peers (Rubin, Bukowski, & Parker, 1998).

As previously noted, the child with DD has significant and sustained delays in a number of behaviors. These behavioral setbacks markedly impede the child from progressing at a normal rate through this developmental social play sequence. Thus, interventions have focused on self-initiation and interactive social behaviors in a play context as a means of assisting these children to gain the skills typically developing children gain with observation and experience. Much of this structured play-skills training has occurred in the preschool setting.

Many structured methods have been developed to promote social skills acquisition in children with DD. Some of these are social games, self-management, peer tutoring, visual cuing, circle of friends, video modeling, peer-mediated trainers, reinforcement schedules and activities, and the Picture Exchange Communication System (often referred to as "PECS"). Reviews of these methods are available elsewhere (e.g., Matson, Matson, & Rivet, 2007). Our discussion here is restricted to methods to promote social competence in the context of play.

Play Characteristics

Therapies focusing on increasing play behavior as a means of enhancing social skills in children with DD have several common characteristics. First, these different kinds of therapies use a behavior analytic framework. Second, they tend to be sensitive to issues of generalization (i.e., the child has difficulty using learned play techniques outside of the session room). Therefore, peers are often incorporated as "cotherapists." Similarly, specific cusp behaviors are selected to focus on, and play is initiated in naturalistic settings. Third, a good deal of preplanning and structure is used, as well as considerable repetition because children with DD often have intellectual impairments or are resistant to change. Fourth, transitioning across play tasks or activities or playing with different children at different times and in different settings is crucial. Children with DD may become fixated on a particular type of toy (e.g., Transformers) or a particular type of movement (e.g., spinning toys). Additionally, they may be tactilely defensive or become upset by particular types of noise. All of these concerns make it essential that play tasks take these unique issues into consideration and introduce change very gradually and systematically. For example, a toy similar to a Transformer might be introduced with the Transformer, with all other aspects of the play routine held constant. Fifth, one-to-one or small-group therapy is typically used. This approach allows for frequent repetition and increases the likelihood that the child will not experience sensory overload. Sixth, these programs tend to be intensive. Unlike many more traditional play therapy programs, which may be for 1 or 2 hours once or twice a week, for the child with DD play and social skills are often worked into programs that cover 20 to 40 hours of treatment a week. These social behaviors are not taught alone but in the context of communication and adaptive skills. Seventh, parent training and involvement during the bulk of treatment is often in place. Again, difficulties with transitions and generalization and the need for constant repetition make this factor crucial. Parents can be involved in a good deal of the day treatment and can replicate many of the same routines in the home environment. Eighth, a careful assessment of the child's strengths and weakness is performed, and socialization training builds on the child's existing strengths (Luckett, Bundy, & Roberts, 2007). For example, if the child is a visual learner or responds best to a particular peer, those elements are incorporated into the treatment when feasible. Ninth, particular emphasis should be placed on initiation of play because children with DD are much less likely to engage in this skill, and it is typically one of the highest ranked cusp skills for any play program for children with DD (Nelson et al., 2007).

Example Play Programs

Most of the research that has focused on play in children with DD has been with those with ASD. We have also located and reported on interventions pertaining to children with ID. The methods used with each have a great deal of similarity. Again, the level of structure, specificity, and directed learning differs markedly from conventional play therapy. However, as noted, the lack of the basic skill set needed for play, easy distractibility, and the proclivity for sensory overload has led to this approach.

Jahr, Eldevik, and Eikeseth (2000) provided a good example of evidence-based play and social skills training for children. Important to the study's success, all 6 children (ages 4–12) in their single-case research design study had had at least 6 months of intensive early behavioral training. This pretraining is essential because children with DD are often deficient in many basic social skills that are prerequisite to socialized play, and these programs cannot be implemented without them (see Matson & Smith, 2008).

The primary components of the training were modeling, verbal description, and imitation, in that order. The child first observed two models demonstrating cooperative play with a toy in a socially acceptable fashion. Children with typical development, other classmates, or siblings usually served in this capacity. Adults (e.g., parents or teachers) may also serve as models; however, children are generally preferred because most natural play is solitary or with other children. The response began when the child touched the toy and ended when he or she let go of the toy or stopped the play activity.

Typical behaviors included feeding a doll, driving a car, or building a railway. Immediately following the modeled cooperative play, the child with DD was asked to verbally describe what had transpired. Then, he or she was asked to take the place of one of the models and help re-create the episode. The trainer initiated play sequences by asking the children to start playing and then at the end of the models-play sequence, questioned the child with DD about what had transpired first. The same play scenario was used until the child with DD could explain and do the sequence successfully for two trials in a row. The children with DD were able to learn a number of cooperative play skills, and these skills were maintained at a 6-month follow-up.

Gillett and LeBlanc (2007) described a somewhat different variation on this type of structured play. They treated three preschool-age children who had major deficiencies in spontaneous speech. Two of these children had autism, and the third had an unspecified developmental delay. In this play-skills approach, the mother served as the partner. The mother placed three items (e.g., books or toys) in front of her child and asked the child to choose one. The mother presented access to the preferred item while playing with it for about 5 seconds in an effort to prompt an unsolicited verbal exchange initiated by the child. If no vocalization occurred, the parent provided a vocalization describing the action of the object (e.g., "Roll the ball"). The verbal comment was made every 5 seconds, up to three times, unless the child modeled the verbal comment. A modeled verbal report by the child with DD resulted in immediate access to the toy or book. To strengthen the verbal response, the verbal response was repeated several times while the child was playing. This emphasis on modeling and practice has proven to be very effective for teaching play to children with DD and thus has often been replicated elsewhere (Paterson & Arco, 2007; van der Aalsvoort & Gossé, 2007).

After approximately 30 seconds of the child playing with the item, the mother would say "My turn." She would then retrieve the item and repeat the sequence, this time using another verbal phrase. The goal was to produce as many and as varied appropriate reciprocal vocalizations from the child as possible during the allotted playtime. Using this strategy, all three children had immediate increases in appropriate verbal exchanges; furthermore, these exchanges continued to increase throughout treatment. Also, the number of spontaneous exchanges increased markedly, as did the length of the social commentary.

Pretend play is an arena children with developmental delays have difficulty engaging in and provides another target for social skills intervention. In an investigation by Goldstein and Cisar (1992), three preschool children with autism were taught to participate in thematic play with two typically developing peers using scripts. Through training sessions in small-group lessons, the target child assumed a role in one of three scripted make-believe play activities (pet shop, carnival, magic show). For example, roles assigned in the carnival game included a booth attendant, an assistant, or a customer. The target child was given prompts and reinforcement to help facilitate behaviors and verbalizations characteristic of the assigned role. Not only did thematic scripted play increase, but spontaneous make-believe play also occurred. This set of skills generalized to a free-play environment and with children not in the children's respective training group. Increases in this play skill have been reported in other studies that have used scripted play and, in addition, other strategies such as video modeling, acting out familiar children's stories, and peer modeling with or without toys (D'Ateno, Mangiapanello, & Taylor, 2003; Neville & Bachor, 2002).

Ingersoll and Schriebman (2006) used a different approach, reciprocal imitation training, to foster the pretend play of five preschool children diagnosed with autism. Reciprocal imitation training has been used, as its primary purpose, to facilitate mutual and reciprocal imitation of play and vocalizations between a therapist and child (Warren, Yoder, Gazdag, Kim, & Jones, 1993). The children who participated in the study had mild to severe language delays and exhibited deficits in spontaneous object play, imitation, and joint attention. Intervention consisted of 2-week phases that emulated the natural imitative progression noted in typically developing children: (a) recognition of imitation; (b) therapist imitation of the child using a familiar action with the same toy, (c) therapist and child imitation of familiar and novel actions with the same toy, (d) child imitation of familiar and novel actions with the same toy with the introduction of therapist imitation of the child using familiar actions with a different toy, and (e) therapist and child imitation of familiar and novel actions with a different toy. The therapist used a combination of linguistic mapping (i.e., providing a running commentary of the actions that he or she and the child are performing), contingent reinforcement, prompting, imitation, and modeling to gain the child's attention, encourage vocalizations, and increase both imitative and novel play. All the children had increases in joint attention, total object imitation, appropriate language, imitative and spontaneous pretend play, and appropriate play. These gains were maintained across settings, toys, and therapists and at a follow-up consultation 1 month later.

Another important component of the social enterprise is the encouragement and development of the ability to share. DeQuinzio, Townsend, and Poulson (2007) described a program to teach this goal with manual guidance, auditory prompts, contingent access to toy play, and social interactions with the teacher. Children were 8 to 10 years old and autistic. Although these children were beyond the preschool years, the treatment these authors described also has relevance for very young children. Handing a toy to the child with DD, manually guiding and reinforcing the child for giving the toy to another, and then having the recipient of the toy engage in joint play with the child were the cornerstones of the intervention. A multiple baseline design across children and 49 training sessions demonstrated the value of this approach in the promotion of sharing in a play context. This sharing response also generalized to other toys and people.

The results of these studies underscore those of previous studies with similar treatments for children with DD that resulted in enhanced play and verbal exchanges (Koegel, O'Dell, & Koegel, 1987; Laski, Charlop, & Schreibman, 1988). Furthermore, these efforts underscore the value that researchers place on initiation of play and of the verbalizations and play skills of young children with DD. Nelson et al. (2007) stressed that these skills are crucial to the successful inclusion of young children with disabilities into the preschool environment. The notion of teaching children with DD to initiate interactions is one, if not the top, priority for research regarding social skills for children with DD.

Programs for Milder Impairments

For children with DD but with less severe social and learning impairments, a less structured intervention model may be practical. The implication here is that these children would have less severe intellectual and adaptive difficulties. Garfinkle (2002), for example, described small-group activities with four preschool children with autism or ID who were integrated into small social play groups with typically developing peers. Modeling and interacting with children with normal development in free-play settings was sufficient to increase both proximity to peers and number of social interactions, as well as general nonsocial engagement in classroom activities. Garfinkle stressed that the less intense nature of the intervention enhances the likelihood that it will be used by teachers. We believe this is a very important but frequently overlooked point in early childhood intervention.

Craig-Unkefer and Kaiser (2002) performed a similar study using small-group intervention to target six preschool children identified as being at risk for developing language delays. These children also engaged in problem behaviors such as aggression and noncompliance and experienced anxiety and depressive symptoms. Using a multiple baseline approach, the children were taught in pairs to plan their play activity, use conversational strategies with each other, and self-evaluate play interactions. The amount of social talk during play and in requests and descriptive talk increased markedly as a result of the program. Talk between the paired children also increased in word complexity and topic diversity, and noncompliance and behavioral issues decreased.

In line with maintaining ease of teacher application, teaching typically developing peers to interact with the child with DD can be a simple way to increase social play in an integrated classroom. Researchers using this method have found it effective in increasing the child with DD's interactions and initiations with same-age peers and for increasing the typically developing peer's desire to engage in play with the target child (Goldstein, Kaczmarek, Pennington, & Shafer, 1992). A study by McGee, Almeida, Sulzer-Azaroff, and Feldman (1992) used this intervention to increase the reciprocal interactions of three preschool children with autism. In their study, peers–classmates were selected who were rated as having high compliance and social skills. A series of 5-minute sessions were conducted during a 45-minute free play. The teacher told the peer and the target child to "come play," at which time an array of toys preferred by the target child were made available. The peer was provided with instruction, modeling, and assistance to complete the incidental teaching process. The interaction between the peer and the target child was typically structured in the following order: Wait for the target child to initiate a request for a toy (e.g., by reaching), ask the child to label the toy (e.g., "Say dog"), exchange the toy when an appropriate label is given, and praise the child for labeling the item (e.g., "Good job! You said *dog*"). The peer was then encouraged to prompt the child to engage in other social activities such as sharing or interactive play. The results for all three target children showed that their reciprocal interactions increased with peer training. The level of social interaction was also maintained after the teacher's level of involvement was faded out.

Naturalistic behavioral techniques, such as incidental teaching, are yet another method to incorporate play-skills training into a typical school day. In a study conducted by Kohler, Anthony, Steighner, and Hoyson (2001), four preschool children with various developmental disabilities received 10 minutes of intervention by their respective teacher during daily free-play time. The teacher was trained by the experimenters to use seven naturalistic teaching strategies to encourage the child's interest, enjoyment, and play and to increase communication and social interaction with typically developing classmates. The seven tactics used by the teachers included use of novel materials, joining activity, inviting choices, incidental strategies, comments or questions, expansion of talk, and interaction with peers. This intervention was successful at increasing the children's social exchanges. The children also had success in using interaction skills at a variety of play areas and taking active roles in classroom activities. Kohler et al.'s strategies have been successfully incorporated into preschool programs, such as the Walden Program at Emory University (McGee, Morrier, & Daly, 1999) and the LEAP program in Colorado (Strain & Cordisco, 1994), to increase play in children with autism and to train peers to encourage communication and play in the classroom.

Another way to incorporate social play into the child's repertoire is to include the child in the school curriculum. Morrison, Sainato, Benchaaban, and Endo (2002) described a program they used to teach relevant play skills to four preschool children with DD. Their program consisted of using activity schedules and teacher prompts to increase appropriate play behavior. The activity schedules were composed of photographs of four specific play stations in the classroom. As play skills increased, prompts were gradually decreased (faded) from the instructional paradigm. Again, however, with respect to children with DD, much of the focus must be on the actual teaching of play skills in a highly structured way because many of these skills do not come naturally to children with DD.

The results of the Morrison et al. (2002) study give further support to an increasing body of literature dictating the usefulness of photographic activity schedules (Bryan & Gast, 2000) and correspondence (i.e., on-task and off-task behavior) training (Baer, 1990) in improving the play skills of preschoolers with DD in school. These researchers, in particular, were able to combine two intervention strategies to show that these children could be taught to express their preferences in play even if there were language difficulties present. Additional observations indicated that the children were able to continue to apply the schedule in the presence of typically developing peers, and an increase in turn taking, verbal interactions, and interactive play was noted. The use of both strategies was shown to be socially acceptable with teachers and professionals because of the ease of intervention approach, the success gained in the children's play, the application to other areas of training, and the potential benefits to typically developing children (Bryan & Gast, 2000; Bevill, Gast, Maguire, & Vail, 2001).

A Final Note on Play Procedures

In a review of play skills for children with DD, Celiberti and Harris (1993) made the cogent point that siblings can be a powerful and useful asset in helping to establish appropriate play behavior and outlined the social benefits that can accompany their inclusion. They stressed that sibling involvement is best during playtime versus academic work or self-help activities and can aid dramatically in enhancing the poorly developed play skills of children with DD (Nulff, 1985). This approach has proven advantageous for many children with DD, including those with ID and autism (Powell, Salzberg, Rule, Levy, & Itzkowitz, 1983). For example, Coe, Matson, Craigie, and Gossen (1991) found that siblings of two autistic children could develop prompting and reinforcement skills, use them in multiple play-oriented contexts, and do this without parental supervision. Thus, sibling involvement can serve the dual purpose of teaching the child with DD important play skills while at the same time enhancing the number of positive interactions and the emotional bonds between siblings.

The procedures we have reviewed constitute the primary methodologies for teaching play and social interaction to children with DD. Often, components of these treatments are also incorporated into more comprehensive and intensive programs. We next provide a case example to illustrate how some of these training components might be used in play skills training. This illustration is by no means comprehensive in its scope, but it is a compilation of many interventions that can be used successfully.

CASE ILLUSTRATION

Jane, a 4-year-old child with spastic cerebral palsy, exhibits significant communication and socialization delays. At the time of treatment she was enrolled in a regular nonspecialized preschool class and was eligible for early intervention services; however, her parents felt that continuing contact with typically developing peers would be best for Jane's social development. Formal testing done at age 3 years, 7 months, using the Bayley Scales of Infant Development, Third Edition (Bayley, 1993) assessed Jane's cognitive functioning as being at the lower end of the average range and her receptive and expressive language as mildly delayed. Jane's vocalizations were noted to include the use of single words, two-word combinations, imitative words, and jargon. Her spontaneous speech was often difficult to interpret, and she frequently relied on contextual cues to comprehend simple directions.

According to teacher observations of playtime, Jane typically sat with an adult or alone and watched the other children play. When her classmates approached her to play, she would look at them and appeared to be interested in playing but ultimately would not respond to their initiations. Jane's peers wanted to play with her, but they did not know how to initiate play with her. This factor was largely due to Jane's significant communication, cognitive, and motor delays, which interfered with her ability to play with her classmates.

Professional Evaluation

Jane's parents and teacher contacted a psychologist who specialized in early intervention techniques for children with DD to give recommendations to help facilitate Jane's interactions with peers and encourage her social development. The psychologist conducted a formal assessment that included several components, such as a social skills checklist tailored to children (i.e., the Matson Evaluation of Social Skills With Youngsters; Matson, Rotatori, & Helsel, 1983), the Vineland Adaptive Behavior Scales (Sparrow, Balla, &

Cicchetti, 1984), role-play, parent and teacher rating scales, and direct observations of Jane during school while she was interacting with the other children in her class. On the basis of these procedures, several social and communication competencies were identified to target for intervention. Jane demonstrated appropriate initiations and responses with a social goal; however, she was not able to attain her goals because of her limited social–communicative skills and her peers' inability to understand her cues. Therefore, the skills that were selected to be targeted for Jane included sharing play materials, establishing eye contact, and responding to peers' initiations by smiling and reaching or pointing to them. These three rudimentary behaviors were thus the cusp behaviors for Jane to use as a means of initiating play with her classmates.

Treatment

The method used to help foster Jane's social communication involved a combination of incidental teaching, modeling, and peer interaction training groups. The intervention occurred in Jane's preschool setting and was conducted by her teacher, who was trained in the delivery protocol. Prompting and reinforcement (i.e., verbal praise) was used to ensure that Jane and her classmates knew what behaviors were expected and to increase appropriate responses.

Treatment focused on structuring the class environment in a manner that would make Jane's transition into play as smooth as possible. Peers were instructed regarding what to expect from Jane. To help Jane transition into therapy, sessions initially were kept brief (i.e., 5 minutes in length). After Jane was able to tolerate short play intervals, training sessions were increased in duration in a stepwise fashion until sessions lasted approximately the same time as an extended free-play break (i.e., about 45 minutes).

First, to ensure that Jane would be able to perform her cusp behaviors of pointing or reaching, smiling, and making eye contact, an intervention using direct instruction in combination with a least-to-most prompting sequence was used. This procedure was followed to ensure that given her motor limitations, Jane was still able to exhibit these behaviors. Training consisted of one-to-one instruction with Jane and the teacher. Once a prompt was given (e.g., "Point to the dog in the book"), Jane would be given approximately 5 seconds to comply with the demand. If no appropriate response was elicited, the teacher modeled the desired behavior while repeating the verbal prompt (e.g., "Point to the dog in the book like this"). If Jane still did not respond, she was physically guided to comply with the demand. For the behaviors of eye contact and smiling, where physical guidance is not applicable, the teacher continued to issue the gestural prompt until Jane complied. Verbal reinforcement was given for an appropriate response to the verbal or gestural prompt. After these behaviors were established, the next phase of treatment began. It should be noted that any time Jane initiated play by using one of these cusp behaviors, the prompting sequence was continued until she could elicit the skills independently.

Treatment Overview

The incidental teaching method involved a simple naturalistic intervention strategy. First, the teacher targeted unstructured activities in which Jane showed an interest (e.g., art). When the teacher noticed that Jane was actively watching other children engage in that activity, she would prompt her to engage in a social-communicative behavior. Next, the teacher would elaborate on Jane's response or model an appropriate response. The final procedural step involved the teacher providing positive feedback and praise to Jane. An example of this type of treatment session follows:

> William and Elizabeth were finger painting in the art area. Jane's teacher observed Jane looking at the children playing. She asked Jane, "Do you want to paint?" Jane looked at her teacher and then at the art table. In response, the teacher verbally prompted Jane to point toward the art table and provided a gestural model to encourage her to smile, indicating that she wanted to play. Next, the teacher physically guided Jane to point to the art table and then led her over to the table. The teacher asked William and Elizabeth if they would share their art materials with Jane. Jane began to paint with her classmates. The teacher said, "Jane, it is nice to see you play with Elizabeth and William." The teacher subsequently praised the other two children for sharing their paint with Jane.

A second strategy was to use peer-mediated activities to teach Jane social–communicative competencies. Same-age peers were identified who had a high level of appropriate social interaction skills and were able to communicate successfully with other children. These children were trained to make social-communicative interactions with Jane and taught how to be responsive to Jane's social exchanges. Jane was taught specific social-communicative skills to use when interacting with peers. Role-playing sessions between Jane and the teacher were used to practice and master these skills in a structured environment. This adult–child role play method was used to give Jane the opportunity to master the targeted behavior and gain some success. After the environment was arranged and training was provided to both the peers and Jane, the teacher continued to use prompting and praise to facilitate social-communicative interactions. An example of this type of training session follows:

> Three children were chosen to become better friends with Jane. Using role playing, the teacher showed these children how to interact with Jane. She told them that Jane would indicate that she wanted to play by looking at them, pointing to them or the area they were in, and/or smiling.

The peers were told to encourage Jane to respond to their initiations and persist at interacting with her by saying her name, asking whether she wanted to play, and smiling.

Jane was instructed on how to appropriately engage in playing with the children. After an array of her preferred toys was provided, Jane was asked, "Would you like to play?" She was given 5 seconds to respond by vocalizing, gesturing (i.e., nodding or pointing), or smiling. If Jane responded, she was given verbal praise and access to the toy; however, if she did not respond, she was asked again and prompted to respond. This continued until Jane responded, at which time she was given access to the toy. These modeling activities continued until Jane could respond appropriately within 5 seconds of the statement.

When Jane was ready to join the other children, she was led to an area close to the play group playing on the floor. The teacher prompted the children to ask Jane to play with them. Mary, one of the children, looked at Jane and asked, "Jane, would you like to play?" When Jane did not respond, Mary repeated her question. Jane then looked at Mary and smiled. The teacher praised Jane for responding. She also praised Mary for asking Jane to play. The children were then allowed to engage in playing on the floor. While the group was playing, the teacher continued to provide feedback and praise to Jane and the children for interacting appropriately.

The last main point of Jane's intervention dealt with increasing her interactive play. A procedure that incorporated peer modeling and modified pivotal response techniques was used. The peer selected to help implement this procedure was Lila, a classmate whom Jane seemed to prefer more than the other children in her class. The concepts that Lila was trained to incorporate into her play with Jane included ensuring Jane was paying attention, giving Jane a choice of toys to play with, playing with many different toys, modeling appropriate social behavior, giving verbal praise when Jane attempted to interact or play, talking to Jane, taking turns, and describing play activities and toys. Next, she was asked to engage in a role play sequence to simulate a play session with Jane. The teacher was also available to provide prompts in case Lila needed them. An example of this intervention in a later stage of implementation follows:

> Lila and Jane were both seated next to each other on the floor amid an array of Jane's preferred toys. The teacher prompted Lila to initiate play with Jane. Lila touched Jane on the arm and said, "Jane." She waited for Jane to make eye contact and then said, "Let's play! Pick a toy." Jane reached for the barnyard animal set and said "Moo!" As the teacher moved the set toward the girls, Lila said, "Good. Let's play farm! Want to be the cow?" Jane replied, "Moo! Yes." "OK, I'm a duck," Lila said. After a few moments, Jane said, "Ducks say quack!" "Yes!" said Lila. "I want the ball. I am going to roll it," said Jane. Lila handed her the ball and said, "Roll to me." Jane rolled the ball, after which Lila said, "Good roll!"

Summary

Young children with DD often have deficiencies in social–communicative competence. In Jane's case, she was experiencing difficulty in the area of initiation and maintenance of reciprocal play with peers primarily because of deficits in language. The approach taken to aid Jane in becoming more socially adept aimed to increase both basic social behaviors (i.e., pointing, making eye contact, smiling) and appropriate skills in the context of reciprocal play (i.e., sharing, talking to peers, cooperative play). In addition to the strategies described in the case illustration, many other methods may be implemented to increase social play.

No matter what intervention methods are used, two additional topics must be considered: generalization and maintenance. *Generalization* and *maintenance* refer to the occurrence of the targeted behavior under nontraining conditions (i.e., across settings, people, time) "without the scheduling of the same events in those conditions as in the training conditions" (Stokes & Baer, 1977, p. 350). In Jane's case, this means that a plan should be formulated to help increase the likelihood that the trained social behaviors will occur outside of the play therapy sessions and will continue to occur long after the treatment has ceased. Strategies such as introducing "new" classmates into Jane's existing play group, incorporating the targeted skills into her curriculum, or organizing playtime outside of the classroom are some examples of ways to help promote generalization and maintenance. In addition, Jane's parents should be given the opportunity to be trained in implementing the treatment strategies at home. Not only would this promote parent involvement, which is crucial to treatment fidelity, but the additional repetitions at home would also help in solidifying these skills into Jane's social repertoire.

CONCLUSIONS AND FUTURE DIRECTIONS

There has been a long tradition of using play as a therapeutic medium for young children. However, children with DD have come to this enterprise with far fewer precursor play skills than typically developing children and a reluctance to initiate play with others. These factors may in large part explain the substantial deficits these youngsters with DD have in development and display of such skills. Additionally, this may be a primary reason why play has taken on a much different character, from a therapeutic standpoint, than what is seen with typically developing children.

The recognition that basic elements of play must be systematically and gradually taught in incremental steps before more advanced reciprocal social play can proceed has been recognized and made a high training priority for children with DD. This training typically has been done one to one or in very small groups. Training is highly structured and focuses on small, discrete units because the child with DD can very easily become overstimulated and/or distracted. Although generally agreed-on training objectives have been established, at present very few studies using the same strategies have been reported. For future research, a broader range of training strategies, efforts to discern the most critical elements of training, and methods to simplify and enhance the user-friendly implementation of play would be advisable. In addition, children have had little input with respect to styles of play, play partners, play items, the content of play, or any number of other relevant factors. All of these issues warrant consideration and attention in the future. Furthermore, developing methods that enhance the ability of children with DD to make choices and increase the unique nature of their play is a goal with considerable merit.

Issues of development affect the type, intensity, and environment in which play occurs, as well as other factors. IDs and other developmental disorders such as autism present unique challenges for the clinician. A given child may have considerable deficits in some developmental milestones but be quite advanced in others. Thus, we should stress that each child's unique strengths and weaknesses must be considered in the play process. To date, there has been little research focusing specifically on developmental disabilities and their severity as a factor in establishing goodness of fit for these play-skill paradigms. Furthermore, efforts have not been made to look at various play strategies and evaluate how data determine effectiveness of programming or maintenance and generalization of social skills treatment gains. Other variables similarly need considerable thought and investigation. The development of efficacious play procedures to enhance the social skills of preschoolers with DD is relatively new. Much has yet to be learned before a standard for such training can be established. However, on a positive note, these early efforts are promising. These young children, once considered incapable of learning or engaging in meaningful play, are now seen as children with great potential. For these and many other reasons, continued clinical and research efforts to enhance the social play of children with DD are both promising and warranted.

REFERENCES

Baer, R. A. (1990). Correspondence training: Review and current issues. *Research in Developmental Disabilities, 11*, 379–390.

Baranek, G. T. (1999). Autism during infancy: A retrospective video analysis of sensory-motor and social behaviors at 9–12 months of age. *Journal of Autism and Developmental Disabilities, 29*, 213–224.

Bayley, N. (1993). *Bayley Scales of Infant Development*. San Antonio, TX: Psychological Corporation/Harcourt Educational Measurement.

Ben-Itzchak, E., & Zachor, D. A. (2007). The effects of intellectual functioning and autism severity on outcome of early behavioral interventions for children with autism. *Research in Developmental Disabilities, 28,* 287–303.

Bevill, A. R., Gast, D. L., Maguire, A. M., & Vail, C. O. (2001). Increasing engagement of preschoolers with disabilities through correspondence training and picture cues. *Journal of Early Intervention, 24,* 129–145.

Bryan, L. C., & Gast, D. L. (2000). Teaching on-task and on-schedule behaviors to high-functioning children with autism via picture activity schedules. *Journal of Autism and Developmental Disorders, 30,* 553–567.

Carlton, M., & Winsler, A. (1999). School readiness: The need for a paradigm shift. *School Psychology Review, 28,* 338–352.

Celiberti, D. A., & Harris, S. L. (1993). Behavioral interventions for siblings of children with autism: A focus on skills to enhance play. *Behavior Therapy, 24,* 573–599.

Chang, C. L. (2007). A study of applying data mining to early intervention for developmentally-delayed children. *Expert Systems With Applications, 33,* 407–412.

Coe, D. A., Matson, J. L., Craigie, C. J., & Gossen, M. A. (1991). Play skills of autistic children: Assessment and instruction. *Child & Family Behavior Therapy, 13*(3), 13–40.

Corsaro, W. A., & Eder, D. (1990). Children's peer cultures. *Annual Review of Sociology, 16,* 197–220.

Craig-Unkefer, L. A., & Kaiser, A. P. (2002). Improving the social communication skills of at-risk preschool children in a play context. *Topics in Early Childhood Special Education, 22,* 3–13.

D'Ateno, P., Mangiapanello, K., & Taylor, B. (2003). Using video modeling to teach complex play sequences to preschoolers with autism. *Journal of Positive Behavior Interventions, 5,* 5–11.

Denham, S. A. & Burton, R. (2003). *Social and emotional prevention and intervention programming for preschoolers.* New York: Kluwer/Plenum Press.

DeQuinzio, J., Townsend, D. B., & Poulson, C. L. (2007). The effects of forward chaining and contingent social interaction on the acquisition of complex sharing responses by children with autism. *Research in Autism Spectrum Disorders, 2,* 264–275.

Eisenberg, N., Fabes, R. A., Guthrie, I. K., & Reiser, M. (2002). The role of emotionality and regulation in children's social competence and adjustment. In L. Pulkkinen & A. Caspi (Eds.), *Paths to successful development: Personality in the life course* (pp. 46–70). New York: Cambridge University Press.

Garfinkle, A. N. (2002). Peer imitation: Increasing social interactions in children with autism and other developmental disabilities in inclusive preschool classrooms. *Topics in Early Childhood Special Education, 22,* 26–38.

Gillett, J. N., & LeBlanc, L. A. (2007). Parent-implemented natural language paradigm to increase language and play in children with autism. *Research in Autism Spectrum Disorders, 1,* 247–255.

Goldstein, H., & Cisar, C. L. (1992). Promoting interaction during sociodramatic play: Teaching scripts to typical preschoolers and classmates with disabilities. *Journal of Applied Behavior Analysis, 25*, 265–280.

Goldstein, H., Kaczmarek, L., Pennington, R., & Shafer, K. (1992). Peer-mediated intervention: Attending to, commenting on, and acknowledging the behavior of preschoolers with autism. *Journal of Applied Behavior Analysis, 25*, 289–305.

Göncü, A. (1993). Development of intersubjectivity in the dyadic play of preschoolers. *Early Childhood Research Quarterly, 8*, 99–116.

Hogan, D. P., Shandra, C. L., & Msall, M. E. (2007). Family developmental risk factors among adolescents with disabilities and children of parents with disabilities. *Journal of Adolescence, 30*, 1001–1019.

Howlin, P. (2004). *Autism and Asperger syndrome: Preparing for adulthood.* London: Routledge.

Ingersoll, B., & Schreibman, L. (2006). Teaching reciprocal imitation skills to young children with autism using a naturalistic behavioral approach: Effects on language, pretend play, and joint attention. *Journal of Autism and Developmental Disorders, 36*, 487–505.

Jahr, E., Eldevik, S., & Eikeseth, S. (2000). Teaching children with autism to initiate and sustain cooperative play. *Research in Developmental Disabilities, 21*, 151–169.

Koegel, R. L., O'Dell, M. C., & Koegel, L. K. (1987). A natural language teaching paradigm for nonverbal autistic children. *Journal of Autism and Developmental Disabilities, 17*, 187–200.

Kohler, F. W., Anthony, L. J., Steighner, S. A., & Hoyson, M. (2001). Teaching social interaction skills in the integrated preschool: An examination of naturalistic tactics. *Topics in Early Childhood Special Education, 21*, 93–103.

Laski, K. E., Charlop, M. H., & Schreibman, L. (1988). Training parents to use the natural language paradigm to increase their autistic children's speech. *Journal of Applied Behavior Analysis, 21*, 391–400.

LeBlanc, L. A., & Matson, J. L. (1995). A social skills training program for preschoolers with developmental disabilities: Generalization and social validity. *Behavior Modification, 19*, 234–346.

Loeber, R., Lahey, B. B., & Thomas, C. (1991). Diagnostic conundrum of oppositional defiant disorder and conduct disorder. *Journal of Abnormal Psychology, 100*, 379–390.

Luckett, T., Bundy, A., & Roberts, J. (2007). Do behavioral approaches teach children with autism to play or are they pretending? *Autism, 11*, 365–388.

Matson, J. L., Matson, M. L., & Rivet, T. T. (2007). Social skills treatments for children with autism spectrum disorders: An overview. *Behavior Modification, 31*, 682–707.

Matson, J. C., & Minshawi, N. F. (2006). *Early intervention for autism spectrum disorders: A critical analysis.* Oxford, England: Elsevier Science.

Matson, J. L., Rotatori, A. F., & Helsel, W. J. (1983). Development of a rating scale to measure social skills in children: The Matson Evaluation of Social Skills with Youngsters (MESSY). *Behavior Research and Therapy, 21*, 335–340.

Matson, J. L., & Smith, K. R. (2008). Current status of intensive behavioral interventions for young children with autism and PDD-NOS. *Research in Autism Spectrum Disorders, 2*, 60–74.

Matson, J. L., & Wilkins, J. (2007). A critical review of assessment targets and methods for social skills excesses and deficits for children with autism spectrum disorders. *Research in Autism Spectrum Disorders, 1*, 28–37.

Matson, J. L., Wilkins, J., & González, M. (2007). Early identification and diagnosis in autism spectrum disorders in young children and infants: How early is too early? *Research in Autism Spectrum Disorders, 2*, 75–84. doi: 10.1016/j.rasd.2007.03.002

McGee, G., Almeida, C., Sulzer-Azaroff, B., & Feldman, R. S. (1992). Promoting reciprocal interactions via peer incidental teaching. *Journal of Applied Behavior Analysis, 25*, 117–126.

McGee, G., Morrier, M., & Daly, T. (1999). An incidental teaching approach to early intervention for toddlers with autism. *Journal of the Association for Persons With Severe Handicaps, 24*, 133–146.

Missiuna, C., & Pollack, N. (1991). Play deprivation in children with physical disabilities: The role of the occupational therapist in preventing secondary disability. *American Journal of Occupational Therapy, 45*, 882–888.

Morrison, R. S., Sainato, D. N., Benchaaban, D., & Endo, S. (2002). Increasing play skills of children with autism using activity schedules and correspondence training. *Journal of Early Intervention, 25*, 58–72.

Nelson, C., McDonnell, A. P., Johnson, S. S., Crompton, A. & Nelson, A. R. (2007). Keys to play: A strategy to increase the social interactions of young children with autism and their typically developing peers. *Education and Training in Developmental Disabilities, 42*, 165–181.

Neville, M., & Bachor, D. G. (2002). A script based symbolic play intervention for children with developmental delay. *Developmental Disabilities Bulletin, 30*, 140–172.

Nulff, S. B. (1985). The symbolic and object play of children with autism: A review. *Journal of Autism and Developmental Disorders, 15*, 139–148.

Parton, M. C. (1932). Social participation among preschool children. *Journal of Abnormal and Social Psychology, 27*, 242–269.

Paterson, C. R., & Arco, L. (2007). Using video modeling for generalizing play in children with autism. *Behavior Modification, 31*, 660–681.

Piaget, J. (1945). *Play, dreams, and imitation in childhood.* New York: Free Press.

Powell, T. H., Salzberg, C. L., Rule, S., Levy, S., & Itzkowitz, J. S. (1983). Teaching mentally retarded children to play with their siblings using parents as trainers. *Education and Treatment of Children, 6*, 343–362.

Rehm, R. S., & Bradley, J. F. (2006). Social interactions at school of children who are medically fragile and developmentally delayed. *Journal of Pediatric Nursing, 21*, 299–307.

Rosales-Ruiz, J., & Baer, D. M. (1997). Behavioral cusps: A developmental and pragmatic concept for behavior analysis. *Journal of Applied Behavior Analysis, 30*, 533–544.

Rubin, K. H., Bukowski, W., & Parker, J. G. (1998). Peer interactions, relationships, and groups. In W. Damon & W. Eisenberg (Eds.), *Handbook of child psychology: Vol. 3. Social, emotional, and personality development* (pp. 621–632). New York: Wiley.

Rubin, K. H., Watson, K., & Jambor, T. (1978). Free play behaviors in preschool and kindergarten children. *Child Development, 49*, 534–536.

Sparrow, S., Balla, D., & Cicchetti, D. V. (1984). *The Vineland Adaptive Behavior Scales*. Circle Pines, MN: American Guidance Service.

Stokes, T. R., & Baer, D. M. (1977). An implicit technology of generalization. *Journal of Applied Behavior Analysis, 10*, 349–367.

Strain, P., & Cordisco, L. K. (1994). The LEAP preschool. In S. L. Harris & J. S. Handleman (Eds.), *Preschool education programs for children with autism* (pp. 115–126). Austin, TX: PRO-ED.

van der Aalsvoort, G. M., & Gossé, G. (2007). Effects of videorecording interactions and counseling for teachings on their responses to preschoolers with intellectual impairments. *Intellectual and Developmental Disabilities, 45*, 103–115.

Volkmar, F. R., Klin, A., Marans, W., & Cohen, D. J. (1996). The pervasive developmental disorders: Diagnosis and assessment. *Child and Adolescent Psychiatric Clinics of North America, 5*, 963–977.

Vygotsky, L. S. (1978). *Mind in society: The development of higher mental processes*. Cambridge, MA: Harvard University Press.

Warren, S. F., Yoder, P. J., Gazdag, G. E., Kim, K., & Jones, J. A. (1993). Facilitating prelinguistic communication skills in young children with developmental delay. *Journal of Speech and Hearing Research, 36*, 83–97.

Watson, L. R., Baranek, G. T., & DiLavore, P. C. (2003). Toddlers with autism: Developmental perspectives. *Infants and Young Children, 16*, 201–214.

INDEX

defined, 199
developmental issues, 200–202
empirical support for, 211
future research, directions for, 218–219
parent-directed interaction in, 206–210
and sociodramatic play, 190–191
theoretical underpinnings, 200
for treatment of anxiety, 111
Parent-directed interaction (PDI), 206–210
Parenting styles, 227–228
Parent involvement, 20–21
Parton, M. C., 305
Patel, A., 33
PCIT. *See* Parent–child interaction therapy
PDI. *See* Parent-directed interaction
Pearson, B., 169
PECS (Picture Exchange Communication System), 306
Peer social coaching, 258–259
Pellay, Y., 38
Persistence, 204, 252, 253
Petersen, I., 38
Peterson, R., 39
Pettit, G. S., 228
Phobias, 36–38, 158
Photographic activity schedules, 312
Physical activity, 41
Physiology, 115–119
Piaget, J., 186
Picture Exchange Communication System (PECS), 306
Play. *See also* Play therapy; Sociodramatic play
  child-directed, 251
  dramatic, 184, 278, 281–282
  experiential mastery, 122–125
  free, 20, 136
  joint, 40
  make-believe, 184–188, 193
  manipulation-sensory, 284
  nurturing, 96
  in Posttraumatic Parenting Program, 79–80
  pretend, 22–23, 308–309
  shared, 136
  structured vs. unstructured, 163–164

symbolic, 134, 184, 282
theraplay, 111
and trauma from domestic violence, 134–135
Play preferences, 284
Play therapy, 3–10
  defined, 5
  development of, 5–7
  international interest in, 9
  and preschool children, 3–4
  recent changes in, 7–9
Poor attention, 48
Positive imagery, 118
Posttraumatic Parenting (PP) program, 71–72, 77–83
Poulson, C. L., 309
Powell, B., 38
Powell, D., 227
PP program. *See* Posttraumatic Parenting program
Praise, 203
Preschool Age Psychiatric Assessment (PAPA), 19
Prescriptive matching, 7
Prescriptive play therapy, 7
Pretend play, 22–23, 308–309
Prevalence rates, of psychopathology, 16–17
Prevention
  relapse, 163, 166
  response, 125–126
  and treatment studies, 247
PRIDE skills, 203–204
Protected space, 224
Protection, 78
Proximal development, 187, 279, 285
Psychoeducation, 161
Psychopathology, 16–17
Psychotherapy (in general), 59, 75–76. *See also* Child–parent psychotherapy; Psychotherapy for children
Psychotherapy for children
  assessment issues, 19–20
  barriers to treatment, 17
  clinical issues, 15–22
  developmental issues, 22–24
  diagnostic issues, 17–19
  empirically supported interventions, 21–22
  parent involvement in, 20–21

ABOUT THE EDITOR

Charles E. Schaefer, PhD, RPT-S, is cofounder and director emeritus of the Association for Play Therapy (APT). In 2006, APT awarded him its Lifetime Achievement Award. Dr. Schaefer is also founder and codirector of the Play Therapy Training Institute in Hightstown, New Jersey. He coordinates an annual International Play Therapy Study Group in Wroxton, England.

Dr. Schaefer is author or editor of more than 100 professional articles and 55 books. Among his books are *Foundations of Play Therapy; Handbook of Play Therapy; The Playing Cure; Play Therapy Techniques; 101 Favorite Play Therapy Techniques; Game Play; Contemporary Play Therapy; Short-Term Play Therapy; Play Therapy With Adolescents; Play Therapy With Adults; Play Therapy With Very Young Children (Zero to Three); Empirically Based Play Interventions for Children; Handbook of Parent Training (3rd ed.); How to Help Children With Common Problems; Teach Your Baby to Sleep Through The Night; Toilet Training Without Tears; and Ages & Stages: A Parent's Guide to Normal Child Development.*

Dr. Schaefer is emeritus professor of psychology at Fairleigh Dickinson University, Teaneck, New Jersey, and maintains a private practice at the university's clinic in Hackensack, New Jersey.